M000284037

WHITEHUNTERS

WHITE
HUNTERS

THE GOLDEN AGE OF
AFRICAN SAFARIS

BRIAN HERNE

A JOHN MACRAE // OWL BOOK
HENRY HOLT AND COMPANY // NEW YORK

Henry Holt and Company, LLC
Publishers since 1866
175 Fifth Avenue
New York, New York 10010
w.w.w.henryholt.com

Henry Holt ® is a registered trademark
of Henry Holt and Company, LLC.

Copyright © 1999 by Brian Herne
All rights reserved.
Distributed in Canada by H. B. Fenn and Company Ltd.

Library of Congress Cataloging-in-Publication Data
Herne, Brian.
　White hunters: the golden age of African safaris / Brian Herne.—1st ed.
　　p.　　cm.
　Includes index and bibliographical references.
　ISBN-13: 978-0-8050-6736-1
　ISBN-10: 0-8050-6736-1
　1. Hunters—Africa—Biography.　2. Big game hunting—Africa.　　I. Title.
　SK15.H47　　1999
　799.2'6'09226—dc21　　　　　　　　　　　　　　　　98-46157
　[B]　　　　　　　　　　　　　　　　　　　　　　　　CIP

Henry Holt books are available for special promotions and
premiums. For details contact: Director, Special Markets.

First published in hardcover in 1999
by Henry Holt and Company

First Owl Books Edition 2001

A John Macrae / Owl Book

Designed by Victoria Hartman

Printed in the United States of America

10　9　8　7　6　5　4

For Diana

Uganda

Kenya

Bukoba

Lake Victoria
Musoma

Serengeti
Nat'l
Park

Loliondo

• Nairobi

Malagarasi R.

Shinyanga•

L. Eyasi

Ngorongoro

Arusha

• Moshi

Mt. Kilimanjaro

Kigoma

• Tabora

Manyara
Nat'l Park

Ruvu R.

Ugalla R.

Tarangire
Nat'l Park

• Kijungu

Tanga

Pangani R.

•Nyonga

•Dodoma

Zanzibar

•Mpanda

L. Tanganyika

Katavi Plain

•Rungwa

Kisigo R.

Mikumi
Nat'l
Park

Dar es
Salaam

Ruaha
Nat'l
Park

Great

Ruaha R.

Rufiji R.

Indian

L. Rukwa

Kilombero R.

Selous
Game
Reserve

Ocean

• Kilwa

Tunduma

•Njombe

Luwegu R.

Zambia

Nachingwea•

•Lindi

L. Nyasa

•Newala

Rovuma R.

Mozambique

Tanzania

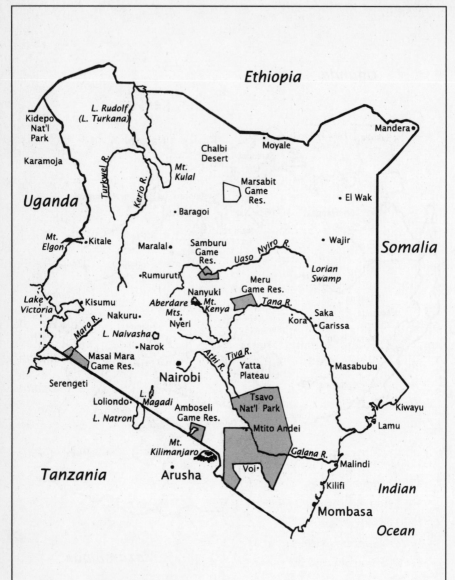

CONTENTS

WHITE HUNTERS

THE FIRST WHITE HUNTERS

In the late nineteenth century the deserts of north Somaliland, or the Land of Punt, as it was sometimes called, ran from the Gulf of Aden to the Horn of Africa, then south to the Juba and Tana rivers where they spilled into the Indian Ocean. It was truly terra incognita, the land of devil dervishes, dust storms, and, it was said, fiendish beasts. Fierce Somali clans roamed this unmapped territory of heat, thirst, and sudden death. Despite such formidable obstacles superb hunting could be had east of Suez, just a few miles into the interior from the sultry port of Berbera. Somaliland's northern coast lay along the direct sea route between England and its Indian empire, thereby making it accessible to a handful of intrepid Victorian adventurers.

Early foreign hunters drawn by the Land of Punt's inexorable romance, mystique, and danger included British army officers stationed in India. Almost all of these amateur hunters set out with the object of bagging a lion. Some were successful, but the lions in many cases kept the score fairly even, mauling or killing many of these daring souls. Hunting was, of course, a long cherished tradition during the Victorian and Edwardian eras in England, just as it was on the European continent and in the United States.

Although the term "white hunter" actually had its beginnings in British East Africa after the turn of the twentieth century, big game hunting was already popular in other parts of the "Dark Continent," notably in South Africa, where amateur and meat hunters, as well as a few ivory hunters, had been active long before Somaliland and East Africa came into vogue. In South Africa the exploits of adventurers such as Gordon Roualeyn Cumming, William Cornwallis Harris, and Charles Baldwin, to name just a few of that era's prolific South African nimrods, were the stuff of legends. These men were after meat mostly;

some were hide or tusk hunters, but all proved capable of remarkable feats of endurance, regardless of quarry. In Cumming's book, *The Lion Hunter of South Africa*, for example, there is a sketch of Cumming swimming in the water alongside a giant hippopotamus, armed with nothing but a sheath knife. His intentions are clear—he is attempting to dispatch the "sea horse," or at least secure it by cutting hand-hold slots in the unfortunate hippo's hide. He titles the sketch, "Waltz with a Hippo."

CORNWALLIS HARRIS was a magnificent painter and a fearless hunter who cut the trails of countless "ferocious beasts." Charles Baldwin wrote a memorable account of his own stirring exploits in the pursuit of big game circa 1852–1860. These South African hunters all remained amateur hunters, not white hunters, who were professionals.

In German East Africa, Carl Georg Schillings, a hunter and a gifted naturalist, had made a series of safaris to the German colony beginning in 1896. Schillings was also an innovative photographer who took great risks to secure some of the earliest pictures of African game. He once stalked to within fifteen yards of a mud wallow to photograph two rhino. Another time he was charged by an agitated herd of elephant and had to shoot his way out of the fix. He experimented with flashlight photographs, having mixed his own flash powder at no little risk. Under the most primitive conditions Schillings developed his massive photographic plates, experimented with some of the earliest telephoto lenses, and explored most of the north-central part of the colony. He took particular interest in the country around Kilimanjaro, and some of his best wildlife photographs were shot across the border in British East around the soda lake at Amboseli. Schillings's pictures of lions taken at night with his infamous flash powder are classics to this day. He was also a fine ornithologist and made a great collection of birds, many of them hitherto unknown. His handsome two-volume book, *With Flashlight and Rifle*, was first published in Berlin and translated into English in 1906. The books were received with great acclaim in Europe and aroused an unprecedented interest in the German colony.

Around 1900 there were fair numbers of white settlers, mostly farmers living in the Rhodesias, who occasionally took friends out for a spot of shooting. Such hunts were normally casual, disorganized affairs. "Shooting" was still the operative word, rather than "hunting."

One of the best pioneer Rhodesia-based hunters was the immensely

Carl Georg Schillings, 1903.

experienced Marcus Daly, who was sufficiently opportunistic to be regarded as both a professional white hunter and an ivory hunter. He began his career as a game trapper near the Zambezi River catching animals to stock Cecil Rhodes's Kenilworth Zoo in England. Daly roamed across Africa, taking paying clients when he could get them, hunting ivory for himself when he could not. He was an accomplished hunter who had a reputation for physical ferocity. Marcus Daly was known to have a habit of sending bullets whistling dangerously close to the feet of uninvited guests to his camp, particularly government officials, whom he loathed on sight. Daly hunted for a while in British East as well as other African countries, and he was friendly with early Nairobi white hunters Bill Judd and Tom Murray Smith, who was later to become president of the East African Professional Hunter's Association.

Some competitive resentment naturally arose between professional hunters operating in different areas. Marcus Daly, for one, must have resented the special aura that attached itself exclusively to the hunters of East Africa, for he wrote, "The term *white hunter* is a purely Nairobi manufacture and was never heard of in Rhodesia where all the best hunters are found."[1]

Whether Marcus Daly liked it or not, the white hunters of Nairobi *were* a breed apart. Lionized by Ernest Hemingway and Robert Ruark, it was the white hunters of British and German East Africa who came to be portrayed on movie screens around the world.

✧

MODERN DAY authorities hold divergent views on the subject of just who should be accorded the title of Africa's first white hunter. There is equal uncertainty about precisely who first coined the term, but what is certain is that the term "white hunter" has been in common use in East Africa since the turn of the century.

Emily Host and colonial historians accord the honor of first white hunter to either R. J. Cunninghame or Bill Judd. White hunter Donald Ker emphatically states it was Alan Black. J. A. Hunter maintained that it was the Hill cousins. It could even be argued that one of the first white hunters was in fact no stiff-upper-lipped Victorian, but a Texan with the grand name of Peregrine (Peary to his clients) Herne. In the 1840s Herne (no relation to the author) roamed the wilderness of the American West, making a living hunting and trapping. At the trading station called Brown's Hole on the Green River, upstream from the Colorado, Herne's path crossed that of an English sportsman, a gentleman of fortune named Robert Barrill. The two men became fast friends, and Barrill proposed that as an "experienced hunter" Peregrine Herne should accompany him to various parts of the world. As Herne wrote, "If I would accompany him on his travels and hunting expeditions, he would take care that I was well provided in every respect." Herne gladly accepted, and may actually have been the first white hunter from that era to have been paid for his services, which included hunting in Africa.[2] In any event Herne's "guiding" activities closely resembled those of this century's first white hunters.

By several reliable accounts it was the chance meeting of hunter Alan Black and a reckless amateur hunter known as "D," the fiery Lord Delamere, that led to the term "white hunter." Delamere had employed the youthful Alan Black to help out on one of his Somaliland safaris in the late 1890s. When Delamere settled in British East Africa he purchased very large acreages of ranching country. At the time he employed a Somali hunter to shoot meat for his employees, and he also hired Alan Black as a hunter. To differentiate between the two hunters, as well as on account of Black's surname, the Somali hunter was referred to as "the black hunter," while Alan Black was always called "the white hunter," and from this difference, or so the story goes, "white hunter" came into common usage.

"Black was, therefore," according to veteran hunter Donald Ker, of

Ker and Downey Safaris, Nairobi, "the first white man to operate in a professional capacity taking out hunting parties for a living." And, Ker adds, "Black was one of the best that ever lived."[3]

Alan Black settled in British East Africa for good in 1903, although he continued to travel overseas during monsoon rainy seasons when he could not hunt. An original "Sportsman's Game License," costing 750 rupees, was issued to Black by the East Africa Protectorate government in June 1906, but that was certainly not his first game license.

IT IS SAFE to say that about half a dozen men started in the safari business at about the same time. Kenya writer Emily Host states, "It seems likely that R. J. Cunninghame and Bill Judd, who came to East Africa in 1899, and George Outram and Leslie Tarlton, who followed in 1903, were among the first to take up professional hunting."[4] Host gives the date of Cunninghame's arrival in British East Africa as 1899, but others believe it was late 1901 or early 1902.

Richard John Cunninghame, known as R.J. (and to the Africans as Masharubu*), was a Scot, born on July 4, 1871. After attending Cambridge he was briefly a whaler in the Arctic, a hunter and naturalist in Lapland, a meat hunter in Mozambique, and a transport rider in South Africa, before arriving in British East Africa.

Whether Cunninghame was the first of the professionals or not, it is generally conceded he was probably the leading white hunter of his day. At a slim six foot two, he was whipcord tough and came to epitomize the finest qualities sought by visiting sportsmen eager to hunt dangerous big game in company with an expert. Among his more famous clients were President Theodore Roosevelt, his son Kermit, and author and amateur hunter Frederick Courtney Selous (on Roosevelt's 1909 safari), and the American novelist Stewart Edward White.

IN 1906 CUNNINGHAME was the white hunter selected by American photographer Carl Akeley to lead an elephant and buffalo hunt in the Aberdare Mountains of British East Africa. Akeley, who had

---

*Although *masharubu* means "mustache" in Swahili—*kidevu* means "beard"—Cunninghame and a few bearded hunters who followed were known as Masharubu, and in some regions as Sharafa—long *flowing* beard.

R. J. Cunninghame may have been the first white hunter.

previously been mauled by a leopard in Somaliland, was a worldwide traveler and frequent visitor to Africa. A recent encounter on Mount Kenya had left him somewhat apprehensive of elephant. On that occasion Akeley and his party were spooring a small herd of bull elephant that they hoped to photograph. He and his tracker had paused to check cartridges for the gun that he carried for protection when a solo elephant suddenly charged them in an unprovoked attack. The elephant hit Akeley with its trunk, breaking his nose and splitting his cheek open to the teeth. The beast got Akeley down on his back between its tusks, and then tried to crush him with its massive forehead. Akeley passed out, at which point the elephant unaccountably lost interest in him, possibly assuming its victim was already dead.

After that Akeley did not wish to take unnecessary chances, and for his expedition on behalf of the Field Museum of Chicago, he took the precaution of signing up R. J. Cunninghame. Akeley's confidence was well placed, for Cunninghame displayed his usual cool skill when working among elephant at close range. The successful safari ended with the two parting with mutual admiration. Cunninghame refused any payment from Akeley, on the grounds that the trip had been a scientific endeavor. "Coming from a Scotchman it was quite unexpected," Akeley wrote, "but it was typical of Cunninghame's generosity and indicative of his interest in scientific work."[5]

Cunninghame's most celebrated safari was with Teddy Roosevelt, in 1909–1910. The story persists that on the toss of a coin by Nairobi safari outfitter Leslie Tarlton, Cunninghame was chosen to lead the safari rather than fellow white hunter Bill Judd, who lost the toss. In reality

Cunninghame had been selected to lead the safari well in advance of Roosevelt's arrival. Judd was, however, invited to join the safari for a while to hunt with Roosevelt and Cunninghame. Of Cunninghame, Roosevelt declared, "I doubt if Mr. Cunninghame's equal in handling such expeditions as ours exists. He combines the qualities of a first-class explorer, guide, field naturalist, and safari manager."[6]

R. J. Cunninghame was not afraid to speak up to denounce the establishment for injustices to native African workers during the early days of the colonial British East Africa Protectorate. At one vociferous meeting in Nairobi, Cunninghame quietly put in a word for amelioration of laborers' conditions. He spoke movingly of improper food supplies and advocated that conditions promised to the natives should be carried out.[7]

RANKED ALONGSIDE Cunninghame, Black, and Judd as one of the top white hunters of his day was Arthur Cecil Hoey, an Englishman born at Wimbledon in 1883. On his first solo journey in 1904 he walked over a thousand miles of country surrounding Mount Elgon and the little-known Cherangani Mountains. Hoey then trekked across the vast plateau known as the Uasin Gishu as far as the Nzoia River. Although a handful of hunters, including the great ivory hunter Karamoja Bell, had traversed the Uasin Gishu ahead of young Hoey, it would be Hoey who would for some years thereafter claim it as his special turf. In his day, none knew it better.

When Arthur Hoey first arrived on what became known simply as "The Plateau" he was surprised to find it empty of human habitation. An ancient people called the Sirikwa had dwelt there once and left traces of circular stone dwellings, but none had taken their place. It was only when Hoey reached the Nandi hills to the north of the Uasin Gishu plain that he encountered any occupied settlements.[8]

Out on the golden short-grassed plains Hoey found massed herds of game. Elephant were plentiful and many carried heavy ivory. Hoey once shot three elephant in half an hour, the best of which had record-class tusks weighing 131 pounds each, and another with tusks weighing 128 pounds.[9] The Uasin Gishu plateau was the best big game region Hoey had yet seen in Africa.

Arthur was so taken by this part of western Kenya that he decided to settle there permanently. In order to reach the land that he wanted for himself, Hoey had to construct a bridge across the Nzoia River, a land-mark that became known thereafter as Hoey's Bridge.* A band of African hunting tribesmen known as the Cherangani D'robo inhabited the mountains of that name close by where Hoey began to farm. Hoey greatly admired the hunting skills of the D'robo, and he was the first white man to live among them.

While Hoey had been befriended by the Cherangani D'robo, he considered another neighborhood tribe, the Nandi people, to be the bravest hunters of all. He often employed the Nandi as gunbearers and trackers on his safaris. Their steadfast courage was often demonstrated during their own lion hunts. A group of near naked and chanting Nandi spear-men led by their veterans wearing war paint and lion mane headdresses would surround a lion, and when the infuriated beast charged the circle of men one would kneel holding his buffalo hide shield before him, his spear at the ready, and then at the last moment he would take the lion's charge on his shield, and thrust deeply with his spear. At that moment his comrades would move in swiftly and pepper the lion with spears. The Nandi hunters often suffered casualties during these hunts, and maulings and deaths were not uncommon.

Over the next few years Arthur became a noted lion hunter and a practitioner of the British East African sport of "riding lions," the comparatively new and exceedingly dangerous method of hunting being practiced by the more daring white hunters in the early 1900s. Lion hunting was considered not only a sport but a necessity in the territory to protect livestock. In those days lions were often hunted at night over kills used as bait, or miserably poisoned or trapped. Such lowly methods were legal, but regarded with contempt by any self-respecting hunter.

Riding lions was considered a far more sporting method. Count Wickenburg, who rode lions before nearly being killed by one in Somaliland, was probably the first proponent of the pastime. The unwritten rules for riding lions required that lions be pursued on horseback. When the lion either turned at bay, or otherwise offered a shot, the hunter was supposed to dismount—the ideal range was variously reckoned at between forty and sixty yards—and shoot before the big cat either ran away or charged. Yet the rules—and the advice—were flexible, and not

---

*Hoey's Bridge is now Moi's Bridge, renamed after Kenya's current president, Daniel Teriotich Arap Moi.

D'robo hunter.

always easy to follow. The sport resulted in numerous maulings and fatalities among its more reckless practitioners.

In 1908 Hoey was sought out by the American writer and preacher W. S. Rainsford, an experienced hunter and accomplished marksman. Rainsford had hunted extensively in the United States and was making his second safari in Africa. While his main interest was lion hunting, he was also keen to study the Cherangani D'robo tribe, so it was inevitable that he would find his way to Arthur Cecil Hoey, an acknowledged expert on both counts.

By his own admission Rainsford was a cautious hunter. He never shot at anything unless he could see it clearly and knew exactly where he wanted to put his bullet. But the preacher was also an indefatigable sportsman, intent on experiencing all aspects of African big game hunting. Once he learned of the risky new practice of riding lions, Rainsford itched to try it for himself.

Before setting out on his safari with Hoey, Rainsford took the trouble to meet and interview some of the leading lion hunters in East Africa, including the territory's first game ranger, Blayney Percival, the most experienced lion rider of all. Percival was a master at what he called *galloping* lions. "To my mind," Percival wrote, "there is no sport equal to galloping lions. From the moment the quarry is afoot till he is dead there is no cessation of excitement!"[10] Percival had his own strate-gies; he advocated "a range of around 150 yards as being ideal." He continued:

> The horse's head should be turned away from where a lion was thought to be crouching, for should the lion charge out you want the very best start you can get. I have often drawn a lion which would not yield to other measures by galloping rapidly past within 25 yards or so of the spot where he lay. Unable to resist temptation he charges and is thus lured out of the cover. I don't recommend this plan for general adoption. It is too risky unless you know your horse well, and he is thoroughly accustomed to lions.[11]

Percival told Rainsford that once when he was well mounted, he was almost pulled down by a lion that he had driven into cover. On that occasion he got too close to the big cat, and although it was unwounded, the lion dispensed with all the usual preliminaries and rushed at him. He turned his horse as quickly as he could and rode for his life. He had fifty yards' head start, yet believed that had he not fired his heavy revolver into the face of the lion when it was almost at his horse's hindquarters, both horse and rider would have been pulled down.

Despite Percival's close call, Rainsford went ahead with his plans for a safari. Hoey took Rainsford to his favorite country along the Sergoit River. "I have never been here yet at this time of year without see-ing lion," Hoey told Rainsford. The words were scarcely out of his mouth before a tiny yellow spot, fully one thousand yards away, caught his eye. Hoey clapped the glass into his pocket. "A lion—and we can cut him off! The going is splendid. He is ours!" The chase was on, and Rainsford wrote:

> A yell, and we are off! The horses need no urging. They see their game and race for dear life. He holds his own, or almost his own for about half a mile. No twining grass or weed hold him back. And then we gain fast. I try and keep within a couple of hundred yards of the racers, and so staunch is the fine mule I am riding and so eager is he not to be left behind, that though in the first keen rush the ponies distance me, I am almost holding my own now. More than a mile and a half we have ridden. Suddenly he halts his

stride, he drops from gallop to trot. Hoey is past him in an instant. He wheels to bay, stands looking first at one pony, then at the other, then back at me. His retreat is cut off, and he knows it. For a moment he lies down and takes his breath, then slowly rises to his feet. His tail swings from side to side—which of the three of us should he tackle?[12]

Hoey, armed with his favorite rifle, a .450 double, calmly backed Rainsford as the American fired two quick shots from his Mauser .350 repeater, killing the lion. During the course of the safari Hoey made sure his thrill-seeking American client had plenty of close contact with the king of beasts. By then Rainsford had learned a few tricks of his own, which he was proud to pass on to others:

There are one or two things that any man riding lions would do well to remember: First, do not follow a lion or lions into cover if you are on horseback—not even thin cover. Once you have chased a lion he is a very different beast from the beast that slinks away from you when you are hunting on foot. In this case he instinctively knows he can get away from you if he cares to. The second lion Hoey and I rode on a memorable morning, when we chased two and shot them in half an hour, had, after Hoey's bullet had only stung him, every chance to walk into the impenetrable stronghold of the river grass, if he wanted to. It grew thickly not twenty yards from where he was hit. But he did not want to do anything of the sort, and angered by the long, hard chase, and casting all idea of further retreat behind him, he came boldly away from the covert he had striven so strenuously to gain, and advanced quickly into the open to grapple with his pursuer.

To follow a lion in such a mood into even short cover is to court death. You are within a few feet or yards before you know it. His terrible striking growl as he rushes in will render your mount unmanageable, and make shooting out of the question. You cannot escape and you are at his mercy. This is of course also the reason why it is folly to ride lion in grass or bush country. You see one or ten galloping in front of you, next moment some of these have vanished. You may not ride into them, but you may, and if so, you are done for; and then, at best, you will do no more lion riding that trip.

Summing up the whole matter, no man can tell what a lion
will do, how he will come, or whether he will come at all or no.
He may die as tamely as a house cat, or he can make you shoot for
your life. And just here is the unequaled fascination a man experiences in pitting himself against the lion in East Africa. Let no fool
persuade you to shoot from horseback.[13]

Rainsford spent a year on safari with Hoey,* hunting with the D'robo
and the Nandi. Of them he wrote, "My teachers were the Cherangani
D'robo, the most interesting natives I met. Neither of these small
mountain communities have ever come in touch with the white man,
till Hoey came among them and won their confidence."[14]

---

*A member of the Game Policy Committee, Hoey influenced the creation of early game
reserves. In 1913 he married the daughter of a safari client, Gladys Wright, and in 1920
selected the site for Kitale town.

2.

NAIROBI, WILD WEST TOWN

At its inception the settlement of Nairobi was described by pioneer railway engineer Ronald O. Preston—who on the way there had shot several man-eating lions at Tsavo railway station—as "a bleak, swampy stretch of soppy landscape, devoid of human habitation of any sort, the resort of thousands of wild animals of every species. It did not boast a single tree. It was unsafe to walk at night after dark between the railway line and what is known as Railway Hill, the whole valley being one series of game pits."[1]

Despite Preston's disparaging comments, the town grew at a great pace. Robert Foran said there was only one hotel of any substance in Nairobi, a corrugated sheet-iron building called Rayne's Masonic Hotel. If the hotel was full one simply camped, or stayed at the other "hotel," a vermin-ridden Goanese hostelry—and only then if one had not yet purchased a camp bed and tent. Next to Rayne's was one of Nairobi's first shops, owned by a Mrs. Bent, a dressmaker who became Mrs. Tate, the steely-eyed wife of a Nairobi railway man. Later Mrs. Mayence Tate became the owner of the now famous New Stanley Hotel, then called Hotel Stanley (in honor of explorer Henry Stanley) on Sixth Avenue. She was known to bar patrons as "Aunty," and one withering look from her was enough to break up a fistfight, according to white hunter Tom Murray Smith, who knew her well.

A congenial man named Tommy Wood had opened a small hotel on Victoria Street, which ran parallel with the town's Main Street.* There was little furniture at Wood's and patrons sat on soapboxes to do their drinking. Charles Heyer opened a gun shop and safari equipment firm

---

*Later Government Road, now Moi Avenue.

in the center of town. The town's first grocery store was a double-storied wood and iron building owned by Rosenrode and McJohn. They tacked onto their building a small bar, which usually did such a brisk business that patrons spilled out to the verandah of the store. Settlers with a few drinks under their belts often set up a wooden crate in the street and used it for pistol practice, forcing townsfolk to race for cover.

Close to the cluttered railhead settlement a squalid Indian bazaar grew up with fetid *dukas*, or shops, made from tin sheeting, and behind the shops were the crowded living quarters of their owners. The British administration had originally brought in Indian coolies from their Indian empire to serve as laborers during construction of the Uganda Railway. In the bazaar's narrow dirt alleys Indian and native prostitutes lurked. Outraged by conditions he found, Frederick Jackson, the deputy commissioner of Uganda, wrote:

> The camps were crowded with prostitutes and small boys and other accessories of the bestial vices so commonly practiced by the Orientals. . . . A dusty street was lined with a few wood and iron houses for railway officials, and beyond on the plain corrugated iron government buildings appeared. The place was an untidy, sprawling eyesore and a health hazard.[2]

His Majesty's Commissioner for East Africa, Sir Charles Eliot (1901–1904), wrote, "At present the township consists of a semicircle of bungalows on a low ridge, and a huge railway station, houses for workmen, a few European shops and an Indian bazaar. The houses are constructed of white tin, and somewhat resemble a mining settlement in the Western States of America."[3]

In 1902, when bubonic plague struck Nairobi killing sixteen people, a keen young medical officer destroyed the rat-infested Indian bazaar in the heart of the town in one fell swoop by burning it to the ground. He then applied his pyrotechnics to the scattered native villages that had sprung up on the town's periphery, and even set fire to the military lines and the railway workshops. This drastic quarantine measure cost the government £50,000—about equal to half its total annual revenue.[4]

Within a few years the Asian community, many of them no longer employed by the railway, began to emerge as a powerful economic force driven by their own industrious efforts, particularly as small shopkeepers, known as *duka wallahs*. When the Duke of Connaught

Nairobi house built of corrugated iron sheeting, owned by Ali Khan, horse and buggy operator, 1903.

became the first of the British royals to visit the colony in 1906, one of his official duties was the unveiling of a bust of Queen Victoria. The monarch's scowling countenance was donated not by a Victorian European or the British government but by an Indian merchant, an unabashed Anglophile named A. M. Jevanjee, Nairobi's first self-made millionaire, who rolled in the cash from far-flung trading stores. Along with the statue Jevanjee also donated to the township a nicely tended five-acre lot in the center of Nairobi where the statue was placed, known as Jevanjee Gardens. Jevanjee's wide-ranging enterprises had even included the *African Standard* newspaper, later sold and renamed the *East African Standard*. It was said of Jevanjee that more of an imperialist could not be found in a day's march.

COMMUNICATIONS BETWEEN Nairobi and the outside world were sporadic. A 320-mile-long telegraph line existed from Mombasa to Nairobi and the tiny railway stations in between, but it was a telegraph mostly in name only, for it functioned intermittently at best. Tribesmen coveted the treasured copper wire for ornaments and jewelry, so conveniently strung between poles, there for the taking. What the tribesmen did not use, giraffes neglected to duck beneath, or monkeys used as a trapeze.

African mail runners were used between stations when a line was down and farther up-country, where there was no line or mail service. It was a high-risk profession. One day two African postmen running in tandem were attacked by two hungry lions. Both lions hit on one man, giving his companion time to shimmy up a thorn tree. From his lofty perch the mail runner watched his screaming colleague being chewed up by the lions below. The lions' appetites unsatisfied, the horror-stricken man realized he was next on the menu when both lions turned their attention to climbing the tree in which he was clinging for dear life. Luckily for him, the tree was too steep, too thorny, and the lions eventually gave up. Lions were part of everyday life for white hunters, pioneers, and tourists alike. Big game often sauntered the streets of Nairobi and buffalo could be seen in the swamp beside the town or even from Ainsworth bridge.

Lions sometimes made kills right in the town and in the gardens of residents.[5] Nairobi's medical officer, Dr. A. D. Milne, returning one evening from a party on his bicycle actually ran into a large maned lion in the center of town and was unseated. It is not known who was more startled, Milne or the lion. Both retreated in opposite directions.

The ivory hunter Robert Foran killed his first lion (it was actually a lioness) on Main Street. Foran's second lion was also killed in Nairobi. On this occasion he was in dinner clothes and strolling back to his bungalow after a party. As it was near midnight, Foran decided on a whim to check up on his Indian police guards at the railway yards. As Foran later told friends, when he approached the first sentry, he was astonished to hear the man banging his ancient Martini-Henri rifle against the corrugated metal sides of the building and yelling "Shoo!" at the top of his lungs. Foran ran toward the man to see what the trouble was, just as the Punjabi policeman was clambering up the only lamppost in the area.

Foran soon saw the reason for the panicked Indian's flight. A big tawny-maned lion was calmly feeding on a freshly killed zebra. Leaving the terrified Indian policeman up his pole, Foran went to the nearest friend and borrowed a .350 Rigby-Mauser rifle from the disbelieving man. He returned to the policeman, still clinging "like a monkey to the lamppost." Foran's first shot hit the lion in the shoulder, but did not kill it. The lion growled and suddenly bounded off into the moonlight. Foran, still dressed in tuxedo, followed the beast through the streets and came up with it near the cemetery wall. The lion was beautifully silhouetted against a moonlit sky, and Foran killed it.

✧

MAJOR G. C. R. RINGER, the proprietor of the Norfolk Hotel, had
come to the British East Africa Protectorate as a safari client. He stayed
on to establish his hostelry at one end of Government Road, with the
railway station a dusty mile away at the other. The Norfolk opened its
doors on Christmas Day 1904 and quickly gained an international reputation for excellence. In the evenings white hunters between safaris
routinely gathered there with their clients for a sundowner, just as they
would for the next eighty years. Elspeth Huxley observed:

> These big-game shooting visitors, in a holiday frame of mind,
> did much to brighten the life of Nairobi in between safaris. There
> was only one place to stay, the Norfolk. Here also came the gayer
> of the colonists, twice a year, to the Christmas and July races.
> During these race weeks a good night's sleep was the most diffi-
> cult thing to obtain at the Norfolk. It was nothing to have an Ital-
> ian baron or an Austrian count thrown through a window in
> the middle of the night. The famous hunters of the day—R. J.
> Cunninghame, Fritz Schindelar, Alan Black and others—looked
> in whenever they were not in the wilder parts tracking lions and
> elephants, and added to the picturesque quality of the parties.
> East Africa began to earn its reputation for unconventionality and
> the picaresque.[6]

Alan Black was once sitting on the verandah having a drink with Bill
Imbert, an employee of the hotel, when somebody came over and said a
few words to him. Black said to Imbert, "Forgive me, but I have to go
out." He had been told there was a hippo on "the bridge," a spot close to
the Norfolk Hotel, and the hippo was holding up pedestrians. Bill
Imbert heard a gunshot. When Black came back, he said simply: "I've
just shot a hippo at Ainsworth bridge," and went on with his drinking.
The hotel was dubbed the House of Lords because of the numbers of
titled people who frequented it, both residents and shooting clients. For
amusement guests would rest comfortably on chairs on the hotel verandah and use the streetlight in front of the police station across the road
for target practice.[7] Lady Nesta Fitzgerald, a well-known figure, once
rode her pony up the steps and into the crowded bar where she shot
bottles off the shelves.[8]

R. J. Cunninghame's hunting client, the American novelist Stewart Edward White, like others in the safari world, made his headquarters at the Norfolk. He described the town as seen from the hotel's verandah in 1911:

> As one sits on the broad hotel verandah a constantly varied pageant passes before him. A daintily dressed, fresh-faced Englishwoman bobs by in a smart rickshaw drawn by two uniformed runners; a Kikuyu anointed, curled, naked, brass adorned, teeters along, an expression of satisfaction on his face; a horseman, well appointed, trots briskly by followed by his loping syce; a string of skin-clad women, their heads fantastically shaved, heavily ornamented, lean forward under the burden of firewood for the market; a beautiful baby in a frilled baby car is propelled by a tall, solemn, fine-looking black man in white robe and cap; the driver of a high cart tools his animal past a creaking, clumsy, two-wheeled wagon drawn by a pair of small humpbacked native oxen. . . .[9]

The dashing Austrian white hunter, Fritz Schindelar, was a frequenter of the Norfolk between his safaris. On one occasion Fritz shot a lion, and then, while the beast was dying, Fritz took the lion's head in his lap and fondled the beast until it expired. A photograph of this remarkable business was taken and hung for many years above the Norfolk bar. Fritz wrote across the picture, "Dying in my arms."

"I remember an argument that took place under this picture," J. A. Hunter recalled, "between Fritz and another white hunter. The discussion grew violent and finally the hunter said grimly, 'One more word out of you, Fritz, and by God you'll be dying in *my* arms!' "[10] The two men were separated. Yet tall, fearless Fritz Schindelar, the expert hunter and dashing horseman, was himself destined to die a slow, bloody death in the jaws of a lion.

Scrapbooks kept by Fritz Schindelar clearly attest to the numbers of beautiful, adventurous European and American women attracted to Nairobi. "One of the most ornamental of these," Elspeth Huxley said, "was a lady transport rider with two weaknesses, for spirits and for firing off revolvers. She used to ride into the bar of the Norfolk on a pony and, after a good many drinks, ride out again, generally facing the wrong way and firing her revolver repeatedly into the ceiling."[11] It was

Government Road, Nairobi, 1906.

rumored that after leaving Nairobi she made her way to the Congo with a male hairdresser, and from there to New York City, where she was shot dead in the Bowery.

BY 1906 Nairobi's population count showed 20 whites at the military cantonment and 559 in town, out of a total population of 13,515.[12] One of Nairobi's principal diversions was horse racing, which was started by Brigadier General A. S. Cooper in 1900. An original gymkhana meeting was held at Fort Machakos in 1902, and this resulted in the formation of the all-powerful Jockey Club of Kenya. The East African Turf Club's first president was lion hunter Lord Delamere, and the first race at Nairobi was held in 1903 under the rules of the Royal Calcutta Turf Club. In 1904 there were six events and sixteen horses or ponies competing on the card for the second race meet. The jockeys were amateurs, with the exception of an Australian white hunter named Henry Tarlton, whose more famous brother, Leslie, was the leading safari outfitter. Wild plains animals grazed beside the race track and herds of zebra, wildebeest, and gazelle were frequently driven off the course so that the races could proceed.

Lions commonly interrupted races. At the first race meeting an unsophisticated lion chased a zebra across the track as a race was in progress. The jockeys are said to have ridden the fastest races of their careers, although a number of them never made the finishing post as their mounts turned on seeing the lion in possession of the freshly killed zebra.

Horse racing was not the only spectator sport in vintage Nairobi. If there were no itinerant hunting safaris to amuse the populace, Nairobi's residents had become adept at amusing themselves. An amateur theater group called the Bohemians regularly put on plays. On the rougher side of local amusements, there was even a cock-fighting club that held semisecret events a few miles out of town. There was also a pack of hounds, known as the Masara Hounds, run by a Mr. Jim Elkington. Incongruous in the African bush, huntsmen wore traditional red jackets, black caps, white breeches, and rode behind imported English foxhounds in pursuit of jackals.

Apart from these diversions there were more intimate social activities. Ivory hunter Robert Foran was at the time a ranking colonial policeman in Nairobi, and observed:

> Whoring was an original pastime in pioneer Nairobi. Behind Main Street were some tin shanties and godowns, chiefly owned by Indians: also a mass of hovels occupied by Masai and other tribal women. There was a thriving establishment called the "Japanese Legation." A group of popular Japanese prostitutes ran their profession and business was brisk, for there was no competition outside of the tribal ladies in their ramshackle brothels. These women were always unobtrusive and well behaved, and I do not recollect a single complaint being lodged against these Japanese love birds, who were still flourishing in 1910.[13]

It was not long before the "Japanese Legation" had serious competition when a young British madam followed it with a house of Syrian beauties on the Athi River road outside town.

One American adventurer did his share to recreate the Wild West in Africa. Sixty-five-year-old Colonel Charles Jesse "Buffalo" Jones, who billed himself, "The Last of the Plainsmen," kept company with a couple of tough Texas cowpunchers named Ambrose Mearns and Marshall Loveless, along with half a dozen expert horsemen and lasso artists including Guy Scull, a personal friend of Teddy Roosevelt's. Buffalo and his men brought their own highly trained cow ponies from the United States, and left the hard-bitten locals slack-jawed with their dangerous antics.

Jones hired an Arusha-based pioneer white hunter named Ray Ulyate to lead his "capture and release" safari. During this safari, which was camped on the Athi plains south of Nairobi, Buffalo and his men lassoed a variety of animals. Several of these beasts were later paraded down Main Street, roped to cowboys on either side, and then to loud cheers they were walked back to the plains and released unharmed. Buffalo's men caught nearly every animal in the neighborhood, with the exception of the gnu, or wildebeest, which swarmed in massive herds across the plains. Wildebeest proved more than a match for Buffalo's men. They had the acceleration of a Ferrari, and in top gear easily outgalloped the horses. Gnus also turned on a dime, zigged and zagged, and their sloping shoulders seemed to keep the skillfully thrown lassoes off course. Wildebeest, the clowns of the plains, could keep up a crackling pace for hours, blowing the best of Buffalo's horses in no time. Yet Mearns and Loveless easily roped a lioness, rhino, zebra, and much else besides.

Once, as Buffalo and his men paraded down Government Road, one of his cowboys broke into a gallop and raced past applauding fellow American, the gigantic Northrup McMillan. In an instant McMillan was astonished to find the man's lariat snaking through the air and pinning his arms to his sides. Another big man, a game ranger named Goldfinch, also enjoyed drinking beer on the Norfolk's patio. He was thus occupied when a lariat whistled through the air, encircled him, and yanked him out of his chair into the dust. He was surrounded by a laughing group of good-natured cowboys. Goldfinch dusted himself off, and happily stood a round of drinks.[14]

Buffalo's big, beautiful horses were the envy of the locals, and many offers were made to purchase them, but Jones would not part with any, taking them with him back to America.

Another of Nairobi's characters was Captain Jackie Lethbridge, who kept a pet lion at his home at Parklands near town. "He had a more or less tame half-grown lion," his son-in-law, white hunter Tom Murray Smith, recalled, "which he used to tether to the steps of his bungalow to keep off thieves, importunate bazaar wallahs, and other sundry visitors he didn't care much about. He took his lion about with him everywhere, into hotels or shops, wherever Jackie went, the lion went with him. It used to ride alongside him in his native-drawn rickshaw and would growl down the neck of the wretched rickshaw 'boy' if Jackie thought the pace too slow."[15]

Lethbridge was a tough old war veteran who had fought the Boers before arriving in East Africa in 1902. At one stage in his rather checkered career, he took forty Indian polo ponies to Abyssinia for Northrup McMillan and sold them to Emperor Menelik in Addis Ababa. The ponies had to be walked the whole way, about 1,500 miles. Not one was lost to lions, sickness, or bandits. The emperor was so pleased with the horses, he invited Jackie to dine with him, recalled Murray Smith. "My father-in-law always traveled with his evening kit as a matter of course, and so he was properly dressed for the palace function. Menelik also appeared in full evening dress, but wore his shirt outside his trousers. Not to be outdone and save his host and himself embarrassment, Jackie promptly pulled his shirt out too!"[16] Although Jackie Lethbridge was never a white hunter, he liked to hunt lions. Murray Smith wrote:

> One day on the Athi Plains he was hunting with a friend who was dragged off his horse by a lion and was terribly mauled before Lethbridge rode up and shot the lion as it straddled the fallen man. He was able to get the man back to camp, but they had no medical supplies. There was only one thing to do and Jackie did it—he rode hell for leather to Nairobi, 30 miles away, having to swim the Athi River which was in full spate as the rains had started.
>
> Arriving in town after sundown, the only doctor he could locate was an Indian, who, realizing the state of the country during the rains, showed some hesitation in turning out, but promptly changed his mind on sight of the business end of a revolver. Both riding fresh horses, they set out on the return journey. Arriving at the river, one sight of the dark rushing flood was enough for the scared Asian, who absolutely refused to attempt the crossing. "Sir, you can shoot me if you like," he said, and meant it. He was terrified. Without wasting words, Lethbridge packed the medical supplies under his hat, and with great difficulty, he and his horse swam the river again, arriving back at the camp around midnight. The mauled man was in a bad way. The

wounds, which Jackie dressed immediately, were severe enough, but it was really a shock to the system which proved fatal. The poor fellow died suddenly at dawn, drinking whiskey for whiskey with his friend till almost the last. Lethbridge left East Africa in 1911, saying the country was becoming too civilized.[17]

3.

HUNTER ON THE
LUNATIC EXPRESS

Twenty-one-year-old John Alexander Hunter was a raw country boy fresh from Scotland when he boarded the Uganda Railway, unofficially known as the Lunatic Express, at Mombasa in 1908. The railway had lived up to its nickname. From the start it was thought an insane undertaking into the unknown heart of Africa. Tracks would have to be laid from sea level across the formidable Taru Desert, then through miles of lion-infested thorn jungles. Farther on there were steep mountain ranges, one over 9,000 feet, not to mention opposition from tribes, wild animals, insects, and a tropical climate. During construction of the rail line's first thirteen miles from Mombasa to Mazeras station in November 1896, work ceased for three weeks due to floods. After one year's toil the line had reached mile 23, where it suffered another delay after 500 workers went down with malaria. At mile 100 the rails reached Voi station, and an Irish supervisor, O'Hara, was dragged to his death by a man-eating lion as his wife and child cowered helplessly in a tent.[1]

In February 1899 progress was halted again at Tsavo River for three months as man-eating lions terrorized workers, mostly Indian coolies imported by the British from eastern India, killing and eating twenty-eight men. The attacks eventually ceased when a railway official, J. H. Patterson, shot the marauders. Work stopped at the appropriately named Kima (minced meat) station after a solitary man-eating lion caused havoc. A railway police superintendent, Charles Ryall, set out to shoot the man-eater. He had his sleeping coach shunted off the main line and parked twenty yards from the station. With two European companions Ryall planned to keep watch over the station platform through the night. Ryall began his shift at midnight, but dozed off. The man-eater entered the open door of the compartment, standing on one of the terrified men who had been sleeping on the floor, and seized Ryall by the throat. The big cat found itself trapped in the compartment as the sliding door had shut behind it. With Ryall firmly in its jaws the lion calmly dragged him through an open window to the platform, ignoring the policeman's panic-stricken companions. The next day Ryall's body was found beneath a bush, partly devoured. His throat was lacerated and one thigh eaten. The lion had disemboweled the man and dragged the intestines a short distance. The railway offered a reward of one hundred pounds for the man-eater, dead or alive. Twelve lions were shot by eager hunters around Kima, but the real culprit eluded them and continued to kill humans. The man-eater was eventually trapped unharmed by two railway employees who constructed an ingenious drop-door trap baited with a live calf. The heavily maned lion was in prime condition and had not been driven to man-eating because of some injury that forced it to prey on humans rather than animals.

In 1908 as John Hunter traveled on the Lunatic Express between Mombasa and Nairobi, he was astounded at the big game he saw from his carriage. Herds of elephant roamed the bush country around Voi, and upon the Athi Plains countless animals of many species grazed in vast herds as far as the eye could see. When he disembarked in Nairobi, the first person he met was white hunter Alan Black, whose hatband bore the tail-tips of fourteen man-eating lions he had dispatched. Soon afterward, J.A., which is the name John Hunter came to be known by in East Africa, met other white hunters whom he considered to be the most colorful group who ever lived. Among these famous men were Bill Judd, Fritz Schindelar, and ivory hunter Karamoja Bell, whose marksmanship was a byword in Africa. J.A. admired these hunters enormously and dreamed of a life as exciting as theirs. He was already an experienced shot having spent his youth hunting wildfowl in the bogs of Lochar Moss, where he shot duck, mallard, and red grouse with his father's Purdey shotgun.

J.A. soon found work as a guard on the Lunatic Express, then switched to hunting lions for the railway. Even when lions were not killing laborers, the men were so intimidated by their distant roaring at night they refused to work. The stretch of line between Athi River station, twenty-five miles east of Nairobi, and Simba (Lion) station and Kima station was one of the most notorious for man-eating lions. Game

The Lunatic Express's maiden run from Mombasa, January 1898.

rangers Captain Woosnam and Blayney Percival often had their hands full trying to deal with lion attacks and were not averse to assistance. J.A., although new to the business, was already beginning to be noticed for his feats of marksmanship with rifle or shotgun. He was often able to sell his lion skins at a good profit and supplement his meager railway salary. At the time a heavily maned lion could fetch as much as twenty pounds. Many of these skins were sold to "dudes," who returned home claiming they had shot the trophies themselves.

J.A. worked with a skilled African tracker, a member of the WaLiangulu tribe, famous for their hunting prowess. Together the two men developed their own method, a very dangerous one as it turned out, for hunting lion. When a report of a man-eater or a cattle killer would come in, Hunter and his tracker would follow the informant back to where the lion was last known to be, and from there would track it down. It was fairly easy spooring in sandy bush country around Tsavo, and the intent was to catch up with the lion when it was under shade having a noontime siesta.

Once J.A. was reasonably certain the lion was in a particular thicket, he would have his tracker lob stones into the brush. The resulting growl often gave Hunter a bearing on the lion, which would usually break cover giving him a flying shot as it tried to make off to better cover; in some instances, it charged straight for him. In J.A.'s words:

> There were few sights in nature more terrible than that of a charg-
> ing lion. A man standing only thirty yards from a charging lion
> cannot afford to miss.
>
> I would stand with my rifle ready while my boy was throwing
> stones to provoke the charge. When the charge came I'd throw my
> rifle to my shoulder and fire instantly at the tawny shape that
> seemed to move with the speed of a shell. If the shot is true the
> lion often turns a somersault and comes smacking down maybe a
> dozen feet in front of you. If a man misses, he is indeed fortunate
> if he has time for a second shot before the lion is on him, with
> fangs busy and hind claws ripping him open.[2]

One lion routinely began visiting Simba and the Indian stationmaster was as terrified as the coolies under him, but he found a large
circular water tank that he set up in his tent as protection, shamelessly
leaving his wretched coolies to their own devices. Apparently he slept
soundly in his metal container, which he crawled into through a small
opening in the top—until the fourth night, when the prowling man-
eater returned and began to sniff around the tank. He liked what he
smelled. The terrified man in the tank tried to make himself as small as
possible, while the lion tried—unsuccessfully—to get through the hole
in the tank. The cat and mouse game continued for some time, during
which the frantic man fainted several times from sheer terror.

When the stationmaster did not appear for duty somebody was sent
to awaken him. The coolie approached gingerly, seeing the tent was
badly shredded. As the man looked around he saw the spoor of a lion,
and soon heard the groans of the stationmaster in the tank. It is claimed
the man's hair had turned white overnight. In any case, the stationmaster refused to spend another night at Simba, and without informing
anyone, boarded the next train passing through Simba. At Mombasa he
hopped on a freighter, not caring where it went, provided it was as far
from Simba station as possible.[3]

During another ten-day period at Simba, half a dozen men were
killed by a huge black-maned lion. A wealthy Indian prince, upon hearing of this magnificent trophy, caught a train to Simba station where he
set up camp to hunt the lion. The prince did not have long to wait. Just
after dark the man-eater jumped into a startled circle of Africans sitting

J. A. Hunter.

around a cooking fire right under the station's lamp. The lion grabbed a man, who screamed the scream of the condemned. The lion nonchalantly dragged him across the railway tracks, then sat down and calmly began to eat his victim in full view of the diners. Those at the station with any sort of gun, including the Indian prince, began firing. This excited shooting caused the lion to drag its victim a few yards farther away, just outside the circle of light shed by the station lamp. Every time a bullet whistled past he let out an earth-shattering roar. Next morning the big cat and its victim had vanished forever.

The most publicized series of lion attacks is that of the Tsavo man-eating lions immortalized by Colonel J. H. Patterson. Twenty-eight Indian coolies and an unknown number of African laborers were killed and eaten by lions in the Tsavo area in 1898. Man-eating lions continued to attack people at remote railway stations for the next twenty years.

Early in his career as a lion hunter J.A. realized that the coolies brought much of their troubles upon themselves. Railway officials tried to induce coolies to bury their dead by paying them a reward to prevent corpses being left out in the bush to be consumed by vultures and other scavengers, including lions. Hunter believed some man-eaters had developed a taste for human flesh by feeding on corpses. Years later during a sand grouse shoot near Simba station, J.A. told me it was his theory habitual man-eaters became that way because of an acquired liking for human flesh and blood, which he claimed is saltier than venison.

However, J.A. would not elaborate on how he came to know human flesh tasted saltier. Since J.A. had made the acquaintance of cannibals in the Congo in the early part of this century one can only assume he had posed the question to them. But he would never say.

The completion of the railway brought a decrease in man-eating incidents along the Uganda Railway. Game ranger Blayney Percival attributed the reduction to the withdrawal of a reward offered by the railways for lions killed within the Mile Zone (the railway claimed ownership of land extending one mile on either side of the tracks), as well as the closing of construction camps and consequent reduction of men along the line.

4

FLASH JACK AND THE KING

White hunter Captain G. H. "Flash" Jack Riddell was among the more flamboyant members of the safari community in Nairobi after the turn of the century. Riddell was the son of a captain in the 16th Lancers who came from a long line of British aristocrats with strong traditions of the hunt. The tall, slim, mustachioed Riddell, a Sandhurst graduate who had served in India and the Boer War, was known as Flash Jack because he liked to make a distinctive sartorial statement in equatorial fashion. He fancied silk shirts, colorful cravats, and a wide-brimmed Stetson. Riddell was known for his wild antics. On festive occasions such as Nairobi race week celebrations, an elegantly attired Riddell would ride his favorite mare, Bess, into the dining room of the Norfolk Hotel where he and the surefooted Bess would jump over carefully prepared dining tables without disturbing a single piece of cutlery or china.

Jack's patrician background and impeccable social connections were useful in his line of work. He always traveled with what he called his "right arms," one of whom was an ancient Kamba gunbearer with the unlikely name of Kazimoto (Hotwork), said to be suicidally brave, and utterly devoted to Riddell. Jack, having been an officer, was accustomed to the services of a military "batman," and in civilian life he saw no reason why the tradition should cease. Thus his other "arm" was an unusual Masai spearman named Nganodudu. Unusual because his name was not Masai and meant "wheat insect" and also because the warlike Masai seldom accept such mundane domestic employment.

Riddell took his friend Winston Churchill, with whom he had served in India, on safari to the Thika River, north of Nairobi. At the end of one portion of their safari, Riddell and Churchill took a bet as to who would arrive back at the Norfolk Hotel first, thirty-five miles from their camp.

Riddell mounted his famous black mare, Bess, saying he could beat Churchill, who was to drive his own car, a Napier vehicle he had brought with him from England. At that time cars were almost nonexistent in the country; only a badly rutted wagon track separated Nairobi and Riddell's camp. As Riddell galloped off, Churchill's car lurched and jolted across bush tracks until the engine overheated and boiled over in the high altitude, forcing Churchill to stop frequently to refill his steaming radiator with water. It was a close race, but Riddell, the expert horseman, won the bet, arriving at the finish just ahead of Churchill.

Churchill also visited Lord Delamere's Soysambu ranch in the Great Rift Valley, where he did some pig-sticking on horseback, pursuing African wart hogs instead of the Indian or European boars to which he was accustomed. Delamere's grand luncheon in Churchill's honor was the year's most important social event in the Rift Valley.

The main part of Churchill's safari was to be a journey to Uganda, which Churchill had dubbed "The Pearl of Africa" during a safari seven years before. By the time Winston's party began making its way along the White Nile there was plenty of accumulated personnel and baggage. In addition to white hunter Riddell, there was now a detachment of the King's African Rifles, several British colonial officers—at the time Churchill was Undersecretary of State for the Colonies—over one hundred porters, and assorted hangers-on. After watching his safari preparing to move on, with the porters shouldering their sixty-pound loads ready for the day's march, Churchill commented:

> It compromises yourself and everybody and everything you take with you—food, tents, rifles, clothing, cooks, servants, porters— but especially porters. This ragged figure, tottering along under his load, is the unit of locomotion and the limit of possibility. Without porters you cannot move. With them you can move about twelve miles a day if all is well. How much can he carry? How far can he carry it? These are the questions which govern your calculations and your fate.[1]

One evening in camp as Riddell and Churchill shared a brandy around the campfire, Riddell told his friend about plans to open up trade in East Africa. At the time he argued that Abyssinia, directly north of British East Africa, would be a good market for Lancashire cotton products. American cotton cloth, known in East Africa as *amerikani*, was then a chief item of barter. Traders measured the cloth by arm's lengths, each length from elbow to fingertip. Four to six arms, or *mkonos*, of *amerikani* could be exchanged for one sheep or goat.*

Churchill agreed with the viability of the proposition, and Riddell launched his new firm, which he called the Boma Trading Company, or BTC. He could supply clients with almost anything and any service, whether they required cattle, donkeys, horses, skins, beeswax, ostrich feathers, or adventurous hunting safaris into the back of beyond. Riddell suggested clients take flannel shirts and undergarments for cold nights in the highlands, "and a fur-lined coat would not be unwelcome," he advised, as well as "a revolver, field glasses, saddle and bridle, compass, blankets, rifles and ammunition."[2] Naturally, for a price Riddell could provide almost any item a customer wanted.

WHEN HE WAS not hunting professionally, Flash Jack had already made a name for himself living on the edge as a horse and ivory trader in Abyssinia (now Ethiopia). He easily induced one of his American safari clients, a wealthy Bostonian by the name of W. G. "Billy" Sewell, who shared Riddell's taste for adventure, to take part in one of his escapades. The two men made a highly illegal raid into Abyssinia to buy prized horses (although the emperor of Abyssinia had expressly forbidden the export of horses) for shipment and resale in British East Africa.

Flash Jack had an archrival in the person of John Boyes, a ferocious and diminutive professional hunter and trader. The two men were exact opposites. Riddell was the suave and sophisticated white hunter, educated and cunning. Boyes was the belligerent bantam cock afraid of nothing, a crude maverick with little book-learning who lived among Kikuyu tribesmen. Riddell and Boyes became fierce competitors, determined to bend any law and take any risk to outdo the other.

J. A. Hunter chuckled over one "holy row" he had witnessed in the Norfolk Hotel bar shortly after he had first arrived in the colony:

> Riddell, one of the best known of the early white hunters, was
> leaning against the bar with a glass of straight whiskey in his

---

*Even in remote regions today elephant ivory is estimated for length by native hunters or trackers as *mkonos* (arm lengths) in the same way as *amerikani* cotton cloth. An elephant with two *mkonos* of ivory might be in the forty-pound class of tuskers, with each tusk estimated at forty pounds. *Mkono ene* (four arms) describes an eighty pounder. *Mkono sita* (six arms) is the prize of all prizes, a hundred pounder.

Self-styled "King of the WaKikuyu," John Boyes, and Kikuyu warriors.

hand and his thumb hooked into his cartridge belt watching a little man who was jumping about in front of him like a furious terrier, and using the most terrible language it had ever been my lot to hear.[3]

Boyes had learned Riddell planned to open a trade route with Abyssinia to trade for horses, donkeys, and camels, and the reason for Boyes's fury was that Riddell refused to cut him in. Always prepared to meet a challenge, Boyes mounted a rival Abyssinian expedition. Boyes and a Scandinavian friend named Selland set sail for Djibouti (then a French port on the northeast African mainland) aboard the French steamer *Oxus*.[4] Before starting out, Boyes had the foresight to obtain a letter of introduction to the emperor of Ethiopia from his old American friend and safari client, the influential Northrup McMillan. With McMillan's letter, permission to trade and the vital passport were granted by Emperor Menelik himself to proceed south from Djibouti.

Riddell was outsmarted by Boyes, for he was never able to obtain the emperor's permission to enter the country. Once in the Abyssinian capital of Addis Ababa, Boyes was requested by the British legation to contract for the transport of a valuable stock of three thousand pounds of ivory, currently buried near the international frontier, with British

East Africa. Boyes was to carry the ivory across the desert and deliver it to the British administration in Nairobi. Boyes knew the ivory would slow him down considerably and also make him a prime target for raiders, but he would never refuse such a valuable cargo. The safari, which by then was carrying a ton and a half of ivory, swelled to 30 Gabbra men leading 32 camels, 21 African followers, 6 Somalis, 28 horses, 48 mules, and 21 head of cattle. With the greatest difficulty Boyes led his safari to Nairobi across the parched lava beds and northern deserts. His exhausted column was attacked and harassed continuously, and he was often unable to purchase grain or food. Somehow Boyes got his caravan safely through to Nairobi.

After Boyes's success, Riddell remained more determined than ever to secure trading rights with Abyssinia. He planned to trade cotton cloth to tribesmen in return for their sheep and goats. In this enterprise Riddell took as partners his well-heeled friends Freddy Ward, formerly of the Irish Guards, the Marquis Gandolfi Hornyold, an Englishman whose titled Italian forebears had settled in England, and the Roy brothers, grandsons of a London shipping magnate. Billy Sewell, Riddell's old hunting companion, could not wait to get started.

Two BTC men, Marquis Hornyold and Fred Roy, were stationed at the remote Northern Frontier post of Mount Marsabit, from which they traveled continually throughout the desert regions. It was a tough way to make a living, but it was the likes of such rogue traders as Flash Jack and John Boyes that the British East Africa colonists were assured a supply of otherwise unobtainable native sheep. The Masai had no interest in trading sheep, but northern tribes such as the Rendille and Samburu would trade animals for *amerikani* cloth. Flash Jack saw beyond cotton and looked to profit from lucrative ivory, camels, donkeys, mules, cattle, and even beeswax.

The Colonial Office knew of Jack Riddell's rumored illicit activities in the past and laid down stiff conditions, stipulating Riddell must respect Abyssinian Emperor Menelik's authority, write reports regularly, and deposit one thousand pounds against good behavior, and also provide route maps.

In 1908 Jack Riddell and two partners arrived in Addis Ababa to once again seek Emperor Menelik's permission to buy ponies, much in demand for their hardiness, but permission was denied. The adventurers rode across the Danakil Desert where they purchased one hundred horses for the equivalent of two pounds per head. The problem remained how to get permission from the local Abyssinian *ras*, or governor, to take the horses across the border into British Somaliland without being caught and castrated. "Bribery and plenty of *tej* [local brew]," Billy Sewell said, "did the trick"—or part of it. As part of the deal the *ras* allowed the raiders twenty-four hours' head start. As Riddell's men crossed the border they saw a long line of horsemen galloping toward them—but just too late.[5] With incredible endurance Flash Jack and his partners drove the horses through Hargeisa to Berbera on the Red Sea, shipped them to Mombasa, and sold them at Nairobi for thirty pounds each.

Flash Jack thumbed his nose at the conditions laid down by the colonial government and continued smuggling operations. Geoffrey Archer,* a colonial administrator for whom Archer's Post in the Northern Frontier is named, recalled meeting Riddell during a foot safari to Mount Marsabit in 1909. Archer wrote, "Captain Jack Riddell . . . lunched amicably with me as I marched in and his caravan marched out. His caravan consisted entirely of 'chop boxes' filled with illicit ivory sawn into small pieces to avoid detection!"[6]

In addition to ivory Riddell found horse smuggling highly lucrative, despite considerable risks. Yet Riddell was not alone in these escapades, for a few others were doing the same thing, among them Abraham Block, who later owned the New Stanley, Norfolk, and Mawingo hotels. Riddell would smuggle horses, Boran cattle, and camels to a secret destination, then exchange the livestock for Masai sheep, which were in great demand and could be sold quite openly. For this purpose Flash Jack used land he had in the Rift Valley while Block used white hunter Bill Judd's coffee farm at Fort Smith.

The government finally closed down Riddell's operations. Flash Jack went back to being a full-time white hunter, a career at which he was far more successful. He continued to be in great demand for important safaris, among them those of the Duke of Connaught, the son of Queen Victoria and the younger brother of King Edward VII, and his family. Riddell's clever planning ensured that the duke would visit the widest variety of game country during three months' safari. There was a dramatic encounter during one stalk when a lioness rushed the hunters and was shot in full charge.

---

*Geoffrey Archer was the nephew of Frederick Jackson, a powerful Nairobi administrator, and later governor of Uganda.

5.

YANKEES ON SAFARI

In 1905 the voyage from the east coast of the United States to Mombasa on the east coast of Africa could be done in between thirty and forty days, at a one-way cost of $500. German Lloyd steamers sailed from New York to Naples or Marseilles, and from there passengers boarded the popular German East Africa Line for Mombasa. The new Uganda Railway carried safari hunters into the heart of big game country with only a twenty-four-hour train journey from the port of Mombasa to Nairobi. Beyond the railway line travel was still agonizingly slow, often held up while heavily laden ox-drawn wagons caught up with those on foot or horseback. Some of the best general hunting areas lay around Nairobi itself, and most of the early safaris utilized these accessible regions.

Trains did not have dining cars; instead travelers would alight at remote stations and there take meals at Dak bungalows, or rest houses, as was the fashion in India. The Daks usually had a few bedrooms that could be reasonably rented for those waiting for wagon transport to German East Africa or other destinations away from the railway line. The dining rooms were catered by a Goanese firm in Nairobi named J. A. Nazareth & Company. Goanese waiters in starched white uniforms sanctimoniously attended tables. With the exception of Dak breakfasts (oatmeal porridge, bacon, eggs, toast, and coffee), few travelers praised the meals, which invariably consisted of soup, stringy beef, potatoes, and cabbage topped off with banana fritters and Ceylon tea. But every traveler arriving at the first Dak, at Voi, just 103 miles from Mombasa, had been on the Lunatic Express for at least ten hours without food or anything to drink (unless they had the forethought to bring their own).

At some small stations refreshments were catered by the Indian stationmasters and limited to tea, a small bun, or *chapati* bread. Many veteran travelers preferred Dak bungalows to dining cars because the halts at stations gave passengers the chance to stretch, walk about, and socialize without the violent motion on the old mail trains. Even so, travelers had to be on the lookout for unseen dangers. One man who had a dog with him attracted a large leopard at Voi Dak bungalow. The leopard killed the dog, and severely mauled its owner.

At Nairobi the sportsman would be met by his white hunter, wined and dined at the Norfolk Hotel, and kitted out with made-to-measure khaki jodhpurs, bush jackets, skirts, blouses, terai hats, puttees, and boots from newly established Indian tailors and cobblers specializing in the business of outfitting clients. These early Nairobi clothiers, like Meghji Ahmed, Ahmed Brothers, and Alibhai's, gained international reputations for the quality and cut of their clothes. Clients would be measured in the morning, and their made-to-fit clothes, neatly pressed and wrapped in brown paper and string, were delivered to the Norfolk next day. Few items ever required tailoring adjustments. The tailors would even customize bush jackets with sewn-in cartridge loops to the exact size specified.

THE EARLY SAFARI clients were often as interesting and daring as their white hunters, and some of them were every bit as tough. Others brought with them a class and elegance not often seen in the country. One of the best known of these pioneer sportsmen was William Northrup McMillan. McMillan first came to Africa determined to explore the unknown reaches of the Blue Nile. Although the Blue Nile was vaguely marked on maps, no European had yet actually penetrated its immense trough, which extends more than three hundred miles from Lake Tana in the Ethiopian highlands to the Sudanese border. To lead the expedition McMillan employed a Norwegian explorer named B. H. Jessen, and at great cost arranged for a number of boats to be transported to Khartoum in Sudan.

In the fall of 1903 the expedition tackled the Blue Nile gorge from two directions at once.[1] McMillan was accompanied by his good-natured wife, Lucy, and her personal attendant, a former American slave named Louise Decker, as well as Englishman Charles Bulpett, who was his general manager.* Jessen was to sail up the Blue Nile from Sudan. The rest of McMillan's flotilla would sail downstream from Lake Tana in Abyssinia. The enterprise was doomed, but not for lack of daring or finances. Jessen found himself blocked by rapids at Famaka in Sudan before he ever got near the Abyssinian frontier. McMillan fared worse. All his boats were wrecked as soon as they were launched into the headlong current. Still, McMillan was philosophical, even though his expedition's purpose was never achieved.† He made the best of a bad situation and turned to hunting big game and collecting birds and butterflies for the British Museum.

Undaunted by his failure to unlock the secrets of the Blue Nile, McMillan encouraged Jessen to try again, although he himself did not make the journey. In 1905 Jessen set off with a mule caravan from Khartoum and entered the gorge from Sudan, but was forced to turn back three hundred miles from Lake Tana.

In September 1905 McMillan, his wife Lucy, Louise Decker, Charles Bulpett, and a friend, Major Ringer, returned to British East on a safari arranged for him by John Boyes, by then known as the self-styled "King of the WaKikuyu." Boyes had daringly insinuated himself among the region's largest tribe, whose chief he had befriended.

McMillan's safari with Boyes had two objectives. The first was to do some big game hunting, and the second was to scout for suitable ranchland. McMillan, Bulpett, and Ringer shot lions near Nairobi with Boyes, until McMillan became unwell and had to break off his safari. John Boyes took Ringer and Bulpett to a hill known as Ol Donyo Sabuk (The Mountain of Buffaloes), thirty miles north of Nairobi, where Ringer purchased a ranch for himself, which he named Juju, after a West African god known as the Big God. While his companions were away on their safari, McMillan bought his own ranch of 22,000 acres of game-rich land not far from Ringer's place, and named his estate Juja, or Lesser God. McMillan's Juja became the most famous ranch in the country. The ranch was set among the rivers Therika, Ruiru, Athi, and N'Derugo. Never one to do anything by halves, McMillan sailed for England and returned with a huge quantity of materials, enough to

---

*McMillan's Blue Nile expedition employed a Greek named Philip Zaphiro as taxidermist. Zaphiro's son, Dennis, a Kenya game warden, accompanied Ernest Hemingway when he was hunting with Philip Percival.

†Nobody succeeded in unlocking the secrets of the Blue Nile gorge until Colonel R. E. Cheesman's expedition mapped the region in 1925–1926.

build several bungalows and storehouses, an electric plant, an ice plant, a machine shop, a water tower, stables, stores, and outbuildings.

So it was as a result of Boyes's safari that these three clients, American William Northrup McMillan and the two Englishmen Charles Bulpett and Major Ringer, stayed on to settle in the country and become important citizens.

Northrup McMillan and some early safari clients were keen to get into unknown territory. One such man was an American friend of McMillan's, a midwestern rancher named Edgar Beecher Bronson, who came to Africa in 1908. Bronson told McMillan he wished to get into country that had not been shot over. McMillan recommended the man who had by then become his favorite—and only—white hunter, Bill Judd. Judd in turn suggested Bronson also hire the crack Australian professional, George Henry Outram, who had been a scout to the Anglo-German Boundary Commission in 1903, and who had traversed the entire border region between British East (now Kenya) and German East Africa (now Tanzania).

Judd wanted George Outram along because Outram had penetrated areas even Judd had not yet seen. The hunters planned to take Bronson into the rich game fields lying beyond the parched inferno surrounding the soda-encrusted shores of the twin saline lakes Magadi and Natron. Until then probably only two professional hunters, George Outram and R. J. Cunninghame, had led safaris into these regions, which, although relatively close as the crow flies, were separated from Nairobi by a belt of inhospitable arid lava wilderness. In this region George Outram had located several natural water tanks, or rain pools, hidden high on volcanic ridges or in deep gorges. These water tanks, few and far between, were known only to the Masai herders in the region and to a few enterprising Kikuyu tribesmen who risked the journey to dig out chunks of rock salt from Magadi, a task they had performed since time began.

Bronson's ultimate destination was the Mara River in Masailand, Judd's main hunting ground. Bill Judd had pioneered safaris into the highlands of Masailand and the area known today as the Masai Mara Game Reserve, but he had always previously approached this country from Kijabe in the north.

The core of Bronson's safari staff was made up of employees from McMillan's Juja ranch, including Regal Wassama, McMillan's cook, a splendid old Somali with great dignity and a culinary skill matching the best French chef; Awala Nuer, Outram's Somali *shikari*, whose one good eye constantly picked out game at distances most humans could never see; and Salem, an experienced coastal Swahili headman. In the safari's vanguard marched 70 *wapagazi* (porters) and 35 tough WaNyamwezi men used to the hardest marching, along with 35 untrained Kikuyu porters. Also on the safari were 7 Abyssinian mules and 22 donkeys to pack native food, chiefly beans and corn *posho*.[2]

Bronson's safari had only gone a few miles when the untrained porters debunked, a common problem on safaris of the time. At Nairobi Judd found the town stripped of porters because a record thirty safaris had been outfitted during November 1908. Judd had to hire thirty-five more untrained porters to take up the slack. It was to be a three-month-long safari, relatively common by the standards of the time. Led by Outram and Judd the caravan trudged southwest taking a line that would become the highway to present-day Magadi town. Marching in single file the hunters made for the nearest permanent water, the southern Uaso Nyiro River, sixty-four miles away. Bronson wrote:

> For this five days' ordinary safari marching, the trail traverses a horrid arid country hot as Death Valley, [with] isolated black volcanic uplifts rearing here and there high into the sky, their rugged grassless slopes, and the plains everywhere strewn with sharp fragments of volcanic rock. The traveller rarely has a chance to set foot upon soil. The thin growth of grass and thorny scrub on the levels and lower hill slopes is for nine months of the year burned gray as ashes and brittle as straw by the fierce equatorial sun blazing twelve hours a day out of a cloudless sky, and making the volcanic rubble so hot one can hardly hold a hand on it for a second. Indeed the route from Ngong to Magadi is only possible after the season of the big rains, when at four points on the way, natural tanks worn by the torrential downpours in the iron-hard volcanic rock are filled and afford a supply of fairly pure water until evaporation, occasional soda porters, and the nomadic Masai herdsmen and their flocks have exhausted it.[3]

The risk of not finding water in the tanks increased when the safari met a group of Kikuyu soda porters hauling blocks of rock salt on their backs, knowing the Kikuyu caravan might well have emptied the tanks. Even so, the safari was now committed and they plunged on. Their luck held and water was found at the second of the tanks, enough for the men, horses, and mules after a stiff march across a lava-strewn plain molten with heat. The heat was so intense it was decided not to march in the noonday hours for fear of crippling the men. Instead they began a series of night marches, beginning at 2 A.M.—"safely and truly piloted by the indomitable, never-hesitating Outram," Bronson wrote. On the fourth day the safari was desperate for water and descended a broad grassy plain full of zebra and Grant's gazelle. Bronson wrote, "Outram led us a mile off our true course, where hid away beneath a rocky ridge on the edge of a lava cliff several hundred feet high, we found several natural rock tanks of sweet rainwater the Kikuyu soda porters had not quite emptied."

The porters and animals were so exhausted they were unable to continue, and the safari took a day to rest in what shade they could find. Far away below the men could see the white, heat-warped surface of Magadi soda lake. An Indian soda caravan desperately tried to pass Bronson's safari, and Outram, suspecting the next water tanks would be low, raced ahead of both caravans so that he could hold the water tanks against all comers. Even so, the tank only held about sixty gallons of water, not nearly enough for man and beast, and the situation was desperate with the Uaso Nyiro River still twenty-five miles away and the footsore men and animals worn out from thirst. All thirty-five Kikuyu porters deserted. Men and animals doubled up on loads and then began a series of slow night marches across the lava beds. Bronson wrote of white hunter Outram:

> Outram's work that night was the most remarkable piece of night travelling I have ever known. Travelling by the stars in a country where we were seldom able to keep a straight course for a quarter-mile, turning sharply on long detours to keep to ground that would not pitch us over a cliff, the ground covered with thick loose volcanic stone and often held up by solid walls of thorn scrub, he brought us just at dawn to one narrow gorge in fifty miles that enables ascent to the next escarpment. It was astounding![4]

At last in the distance the exhausted caravan saw tall green timber marking the course of the Uaso Nyiro. With shouts to encourage each other, the travelers made for a campsite beside the river, shaded by giant ficus trees. In less than an hour Judd and his two companions caught forty-five catfish, one-half to one-and-a-half pounders, while the safari crew caught them by the scores. That night everybody in camp feasted on Kumbari à la Regal (catfish) and roast guinea fowl.

The hunters moved west across the Uaso Nyiro Valley, and on the way Bronson shot a rhino with a front horn of 23½ inches, and a couple of record-class buffalo, one of them with a huge 17-inch boss. With meat for the porters the hunters climbed the 2,000-foot lava-studded shoulders of the Nguruman escarpment, to reach another rain pool found by Outram. Now at 5,000 feet on the cool plains of the Loita plateau, Bronson shot a fine roan antelope and a number of common plains animals for the porters. The safari had tramped twenty-three days just to reach their chosen hunting area. As they trekked across the breezy highland savannahs, in the distance trees broke the plain marking the course of the Mara River—or the Amala River, as it was then known. Near their camp a group of Mara Masai told Judd that apart from Outram and one white elephant hunter, no white man had ever before been among them.[5] The safari was now in a part of the Mara not even the redoubtable Judd had yet traversed.

Bronson, like his friend McMillan, had found his bit of unknown territory, and his Yankee ingenuity had equipped him to deal with its rigors. He was so pleased he extended the length of his safari to seven months.

ANOTHER AMERICAN equally enchanted by Africa was a millionaire Ohio banker, Kenyon Painter, who hired Bronson's hunter, George Outram, and Arusha hunter Ray Ulyate for a three-month safari to German East in 1907. Painter's first safari led to an astonishing collection of wildlife and bird specimens. Between 1907 and his death in 1940, Painter made thirty-one extended hunting safaris. Although little known today, Painter was one of the first to exploit business opportunities in German East on a grand scale, far greater than most pioneer hunter clients in British territory.

Painter returned on his third safari in 1910–1911, but this time he brought his young bride, petite New Yorker Maud (née Wyeth). At Nairobi, Roosevelt's safari, which had been headed by R. J. Cunninghame, had just returned from Sudan, and the Painters purchased much of Roosevelt's outfit. Teddy, who was a personal friend, had given Painter his leather writing case fitted with glass shades and candles, and even a pair of his massive knee-high safari boots, which tipped the

Kenyon and Maud Painter (center and right, on oxcart) during their three-month honeymoon safari, 1911.

---

scales at a staggering 4 pounds 11 ounces each. Kenyon and Maud's honeymoon safari was led by unknown Arusha white hunters named Twigg and Smith.* The Painters were as intrigued by Smith's beautiful coffee estate as they were with the tiny frontier town of Arusha. Unlike downtown Nairobi's flat-as-a-pancake landscape, Arusha was beautifully sited at the southern base of Mount Kilimanjaro's sister mountain, Meru, amid rolling green foothills. Towering above Arusha township is the 14,979-foot cone of Mount Meru's extinct volcano, which is more reminiscent of an Alpine landscape than of tropical Africa, for sometimes the peak is dusted with snow. Three swift, gin-clear mountain streams flow through the perennially green, well-wooded settlement, which had originally grown up around a German fort or *boma* (Swahili for cattle corral). The well-fortified *boma* was garrisoned with a platoon of soldiers and staffed by a handful of German civil administrators and police.†

---

*One of the Smith brothers was killed in action by General Paul Emil von Lettow-Vorbeck's *Schutztruppe* at the Battle of Longido Hill in 1915. Hamilton Twigg died of blackwater fever at Kondoa Irangi in 1916 during the British advance on von Lettow's positions.

†The fort's stone-rag, or uncut stone, structure endured and remained in use as a police station, jail, and administrative offices until 1965, when it became a museum.

◇

WHEN KENYON PAINTER had first arrived at Arusha by ox wagon and mules back in 1907, the town boasted one tiny hotel, known by the name of its Jewish owner, Bloom's. Bloom's was nothing more than a whitewashed, mud-brick building with a roof of corrugated iron sheeting. It had a dozen bedrooms, a chintzy lounge, and a bar cum dining room overlooking a fast snowmelt stream called the Themi River. Sunburned German settlers routinely gathered for schnapps and songs on the verandah. The few British residents slouched in for pink gins much as they did in the more sumptuous surroundings of the Norfolk in Nairobi.

Adjacent to the hotel was John Mulholland's Store, which dealt in everything from rhino horn and ivory tusks to trophies of every sort, along with the best groceries in town. He also sold rifles, pistols, *likker*, vegetables and tinned goods, tents, bedding, mosquito nets, pots and pans, saddles and tack. Arusha was made up of a few modest dwellings, a telegraph office, a couple of rickety Indian-owned mud *dukas* with false storefronts, a German blacksmith, livery stables, and half a dozen shops owned by Germans, Greeks, and South Africans trading in farm implements, seed beans, cattle, and goatskins. In the town lived several hundred Africans, mostly members of the Wa-Arush, a mixture of intermarried Masai and Meru tribesmen who were sedentary subsistence agriculturalists growing bananas, corn, and cassava. Surrounding the town were German-developed small holdings carved out of nothing and growing everything from cereals to cherries, apples, citrus, coffee, cocoa, vanilla, and rubber.

Kenyon and Maud Painter could not wait for their fourth safari, led this time by George Outram. Painter shot a Roosevelt's sable in the Shimba hills south of Mombasa. His trophy was the last Roosevelt's sable legally shot, for game ranger Blayney Percival made the species "Royal" or protected game.*

During his safari with Outram, Painter wounded a lion with a shot in the neck. The enraged animal promptly charged Painter's gunbearer, who fired at it but missed. The gunbearer's bullet struck the wooden fore-end of Painter's .350 Mauser rifle; otherwise Painter would have

---

*Roosevelt's sable was never prolific in Kenya in this century. Mostly confined to the Shimba hills, twenty miles south of Mombasa, the modern Kenya sable population probably never numbered more than two hundred, although their number was once much larger.

Gunbearers with Painter's black-maned lion near Arusha, 1911.

been killed. Cool-headed Outram shot the lion through the brain as it savaged the gunbearer.[6] The experience did nothing except further spur Painter's fascination with lion. Several days later he shot a magnificent old black-maned specimen on the Ardie Plains, a few miles from town.

On his next trip to Africa Painter hired two little-known Arusha hunters by the names of Thompson and Noadi. Their safari camp was again pitched on the Ardie Plains, and almost immediately they encountered lion. An entry in Kenyon's diary shows their luck ran out with the King of Beasts:

> The porters told us they could not get water because a large lion was by the river. I went out and shot it. The lion roared and went into the bushes. By this time John [John Wyeth, Painter's brother-in-law], Noadi and Thompson joined us. We told Thompson not to go into the bushes but he went in, and was bitten severely in the arms, legs, chest and thigh in about 24 places.[7]

The badly savaged white hunter, ashen-faced and bleeding from his wounds, asked his partner, Noadi, whether or not the lion was dead. Noadi was uncertain, and said he would give the lion a final shot to be sure. The second mauling that followed was recorded by Maud Painter:

Kenyon Painter's world-record rhino (front horn 53½ inches).

He [white hunter Noadi] fired. Then the lion jumped on top of Thompson again; Noadi was knocked over by the jump and his first shot missed. The second shot hit Thompson's gun, went through it and got the lion in the back of the neck, but only wounded it. The lion was trying to get Thompson's face as he lay on the ground, but he had his arms up protecting himself. The lion chewed one arm then the other. Noadi got his gun in the lion's ear and killed it. Noadi had to drag the lion off Thompson and take its teeth out of his arm, and a claw out of his back. This all happened in less than 10 seconds!

He was so brave. John gave him a drink of whiskey. His last wound I dressed seemed very painful, but I stuck to it. Poor fellow was exhausted by then. Everybody was working pulling bandages off the reels and getting adhesive tape. John drove the car, Noadi beside him, with Thompson in the back on pillows with a boy to hold his feet. There are no roads. They had 40 miles across the plains with a hole every 20 yards. Then they struck the main road which was something awful. Rocks and ditches and perfectly terrible. They arrived at the hospital at 6 A.M. It takes three days for blood poisoning to set in, so we were terribly worried until we got word he was O.K.[8]

On a later safari Painter shot the world's outright record rhino. He was camped with white hunter George Hurst near the tree line above the plains on Mount Meru's western slope, where rhino were common. The two had tracked a rhino for many hours and found it in a small forest glade. Painter's remarkable trophy had a front horn of 53½ inches and a rear horn of 18 ¼ inches.

6

THE HUNTER'S HUNTER

When the Boer War began in South Africa on October 10, 1899, the young hunter William Charles "Bill" Judd* rushed to join up as a cavalryman in a band of British irregulars, and he saw plenty of action. Following the war Judd decided to look for adventure of a different kind. He returned to his old hunting grounds in the Portuguese territory of Mozambique, this time with a job shooting Cape buffalo on the Incomati sugar estates. It was dangerous work, which earned him 5 shillings (about $.80) for each buffalo hide. Sometime over this period he met R. J. Cunninghame.

"Cunninghame and Bill Judd were professional hunters of buffalo on the Pungwe in Mozambique in 1899," according to author and artist John G. Millais, "and shot buffalo daily for a living." Millais, who later hunted with Judd as a safari client, observed that "Judd adheres to his original opinion that the buffalo is the most feared, as he is so hard to stop on charge." Judd remarked to Millais, "I personally have had more close shaves from these brutes than I have had from all other game put together—lion and elephant included."[1]

From the Portuguese port of Beira Judd followed his friend Cunninghame to British East Africa, landing at Mombasa in 1902. He immediately began hunting ivory, traveling deep into the eastern Belgian Congo, before returning to Nairobi, where he met American settler Northrup McMillan. The two men hit it off so well that McMillan promptly hired Judd to arrange a shooting safari for him. McMillan's generosity and friendship was a windfall for Judd and enabled him to become a full-time white hunter. It was the beginning of a long and

---

*Bill Judd was born in Greenwich, England, February 2, 1870.

Bill Judd, 1905.

highly successful career that made him famous. McMillan went on to engage Judd on five more lengthy safaris over the years. McMillan's international connections also resulted in numerous celebrity safaris for Judd, including those of Baron Goldschmidt, Sir Edmund Lechmere, Baron Rothschild, Congressman Tinkham, Teddy and Kermit Roosevelt, and Frederick Courtney Selous, among others.

By this time the Africans had nicknamed Judd "Bwana Ngozi" (Mister Skin) on account of his preference for wearing leather riding chaps, or leather breeches. Five foot ten inches tall, dark-haired, brown-eyed, and mustachioed, Judd was regarded with awe because of his great physical strength, demonstrated when he once lifted a grown donkey.

IN MAY 1908 Americans J. J. White and the preacher Dr. W. S. Rainsford asked Bill Judd to outfit a safari for them. Hunting near the Nzoia River White shot an antelope, but before he and Judd reached the dead animal, three big black-maned lions materialized out of the grass and promptly seized possession of the carcass. So intent were the lions on their meal they did not notice the approach of the hunters. It was White's first crack at a lion, and not only was he nervous, but he was using an untried .350 Mauser rifle, a light-caliber weapon then in common use. He took a bead on his lion and fired. He thought he had missed. But in fact his bullet had passed low through a foreleg, slightly wounding the lion, but without breaking a bone. Judd, waiting for his client to have a fair shake at the lion, hesitated before loosing off his own shot. By then the winged lion was in top gear racing for cover along the Nzoia River, but inexplicably White did not fire.

Judd knew that if the wounded lion got into thickets it would be very bad medicine indeed. Judd decided he could wait no longer for White to fire. By then the lion was over a hundred yards away and moving fast. Bill threw up his own .350 Rigby Mauser and drew a bead on the galloping yellow speck, firing two shots in quick succession. He heard the distant smack as his soft-nose bullets connected, and from long experience knew the shots were too far back and could not be immediately fatal.

According to Rainsford, Judd and White "recklessly" followed the blood spoor into the riverine thickets. "Nothing," Rainsford wrote, "would have induced me to allow, so long as I could prevent it, anyone to enter such a place, had I not had the most positive assurances from J.J.W.'s [White's] hunter [Bill Judd] that he knew where his bullets were placed."

Judd, of course, had no intention of leaving a lion that had been wounded. He would go in and finish the business, no matter how unpleasant. Judd's mistake, if it had been one at all, was permitting two greenhorns to accompany him in such dangerous circumstances. It was a lesson that taught him never to allow such folly again. Near the dense riverine thickets Rainsford joined White and Judd. Rainsford wrote: "Everything looked like a dead lion. So we went in. We formed the beaters in a line, only a few feet apart, with a gunbearer or an *askari* carrying a double gun here and there to give the men heart, and slowly, foot by foot, began our advance into the semi-darkness. In all, the beaters line had quite a massive line of artillery, for there were twelve rifles and double barrels in all."[2] There was an awful roaring coming from the middle of the line, and a fusillade of shots from all sides, but none of the untrained beaters could shoot properly, and none hit the lion. Suddenly there was silence, then a loud cheer.

Momba, Judd's trusted Kikuyu gunbearer, had come upon the lion on the riverbank. Momba was positioned on the extreme right wing of the beaters. The lion was hurt, "nearly done," Rainsford says, yet as Momba broke through the cover, the lion raised his head. Momba fired two or three times at the lion from a range of several feet. The lion seized Momba's arm in its jaws, and along with it the stock of his rifle.

The lion's teeth sank into the rifle stock, lessening the wound, because only its upper jaw was able to bite the man's arm. The lion let go and obtained a better jaw-hold on Momba's arm but soon broke off, running back through the advancing line of beaters where White and Judd were. According to Rainsford, "All three men fired their .350s. Two bullets took the lion in the chest and he fell at their feet, the bullets in all likelihood fired by the hunter, as J.J.W.'s Somali gunbearer, although brave to the point of suicide, was a very indifferent shot."[3]

The men cheered when the huge lion fell, but few at that point realized that Momba had been mauled. Soon his companions heard his cries and carried him out. Of Momba's bravery, Rainsford reported:

> He had made no outcry when the beast gripped him, though the wounds of the great teeth, almost through the forearm, showed plainly the sideways tug he had received—and flesh and sinew were forced outward by the straining. But he cried pitifully when the fierce burning current of disinfectant was forced into all the wounds. Poor Momba had seventeen wounds in all. . . . It was fortunate that I always carried in my saddlebags permanganate of potash, lint, bandages, and strong syringe; also that my syce carried my water bottle full of boiled water. These were to hand in a few minutes, and I did with them for poor Momba what I could.[4]

Bill Judd was a meticulous diarist, and he had a very different perspective of these events. In his diary of Sunday, 31 May 1908, he wrote:

> Had carpet lecture from Dr. R. on the sins of leaving Mr. W. by himself whilst I was looking for the lion yesterday. Left camp at 8 o'clock with 20 porters to look for the lion. I formed the boys 10 paces between each and started through the bush. A grunt told us the lion was still alive. Next thing a fusillade of shotguns and Sniders told us they had come in touch with Leo. Hurrying to where the shots were being fired I just caught sight of the lion passing through some scrub and potted at him, but missed, for he came on and emerged near me, about 6 paces off. I let him have two .350s in the chest and with a last growl he fell over dead. Three cheers were given as is customary, but they had hardly died away when my boy, Momba, called out that he was hurt. In a minute I was by his side. He was holding his arm which we saw

the lion had bitten. I cut off the sleeve of his jersey and found very deep tooth marks which were bleeding freely. Fortunately I had antiseptics and bandages in my saddlebags and these were quickly to hand, and in the water bottle I soon had a solution of Condy's ready with which the wound was well washed and afterwards bound up. Fortunately no bones were broken. I gave him 2 grains of opium and he seems to be getting a good rest.[5]

White's safari marched off the Uasin Gishu plateau and several weeks later arrived on the Laikipia plateau, where they happened upon a medical missionary who looked over Momba's wounds. Rainsford noted:

He probed and lanced the arm, leaving in drainage tubes so that in a week, all swelling had gone. Nine weeks after his mauling, Momba marched off joyously on an eighty-mile tramp to greet his four expectant Kikuyu wives, dropping hints that as he was now possessed of seventy-five rupees he might add to their number.[6]

Rainsford's savage criticisms in a later book undoubtedly hurt Judd's reputation, for although he never mentions Judd by name the descriptions left no doubt in anybody's mind that he was referring to Judd.

ONE OF BILL JUDD'S clients, William D. Boyce, a millionaire Chicago newspaper publisher, hoped to be immortalized as the first to take aerial wildlife photographs from a balloon. Boyce set up his apparatus beside the Norfolk Hotel. Fascinated Nairobi townsfolk gathered to witness the magic and guess what the strange Americans would dream up next. The balloon attached to its cable ascended to a dizzying five hundred feet, when the first aerial pictures of Nairobi were made with a hand-cranked movie camera. Judd loaded the entire Boyce safari on the train for Kijabe (Wind) station, where the balloon was supposed to soar over the Rift Valley, but at Kijabe the balloon could not be coaxed any higher than two hundred feet. Abandoning his Balloonograph Expedition, as he called it, Boyce concentrated on his top trophy priority, elephant, which was to be followed by a trip to the Mara River for lion.

At a camp in Kisii, Judd left Boyce to rest, while he went out with his trackers to scout for elephant. In Judd's absence Boyce stupidly decided to hunt on his own. From a ridge Boyce saw the back of an animal in tall grass, and because he could not speak Swahili, he could not understand what his gunbearer was telling him. Thinking it was a rhino, Boyce got off his horse and entered the tall grass. Boyce wrote:

> I saw right in front of me and not ten yards away, a trunk wave in the air, two big ears flop, and an elephant looking at me as much surprised as I was. I threw up my double-barrel .500 rifle and pulled both triggers, tossed the gun away and ran back the way I had come.[7]

Badly shaken but thanking his stars he was still in one piece, Boyce made it to camp guided by his gunbearer. Later he wrote:

> Judd came in later and gave me a "blowing up" for having gone out alone. He said that I might have been killed and that would have ruined his reputation. The gunbearer told him that I had hit the elephant. Anyhow the gun had to be recovered, as it cost $600, and they went out, and they found the gun and two hundred yards away a dead elephant. My greatest disappointment was that it was a cow, with only thirty pounds of ivory. As it was against regulations to shoot cows and the ivory was underweight, I had to pay $125 [fine] for killing the elephant and was supposed to have the ivory confiscated. However the Governor of B.E.A., who was reared in New Orleans, permitted me to keep the ivory. Judd would not permit me to go out alone again.[8]

Judd moved camp once more, this time to the high Loita Plains country, where the safari quickly made contact with a big maned lion. Boyce recalled:

> He came straight for us with tremendous leaps, and at a speed faster than anything I had ever seen in a four-footed animal. With Judd holding his fire for an emergency, I let the lion come for about forty yards. His big chest was a fair mark and I hit it flush. He never lashed his tail after that. The bullet had passed through his heart and carried thru almost into his hindquarters. He measured ten foot six from tip to tip.[9]

LATER THAT YEAR Judd made an astonishing safari marching with a group of clients across western Kenya into W. D. M. Bell's great

Bill Judd on safari.

elephant-hunting country in the Karamoja district of Uganda. The safari hunted all the way en route to Sudan, collecting excellent specimens of elephant, buffalo, lion, leopard, and greater kudu. Reaching the Nile at Nimule, Judd turned north, following the river to the old British outpost of Gondokoro on the east bank of the Nile, where they sailed aboard a paddle steamer down the river. Judd and his men parted company with the clients at Port Said and sailed back to Mombasa via the Red Sea. This incredible distance was covered in only four months. While in Sudan Judd discovered two new butterflies, which were named after him.

His Fort Smith coffee plantation and Naivasha ranch were doing well, and Judd now considered retiring from safaris to spend more time with his family. Yet his energy and great strength had not diminished. Old settlers recall that when Judd had his first safari car, a Model T Ford, he never bothered to use a jack to change punctured tires. He simply lifted the car off the ground while his equally powerful son, Jack, changed the tire.[10]

Nobody really believed dynamic Bill Judd would retire. Yet more and more he spoke of his "last safari." He would do one more, he said, and get a great tusker, just one magnificent trophy for himself, something he had always wanted; something he could set around the big fireplace in the living room at Fort Smith; something to admire in old age. Then he would hang up his well-worn guns, a .256 Mannlicher Schoneaur, a .350 Rigby Mauser, a .450 Army and Navy double, and his trademark trusty .577 Westley Richards double rifle. And that would be the end of it. Besides, his son Jack, like his father, was a thoughtful, muscular youth showing great promise as a hunter. Jack Judd knew he was expected someday to take over the whole shebang and the formidable Judd reputation. It seemed that time had come at last.

Father and son loaded Bill Judd's brand-new Chevrolet truck, and with old Momba and a younger gunbearer, along with a Jaluo cook, that last safari left Nairobi on November 9, 1927, headed for Kibwezi, a heavily wooded thornbush area 120 miles from Nairobi. Kibwezi was the haunt of great elephant herds and astonishing numbers of black rhino, buffalo, and big cats. The Judds drove east on the corrugated dirt highway to Mombasa, but the road was so rough they could average only 20 miles per hour. They arrived to pitch an overnight fly camp* at Simba railway station at seven that evening, satisfied with their progress. The new Chevy was so heavily loaded with camp gear, food, and fuel that Judd did not want to risk losing time with smashed springs by speeding on the potholed dirtway.

The following morning the safari eased off the wide game-specked Soysambu Plains, past Kiboko (Hippo) station, riding along in high spirits. Instead of turning off at Kibwezi railway station to head up the track to the Yatta plateau as they had originally planned, they paused instead to consult two Kamba trackers they had picked up at Kibwezi. The Judds were in any case already in the heart of some of the very best elephant country on earth. Dense rolling thorn-scrublands covered the area, with thickets of spiny sansevieria plants broken by many beautiful giant baobab trees, laced with dry sand streams. The local trackers thought they would do better farther east. Judd agreed and turned off the Mombasa road heading along an overgrown track to Masongaleni railway station. Because water was available at the station they camped nearby in the shade of acacia trees.

At the time Masongaleni was swarming with great herds of elephant; some of these huge mating herds numbered many hundreds of animals, but Bill Judd hoped to find a small herd of bachelor bulls,

---

*This refers to the outer canvas flysheet of a tent used for temporary camps to keep off heavy nighttime dew.

which he knew usually held the best chance for heavy ivory. For days the hunters walked through the Masongaleni bushlands hunting for a big set of elephant tracks. On December 20, 1927, they turned their attention in the direction of Darajani, twenty miles to the east. Almost immediately after dawn they came upon the steaming hot dung and spoor of a solitary bull elephant with huge, smooth-heeled tracks—the sure sign of an old tusker. Elated at the prospect of catching up with a trophy bull the two hunters and their men remorselessly tracked the elephant through the intense heat of the day, but by late afternoon when there was no sign they were catching up with their quarry, they debated calling it quits. The Judds had not rested on the spoor in over ten hours of concentrated tracking. Dead tired or not, old man Judd did not want to give up the chance of a prized tusker just because he was a little weary. The light easterly breeze that had held steady all day began to shift in little eddies, and the hunters paused to see if the wind would settle. Bill squinted into the tiny cloud of wood ash that came from the cotton ashbag his tracker carried. As the man tapped the bag, wood ash floated this way and that on the breeze. After a pause it seemed the wind settled, at least for the present, and the Judds jubilantly pressed forward into a dense thicket. Suddenly the hunters were aware the elephant was right there moving along ahead of them. Just as suddenly they knew the great animal had stopped moving. There was total silence. Had he heard them? Or had he caught a slight whiff of their presence? Because the bush was very thick at this spot, Bill Judd cautiously knelt down to look beneath the thickets.

On one knee, his heavy double rifle cradled in his arms, Bill could see the elephant's feet and the massive ivory tips of a big set of tusks. On hands and knees the two men crept deeper into the thicket, when Bill suddenly knelt down, sighted his .577 Westley Richards, and fired two quick shots. The elephant wheeled around and came straight for Judd, ears flattened back against its skull, eyes bulging. There was no shriek, no trumpeting, no sound but the awful crack of branches as the elephant ploughed through the brush in a full-out charge. Judd, who had faced many elephant charges in a lifetime of hunting, always carried two rounds of the cigar-size .577 shells between the fingers of his left hand. He quickly ejected his two spent shells, reloaded, and was able to snap two more shots off as the elephant bore down on them, smashing trees and flattening thorn scrub as it came at full speed. Young Jack fired a shot of his own, but nothing stopped the enraged elephant.

After young Jack had fired his shot, and as he backed away reloading, he tripped, falling over backward. At that moment the elephant grabbed Bill with its trunk and smashed him to the ground like a rag doll. It snatched him up in its trunk, and pulled him onto a tusk, skewering him through the abdomen, then with its trunk around Judd's waist it jerked him off its tusk. The elephant smashed the pulped body to the ground again, and this time the elephant kneeled on Judd, mashing him into the iron-hard red earth. In the meantime Jack, horrified at the sight, quickly worked another round into the breech of his .350 Rigby-Mauser magazine rifle. Throwing the rifle to his shoulder he slammed a bullet into the elephant's heart region as it knelt on his father. But the elephant ignored the shot. Young Jack raced up to the elephant and from a range of about fifteen paces fired a side-brain shot, dropping the elephant, which fell beside what little remained of his father.[11] Bill Judd was fifty-seven years old.

JUDD'S FAME as a white hunter was such that newspapers around the world carried assorted accounts of the tragedy. In London and Boston and Sydney it was front-page news. His son, my uncle Jack Judd, a broken young man, never hunted again.

7

FUNGA SAFARI!

In early 1904 two enterprising Australians named Victor Marra Newland and Leslie Jefferies Tarlton opened an international professional safari outfitting firm, the first of its kind anywhere in Africa. Newland and Tarlton, with Leslie's brother Henry Tarlton and Claude Tritton as partners, started their company with a ludicrously small sum of capital, a mere 200 British pounds sterling. Newland opened an office in Nairobi while the socially well-connected Tritton, formerly the owner of a thriving agricultural seed business, returned to London to open a Newland and Tarlton branch above the site of Rowland Ward's famed taxidermy studio at 167 Piccadilly.

Victor Newland and Leslie Tarlton had come to British East Africa in 1903. Tarlton, a spare, redheaded young man, had been born in 1877 on the Emu Plains in Australia. Like Newland he arrived in Africa as a soldier in the Boer War in South Africa. After the war the two friends went together to East Africa in search of their fortune. At Nairobi they saw an opportunity as overseas interest in African safaris gathered momentum. Newland and Tarlton, or N&T as they were usually known, recruited the loose confederation of independent white hunters then operating their own safari businesses. Leslie Tarlton was the principal in the hunting department while Newland was the manager.

Unlike his partners, Leslie Tarlton was a hunter first and foremost. His prowess quickly earned him a formidable reputation as a sportsman in the fledgling colony. The American taxidermist and photographer Carl Akeley ranked him "one of the best rifle shots of all time, and the best shot I have ever known."[1] Tarlton also exhibited considerable skills of horsemanship. A type of ostrich fever gripped East Africa in those days, and Tarlton drew much admiration for his singular ability to round up one hundred cock ostriches at a time.[2] As a sideline Tarlton had his own ostrich enterprise.

Newland and Tarlton's first safari client was Carl Akeley.* At the time Akeley was looking for a place to store his taxidermy equipment. Akeley stumbled upon Leslie Tarlton's corrugated iron house upon hearing the furious sounds of a typewriter hammering away. "Tarlton afterwards confessed to me," Akeley wrote, "that the typewriter that first attracted my attention would not write at all. Its only use was to make noise when a prospective client came in sight."[3]

In time Newland and Tarlton had gathered together the leading lights of the safari world. Before the First World War they already had the best white hunters in the country on their books: R. J. Cunninghame, Fritz Schindelar, George Outram, Alan Black, A. C. Hoey, Bill Judd, Philip Percival, and Al Klein. The firm came to represent quality sport and dashing white hunters whose collective reputations drew a clientele that included celebrities and royalty. Newland and Tarlton's recognition was such that their name on a package guaranteed delivery. N&T's cable address, SAFARI, was freely used by many Nairobi citizens.

THE MAJORITY OF N&T clients went first class. A shooting safari could last anywhere from a few months to a year or more. First class meant a top-notch white hunter; Goanese cooks; Somali gunbearers; WaKamba and WaLiangulu trackers; WaNyamwezi, Jaluo, and Swahili porters. It also meant good tents, horses, mules, bullock carts, and camp equipment. Champagne safaris were the order of the day, and no effort was spared to provide every comfort possible. All manner of luxuries, including champagne (in preference to wine, which did not travel well on the heads of porters) and caviar, were transported into the wilderness at great cost.

In those days safaris would form up beside the Norfolk Hotel prior to departure. There was always an air of great festivity at the arrival and departure of big game hunting expeditions. Sometimes a flag was carried by a proud bearer leading the safari out, the flag representing the client's nationality. White hunters, clients, headmen, horses, mules, pack animals, ox wagons, gunbearers, syces (horse grooms), *askaris*

---

*By chance Tarlton and Akeley wound up at the Nairobi hospital in 1911, both critically ill with blackwater fever. Akeley recuperated at Tarlton's Parklands home.

(guards), *m'pishis* (cooks), and *pagazi* (porters) were assembled in a noisy, excited rabble as loads were made up. Each porter would carry sixty pounds of baggage, usually on his head. Among the tangled mounds of equipment were chop boxes for food, folding tables, Rajah chairs, tents, bedding, cots, hurricane lanterns, and bags of alum and trophy salt used to cure hides. At least thirty African *pagazi* were needed per visiting sportsman. For two or more clients, between eighty and one hundred porters were required. If the safari headed for the Northern Frontier camels were in the cavalcade along with horses and mules. Each member of the African crew was dressed in uniform khaki shorts and blue jersey with the six-inch-tall legend *N&T* embroidered in red. All wore puttees to protect their shins against thorns. Men were issued two blankets and a pair of boots, which were such a novelty they were commonly worn with laces tied around the neck. No matter what the terrain, boots were seldom used as footwear on the march itself. Instead such prized commodities were worn in town as a symbol of prestige. The men carried a three-pound sack of daily *posho* ration tied around the waist, and a flat metal water bottle stitched with felt.

When safari preparations were complete, a headman's signal stirred the mob, who formed a line stamping their feet, chanting marching songs accompanied by kudu-horn trumpeters and the haunting sound of conch-shell horns. One of Nairobi's first European settlers, and its first professional photographer, "Pop" Binks, recalled: "N&T ran a posh outfit and it was exciting just to watch the preparations. Everybody knew the safari would be gone for months, and there would be danger and hardships, but the departures were festive events."[4]

At that time clients could choose any sort of safari they wished, and at varying rates. Leslie Tarlton had a supply of white hunters to suit all requirements and purses. To keep expenses down, clients could skimp on this piece of equipment or that, take fewer porters, fewer pack animals, cut out luxuries, and use the train to get their gear a few miles from Nairobi. In 1907–1908 the price of a self-organized hunt ranged from $350 to $500 per month, which covered rations for the African staff but did not include the client's own food. It was suggested hunters buy provisions at the Army and Navy stores in London, then have them specially boxed and transported to Nairobi by steamer and railway. For short trips that used the railway to get out of town, Newland and Tarlton provided the sportsman with thirty porters, one headman, two *askaris*, one cook, one tent boy, and a couple of gunbearers. A safari of

Trackers and gunbearers on a turn-of-the-century safari.

that type did not include a white hunter, his food, or train fares. Some
clients chose to do without the expense of a white hunter and made do
with an African headman, an invaluable person called a *neapara*, who
was an interpreter as well. These old *neaparas* were remarkable men,
some of whom had been guides on early Arab slaving caravans or had
marched with famous explorers.

Leslie Tarlton had one of his most challenging assignments in 1909
when he was selected to outfit the African hunting and collecting expedition of Theodore Roosevelt. It was to be the biggest safari of all. The
former president's retinue was the largest ever assembled, with five
hundred porters in addition to camp and hunting staff. Tarlton named
R. J. Cunninghame as leader of the safari.

Richard Cunninghame was a well-mannered graduate of Cambridge
University. As the person in overall charge of the safari, Tarlton gave
him the task of overseeing most of the actual hunting. Other well-
known white hunters were invited to join the safari from time to time,
and a number of them hunted with Roosevelt, including Sir Alfred
Pease, a former member of British Parliament who had hunted in Somaliland with Lord Delamere and Alan Black. Also invited to hunt with

the president were the lion-hunting cousins Harold and Clifford Hill, as well as Bill Judd. Leslie Tarlton gave a hand with every facet of the president's safari and accompanied the expedition on most of its British East Africa portions, although it seemed he had to make frequent trips back to town for various "supplies." In fact, Tarlton had recently been married.

Before Roosevelt set foot in Africa he had studied his subject, especially its natural history. He listed as probably the three most valuable books available at the time the British soldier-sportsman F. C. Selous's *African Nature Notes*, the great German hunter and photographer C. G. Schillings's *With Flashlight and Rifle*, and artist John G. Millais's *A Breath from the Veldt*, all of them classics to this day. Roosevelt and Selous were guests at McMillan's Juja ranch. Here's Roosevelt's account:

> My host [Northrup McMillan] was about to go on safari for a couple of months with Selous, and to manage their safari they had one of the noted professional hunters of East Africa, Mr. W. Judd; and Judd was kind enough to take me out hunting every day we were at Juja. We would breakfast at dawn and leave the farm about the time it was light enough to see. . . . One day Selous while on horseback saw a couple of lionesses, and galloped after them, followed by Judd, seventy or eighty yards behind. One lioness stopped and crouched under a bush, let Selous pass, then charged Judd. She was right alongside him, and he fired from the hip; the bullet went into her eye; his horse jumped and swerved at the shot, throwing him off, and he found himself sitting on the ground, not three yards from the dead lioness.[5]

Juja was famous for its lions, but it was a leopard that caused the most grief on this portion of the Roosevelt trip. One day the president's son Kermit, who had accompanied him to Africa, went off on a separate hunt with his host McMillan. They were with a group of Africans beating a bush-choked ravine for lion when they unexpectedly put up a small leopard, which retreated into dense cover. Kermit's beaters continued in hopes of flushing the cat again so Kermit could get a shot at it. Teddy Roosevelt wrote:

> But the leopard did not want to be driven. Without any warning out he came and charged straight at Kermit, who stopped him

Bill Judd doctors a beater mauled by a leopard.

---

when he was but six yards off with a bullet in the forepart of the body; the leopard turned and as the leopard galloped back Kermit hit him again. . . . The wounds were fatal, and they would have knocked the fight out of any animal less plucky and savage than this spotted cat.[6]

One of the beaters pressed forward, and the leopard went for him in a flash, even though it was crippled. The beater ran, but the leopard charged after him. It was McMillan, standing on an anthill nearby, who saved the beater from a certain mauling or death. He swiftly fired a shot hitting the leopard, but despite this the leopard still caught the unfortunate beater and knocked him down. Roosevelt reported, "It seized him worrying him with teeth and claws; but it was weak because of its wounds. . . ."

The beater, a big, powerful African, wrenched himself free, while McMillan fired yet again into the cat. Even then the leopard was not dead and it made off into long grass. McMillan sent for some Boer-owned dogs that he hoped to use to flush the leopard. While McMillan and Kermit waited for the dogs to arrive, they were surprised by the leopard again making a rush at them, and this time it dropped to Kermit's bullet. When R. J. Cunninghame and Bill Judd arrived on the scene, Judd quickly opened up his saddlebags and doctored the injured beater.

Meantime not far away from Juja on the neighboring Juju ranch, McMillan's old safari companion from the Blue Nile expedition, Charles Bulpett, a keen amateur hunter, spotted a very big lion. He stalked it, and just as he fired the lion saw him. Taking the bullet, the lion made straight for Bulpett, knocking his rifle from his hands. As man and beast struggled in the dust, Bulpett's Somali gunbearer, his only companion that day, threw himself at the lion, ramming his bare arm into the lion's mouth. Meanwhile Bulpett was able to retrieve his rifle and kill the lion, which still had the brave Somali's arm in its jaws.

CUNNINGHAME LED Theodore Roosevelt's massive expedition across British East Africa into the Uganda Protectorate. At Kisumu the party boarded a steamer on Lake Victoria for the twenty-four-hour crossing to Entebbe, the seat of the British government in Uganda. On land the safari covered one hundred and sixty miles in ten days as they marched west to the port of Butiaba on Lake Albert. There Cunninghame and Roosevelt boarded the steamer *Kenia* and sailed north to the Albert or White Nile.

At a spot called Koba Roosevelt was warmly welcomed by the local Africans when the steamer drew alongside a mud bank on the river. At that time Koba was used as a convenient base by a loose confederation of renegade ivory hunters who poached elephant in the Belgian-claimed territory across the river on its west bank. Known as the Lado Enclave, it then included West Nile Province in Uganda and a large part of Sudan. At Koba white hunter John Boyes grandly hosted a party for Roosevelt, inviting those ivory hunters presently in the region to attend.* Roosevelt missed the most famous ivory hunter of all. Karamoja Bell was nowhere near Lado, but far out in the bush unaware of the celebration.

At Koba Cunninghame collapsed with one of his periodic bouts of recurrent malaria. Ivory hunter Quentin Grogan, then only twenty-five years old, was already one of the most successful Lado hunters, and

---

*Among the daring band of Lado ivory hunters that met the president at Koba were John Boyes, Bill Bennett, and the Brittlebank brothers, Dickenson and Ishmael. Prominent members of the Lado fraternity that missed Roosevelt included: Mickey Norton, Bill Buckley, F. G. "Deaf" Banks, Billy Pickering, the Craven brothers, Pete Pearson, and J. W. "Yank" Rogers.

he had an intimate knowledge of the country. Quentin's more famous brother, Ewart, had been the first—and only—person to make the fearsome journey from Cape Town to Khartoum accompanied by a small band of African followers. Ewart Grogan's historic walk had led him through Lado following the Nile to Khartoum back in 1899. Quentin helped Roosevelt get a white rhino for the Smithsonian Institute in Washington.[7]

In describing the ivory hunters he met at Lado Roosevelt wrote:

> We were warmly received by the district commissioner, and there we met half a dozen of the professional elephant hunters, who for the most part make their money at hazard of their lives, by poaching ivory in the Congo. They are a hard-bit set, these elephant poachers; there are few careers more adventurous, or fraught with more peril, or which make heavier demands upon the daring, the endurance, and the physical hardihood of those who follow them.[8]

The Roosevelt safari was royally entertained by both Belgian and British officials as well as military officers as it passed through some of the loneliest outposts on earth. Belgian authorities went to considerable lengths to assist Roosevelt and granted permission for him to hunt in the Lado Enclave from a camp he characterized:

> We made our camp close to the river's edge, on the Lado side, in a thin grove of scattered thorn trees. The grass grew rank and tall about us. . . . The nights came hot and the days burning: the mosquitoes came with darkness, sometimes necessitating our putting on head nets and gloves in the evenings, and they would have made sleep impossible if we had not had mosquito biers. Nevertheless it was a very pleasant camp, and we thoroughly enjoyed it. It was a wild lonely country, and we saw no human beings except an occasional party of naked savages armed with bows and poisoned arrows. Game was plentiful, and a hunter always enjoys a permanent camp in good game country.[9]

The Roosevelt safari was also a full-scale scientific expedition under the patronage of both the Smithsonian Institute, for which the Roosevelts were to collect birds, mammals, reptiles, and plants, and the National Museum in Washington, for which they were to collect speci-

Leslie Tarlton,
cofounder of the
world's first safari
company, with Teddy
Roosevelt, 1909.

---

mens of big game. The large support staff included three distinguished
American naturalists, Surgeon Lieutenant Colonel Edgar A. Mearns,
Edmund Heller of California, and J. Alden Loring of Oswego, New
York.* Many specimens were collected as the safari made its way down
the length of the Nile. Roosevelt wrote, "In the Lado we found rats,
mice, and shrews abundant, but the number of species limited. . . .
Some of the bats were different from any yet obtained; the same may be
said of the shrews.[10]

During this historic safari substantial scientific discoveries were
made in East Africa. Heller and Loring gathered an astonishing collection of unknown or little-known species, including small rodents such
as the iridescent creek rat *(Pelomys roosevelti)*, the masked tree rat
(Thamnomys loringi), the Masai mouse *(Epimys panya)*, and the Athi
gerbil *(Tatera pothae Heller)*.

Despite its other objectives, the Roosevelt safari was primarily a
hunting safari. Of the Big Five, Roosevelt shot 9 lion, 6 buffalo, 8 ele-

---

*Also on Roosevelt's safari was a young man who helped collect small mammals, Hugh
Stanton, later famous as a collector for the world's zoos.

phant, 8 black rhino, and 5 white rhino. Kermit shot 8 lion, 4 buffalo, 3 elephant, 3 black rhino, and 4 white rhino, as well as 3 leopard.

To some, Roosevelt's trophy bags on his Newland and Tarlton safari seemed excessive, and by today's standards they were. But in Roosevelt's day his bags were for the most part relatively modest. Roosevelt himself commented, "The mere size of the bag indicates little as to a man's prowess as a hunter, and almost nothing as to the interest or value of his achievement."[11]

The sheer scope of Tarlton's arrangements for the remote Uganda and Sudanese portions of Roosevelt's safari would rival any of those made by the best of modern-day outfitters, even given advanced equipment and motorized transport. By 1910 when Roosevelt's safari ended, Newland and Tarlton was the biggest private employer of native labor in the entire country. Tarlton also employed thirty-seven Europeans at an average salary of £500 per year.

Roosevelt's safari brought with it the enormous prestige the American ex-president enjoyed and ensured almost unlimited publicity for both East Africa and its white hunters. The public had been kept well informed of its progress. Former ivory hunter Robert Foran* had joined the safari and wrote articles for the Associated Press, which focused international attention on the president's adventures.

During the course of his safari Roosevelt endeared himself to the rugged Kenya pioneers and hunters, perhaps because he shared so much in common with their love of the outdoors. Those who had been initially skeptical or critical of Roosevelt appeared to have been won over after meeting him. Some of the white hunters had viewed Roosevelt with suspicion because of his reputation as a teetotaler, a rare trait among the first lot of hard-bitten hunters of the day.

AT THE SAME TIME he was operating the first safari company in Africa, Leslie Tarlton was making his own name as a white hunter. Carl Akeley recalled Tarlton once confided that he was going to give up lion hunting. What had brought him to this conclusion was that he had just had a close call from a charging lioness:

---

*W. R. Foran was well acquainted with the Lado Enclave and all its ivory hunters, for he had himself poached there for several years prior to Roosevelt's safari. He returned to poach at Lado again in 1910–1911.

He hit her three times in the chest, and still she came on. She died on his feet. Examining the bullet wounds, Tarlton said all three bullets were grouped in a three-inch radius and every one should have been fatal. Yet the lion had almost reached him despite his fast and accurate shooting.[12]

Leslie Tarlton did not give up lion hunting soon enough, for he was caught by a big maned lion near Thika, and badly mauled. In his time Tarlton shot 284 lions, a staggering number and horrific by today's standards. However, it must be remembered that in Tarlton's early days lions were both extremely numerous and universally regarded as a menace.

8.

THE ELEMENT OF STYLE

One of the assistant white hunters on Teddy Roosevelt's safari was young Philip Hope Percival, who apparently made a lasting impression. Roosevelt later wrote of him:

> At Bondoni was Percival, a tall, sinewy man, a fine rider and shot—like so many other men whom I met, he wore merely a helmet, a flannel shirt, short breeches or trunks, and puttees and boots. I shall not forget seeing him one day as he walked beside his twelve-ox team, cracking his long whip, while in the big wagon sat pretty Mrs. Percival with a puppy, and a little cheetah cub, which we had found and presented to her and which she was taming.[1]

Philip's older brother Blayney had preceded him to British East Africa, where he became a game warden.* Blayney sent colorful accounts of life in the colony back home to his brother Philip. When Philip inherited a small sum of money at the age of twenty-one, he boarded a ship and sailed for Mombasa. Within days of Philip's arrival in 1905, the reunited brothers were out hunting together, and Blayney had

---

*Born at Newcastle-on-Tyne in 1875, Blayney was eleven years older than Philip. He was an ornithologist for the British Museum in Arabia and South Africa, then walked to British East from South Africa in 1900. Sir Charles Eliot made Blayney "Ranger for Game Preservation" on May 10, 1901, although the Game Department was not a separate branch of the colonial service until 1907. Blayney served under Lieut. Colonel J. H. Patterson, famous after publication of *The Man-Eaters of Tsavo*. Patterson was embroiled in a scandal involving a married couple he accompanied on a shooting trip, in which the husband was shot to death. Patterson was replaced by R. B. Woosnam.

a dramatic opportunity to display his prowess at riding lions. Philip described the day:

> I nearly finished my hunting days before I even started. . . . We were riding through some long grass and over-rode a lion. The lion went for me, and as it came alongside my saddle, I shouted in its face, but Blayney seeing the situation rode up at full gallop and drove the lion off.[2]

In addition to Blayney, Philip credited the Hill cousins from Machakos, Harold and Clifford, for teaching him the basics of African hunting. He bought a farm at Mua hills, and, like the Hill cousins, he at first went into the business of ostrich farming.* Percival's ostriches proved to be just as effective lion bait as had the Hills', and Philip soon had plenty of experience in tracking and hunting lions. When he was not hunting lions with the Hills, Phil began to take clients out on lion hunts, charging ten British pounds per week and twenty-five pounds per lion. Like the Hills, Phil provided only a wagon, trek oxen, horses or mules, and a couple of Africans to assist him. The "sportsmen" provided their own food, drink, tents, bedding, and furniture. It was rough-and-ready outfitting, but Percival was feeling his way in a brand-new profession that had no guidelines. Most important, he was gaining a wealth of experience in dealing with dangerous game.

Another of the Percivals' neighbors at Machakos was white hunter Sir Alfred Pease, who had been the individual responsible for first inviting Theodore Roosevelt to hunt in East Africa. Pease, like Percival and the Hills, also raised ostriches between hunting safaris, and was the proud holder of a local record, having shot fourteen lion in one day on his nearby Kitanga ranch. Pease, a close friend and hunting partner of Lord Delamere's in Somaliland, was a former magistrate and British member of Parliament. He had explored and hunted remote regions of the Sahara, Sudan, and Abyssinia before settling in East Africa.

On a visit to Washington, D.C., Pease had met Colonel Theodore Roosevelt and had expansively asked him to come to Africa as his guest on Kitanga ranch for a lion hunt. Never dreaming the president would take him up on his offer, Pease now scrambled to build a hunting lodge

---

*Philip returned briefly to England to marry his childhood sweetheart, Vivian Smith-Spark.

for his important guest. After his safari Roosevelt described Pease as "a singularly good rider and one of the best game shots I have ever seen. It would have been impossible to have found a kinder host or hunter better fitted to teach us how to begin our work with African big game."[3]

When Roosevelt began to plan his African expedition in earnest, it was to Philip Percival's brother Blayney that he wrote for information about the country and its game. As early as 1902 Blayney had been instrumental in writing new game regulations, first formulated as "Queens Regulations" in 1897. The first practical game ordinance in British East Africa was largely his doing. Although he was a keen hunter, Blayney was also an ardent conservationist and preservationist, and he was the driving force in the establishment of two new major game reserves, one in the south in central Masailand, the other in the Northern Frontier.*

Roosevelt had written to Blayney on August 8, 1908, asking for advice about his proposed hunting safari on behalf of the National Museum in Washington. "I doubt," Roosevelt wrote, "if there is anyone who can tell me better than you can exactly where to go to get game." In the same letter Roosevelt adds, "I am exceedingly anxious to get lion, elephant, rhinoceros, buffalo, giraffe, hippopotamus, eland, wildebeest, roan, oryx, waterbuck." In conclusion, Roosevelt added, "Everyone tells me that you are of all others the best able to give me the information that I desire."[4]

WHEN PHILIP PERCIVAL returned from Roosevelt's safari, he decided his future would be as a full-time white hunter. Following the enormous publicity generated by Roosevelt's expedition, sportsmen from all corners of the globe began arriving in East Africa and safaris were rapidly becoming big business. Philip Percival's first solo safari client was with a man named Martin. "He was an Englishman," Percival recalled, "a good hunter and a tiptop fellow. We went up to the Lorian swamp and had a very successful hunt." According to white hunter Tom Murray Smith, "Phil followed up this safari with a hunt for Baron Rothschild, so he got off to a good start."[5]

In 1910 when the Duke and Duchess of Connaught returned to East

---

*Prior to 1902 British East Africa theoretically had three game reserves: Athi Plains, Sugota, and Jubaland (in Samburuland). Uganda had two reserves, at Budongo and Toro.

The Duke of Connaught's safari with Jack Riddell, fifth from left, and Philip Percival, third from right.

Africa, Flash Jack Riddell selected Philip Percival as his assistant hunter. The trip was the first of a number of royal safaris Percival was to conduct. "It was a nice safari," Percival remarked, "but as usual on royal safaris there were too many ladies-in-waiting and so on." Even so, Percival found royals pretty regular folks. "Royalty is usually no trouble at all—anything goes and they are easy to get on with."[6]

One of Philip's clients was Hollywood actor Gary Cooper, who came to Africa to hunt with Philip in Tanganyika, but also to visit his old friend Gerry Preston and his glamorous wife, Kiki. The Prestons were wealthy Americans who owned a ranch at Lake Naivasha. Kiki's outstanding beauty was much admired. She never rose before dinner, as she loved parties and was up all night, sometimes playing backgammon with her friend Cockie Birkbeck, when Cockie was married to Bror Blixen. Kiki was on the fringe of Lord Errol's so-called Happy Valley set, an infamous group of British settlers living at Wanjohi Valley, on the slopes of the western Aberdares. They were known for wife swapping, drugs, and endless parties. Kiki committed suicide in New York City in 1946.

Another Percival client was George Eastman, of Eastman Kodak, who was accompanied on his safari by friends Daniel Pomeroy and Dr.

Audley Stewart, who in turn had their own hunter, Pat Ayre. Also on the safari were wildlife photographers Martin and Osa Johnson, whose numerous African expeditions were launched from bases at Nairobi and Marsabit, and who produced some of the finest wildlife footage and stills ever shot. Martin and Osa were both avid hunters as well as photographers.

Percival commented to Eastman that his caravan of five trucks and two passenger cars was the largest motorized safari ever to leave Nairobi.[7] The safari had 35 African staff, but would have required at least another 150 porters if motor transport had not been used. Eastman was surprised by the numbers of cars he saw in Nairobi. "There are a great many automobiles," he wrote, "mostly touring cars and trucks. Ford, Chevrolet and Buick seem to be the favorites. Gasoline is about 85 cents a gallon."[8]

The African rainy season had no respect for modern technology. The party was brought to a standstill by late monsoon rains, and all the roads around Nairobi became impassable. Percival had the clients and vehicles transported on railway flatcars to Limuru station, twenty-five miles outside of Nairobi, from where they were able to proceed westward to the drier Kedong Valley, as this part of the Great Rift Valley is locally known. There they hunted from a place Percival referred to as Bailey camp, so named because Kathleen Bailey (later Mrs. Seth-Smith, mother of white hunter Tony Seth-Smith) was seriously gored by a rhino the week before Eastman's party arrived. Kathleen had followed a couple of rhino with two trackers across the slopes of an extinct volcano called Mount Suswa. When she caught up with the rhino, one of them charged and horned her, tearing away a part of her scalp.[9] Miraculously Kathleen survived, although badly injured in the attack. To this day her son still has the rhino's horn with a piece of his mother's scalp, hair still attached, wrapped around the horn. The size of the horn proved she was a good judge of trophies, for it measures 24½ inches.[10]

Near Bailey camp George Eastman missed a big lion just after the hunting got into full swing, but redeemed himself three days later. Back in Nairobi, as the hunters waited for the country to dry out, the clients stayed at Muthaiga Club and took their meals at museum collector Carl Akeley's home nearby, with Osa Johnson helping out in the kitchen. In the end the Eastman safari was successful in the Northern Frontier, and later on the Serengeti Plains in Tanganyika, where they ran into Alan Black hunting lions with the Ralph Pulitzer party from New York.

◇

ONE OF PHILIP PERCIVAL'S many admirers was his pupil, Sydney Downey, who was to have his own measure of fame in another generation of safari hunters. By then Philip was past middle age, although still a rugged man of middle height with graying hair and rubicund face. With a tall glass of whiskey around the campfire he might be induced to dig into his vast repository of hunting stories.

Sydney Downey, who became a leading hunter, claimed that "Old Phil Percival was *the greatest* white hunter of all time!" Percival, though considered congenial and diplomatic, knew how to get his point across and keep his clients in line if need be. An example of this occurred when one of his clients produced a light rifle sold to him by a London gunsmith, which he proposed to use for lion hunting. Percival grasped the rifle and studied it with obvious distaste, saying, "I do not wish to see that again in the course of this safari."

Downey says that later the three of them were hunting for a big maned lion that was surrounded by lionesses. As the men crept along Philip signaled Downey to remain where he was while Percival and his client continued, with Percival nonchalantly "brushing lionesses out of his way." The client was wildly excited, and at that critical moment he accidentally fired his rifle into the ground. The lions bolted, and the hunt was ruined. Percival did not say a word. Hours later he had still not said a word. The client was distraught, and by the time they were around the campfire with a drink, he was anxious to open some conversation. The client remarked that he would have been more accustomed to the rifle that Percival had not allowed him to use. Then he asked if such a rifle could have killed the lion. Percival's icy response was, "I imagine that the lion might have enjoyed a good laugh." After that Percival acted as if the incident had never occurred.

On occasion, Downey said, Percival could be something of a martinet. "The rank or prerogative of a client meant nothing to him. He would give of his best in producing trophies and amenities and excitement, but he liked to say, 'By 6 A.M. I do not mean 6:20 A.M.' Everything had to be done his way."[11]

Percival's close friend Tom Murray Smith said there had never been a more successful professional hunter—or a better one,[12] an opinion shared by Percival's clients and colleagues. Philip was one of the very few white hunters who escaped serious injury during his long career, but there were some close shaves. One time he was following up a buffalo wounded by a client in the Embu country. The buffalo charged. Philip fired his .450 Number 2 double rifle and broke the buffalo's neck, but the animal's impetus carried it forward and it fell on top of him. "I was underneath his chin and smothered with his blood. Messy business!"

Another time, hunting in dense brush, Percival came close to being horned by a charging rhino. Philip was hoping he would not have to shoot in self-defense, and he tried to get out of its way. But he knew at the last minute there was no escape on the narrow, thorn-choked trail. Instead he wound up with a dead rhino shot through the brain, with its head between his feet and its rather long horn delicately resting between his legs.

In assessing his early years as a white hunter, Philip Percival was characteristically modest. "Why, I can remember way back, when *real* hunters like Alan Black and W. D. M. Bell would be around, we would hardly dare even look at them. I can remember the time when I would practically bow to Alan Black's shadow."[13] High praise indeed coming from a man whose own name was the inspiration to a dozen young hunters he would train.

9

A WHITE HUNTER CALLED BLACK

Alan Lindsey Black* was a Big Game Hunter pure and simple. He was a powerfully built man, five foot ten inches tall, with a deeply tanned face, close-cropped dark hair, and striking cobalt eyes. Early in his long career Black was considered a clever hunter, being renowned both as a fine rifle shot and a skilled archer. Yet he had little opportunity of gaining experience with elephant, and one of his first elephant hunts left him with a permanent scar as remembrance. Fortunately for Black, the incident occurred in company of the maestro, R. J. Cunninghame. Cunninghame later noted with typical understatement, "I have fortunately never had a fatal accident when hunting elephant, but I very nearly had one when out with a man who was learning how to shoot elephant. Alan Black and I were both charged at the same time by two elephants. I got mine. Black was knocked unconscious. Arm and ribs broken."[1]

Alan Black hunted all over British East Africa and Sudan from about 1900, often for himself or as a meat hunter for others. He was content with his own company for long periods, a true loner, who was tight with money and eschewed all personal comforts. Yet he was universally liked and much admired by colleagues. He was one of the first sought out by Victor Newland and Leslie Tarlton in 1904 when they were recruiting white hunters, and he enjoyed a highly successful career with the firm until 1919.

Between safaris to Uganda and Sudan, Black would return to Nairobi, most often with a good haul of ivory. He said that some of the finest

---

*Alan Lindsey Black was born August 14, 1881, the only son of a prominent London family.

hunting he had ever seen was in Uganda, a country he came to know well.

In 1911 Leslie Tarlton sent Black out with a coal-mining heir from the state of Mississippi, Paul J. Rainey, to lead a specialized lion hunt. Rainey, a courtly southern gentleman, had already made a number of safaris. He had become a resident of British East Africa and maintained a home called Falcon Glen outside Nairobi at Parklands, as well as a large home and cattle ranch at Lake Naivasha in the Great Rift Valley.

Lion were exceedingly numerous around Rainey's ranch on the western shores of Naivasha. Throughout the Lake Naivasha region, as elsewhere at that time, lion were regarded as nothing more than dangerous vermin. Riding lions by the likes of Cecil Hoey and Bill Judd was considered a sporting way of hunting. It was also the most dangerous way to go about the business; that is, apart from the native method of spearing lions on foot, as practiced by the finest warriors of the Nandi, Lumbwa, and Masai tribes.

Paul Rainey was neither fainthearted nor content merely to listen to the accounts of others. Rainey was a keen hunter. He was also a skilled rider, a fine shot, and generally well liked in Africa. Rainey had successfully ridden lions, and at the time he hired Alan Black he was ready to explore a new way of hunting them. It was Rainey's theory that his hunting hounds could be trained only to follow the scent of lion, and taught to ignore plains animals when they were coursing. To test his theory he had imported packs of trained bear and cougar hounds from the United States, along with his own personal dog handler, a man named Er Shelley.

Precisely what professional hunter Alan Black thought of Rainey's theory is not known, but Shelley, commenting on Black later, wrote, "He was probably the best in the country. I soon decided, however, that he was not overenthusiastic about hunting lions with dogs. I rather think he looked upon this as a risky business and was afraid somebody was going to get hurt."[2] Whatever his true feelings, Black agreed to participate in Rainey's scheme.

For Rainey's lion safari Black was to be assisted by fellow Newland and Tarlton white hunter, the highly rated Australian George Outram. It happened that Outram kept some young lion cubs at his house near the racecourse outside Nairobi. To prepare for Rainey's hunt, each day Outram would "lead" the lions to their food placed some distance from his house. Rainey's dog handler, Er Shelley, and his American cowboy assistants would then lead Rainey's pack of "strike" hounds after the lions, so that the dogs could "hit" the lion trail. In this way Rainey hoped to train his dogs to scent lions. In time Rainey's hounds were taught to ignore other game and to stick to the lion's scent.*

When Rainey and Shelley thought the hounds were ready to try a real lion hunt, Black and Outram got the safari under way. Rainey had employed an American movie camera operator named John Hemment to record the event on film. In addition Rainey had brought along Edmund Heller, the taxidermist from the Smithsonian Institute who had accompanied Teddy Roosevelt; his friend Dr. Johnson; and a full camp crew, including gunbearers, syces, and over two hundred porters. Three big ox wagons, each carrying five tons of provisions, made up the safari. The entire party boarded a freight train at Nairobi and traveled to the edge of the Great Rift Valley, where they left the train at Kijabe station and began their march south along the floor of the Great Rift to Maji Moto (Hot Water Springs) in Masailand.

BLACK AND OUTRAM agreed that a pair of small rocky hills on the Loita Plains were likely places to find lion. After eight days of marching the safari broke out of dense belts of brush to reach the open plains bordering the Loita hills, and a luxurious camp was set up in a grove of yellow-barked acacia trees. First thing next morning Black positioned Rainey and Johnson where he thought they were most likely to get a shot if lions came off the hill. Shelley, leading a few of Rainey's best hounds, went out with George Outram, the taxidermist Heller, and 150 of their safari porters to make a long line, almost shoulder to shoulder, to "beat" the hill.

When Outram's party got to the summit they saw two huge male lions, "swinging their tails in circles and growling," according to Shelley. The two big lions went down the hill as expected to where Black, Rainey, and Johnson were in position. As Outram and the beaters progressed, three more lions were flushed, but this small pride raced off between the hunters and the beaters, and escaped. From below the hill

---

*Other lion-fighting dogs, which included English retrievers and Airedales, were kept separately and were never allowed to run with the "trailing" or "strike" hounds, because they would break up the hunt.

Alan Black at the height of his fame in the 1920s.

Outram heard a couple of shots, and sure enough, Rainey and Johnson each shot one of the two large lions driven toward them by the beaters. To test his dogs Shelley released them after Rainey had killed his lion, and the hounds went straight after the trail, ending up beside Rainey's dead lion. Both Rainey and Shelley were pleased the dogs had done so well on their first attempt after wild lions.

The following day Alan Black split the hunting party again and tackled the second rocky hill. This time two more very big lions were flushed, but Rainey would not shoot. He wanted his dogs to be further tested, and a runner was sent to fetch the handler Shelley and the hounds. Meantime Black, Rainey, and Johnson mounted and rode after the two big cats as they bounded over the plain. The largest of the lions went only about two miles and then turned at bay to face the three horsemen. The big cat was worked up, growling savagely, with his tail swinging madly—a sure sign of anger. Black knew it would only be a second or two before he went for somebody. Black was not about to let that happen, and he drew his clients off to a safe distance while the bayed lion moved across a gully to join its companion. The horsemen remained in their saddles watching, as they waited for Shelley and his dogs to come up.

Shelley appeared with the hounds, but not knowing about the two lions he crossed the place where the lions had gone over the gully, and immediately the dogs wanted to "open" on the trail. Shelley thought his dogs were trying to open on a nearby herd of impala, and he tried to stop them, but the dogs seemed determined to run, as in fact they had the large lion's trail. Dr. Johnson, contrary to Black's orders, rode after Shelley to tell him it was a lion the dogs were following, and that the lion was under a bush just a few yards from Shelley. Shelley, not knowing all this, had dismounted, and at that moment the infuriated lion rose up growling just thirty feet away. Shelley was saved from almost certain death only because his dogs immediately surrounded the lion. The lion was so distracted he did not go for Shelley, and gave him a chance to mount and get away. Rainey came up to the bayed lion with the others and shot it.

A couple of days later the hunters put up a pride of eighteen lions on another small hill. The lions scattered in all directions with the dogs after them. A Somali *askari* armed with an old Martini-Henry rifle took a potshot at a lion and bowled it over, but did not kill it. The greenhorn photographer, Hemment, came running over, yelling at the Somali not to shoot again. Hemment hastily set up his movie camera as the astonished Somali watched, hardly believing his eyes. Here was a supremely dumb white man just fifty yards from a wounded and very angry lion, thinking he was going to get some nice pictures. Hemment got his head under the hood and began to crank the camera. Just then Alan Black and Rainey rode up to confront the angry cat. Hemment hastily assured Black the lion was harmless. Hemment asked a native boy standing nearby to throw a stone at the lion, as he wanted some action.

As soon as the stone landed near the big cat, it broke into a furious charge racing headlong for Hemment. According to Er Shelley, who witnessed the event, two shots rang out as the lion was in full charge. One bullet struck the lion in the head, and it came slithering to a halt forty inches from the shaken Hemment's camera. The hunters bagged nine lions that day, and the Masai chiefs in the area came to shake hands and congratulate them, because as stockmen, lions were their worst enemy. During that six-week safari with Alan Black, Rainey and his party shot twenty-seven lions.

Frederick Jackson, the British official then in charge of issuing game licenses, noted:

Paul Rainey, with his highly trained bear dogs, claimed, I believe quite correctly, to have killed a greater number of lions, and more in one day, than any man living; and if it should give him any satisfaction to know it, it is highly improbable that his records will ever be beaten. Whether his method of killing them is sport or not, is a matter of opinion, and was certainly a much disputed point; in any case it cannot be compared with hunting on foot.[3]

ALAN BLACK'S SAFARI with Paul Rainey attracted national attention, much of it highly critical. But Rainey was not by any means alone in the awful numbers of lions killed. Later that same year, in 1911, when white hunter Sir Alfred Pease inquired as to how many lions Newland and Tarlton's clients had accounted for that season, Leslie Tarlton replied, "In a letter to our London office sent some months ago, I made a return of the number reported as killed for the year (I think) ended December 1911. The exact figure I do not remember, but I believe the total was either 695 or 795." Tarlton went on to say the largest bag by one individual was that of Mr. Paul J. Rainey and his friends, who had accounted for 120 lions using dog packs.[4]

It was not long before this controversial slaughter was noticed in England and elsewhere, and the rumblings of righteousness were only beginning. Most of the stockmen in East Africa thought lions so numerous and destructive they should be destroyed entirely, or at least considerably thinned out. Many white hunters had second thoughts about the mass destruction of lions, including Black, and in time they urged (and years later eventually secured) legislation that put lions on a game license and banned all sport hunting with the use of dogs. Yet another small faction took the side of the ranchers. But in the meantime the killing continued.

At the time game ranger Blayney Percival felt that hunting lions with dogs was justified in the circumstances. He wrote:

> I believe this method has been criticized as unsportsmanlike by some people in England, and, before saying anything of it, should like to point out that the lion is not to be regarded only as a beast that provides sport. Under these circumstances it becomes legitimate to destroy the too numerous lions by any possible means, and hunting them with hounds is at least one degree better than

taking them with traps or poison, both of which methods are held proper for the destruction of vermin much less dangerous than the lion.[5]

Blayney Percival observed Rainey's dog pack in action and thought they resembled lightly built bloodhounds, but the pack also included "a scratch lot of fighting dogs, Airedales being the favorites, as they have such pluck." Percival wrote:

> Racing along under the guidance of the American hounds, they soon put the lion up, but if "set up" in light cover, he will as a rule break away and try to reach denser bush or rocks. Once he really stands to bay the hounds surround him, and, yapping about him, occasionally getting hold for a moment, they keep him till somebody with a rifle can get to close quarters and kill without risk of injuring the dogs. It is most important that the shot delivered should kill outright, as once the rifle is fired the dogs in their increased excitement "pile in," when should the lion only be wounded, some of them are sure to be mauled. On the whole Mr. Rainey has been very lucky, comparatively few of his dogs have been hurt or killed.[6]

Having watched Rainey's hounds at work, Percival conceded that this was not a particularly dangerous form of hunting. For all the hoopla attached to Rainey's lion-hunting methods, one incident at his Lake Naivasha ranch put lion hunting in perspective for the American thrill seeker. Carl Akeley recalled a day when Rainey's men reported that a lion had invaded a cattle *kraal* the previous evening. Rainey mounted his horse and, with two Masai boys armed with spears, set off in search of the lion. The dogs soon picked up the scent and brought the lion to bay beneath a single acacia tree on a grassy plain. The sun had just risen above the hills on the other side of the lake. Long shadows of tabletop acacias lay across the plain, with the lion standing beneath in the flat sunlight. Rainey jumped off his horse, threw the reins over a bush, and grabbed his rifle from its boot. Much to his astonishment he saw the two Masai boys nonchalantly jog on toward the lion. As they approached the infuriated cat standing his ground ready for battle, now with its lip dangerously curled and a deep snarl breaking from bared teeth, one boy drew back his arm and threw his spear, but missed. The

Lion were common around the Loita hills in Masailand.

boys were between Rainey and the lion, and he could not shoot. Then the boys stood stock-still till the lion was in midair in his final spring. The one with the spear stepped to one side and thrust his spear into the lion's neck, killing it instantly. The lion fell at their feet. As the boy withdrew the spear and carefully wiped the blood off on the corner of his breechcloth, he remarked to Rainey, "You see, Master, it is work for a child."[7]

WHEN ALAN BLACK was later approached by Paul Rainey to lead yet another lion safari, he listened carefully to Rainey's plans, then politely declined, thinking the American's latest scheme suicidal. In the past Rainey had made commercial movies with acclaimed wildlife photographers Cherry Kearton and his brother Charles. Apart from his lion hunts, Rainey made some outstanding wildlife and tribal films. His first major motion picture success, *Water Hole*, had been filmed by a cameraman named Lydford and showed big game around a desert water hole called Laisamis.[8] His later films, *African Hunt* and *Common Beasts of Africa*, were both hugely successful in the United States, as was his tribal account, *Military Drill of the Kikuyu Tribes and Other Native Ceremonies.*[9]

What Rainey now wanted was to obtain the one big action scene that had eluded him—a charging lion. Together with his friends Rainey had already obtained remarkable wildlife motion pictures, including lions, yet—even though Rainey had himself faced a number of provoked lion, as well as charging lion—he had never actually filmed a direct life-threatening charge. Now Rainey meant to put that matter right. After being turned down by Black, who was by then an old friend, Rainey approached George Outram to organize his next death-defying experiment. Outram listened to the plan and then also refused. Next Rainey went to Harold and Clifford Hill, who had previously been hired by Rainey to help make motion pictures of lions being hunted with dogs on the Athi Plains. After talking the matter over in their usual quiet manner, the cousins decided no amount of money could compensate for the dangers involved. Rainey's requirements were so dangerous and so extreme that the Hills also politely declined Paul's offer. It seemed no one, least of all Alan Black or any of his colleagues, would take up Rainey's dangerous proposition. In the meantime Paul had vaguely heard about a daredevil white hunter named Fritz Schindelar, but he did not know him. He mentally filed away Schindelar's name.

Ironically, it was not long afterward that George Outram was himself caught and badly savaged by a lion while on another safari, this time near Thika, in 1913. Outram, one of the best hunters in any era, did not give up lion hunting soon enough. Nine years after being mangled at Thika, he was killed by a lion while trying to save his gunbearer as he was being mauled near Mackinnon Road railway station.

Alan Black went on to other clients and other safaris. Omar Rees, an old-time white hunter, recalled a conversation he had with Black in Nairobi, during which Black stated, "I'm fed up with shooting charging lions."[10] At the time Black had been out with a bow-and-arrow hunting client,* but his words no doubt expressed his sentiments regarding Paul Rainey's proposition.

---

*Black became disgusted with the inhumanity of bow hunting and gave it up. He once accompanied two American archers to the Serengeti in the early twenties. The arrows used were not poisoned. Black said that in eight lion encounters, half the lions when hit with an arrow immediately attacked and had to be killed with a rifle shot. White hunters were later instrumental in outlawing bow hunting in Kenya, Uganda, and Tanganyika.

10.

THE SHORT MYSTERIOUS LIFE
OF FRITZ SCHINDELAR

Not much is known about Fritz Schindelar's life before he arrived in British East Africa, and even the date of his arrival is uncertain. It is thought by some historians that Schindelar arrived in 1906.* What is known for certain about Schindelar is that he was not what he claimed to be when he turned up at Nairobi. The tall, rangy stranger said he was a headwaiter and a hotel baggage porter. But in fact he was almost certainly an aristocrat. After his death a rare photograph was discovered among Schindelar's things that showed him as a youth in the uniform of a commander of a crack regiment of Hungarian Hussars. For a man as young as this to be in command of such an elite corps is a fact that argues he was of royal blood.

People who got to know easygoing Schindelar in East Africa quickly realized that here was no ordinary person. He was an absolutely outstanding rifle shot, no matter whether the target was stationary or moving, coming or going. With a heavy rifle Fritz once shattered half a dozen roof tiles torn off a building on Government Road and thrown in the air by a willing accomplice. And he was a magnificent horseman—a trick rider who could gallop his horse as he stood in the saddle. Schindelar was reckoned to be the best polo player in the colony, which is saying something in a horse-crazy society such as Nairobi. Herbert "Pop" Binks, Nairobi's first professional photographer, once watched in fascination as Fritz casually "tossed" a 240-pound sack of oats onto a wagon as if it were no more than a small box of toffees.[1]

Schindelar had expensive tastes. He knew good food, wine, and

*Stated by Kenya historian Jan Hemsing.

clothes. He was articulate and perfectly at ease in the company of just about anybody, whatever their social standing. A widely believed rumor was that Schindelar had hurriedly left Europe over some scandal involving a woman. But in Africa most people, men and women, liked Fritz and admired him enormously. Within a few years he was among the best known of the white hunters. It was said of him that there was nothing he would not do for a safari client; no risk was ever too much for him; no situation was so difficult or dangerous that he would not tackle it.

J. A. Hunter remembered that Fritz loved to gamble, and he could often be seen at the Norfolk Hotel with several hundred golden sovereigns laying on the table before him.[2] Numerous events fueled talk and speculation that Fritz Schindelar had utter contempt for danger or death. An example of this behavior took place during one of Schindelar's safaris when his clients were Mr. H. Barclay, the owner of a bank, and his two pretty daughters. An irate rhino chased the eldest girl, and put her up a tree. She screamed for Fritz, who galloped up on his swift white Arab mare, dismounted, sent his horse on its way, and then played tag with the infuriated beast around the trunk of the tree before shooting it. On another occasion he threw bottles at an angry lion that had been wounded by a client, in an effort to make it charge him. J. A. Hunter observed, "Fritz did many curious things that would require a psychologist to explain."[3] A light side to Schindelar was often apparent and he was invariably in good humor. The hunter, elegantly dressed in city clothes, was a favorite with the African staff at the Norfolk Hotel. He amused them highly when he would walk around in an exaggerated fashion and serve customers as if he were a hotel employee.

PHOTOGRAPHER Pop Binks was in his Nairobi studio on a fateful day in 1914 when the American Paul Rainey entered the premises. Rainey and his cowboys were the first Americans Pop Binks had ever met, and to him they were memorable characters. Binks wrote, "A great big slab of a fellow walked into my photography shop and introduced himself. He could see I was taken aback by his size.

" 'I know I'm a hunk of a guy,' he said. 'There are six feet four inches of Paul Rainey.'

"I looked him up and down and agreed with him. 'There is a lot of you—I'm five-foot-eight-inch Binks, can I do something for you?' "

African horse syce, Bill Judd, and Fritz Schindelar, 1913.

" 'You can,' he replied. 'You can come on my safari and take pictures; we are going up Gilgil way for lion.' "

Rainey provided the movie cameras, which he hauled out of a rickshaw and demonstrated to Binks. "Here is the book of words, and here is the pump," Rainey instructed. "The cameras are driven by compressed air. You have to fill the air container which supplies enough power to run thirty feet of film."

Binks asked, "And what if she runs out of air when the lion is charging?"

Rainey replied, "Why, you throw the camera at the lion and get the hell out of it!"

"I could see Paul was a man I would enjoy working for," Binks said. "Undoubtedly they were great showmen; in fact, they were great big boys. No gloomy creases disfigured their brows—everything was play. To Rainey the novel idea of riding lions after the manner of a fox hunt was irresistible." Binks immediately accepted the job offer, but not without considerable misgivings, for he well knew from past experience the risks of fooling with lions.

Rainey still needed the expertise of a white hunter to set up spectacular charging-lion photos. The white hunters Alan Black and George Outram and the lion-hunting cousins Clifford and Harold Hill had all turned him down, saying Rainey's proposal was far too dangerous, and could only end in disaster. It was then that Rainey recalled the name of Fritz Schindelar, and he went looking for him.

Schindelar met his soulmate in Paul Rainey. He was immediately drawn to Rainey and the dangerous challenge of his proposals, and became Paul's white hunter. When Clifford Hill heard about the arrangement, he said to Fritz in his usual, quiet way, "Dangerous work, Fritz."

Schindelar replied, grinning, "For what Paul's willing to pay, it's worth the chance!"[4]

Pop Binks observed, "Although riding lions with his fleet-footed Arab polo pony was something Schindelar had done many times over, the trick this time was not simply to kill a lion, but to ride it, and then get it to charge not a horseman but a cameraman."[5]

The safari party set off for Rainey's comfortable Naivasha ranch, eighty miles west of Nairobi, where Rainey kept a small menagerie for his filmmaking, including a pampered tame chimpanzee named Dooley. The chimp had been measured for a suit of safari clothes at Ahmed Brothers in Nairobi, and he was sometimes seen smoking a cigarette, lounging in Rainey's Ford car. As chimpanzees were unknown in this part of Africa, Dooley's antics in small towns drew large crowds of African onlookers who were always doubled over with laughter. The Swahili name for chimpanzee is *soko mutu*, forest person. Just the same the crowds kept a respectable distance from Dooley the forest person, who occasionally gazed absently in their direction as he blew smoke rings, well aware he was something of a sensation.

At the ranch Rainey kept his packs of bear dogs and fighting dogs. A sizeable group of friends assembled for the hunt: a rancher called Boy Long,* who had for fifteen years been Delamere's Soysambu estate manager; Al Klein, the American white hunter, who was along for the ride; as well as Rainey's American cowboys, cameramen, Somali syce, several first-class African gunbearers, Schindelar, and Pop Binks.

The entire region was still crawling with lions in 1914. Land around the Great Rift Valley lakes of Naivasha, Nakuru, and Elementeita was being opened up for ranches and farms. In addition to ranchers who hunted lions in defense of stock, three game rangers—Blayney Percival,

---

*Caswell "Boy" Long married a wealthy, pistol-packing beauty, a safari client of Bror Blixen's named Genessie.

and Messrs. Woodhouse and Woosnam—frequently shot lions in an effort to thin out the population. For this reason some Naivasha lions knew all about hunting and had heated temperaments to match.

In just fifteen days hunting with Schindelar, Rainey's party killed eleven lions, but they had not yet managed to film a charging lion. When a lion did charge, the cameramen had been out of range, or there was no time to set up the big tripods before the lion was in a full rush, and Schindelar or Rainey had to shoot in self-defense. On the sixteenth day Rainey, Schindelar, and the hunting party set up camp some distance from Rainey's ranch. The country southeast of Lake Naivasha is rough. Much of the terrain is black volcanic rubble, broken with open grasslands, and dense thickets of a bluish-leafed bush known by its Masai name, *leleshwa*.*

At Rainey's new camp beneath Mount Longonot, a stark 9,000-foot cone of an extinct volcano, Pop Binks left the safari on the eighth of January 1914 and returned to Nairobi on the train to develop the film at his Victoria Street darkroom. The following day Schindelar, Rainey, and the hunting party set out in search of another lion. The hunters made for Ngasawa Gorge, a rocky defile where a lion was seen at the mouth of the chasm. In moments the hounds were on the heels of a huge and very alert maned lion. This lion had very likely been hunted before, perhaps by the Game Department, for he wasted no time putting distance between himself and his pursuers. Instead of holing up in the gorge the cat raced toward Mount Longonot headed for the cover of a broad expanse of *leleshwa* brush.

Fritz Schindelar spurred his horse trying to cut the lion off as he galloped over a low ridge of hills, but the going was hard, and by then the party had split up. Rainey and Klein were on one side while Fritz paused on a ridge to check the lion as the others caught up with him.

The hounds were still after the lion, but Schindelar observed that now and then the maddened lion would spin about and go after the dog pack, scattering them in all directions. Then the chase would resume. Schindelar knew this lion was different than any they had so far encountered. He was sure the lion would die fighting, and they would

---

*Leleshwa, *Tarchonanthus camphoratus*, is a dioecious shrub that can grow to twenty feet, with leaves smelling like camphor when crushed. The Masai use the shoots to make knobkerries. Because of its high oil content, *leleshwa* will burn even when green.

get the long-sought charging photos. The hunters followed Fritz as they rode into the valley, led on by the barking dogs, which by then had the lion bayed in dense *leleshwa*.

Near the thickets Rainey dismounted and set up the camera tripods twenty yards from the edge of the brush, while all hell broke out with the bark of the dogs and the growls of an aroused lion, still well hidden in the *leleshwa*. At this point the problem was how to get the lion to break cover and charge. Fritz told Rainey he would try to find an opening in the *leleshwa* and ride into it to draw the lion after him. Schindelar galloped his white polo pony right to the edge of the brush, wheeled, and sped away, but the lion would not be drawn.

Fritz came back warily toward where the lion lay hidden, ready to try again, but this time he went at the brush from a different angle hoping to get the lion to charge the cameras. There was no warning when the lion made his move. The big cat broke cover in a long bound as Schindelar wheeled his Arab to escape the ferocious rush. But Schindelar was too close, and the lion was on top of him. The impact of the lion's charge almost bowled the pony over, and the attack threw Schindelar out of the saddle. He landed on his feet, crouching as he faced the lion with his big double rifle in his hands. In a moment the lion went for him as Fritz calmly fired into the open jaws at near point-blank range. The lion knocked Fritz down and in seconds straddled him, tearing out his stomach with its teeth. Just as quickly the lion left Fritz and charged the rest of the party as they opened up with a barrage of shots. The lion fell to their bullets as Rainey and his men rushed to Schindelar's aid.

Fritz rolled in the dust in agony as a solution of permanganate of potash crystals was dissolved in water and squirted into the gaping stomach wounds and torn bowels. Rainey's men bandaged Fritz while a makeshift stretcher was made from saddle blankets. They immediately carried Schindelar toward camp while Rainey mounted his horse and raced back to get his car and head for Naivasha railway station, where he ordered a special train via telegraph. In the tiny town Rainey found a traveling doctor at the Rift Valley Hotel. The two got Fritz to the train late that evening as they set out on the six-hour journey up the eastern wall of the Great Rift Valley to the Scott Sanatorium in Nairobi. The next day Pop Binks visited Fritz in the hospital. Pop says Fritz kept moaning, "My God, what a blow!"[6] Fritz Schindelar died in excruciating pain two days after he was mauled.

Game ranger Blayney Percival officially investigated Schindelar's death. He said Fritz's condition was hopeless right after the attack because the abdomen had been ripped apart. Percival added, "Fritz Schindelar was one of the most daring men I ever met where game was concerned; it has always been a marvel to me that he escaped accident so long."[7]

Mysterious Fritz, an Austrian, or perhaps a Swiss or Hungarian, the nobleman, cavalry officer, and ice-cool shot who was a master of the heavy double-barreled rifle, so good with it nobody ever remembered seeing him miss anything, had somehow missed a lion at a range of a few feet.

11

WAR CLOUDS ON THE EQUATOR

News that war had been declared reached Nairobi on August 4, 1914. At the outbreak of hostilities British East Africa's European settler population numbered seven thousand, of whom many had at least some military background. At remote up-country farms and ranches men saddled up their horses and rode for Nairobi. In the urgent need to meet the threat of German attack, personal considerations were set aside as the territory's residents clamored to join up in a patriotic wave.

In Nairobi there was bedlam as enlistment fever broke out, and volunteers poured in to the main recruiting office at the railway station. Some enthusiastic would-be combatants galloped through the streets of town armed with bamboo pig-sticking spears. Others showed up at recruiting offices armed with everything from elephant rifles to light hunting rifles and shotguns. They came mounted on an assortment of strange transport—bicycles, buggies, mules, ponies, and even race horses. Some were dressed in worn khakis with broad-brimmed terai hats and had bandoliers of ammunition slung across their shoulders. Others wore fashionable jodhpurs with silk shirts and colorful neck scarves. In this motley collection were the colony's dozen or so white hunters.

Nairobi swarmed with volunteer cavalry raised by ex-army officers. It was said there were so many ex-officers available one could have been a captain in a famous British regiment but could only be given the rank of a sergeant in a local regiment's Maxim gun section.

Residents in British territory who were of foreign nationality were keen to exhibit their patriotism and unquestioned loyalty to the allied cause. Swedish white hunter Bror Blixen met with fellow Swedes at his house in August 1914, one day before war was declared. Bror and his friends, Baron Erik von Otter, Helge Fagerskold, and Emil Holmberg,* feared that Sweden sympathized with Germany. Thinking an alliance between Sweden and Germany possible, he and his friends determined to offer their services to the British and their adopted country, with the reservation that they should be freed from military service if Sweden joined Germany. The next day Bror with von Otter cycled to Nairobi to the recruiting office. Bror joined up with his friend, the brawny and mustachioed hunter Bowker Douglas, who had raised his own group of fighting men and given the unit the romantic name "Bowker's Horse."

A cavalry unit known as the East African Mounted Rifles (EAMR) was raised in Nairobi. One of the EAMR's squadrons was called Monica's Own, in honor of the daughter of Sir Henry Belfield, the territory's governor. British East Africa earned the distinction of having the only army that fought first and trained afterward.

Most of the unit's recruits wore informal uniforms, with the only insignia being a patch bearing the letters *EAMR*. Coats or tunics, if worn at all, were mostly cut off at the shoulders. Headgear ranged from smart khaki helmets to felt terais. Volunteers brought along their favorite hunting rifles since weapons were in short supply during the first months of the war. The medical officer of the EAMR, Captain C. J. Wilson, recorded that "An East African Mounted Rifleman on the warpath was a wonderful sight. Straddled across a primitive mule and slung around with rifle, bandoliers, haversack and water bottle, with perhaps a bush knife, revolver, field-glasses, and the odd billy-can or two."[1]

The East African Mounted Rifles was soon 1,166 strong. Among their ranks were white hunters, Boer trekkers from South Africa who had previously fought the British, as well as aristocrats, deadbeats, remittance men, con men, sanitary inspectors, and drunks. The unit's first commander, Boer War hero Colonel D. P. "Jim" Driscoll, D.S.O., was so confident of success that he made an astonishing offer to the London War Office. Driscoll wanted to invade German East Africa with his EAMR *alone*.[2]

WITHIN A FEW months 85 percent of British East Africa's able-bodied males were engaged in some type of military unit. In the balmy days

---

*Father of contemporary white hunter, Anders "Andrew" Holmberg.

building up to real fighting, the war was thought to be a wonderful adventure.

At war's outset, the prevalent opinion was that hostilities in East Africa would end in a speedy victory for the British forces. However, delusions of a rapid Allied victory were to be shattered. In their splendid naïveté the colonists had not reckoned with the greatest guerilla leader of all time, the brilliant and unassuming General Paul Emil von Lettow-Vorbeck, who led the forces in German East. As events would later prove, Driscoll and many of his fellow officers, for all their bluster and bravery, had sadly underestimated the opposition.

At the start of the war the whole of British East Africa and Uganda combined had only one battalion of the King's African Rifles, or KAR. These troops comprised 1,900 African *askaris* commanded by five dozen European officers drawn from the 3rd King's African Rifles, the 4th KAR (Uganda), and four companies of the 1st Battalion KAR from Nyasaland (Malawi). The so-called Royal Artillery consisted of ancient Maxim guns mounted upon Model T Fords. Two of these guns had jammed for Lugard, the early British administrator, on his expedition of 1891 and continued to malfunction during the British-German hostilities.

Across the border in German territory, the enemy was far better prepared. Their forces included 2,540 African *askaris* and 2,154 German soldiers armed with forty modern field guns and seventy machine guns. There were also forty-five Germans in the colonial police force.[3] Once the fighting began, the British forces received regular supplies and reinforcements; however, the German troops under von Lettow could expect no help or resupply from the fatherland because the British Royal Navy had a blockade in the Indian Ocean. Instead von Lettow had to rely on his own thoroughly drilled *Schutztruppe* and highly trained African *askaris*, all of whom worshipped the ground he walked upon. Von Lettow knew that protracted set-piece battles were out of the question. His only recourse would be lightning hit-and-run fights and clever guerilla tactics. His brilliance was quickly established in the first major battle of the war, on November 1, 1914, when von Lettow easily defeated the just-arrived British Expeditionary Force of eight thousand at the German's second most important port of Tanga.

Von Lettow had only four hundred men at the start of the attack, but quickly obtained reinforcements from his up-country garrisons via the German's northern railway. The general himself commanded the attack, and in the heat of battle he rode a bicycle among his troops with

General Paul Emil von Lettow-Vorbeck, undefeated commander of German East Africa's army.

bullets whining around his head. Under withering German fire British forces made an ignominious retreat back to the sea. The British generals in this rout were blamed for the stunning defeat, as were East Indian troops under their command, most of whom abandoned weapons and equipment in their hasty flight across Tanga's muddy beaches back to the cover offered by coastal mangroves.

After Tanga the sound of von Lettow's guns were no longer imaginary. In 1914 the King's African Rifles were hurriedly deployed along the Anglo-German frontier near Kilimanjaro. An armored train patrolled the line between Nairobi and Mombasa, fearing raids that might blow up railway bridges. For all that the Germans made lightning attacks along the railway using fast horses and small bands of guerillas. Enemy forces even blew up the Athi River bridge just twenty miles out of Nairobi. Then they sent two locomotives into each other in the night. The debris was strewn along the tracks for months.

Bloody battles were fought across the full length and breadth of German East, from the coast to the elephant country around Kasigau Hill, and west all the way to Lake Victoria. Some of the first to fall in battle were young hunters including Lionel Tarlton, Leslie Tarlton's nineteen-year-old son. He was shot down in an exchange of fire at Longido Hill, along with other volunteers from famous families, including F. Sandbach-Baker, Alton Forrester, and Drummond Smith.[4]

Despite their small numbers and heavy casualties the Germans expanded their raids much farther afield and right into the frontier districts of Uganda, Belgian Congo, Rhodesia, and Nyasaland in the opening months of the campaign.[5]

WHEN WAR BROKE out, Teddy Roosevelt's white hunter R. J. Cunninghame had been on safari in German East Africa with a client, R. L. Scott. It was widely reported in Nairobi that Cunninghame had been taken prisoner by the Germans. In fact, the legendary hunter and his client were still out on the Serengeti Plains. The Germans knew where the hunting party was and had sent patrols after them. As the Germans neared Cunninghame's camp, D'robo tribesmen warned of their approach. Fearing an ambush, Cunninghame discarded his plan to march north, directly back to British territory via the Loita hills, and instead turned eastward, descending the ragged lava escarpments to Lake Natron. By holing up in the intense heat of the day, the white hunter then led his caravan back to British territory with a series of forced night marches.

Once back in Nairobi, Cunninghame joined up with British military forces. Although he had unrivaled knowledge of the border regions of German East Africa, with typical military logic he was promptly shipped to France, a country he did not know, and assigned to an American ambulance corps. Later he wangled a transfer back to East Africa where he became a political and intelligence officer, gaining the rank of major, and was awarded the Military Cross for valor. Dennis Lyell states in his book, *African Adventure,* "There are men alive today who would be dead had it not been for his good shooting and coolness in danger." Lyell added, "Unlike many of his contemporaries, in peacetime Cunninghame typically never used the title of his military rank, 'Major.' "[6]

Also on safari when war was declared was author Frederick Courtney Selous, who was back in East Africa on what was to have been his last hunting safari with white hunter Bill Judd. Instead, Selous ended up joining the Legion of Frontiersmen, a unit of the 25th Battalion Royal Fusiliers, and the first unit of Lord Kitchener's Army.

The same 25th Battalion numbered some famous hunters among its officers, including Alan Black, George Outram, and Martin Ryan, a Rhodesian hunter who was later killed in a fire-fight with the German *Schutztruppe,* and Major P. J. Pretorious, the Boer ivory hunter who later displayed great bravery for his role in the sinking of the mighty

German battleship *Konigsberg*, which he found hidden in the swamps of the Rufiji River delta.

Feisty bantam-cock white hunter John Boyes also served in the Legion of Frontiersmen. At the time Boyes was still being berated by officialdom for his role as the self-styled "King of the WaKikuyu." Colonel Richard Meinertzhagen, the redoubtable professional British soldier and most ardent of amateur hunters, did not like Boyes and referred to him as a cheerful little rogue. He believed that Boyes had looted livestock from his opponents on more than six raiding expeditions. There was no denying Boyes had plenty of gall and guts. "He had a heart of gold, the cunning of a babu, and the presumption of a white man," recalled David Herne, who knew him well.

John Boyes's nemesis, white hunter Flash Jack Riddell, by a coincidence served with Meinertzhagen's Intelligence Corps at Moshi, in German East Africa. Riddell's extensive knowledge of the country, gleaned on numerous hunting safaris, was invaluable to the Allied forces.

IN BRITISH territory game ranger Captain R. B. Woosnam headed an Intelligence section that included Philip Percival. Blayney Percival commanded a band of WaKamba tribal bowmen armed with their traditional weapons—arrows tipped with deadly *ackokanthera* poison, for which there is no known remedy. Almost any wound, even a scratch, from this poison, if fresh, results in death in three minutes or less.

Under Woosnam, lion-hunting Lord Delamere was in charge of Intelligence on the Masai border. Woosnam used three Swedish hunters—Bror Blixen, Nils Fjasted, and Ture Rundgren—to arrange communications between Delamere and Nairobi. The three rode bicycles to get about in the bush, and in country where they could not ride they used African runners to transmit information. Woosnam assigned white hunter Bill Judd, a veteran of the Boer War, and a South African hunter, J. Postma, to scout the blistering frontier soda lakes of Natron and Magadi. Postma went behind German lines in search of positions with two D'robo hunters. The party was ambushed and captured by a German patrol, then marched to the German camp. One night while Postma's guard was out of sight he grabbed a gun lying nearby and fired into the air as German *askaris*, whose rifles were stacked, took cover. In the melee Postma and the D'robo hunters escaped in the dark as bullets whined overhead. The trio made it back safely to British lines. A few days later Postma rode into a pride of lions. His horse shied, throwing the hunter as a lion promptly went for him, knocking him down and savaging him with bites in the hip. Postma killed the lion with a revolver shot to the head. Although badly injured from the mauling, Postma somehow found his terrified horse and rode back to camp.

ON ANOTHER occasion when British forces were advancing toward the enemy, an ox-wagon caravan drawn by sixteen oxen, and driven by Bror Blixen's wife, Karen (later known as the writer Isak Dinesen), was following with supplies. After three days' march, a pride of lions attacked the oxen. Karen Blixen was unarmed, as her rifles were stowed out of reach on the wagon. When two lions jumped onto an oxen's back, Karen fearlessly waded into the lions with only her *kiboko*, a stockman's whip made from hippo hide. Bror Blixen admiringly wrote, "My wife literally whipped the lions away from the oxen." Later reproached by Bror for this exceedingly dangerous but brave act, Karen said, "What else could I do? If I'd had a gun I'd have used it of course; but the stock whip isn't to be despised, as you see."[7]

Bror Blixen served in Captain Woosnam's Intelligence unit, but when Woosnam was transferred to the Palestine front, Blixen unwillingly had to return to his coffee farm near Nairobi, though he made it clear his services were available if required.[8]

MUCH OF the rough terrain in the northern part of the battlefields along the border separating British and German territories was arid thorn scrub, sometimes broken with lava beds. The bush country was variously known as the *bundu*, the *nyika*, or the *porini*. The dangerous game populating the region could be as unsettling as enemy troops. One dark night near Kilimanjaro, Denys Finch Hatton was bivouacked with Lord Cranworth, and the two listened as lions roared close by in the darkness. As the lions prowled the camp their awe-inspiring roars actually shook the glasses on the table.

ON THE BRITISH side of the border the dreaded Seki water hole was notorious for the large numbers of lions that visited it. After one skir-

East African Mounted Rifles, Longido Hill, 1916.

mish, a column of troops from the East African Mounted Rifles went to rescue a patrol that had been caught in a German ambush. Near Seki the British horsemen came upon the body of young John Dawson, a promising white hunter. Beside Dawson's body were two badly wounded troopers.* One of the troopers had been shot in both legs. He told his rescuers that the German soldiers had confiscated their weapons, but then tended their wounds, leaving them with food, and beneath the shade of a bush. That night the lions arrived in force and the men lay helpless in the darkness, listening to the big cats crunching the bones of their shot mules and horses a few yards away.[9]

Soon afterward a squadron of EAMR horsemen tried to occupy a position on Longido Hill from which they had managed to dislodge the Germans, but their advance was held up by seven lions. It was not the first time a column was met by lions rather than the enemy. Appropriately enough, the East African Mounted Rifles eventually came under the command of white hunter and lion expert Major Clifford Hill.

---

*Seki water hole lies in the hilly thornbush country south of the Masai village of Bissell, in southern Kenya.

Despite the terror and heavy casualties on both sides, the bush war was not without amusing incidents involving the region's wildlife. Soldiers from a newly arrived British regiment once started a pitched battle with a troop of surprised baboons, having mistaken them for the enemy as the creatures crept about the rocks at night.[10]

APART FROM the ground war, British forces were also in the skies above East Africa. Pilots in the African bush war were a stouthearted lot. They were not required to drill or stand formation, and some had ample time to make themselves unfit for combat by treating their malaria with whiskey and champagne.

Royal Flying Corps Squadron No. 26 was the army's daredevil elite. They provided important support for the Allied commander, a South African general named Jan Smuts, who was then making a dogged advance on the eastern side of Mount Kilimanjaro. The squadron's eight BEC2C biplanes were worn-out relics from the European front. Their design made them look more like butterflies than aircraft and gave awful meaning to the word "crate." The planes were hard to maneuver and had been brought down like flies by German fighters over France.

Because of atmospheric conditions the rickety British planes could not get off the ground in daylight hours, and flights took place exclusively at dawn or dusk. This meant it was much easier to stray off course, with a risk of being forced down behind German lines during evening flights. In low-level attacks the BEC2C's lumbering flat-out sixty miles per hour invited machine-gun and rifle fire. A pilot never knew when his plane's rough-running seventy-horsepower engine would die on him, but he knew this would happen without warning several times during short flights.

W. D. M. "Karamoja" Bell, the legendary elephant hunter, had rushed back to England to train as a fighter pilot hoping to see war action on the western front. To his dismay he was instead shipped back to East Africa to fly "crates." As a flight lieutenant, Bell never flew his stuttering BEC2C with an observer, because anybody sitting in the open-front cockpit would block his field of fire as he shot at the Germans with his sporting rifle. Bell was angry at being grounded for two weeks after the arrival of a newly uncrated aircraft assigned to him. He took off and tested the plane with a series of loops, which outraged his C.O., who had doubted the machine's ability to hold up under the stress.[11]

DEEP IN German East Africa, with overwhelming pressure on their rear and flanks, the Germans fell back again and again. Before the war they had set up a series of small, well-defended outposts along both the Rufiji and Behobeho rivers, in what was already a game reserve under the German colonial government. As the Germans retreated toward the Rufiji River in the face of an onslaught of Allied troops, a brave German commander decided to stand his ground to engage General Sheppherd's huge advancing force. During the ensuing battle aging folk hero Frederick Courtney Selous took a sniper's bullet in the mouth and died instantly. The place where Selous fell and is buried at Behobeho would one day be named the Selous Game Reserve, the world's largest, an area designated solely for controlled hunting safaris.

AFTER LONG YEARS of an honorable and magnificent campaign, General Paul Emil von Lettow-Vorbeck, the grandmaster of guerilla warfare, was never defeated. He "surrendered" only reluctantly after the fatherland had handed in its own surrender. Von Lettow accepted General Edwards's offer at Abercorn, Northern Rhodesia, on November 23, 1918. At war's end his brave forces consisted only of Dr. Schnee, the governor of German East Africa, 155 European *Schutztruppe*, 1,165 African *askaris*, 2,891 other natives (including women), one small field gun, 24 machine guns, and 14 Lewis guns. In recognition of von Lettow's exceptional honor and bravery, the Allied Commander Van Deventer allowed his captives to keep their weapons.

12

FRONTIERSMAN IN AFRICA

During the war, an unusual American maverick had found himself attached to Lord Delamere's scouts along the Anglo-German frontier in East Africa. He was a giant named Charles Cottar, a man to be reckoned with, whose ferocity and determination were rooted in the American heartland. The Cottar family was as much a part of the North American Wild West as Samuel Colt's pistols.

Newspaper accounts of Roosevelt's adventurous African safari in 1909–1910 were the catalyst that sparked Cottar's quest for his personal Holy Grail. After reading of Roosevelt's exploits, Cottar had immediately made his own arrangements for a safari to British East Africa. Charles left his family behind in Oklahoma and sailed from New York, arriving alone at Mombasa in 1910. From Mombasa Cottar journeyed up-country on the Uganda Railway to Nairobi. Once in the safari capital he went to Newland and Tarlton and hired a few African porters, then outfitted himself with a bare minimum of equipment, before setting out to hunt in the wilds of Africa, alone and on foot. Cottar quickly realized Roosevelt had been right—it was a big game paradise, and there was no shortage of wide-open spaces. Besides, he fell right in with the British pioneers. Cottar recalled:

> In those days, there was a breed of men out there I could understand. They were Englishmen, yes, but the kind of Englishmen that settled America in the sixteen and seventeen hundreds. They were dying off fast, many of them under the feet of elephants, but while they ran the country, it was a *real* country!!¹

At Nairobi Cottar made friends with Alan Black and David Herne of the Uganda Railway, and perhaps most important with game ranger

Blayney Percival. All three held him in high esteem for his strong, defiant character and his seemingly inborn skill as a hunter.

Cottar returned to the United States more than a year later, laden down with an assortment of African trophies and also with quantities of film. Back in Oklahoma, people who learned of his adventures through local newspapers came from miles around to examine his trophies and view his pictures at county fairs. Cottar's exploits created a great deal of interest.[2]

WHEN CHARLES COTTAR returned to East Africa he brought with him the proceeds from the sale of his businesses and investments in the United States. The family purchased twenty acres of land a couple of miles west of Nairobi, in an area then known as Groganville (named after Ewart Grogan, the Cape-to-Cairo walker, who owned most of the land in that part of town), now the modern suburb of Westlands. On a blank, sun-bleached plain Cottar constructed a wood and iron (sheeting) house upon stilts in the tropical style of the time.[3] Some years later the family moved a short distance north of Nairobi to Parklands, on the edge of the Karura forest. The ten-acre site on Livingstone Road was infinitely more attractive than the treeless plain at Groganville. Cottar's neighbors were Leslie and Jessie Tarlton, Alan Black, R. J. Cunninghame, Blayney Percival, and across the road a young man named Paul Zimmerman, who arrived in the colony in 1911 from Silesia, and would become the country's most famous taxidermist.[4]

With his large family* installed in a comfortable new bungalow, Bwana Cottar (as he liked to be called by Europeans and Africans alike) left on an extended ivory hunting safari to Uganda. He shot enough ivory for a small grubstake, but on the return trip he fell ill with deadly spirillum tick fever. Comatose, Cottar was carried by his native bearers over four hundred miles on a makeshift stretcher all the way from the Nile Valley in Uganda to the railhead at Port Florence (now Kisumu) on the shores of Lake Victoria, and then over two hundred miles by train to Nairobi. Somehow Cottar survived this extraordinary journey and eventually recovered, but the effects of this dreaded, often fatal disease remained with him to the end of his days.

---

*Charles and Annette May, known as Anita (née Bennett), Cottar had six daughters: Marie, Myrtle, Gloria (Biddy), Evelyn (Dutchie), Thelma (Muggy), Audrey (Baby); and three sons: Charles (Bud, also known as Pat), Mike (William Calvin), and Ted (Theodore).

Bwana Charles Cottar, patriarch of the Cottar clan, 1930.

Charles Cottar, along with a number of ivory hunters, continued risky poaching forays into Belgian territory over this period, while the British administration looked the other way. A good number of these adventurers paid for their impertinence with their lives.

AFTER THE WAR Cottar became intensely interested in films, and often took enormous risks to obtain dramatic footage. In 1919 Cottar's film *Cameraring Through Africa* was shown at the Old Globe Theater in New York. His daughter Dutchie recalled:

> It was among the first full-length films of African pictures ever shown in America. He had a great disdain for the processors of his movie film as they helped themselves to prints of his films which then showed up in some unexplained places. To thwart this he included whenever possible a vehicle or something with the Cottar Safari Service logo in his movies.
>
> In taking those early pictures, he was his own cameraman and bodyguard. He would grind away until the last moment in the face of a charging beast, and then snatch up his rifle. He did indeed get his pictures at the risk of his life. With no sponsors to finance him and no hired hunter to cover him, his efforts were

considered noteworthy compared to others who earned fame in the picture world with much less effort and merit.[5]

While hunting a buck for meat, and armed with a repeating .30/.06 Winchester Springfield, Cottar saw a leopard with his head buried in the feathers of a guinea hen. Dutchie recalled: "Dad fired and the cat came straight for his face and landed on his head. It slithered down his back tearing his back and scalp. Within his great strength he threw the leopard off expecting to see it ready for action, but it lay dead where it had fallen." It was the first and lightest leopard mauling Cottar received in his long and bruising career. He would be severely mauled by leopard on two more occasions, and he would take a thorough hammering from an elephant, then a buffalo.

The second time he tangled with a leopard Cottar was permanently crippled. Dutchie Reidy recalled, "That mauling was the eventual cause of a stroke. Papa was taking movie pictures and ran down a big tom leopard on horseback. He managed to rope the leopard around the neck, dragged it a few yards, then dismounting, he took off his lariat and hobbled its hind legs with rawhide." Leaving the leopard to recuperate while he set up the motion picture camera, Cottar returned to fetch his wife, Anita, and twelve-year-old son, Mike, who was supposed to protect his mother while she cranked the movie camera. Dutchie recalled: "When the leopard saw Papa come up he went for him with amazing leaps, even though his back legs were hobbled. Papa stepped backward and fell into a pig-hole hidden in the grass. Before he could recover, the leopard was on him." Young Mike ran in, but the old man yelled not to get close and not to shoot. Cottar swung his rifle at the leopard's head, yet the leopard bit him in the face, shoulders, and legs. Using the rifle as a stave Cottar threw the leopard back and shot it.

Anita kept filming during her husband's battle, but her efforts were in vain. "The picture was no good. Mama had not failed to turn the crank, but she fouled the film," Dutchie said.

Nairobi doctors told Cottar he had blood poisoning from his wounds, and they insisted he must have one mutilated leg amputated to save his life. Cottar refused. To everybody's surprise but his own, Bwana Charles made a good recovery and kept his leg. Over this period Cottar, whom some mistakenly thought of as simply a rough-and-ready fellow, actually wrote many articles on guns, ballistics, bullet performance, and African game for magazines such as *Outdoor Life* and *Outing*, for which he developed a fascinated following.

IN 1920 Cottar's Safari Service, which had been established after the war at the end of 1918, was an active outfitting operation. The post–World War I complexion of safaris was rapidly changing. No longer would white hunters exclusively engage huge teams of porters, wagons, oxen, and horses, for the era of the motor car had arrived in East Africa. Bwana's two oldest boys, Bud and Mike, eagerly joined their father as professional big game hunters. Ted, being the youngest, helped out with errands. The Cottars imported some of the first safari cars into Kenya. Four Ford vehicles were ordered from the States and shipped unassembled in packing cases. A Union Castle liner, the *Berwick Castle*, sailed into Mombasa's Kilindini Harbor carrying the Cottars' cars, but before they could be unloaded a fire broke out in the ship's hold and the precious cars sank with the ship in the harbor.

The sodden crates were finally retrieved three months later, and railed to Nairobi, where the crestfallen Cottar clan hauled the crates in bullock carts back to their compound at Parklands. Cottar and his boys held out little hope for the cars that had been submerged in seawater for so long. Dutchie recalled: "But lo and behold! The parts had been coated with a heavy tar-like grease which wiped off clean as a whistle, and before long four neat box-body Fords stood ready to take the place of the old transportation."

THE LORE and legend of the Cottar clan grew, and soon they had as much business as they could handle. Bwana Charles was not confined to the vastness of east and central Africa. He extended his reach to include *shikaris* operating from Saigon, Indochina, as well as Nepal and India. His friend the Maharajah of Nepal even made his palace available to the Cottars and their clients for tiger shoots.

13.

THE HONORABLE BEDAR

Although Denys Finch Hatton arrived in Africa before the First World War, in March 1911, at the age of twenty-four, he did not become a white hunter until 1925.[1] Despite his robust athleticism and store of amateur hunting experience, Finch Hatton was a ripe old thirty-eight years of age before he turned professional.

The Honorable Denys George Finch Hatton had been born in London in April 1887, the third child of Henry Stornmont, 13th Earl of Winchilsea and 8th Earl of Nottingham. Denys received a gentleman's education at Eton and Oxford. He took up a nomadic way of life in East Africa, and made a number of lengthy trading safaris, during which he spent time hunting for himself in central Kenya and Somaliland.

Among his acquaintances in postwar Nairobi were Baron Bror von Blixen-Finecke and his wife, Karen, known to her English friends in Kenya as Tania. Denys was to have a long love affair with Bror's wife. After the Blixens' marriage ended Denys lived with Karen Blixen for some time, but he also had an affair with famed transatlantic aviator, the tall and glamorous Beryl Markham,* who in turn had numerous lovers, including Bror Blixen.

Denys Finch Hatton was known to the Africans in the rather comical way they pronounced his name, "Pinja Hatterni." Because he was bald he later acquired a Somali nickname that was quickly picked up by Karen Blixen's African plantation employees and their children. They called him Bedar—the Bald One.[2] Finch Hatton came to love Kenya and its cheerful indigenous people. He was fortunate to secure the

---

*Beryl breezed through three marriages, keeping the name of her wealthy last husband, Mansfield Markham. Even in her fifties Beryl had a flirty eye, and made no bones about her attraction to Norris Kirkham, a dashing former Battle of Britain pilot, who also happened to be married to one of my aunts.

friendship of some of the leading white hunters of the time, including Bror, Andy "Mguu" Anderson, and prewar hunting veterans Philip Percival, J. A. Hunter, and Alan Black. Once Denys decided to turn professional he and J. A. Hunter made a number of safaris together. Without a doubt the amateur hunter Finch Hatton benefited greatly from his association with J.A., a highly regarded professional.

One of Finch Hatton's safari clients was an American named Frederick Patterson. For his safari Patterson arrived by sea at Mombasa, then caught the train to Voi Junction, one hundred miles up-country. There he was met by Denys, who drove him to camp in a Dodge safari car. During the night drive along the winding dirt road in the Taita foothills, the headlights picked out the shining green eyes of a leopard, startled herds of Coke's hartebeest, and, as the road swept off the foothills onto the Maktau Plains, herds of Grant's gazelle and impala. They reached the safari camp near Maktau railway station at two o'clock in the morning.

Patterson and Finch Hatton hunted the Maktau region and spent much time taking photographs. The safari lasted five months, which in those days was not an unusual length of time for a shooting trip. This was still the transition age between motor cars, bullock carts, and porters. Truck transport to carry heavy tents and equipment was still rarely used, and Patterson's expedition employed almost as many porters as had the old foot safaris.

While crossing a shallow stream one day near Tsavo a young crocodile attacked Finch Hatton, grabbing him by the leg and holding him until the gunbearers beat the thrashing reptile off. As it was, Denys suffered a bad laceration. Had this been a big crocodile Finch Hatton's luck might have run out there and then. Just the same his client was miffed because he thought it a preventable accident, for normal safety precautions had not been followed. When crossing streams Africans usually carry sticks with which they beat violently into the water, and this is supposed to make invisible crocs back off. Patterson had to wire Nairobi from a railway station for a replacement hunter until Denys was fit enough to resume the safari. In camp Patterson dressed Finch Hatton's wounds daily. It took many weeks for Denys to recover.[3]

AFTER THE SAFARI moved to Klein's camp in Tanganyika, Patterson recorded seeing and photographing over one hundred lions in the space

Denys Finch Hatton, "The Honorable Bedar," with a trophy elephant.

of two weeks. With the marvelous freedom of movement then possible, the safari headed north again back into Kenya, all the way to the Lorian swamp in the Northern Frontier District, in search of elephant.

The hunters soon made contact with elephant. Finch Hatton maneuvered Patterson alongside a trophy-class bull as it moved among olivegreen *m'swaki* (toothbrush) thickets.* Denys slipped Patterson to within forty yards of their quarry. The client fired for the brain, and the great bull fell, but was up again almost immediately. Patterson was dismayed to see the giant on his feet so quickly, for the animal had merely been stunned. The bull whirled in fury and went straight for the hunters, ears back and trunk rolled up in rage. When just a few steps separated the elephant and Patterson, he shamelessly decided to escape the oncoming locomotive, and as he ran to get out of the way, there was a single gunshot. Denys had dropped the beast cold with a frontal brain shot.[4]

Back in civilization Frederick Patterson found life congenial in the capital of Kenya colony:

M'swaki bushes are so named because Africans make toothbrushes from the stems.

It has a population of 25,000, of which 3,000 are whites, and 10,000 Asiatics. The balance are native blacks. The town looks down at heel when one approaches it. But once inside the traveler finds himself amid modern surroundings. Automobiles dash down the main street. Beautifully clad ladies and smart businessmen are to be seen everywhere. Natives thread their way in and out of the crowds with baskets on their heads carrying fowls to hawk to the housewives. Ridiculous looking "dudes" roam up and down the street dressed in khaki and bulging with firearms. There is a good deal of gaiety in Nairobi too; polo, dancing, movies, races and so on. There are five hotels, several movie theaters, a country club and three or four other clubs of various kinds, a daily newspaper, a Mohammedan mosque, a Jewish synagogue and three churches. Swift rickshaws weave their way to the tinkle of little bells. They carry fashionable ladies and are drawn by natives. Traffic policemen are black natives trained like "bobbies."[5]

LATER FINCH HATTON was on safari with J. A. Hunter in Masailand. A Masai herdsman reported two lions had killed five of his cattle in two days, and the desperate warrior asked for their help. The two men followed the Masai man through patches of thorn scrub and abruptly came upon the lions at close range. The startled lions loped into the brush and out of sight, but as the men followed them one of the lions immediately made a rush at Finch Hatton, quickly followed by the second lion. Finch Hatton, who was a very good rifle shot, dropped both lions with a right and a left from his double rifle as coolly as if he were at a fairground shooting gallery. Most hunters using doubles are able to get the first shot off accurately, but mighty few can get the second barrel fired with any accuracy right after the first, because they have not had time to recover from the massive recoil after the first shot. Hunter was suitably impressed by Finch Hatton's seemingly effortless skill with a big rifle, and his calm demeanor when the chips were down.[6]

Finch Hatton began to take an active interest in conservation matters, and between his safaris he wrote letters registering energetic protests to the *Times* of London, as well as to local newspapers about indiscriminate slaughter of game, including lion and buffalo by so-called tourist hunters in Tanganyika. His well-crafted letters drew much applause from colleagues. Finch Hatton had the courage to denounce the Tanganyika Game Department for turning a blind eye when major game laws were broken. He was particularly incensed by the despicable practice of running down and shooting game from cars. His outspoken stand won him many friends, and not a few enemies.

DENYS REGULARLY flew his aircraft, a single-engined De Haviland Gypsy Moth G-ABAK. He scouted for elephant and other game, reconnoitering elephant herds, camp locations, and water holes as well as learning the country in intimate detail. The use of aircraft for these purposes was not considered unsporting then or even fifty years later. When the practice of using aircraft was debated by the East African Professional Hunter's Association under the presidency of Philip Percival in 1936, Percival bluntly stated he could see nothing wrong with it, and his committee agreed with him.

Several other hunters of the day, including Bror Blixen, came to use light aircraft. Philip Percival, who had been in charge of the Martin and Osa Johnson safari when reliance on road transport had stranded the expedition, was quite at ease addressing the issue every time it arose during his fifteen-year presidency of the EAPHA, as it was known.

Finch Hatton had a palm-thatched coral-block bungalow on a low ridge above Takaungu creek on the Kenya coast. Takaungu was his hideaway between safaris. There he could get away from it all, especially the dreadful small-town gossip of Nairobi, where it was said, "If they don't know what you're up to they'll bloody well find out, and failing that they'll make it up." He had brought Karen Blixen here for quiet lovers' interludes among the coconut palms and baobab trees. From the seclusion of this romantic cottage the lovers could hear the Indian Ocean surf just below them as it pounded the coral cliffs at high tide.

FINCH HATTON, accompanied by one African employee, was flying back to Nairobi in his Gypsy Moth in May 1931 after a routine visit to his Takaungu bungalow. On his way Denys scouted Voi sand river and the Sagalla hills for elephant. He stopped over at Voi railway junction where he spent the night with the district commissioner and his wife. Also guests of the D.C. were J. A. Hunter, who happened to be passing through, and his American client, Lea Hudson. Hunter remembers bidding Denys goodnight.

The following morning, May 14, 1931, Denys and his Kikuyu servant, Kamau, took off in his open cockpit Gypsy Moth, circled twice over Voi, and headed for Nairobi. At exactly that moment J. A. Hunter and his client were getting into their safari truck to leave. Lea Hudson suddenly grabbed J.A.'s arm and pointed to clouds of black smoke arising from the nearby aerodrome. "Fearing the worst, we hurried to the scene. Denys had crashed . . . the plane was a blazing inferno, we were held off by the intense heat, a few blackened oranges rolled out of the wreckage."[7] Hunter delayed his safari to take the charred remains of Denys and Kamau back to Karen Blixen in Nairobi.

Finch Hatton was forty-four years old when he was killed. He had been a white hunter for about six years.

Denys's older brother, the Earl of Winchilsea, had an imposing obelisk mounted atop a concrete plinth on Denys's grave. The grave is on the eastern slopes of the Ngong hills, overlooking the Athi Plains and Karen Blixen's old coffee estate across the Mbagathi River. Into the obelisk was set a neat brass plaque with a quote from "The Rime of the Ancient Mariner," one of Denys's favorite poems:

> *He prayeth well, who loveth well*
> *Both man and bird and beast . . .*

The London *Times* published Denys Finch Hatton's obituary in 1931, describing him as "a lover of poetry and music; he had a wide and firsthand knowledge of birds and animals, and he was a shrewd observer of his fellow men and women. . . . He always left an impression of greatness—there is no other word—and aroused interest as no one else could."

14.

BARON OF THE BUNDU

Bror Blixen was perhaps one of the greatest hunters, but his accomplishments were often overshadowed by other dramatic events and personalities in his life. His brazen love affairs were legendary in his day, even in a country well known for scandalous indiscretions. British East Africa seemed to attract gorgeous, adventurous women from all parts of the world, and Blixen had no trouble finding agreeable company. Women flocked to him, drawn by his charisma and charmed by his banter and sense of fun. Although Blixen was big and heavyset, he was by no means as handsome as some of his hunting colleagues, such as the lean, clean-cut Alan Black, who had dark, drop-dead good looks.

Blixen's tireless stamina on the tracks of a big elephant in uncharted country was matched only by his single-minded pursuit of pleasure back in town. Yet men of all professions eagerly sought his company or advice, for Blix, as he was commonly known, had no pretensions. He did not care a hoot whether he was in the company of royalty, millionaires, or naked Congolese pygmies; all were treated with the same admixture of respect, friendship, and humor.

Bror was readily accepted as a brother-in-arms by the leading hunters of the day, particularly by the important and well-established pre–World War I hunter, Philip Percival. Blix became a professional after the war, in 1918. He may have been motivated by financial necessity as much as by his love of hunting. Blixen became one of the most sought after white hunters in the 1920s. It is apparent he possessed that rare quality, a hunter's *inborn* instincts—something that cannot be taught, no matter how much hunting experience is gained. And Bror Blixen was physically tough enough to make the most arduous foot safaris into the trackless Central African rain forests for months at a time, and to return with the prizes of his skill and endurance, proven by the consistently high quality of magnificent trophies he routinely produced for clients. The Africans with whom he worked viewed his far-ranging travels as the inspiration for the unusual name they bestowed on him. Bror's nephew, Romulus Kleen, says his native name was *Waboga,** "The Wild Goose."[1]

Baron Bror Frederick von Blixen-Finecke and his twin brother, Hans, were born in Sweden in 1886. Neither boy liked school, but they were madly keen on hunting, horses, and dogs, and both were deadly shots even as children. Their family estate at Nasbyholm, Sweden, had some of the finest shooting in Europe. Bror attended an agricultural college, then managed a small estate. He met his wife to be, Karen Dinesen, in 1912. After hearing wondrous stories from a relative who had recently returned from a safari, the two lovers came to share a dream of owning a farm in Africa. Bror sailed off to British East Africa with enough family money to buy a few hundred acres. He arrived in Nairobi before the start of the First World War, in 1913, aged twenty-six. After scouting around Nairobi, Bror concluded that coffee would be the most profitable venture.

Karen Dinesen followed Bror to Mombasa by sea, accompanied on the ship by, among others, Prince Wilhelm of Sweden, brother of Sweden's future King Gustaf VI.† When Karen's ship arrived at Mombasa in January 1914 she was met at Kilindini Harbor by Bror. The couple was immediately married in Mombasa. After the wedding the couple traveled by rickshaw down Kilindini Road, Mombasa's main thoroughfare, to the railway station where Prince Wilhelm's personal coach was at their disposal for the overnight journey to Nairobi. Dinner was prepared on the train by Northrup McMillan's safari chef, the grandly named Somali, Regal Wassama. The following morning the Blixens enjoyed breakfast while viewing endless herds of plains game as they crossed the Athi Plains.

For the newlyweds life was wonderful. There were shooting trips, parties, and numerous friends. The Blixens purchased land ten miles west of Nairobi in an area that would later bear Karen's name, and began planting coffee. Karen was an eager hunter and Bror taught her to

---

*Swahili for goose is *bata bukini*. *Waboga* is thought to be an Mbulu word.

†Prince Wilhelm of Sweden kept a home outside Nairobi at Rosslyn Estates, which he used as a base for his hunting safaris.

shoot, presenting her with a Mannlicher Schoenauer .256 magazine rifle fitted with a scope. By her own account she was a good hunter.

DURING THE YEARS of World War I Karen Blixen was treated with suspicion by many British settlers because of her shipboard friendship with German General Paul von Lettow-Vorbeck.* Those skeptical of Karen's Scandinavian loyalties were firmly put in their place when Karen's brother, Private Thomas Dinesen, with whom she was very close, was given Britain's highest and rarest award, the Victoria Cross, for extreme gallantry while serving with the Canadian Quebec Rifles. He also received the French Croix de Guerre and the Danish Order of Danneborg. On October 26, 1918, King George personally gave Thomas Dinesen his V.C. at Buckingham Palace.[2]

If the British in Africa at first treated Karen Blixen with reserve, none of the natives shared their restraint. In the eyes of numerous Kenya tribes, as well as the Somalis, both Bror and Karen were immensely popular, even revered. Karen's Somali nickname was Arda Volaja—The Good, the Great, the Wise.[3]

The Blixens' near idyllic life in British East Africa did not last long. Bror wrote, "The autumn came—the autumn of 1914. The war. The price market was chaotic, communications were chaotic. Difficulty upon difficulty arose. The plantation had to be sold—my home was broken up. I stood there in the forest empty-handed. But I still had my sporting rifle."[4] He also had an enormous enthusiasm and zest for life, but his marriage was in trouble.

By 1919 Bror Blixen's name was outrageously linked with beautiful women, high-spirited revelry, and famous safari clients. But it was also linked with debt. Bror's coffee estate, which had been financed by Karen's family, was never successful, partly because it was badly managed, and partly because it was in the wrong place for quality coffee. Just eight miles as the crow flies north of the Blixen estate Catholic priests were already growing excellent coffee at Saint Austin's mission. Bror and Karen Blixen's life was continually shadowed by the specter of

---

*Karen Blixen's friendship with von Lettow-Vorbeck endured. Anastasia Olga Pelensky (*Isak Dinesen: The Life and Imagination of a Seducer*, p. 174) says Karen visited von Lettow in Bavaria the year before she died, then sent him flowers and a kiss on his birthday. The ninety-five-year-old general replied she would have to claim the next one in person!

financial ruin. Mounting debt and Bror's wandering eye were a fateful combination.

By 1921 the Blixens were separated, and soon afterward divorced. The magnificent, bankrupt Blixen estate, known as the Karen Coffee Company, which by then encompassed two thousand acres, was ultimately carved up into small holdings, either ten- or twenty-acre lots, which sold for a fire-sale rate of from £15 to £32 per acre.

FOLLOWING HIS divorce Bror fell madly in love with a fun-loving married English woman named Jacqueline "Cockie" Birkbeck (née Alexander), whose husband was away in England. Bror was, as usual, deep in debt, offering numerous IOUs to a Nairobi general store known as The Dustpan in exchange for most of his daily needs. At one point when The Dustpan's owner, a Mr. Jacobs, was threatening legal action, Cockie became so alarmed about the chance of Bror's imprisonment that she offered up her pearls in settlement of Blix's debts. Jacobs, in turn, was so touched by Cockie's entreaties that he refused her pearls, and quietly assured Cockie, "No more will be heard of this little difficulty."[5]

Bror and Cockie's red-hot romance resulted in her divorce and their subsequent marriage in 1928. But Bror did not change his ways. He continued to run up endless debts. Romulus Kleen says that once when Blix was on the run from his creditors, his numerous friends got together, reached an agreement with the creditors, and settled the amount among them.[6]

Broke or not, Blixen had no trouble finding safari clients, no matter how many world recessions came and went. When there were no safari clients on the horizon, Blixen went off on his own in search of big tuskers to tide him over. Blixen did not care how far or hard he had to travel to succeed with his hunting, and although not widely credited as being a great elephant hunter, he was indeed one of the best, as in time his astounding results in that very exacting business would show.

Bror blazed trails through some of the hottest, driest, and least hospitable thornbush country in Kenya. His hard-won motor tracks were hacked out by hand with teams of sweating *pagazi*, or porters, slashing away with machetes for mile after trackless mile of *porini* wilderness long before the advent of the four-wheel drive vehicle. Blixen went from water hole to water hole, sometimes following elephant roads, sometimes taking a bearing on the stars. Even years later, his pioneer-

The Tiva River. Blixen hunted pristine country north and east of Tsavo.

ing efforts in the region, which later became the Tsavo national park, and the areas surrounding it, particularly to the north and east, were used by such famous national park wardens as G. W. MacArthur, Tiger Mariott, Bill Woodley, and Peter Jenkins. They resurrected Blixen's faint hunting tracks to the Tiva River, Dakadima, and Mutha hill for their anti-poaching patrols.

Blixen readily attributed some of his great hunting success to a native, a WaLiangulu hunter from Voi named Simba. Bror rewarded him well for his skills. "The ivory has brought him cattle, and three wives till his durra field. Like his temporary employer, he is very fond of beer; mead is brewed in big casks in his secluded village, and when we hunt in these parts a calabash of fresh-brewed beer often comes to Simba's table. He has been all over Africa with me twice. He has ridden on camel-back along Lake Tchad, he has motored to Timbuktu, and gone by boat the whole way round the Cape from Dakar to Mombasa. . . . But for him the monotonous thorny scrubland by the sandy river Voi is the most glorious place in the world—home!"[7]

THE AMERICAN celebrity polo player Winston Guest hunted regularly with Blixen. In the early twenties Guest arrived with five thorough-bred horses from the United States to be used for the express purpose of "riding down a Cape buffalo." Blixen would go to almost any length to keep his clients happy, and if they wanted unusual thrills, so be it. Blixen hired porters and an additional twenty horses and struck out for the plains beyond Rumuruti, where buffalo could be seen in fairly open country.

The hunters soon found a herd of thirty buffalo grazing in a meadow on the other side of a ravine. What followed must have presented a strange spectacle. "We made our way into the valley," Bror wrote, "and gradually approached our still unsuspecting buffaloes. We gave them 200 yards start and then off we went. Nothing can be more exciting than that—bellowing at intervals, bushes that nearly flung one off one's horse—the whole in a reeking cloud of dust. To fire is impossible, to photograph equally so. There is just the joy of pursuing and seeing what it is like." Chasing African buffalo on horseback is not like chasing American bison. The African Cape buffalo can turn on the rider in a moment, and with its strength and ferocity destroy both horse and rider. "Our buffaloes knew the ground well and were soon in thick brushwood, into which we could not follow them."[8]

ONE OF Bror Blixen's most notorious English safari clients during the 1920s was Sir John Henry "Jock" Delves Broughton, who inherited a baronetcy along with vast estates in England in 1914. Following the First World War Jock indulged his adventurous first wife, Lady Vera (née Boscawen), an avid huntress who craved excitement, by arranging for her to hunt with Bror Blixen. Jock was dragged along on all these safaris between 1923–1927, until Vera dumped him for Lord Moyne in 1935.* Jock, in turn, then married a young English beauty named Diana Caldwell.

---

*Colonel Richard Meinertzhagen in his *Middle East Diary 1917–1956* (p. 193) reports that Lord Moyne, an Arab sympathizer serving in Palestine in 1944, was murdered by Jewish extremists.

Bror Blixen and his nephew G. F. V. "Romulus" Kleen.

James Fox's book and, later, a film, *White Mischief*, relates the tale of Broughton's marriage to beautiful Diana and her subsequent adulterous affair with Josslyn Hay, the dashing 22nd Earl of Errol, a prominent member of Kenya's so-called Happy Valley set of mostly well-bred but exceedingly debauched British settlers. Jock Broughton became the prime suspect in the murder of his wife's lover.[*] Following police questioning Broughton decided to get away from it all. He engaged J. A. Hunter to lead a vigorous eight-day hunting safari to the Mara River, where Diana shot a lion. Shortly after the safari returned to Nairobi, Broughton was charged with the murder of Joss Hay. Broughton's murder trial and his subsequent acquittal was one of the most sensational scandals in Kenya, and remains a topic still much debated to this day.[†]

Another of Blixen's English safari clients was a wealthy and popular war hero named Colonel Richard A. F. Cooper, known as both Raf and Dick. Cooper made a number of lengthy hunting safaris in East and

---

[*]In January 1941 Lord Errol was found in his Buick car with a bullet hole in his head. The car was on the Ngong Road, not far from the old Blixen estate.

[†]Jock Broughton committed suicide in England in 1942.

Central Africa with Bror as his white hunter, even trekking through the rain forests of the Belgian Congo in search of heavy ivory. Cooper owned homes in Miami, Cuba, England, and Tanganyika, and was well connected socially. Among his numerous friends were Ernest and Mary Hemingway, who always hunted with Bror Blixen's safari partner at that time, Philip Percival.* Hemingway was quick to spot Bror's keen intelligence and wit. He was fond of using one of Bror's favorite quotes: "Riding is riding, and fun is fun, and as old Blicky used to say, 'It's always so quiet when the goldfish die.' "[9]

It has been speculated that because of his great friendship with Hemingway Blixen was the model for Hemingway's white hunter hero Robert Wilson in "The Short Happy Life of Francis Macomber." Others think Wilson's character was based on Philip Percival, "The Dean of Hunters." At any rate it is true that Hemingway was a friend and admirer of both hunters. Romulus Kleen, who knew Philip and Bror well, believes that the character of Wilson was drawn from the real life adventures of both men.[10]

IN 1927 Dick Cooper engaged Blixen for a three-month safari. Blixen was on hand to meet his client on the docks at Mombasa, and the safari was soon making its journey inland. At Mombasa Blixen signed on a new cook, who traveled with the gunbearers atop a mound of luggage stacked on Blixen's Chevrolet truck.

When the safari reached Blixen's camp, south of Voi railway station, Cooper, being English, wanted a cup of tea. But the cook was nowhere to be found. He had tumbled off the truck during the journey up from the coast. Cooper was amazed that the rest of the safari crew, also riding atop the truck, had said nothing. "Why didn't you call out, you idiots?" the Englishman cried, exasperated and hungry. But Blixen was quite unfazed. Tongue-in-cheek, Blixen wrote:

> Musa was a superior person, and if he chose to disappear sud-
> denly, it was perfectly in order. What was to be done? Should we
> drive back and pick up the cook or let him fend for himself and

---

*Philip Percival and Bror Blixen were for a time in a partnership. Blixen's branch of the firm was Tanganyika Guides; Percival's, African Guides, based in Kenya. The partnership was managed by J. M. Manley.

prepare our own dinner? Our aching bones led us to choose the second alternative, and it was a good thing we did, for in the middle of dinner Musa turned up. It was true he had been flung off the truck at a bend, but he came down in a sitting position and did not even feel a tender spot anywhere. He had run after us for a while, but when he suddenly heard the sound of an approaching train puffing up a hill, he hurried to the railway track close by, climbed on to a buffer of one of the rearmost cars and rode on it to Voi—a smart bit of work![11]

Blixen subsequently took Cooper into Tanganyika to hunt in the area surrounding Ngorongoro crater. In 1927 there were still no roads in the region, which teemed with an assortment of wildlife. Bror had engaged porters at Ngaruka Springs, northeast of the crater, and the safari had trekked up the steep slopes to the forested rim at eight thousand feet, then down the other side to the floor of the crater at six thousand feet.

Blixen had obtained permission to camp in the crater so that Cooper could obtain exotic wildlife films. Before the war two German brothers named Siedentopf had lived on the crater floor and killed thousands of wildebeest in order to can the tongues, which were carted out on the backs of porters all the way to Arusha. One of the brothers, Adolf, wound up dead with a Masai spear through the abdomen. Arusha white hunter George W. Hurst was subsequently granted a 99-year lease on the crater. When Hurst was later killed by an elephant, the lease passed to an Englishman named Sir Charles Ross, manufacturer of the Ross bolt-action rifle, and its advanced .280 Ross cartridge (.280 nitro). Ross had first visited the crater on a foot safari during which numbers of rhino, lion, and other game were shot, but once he acquired a proprietary interest, his attitude changed, and he took measures to reduce hunting and protect the animals, many of which were migratory.

Following their hunt, Dick Cooper obtained an isolated parcel of virgin bushland at Magara, just south of Lake Manyara, where so many expatriates were then eagerly seeking a precarious foothold in Tanganyika. After Bror married his second wife, Cockie Birkbeck, Dick Cooper knew the couple were so broke they had no place to go, even though Bror was certainly among the highest-paid white hunters in Africa. When Dick Cooper offered his congratulations to Bror and Cockie on their marriage, saying to her, "I hope you'll be very happy," her reply had been, "So do I, but it may be difficult without a penny to our names."[12] His response was to offer Blixen and his new wife the handsome sum of £800 a year to live on his Tanganyika farm and plant coffee. Blixen was not ungrateful. Years later he wrote of Dick Cooper, "After nearly ten years of hardships endured together and many bottles of whiskey shared, I dare to affirm that we are the best friends in the world."[13]

According to Romulus Kleen, who worked for Blixen at Cooper's Singu Estates, near Magara, "It was a hard life. Before they could begin to farm they had to clear the bush and build a shack in which to live. Their only water supply was from their corrugated tin roof. In the rainy season, though, they had so much water that they were often marooned for weeks at a time. Still, Cockie recalls these years as the happiest of her life."[14] The primitive nature of Singu Estates drew the attention of the Prince of Wales when he hunted with Blixen in 1928. During the safari the prince took Bror aside and said reproachfully, "I say, Blixen, you really oughtn't to let your wife live in a tumbledown place like this."[15]

BROR CONTINUED to hunt professionally from time to time while working on Cooper's coffee estate. But storm clouds soon formed over Bror and Cockie's happy marriage with the arrival of a tall, leggy Swedish beauty named Eva Dickson, a blonde with a mannequin's face and figure who mysteriously turned up at Singu Estates in her own car. Eva apparently arrived already fixated on the world-famous hunter. The parting of Cockie and Bror's ways came about soon afterward, and Eva moved in with Bror.

At first it was generally thought Bror Blixen had married his stunning blonde live-in companion. Blix, however, confided to his friend Romulus Kleen at Singu Estates, "If it amuses her to call herself Baroness, let her do so." Unfortunately, Eva, who had been eavesdropping at the door, heard Blix's quiet confidence and came storming into the room accusing Blix of not being able to keep a secret and of breaking his word.[16]

Dick Cooper, who had become close to Ernest Hemingway in Cuba, was one of Hemingway's hosts during the writer's safari with Philip Percival in 1934. Hemingway joined Blix and his partner, Percival, and their client Alfred Vanderbilt on a billfishing trip to Malindi, a small resort town on the northern Kenya coast. Hemingway caught a sailfish weighing almost one hundred pounds.

Ernest Hemingway's twenty-four-year-old mistress, Jane Mason, wanted to see Africa for herself, and she engaged Bror Blixen for her own safari in Tanganyika. During the trip she bagged a number of trophies, including Blixen's benefactor, the easygoing Colonel Dick Cooper, who was captivated by the tall, blue-eyed blonde. Dick Cooper came to a sorry end after his affair with Jane Mason, and ended up drowning in Lake Manyara, close to his Singu Estates.

BLIXEN WAS among the first to exploit the use of low-flying aircraft to learn the geography of the country, and to scout for elephant. He did not fly himself, depending instead on Beryl Markham, who was a pioneer in the business of aerial safari scouting. The glamorous Beryl was the first female pilot to work on scouting missions for white hunters. She was also the first female commercial pilot in Kenya. Beryl was hired by Bror to fly "reccies," as they are called, for him in the Voi, Maktau, Kasigau, and Kilibasi areas of Kenya. Beryl would drop messages from her aircraft to Blixen on the ground, and armed with this information Blixen would lead his client and trackers in the direction indicated by Markham. The method was not always successful, but Markham's daring and skillful piloting were soon common knowledge, and she got occasional work from other white hunters.

The aerial surveys and continued propinquity inevitably led to an affair between Markham and Blixen, both of whom were promiscuous. Errol Trzebinski in her biography of Markham says Beryl's explanation for her affair with Blix was uncomplicated: "We were alone . . . in elephant country . . . drinking champagne. He said to me, 'Darling (he called everybody darling), do you realize, we get paid for this by the hour?' "[17]

Spotting elephants from the air was one thing, meeting them in the bush at close quarters on foot proved to be another for Markham. With Blix she once trekked after elephant near Makindu. Closing with the elephant herd Beryl attempted to take a photograph but was put to flight when a bull advanced with its trunk up, emitting shrill blasts. Beryl later said, "By Jove, I've never been so frightened in my life."[18]

On another safari with Winston Guest and his sister in remote territory east of the Yatta plateau, in what is now Tsavo national park, Beryl and Blixen spotted two very large elephants. Landing at his camp, Blixen and his clients took up the pursuit of the trophy bulls on foot. When they came up on the elephants, Blixen had Winston shoot the larger of the two bulls. The hunting party next turned their attention to the second bull and raced after it. In due course Blixen and Diana Guest closed with the second elephant, and she shot it. The tusks from the second elephant weighed an incredible 130 pounds apiece.

Blixen returned to where Winston had shot the first elephant, but much to their amazement the animal had vanished. Blixen and his trackers went after it, and spoored it relentlessly for two days, but near Sala hill they lost the tracks when a huge herd of elephant passed by, obliterating the spoor.

Six months after Winston lost his trophy elephant, an amateur Afrikaner hunter near Voi sand river came across the skeleton of a mighty elephant with the ivory still encased in the skull. The elephant had been dead for a long time, but although it was not the Afrikaner's trophy, he tried to make it look like his own. To do this he shot a dik-dik, a tiny antelope common in the area, and smeared the fresh blood of the antelope over the found ivory, hoping to make it look as though the elephant had been freshly killed. Then he took the tusks, as the law demanded, for weighing and registration to the local game warden, C. G. MacArthur, at Mtito Andei, where he passed the ivory off as his own. To MacArthur, an experienced warden, it was quite apparent the tusks had been dried out by the sun. Confronted with his ruse, the Afrikaner admitted the ivory was not his. When ivory is dried out and weathered it loses a good deal of its weight. Despite this weathering process the tusks still tipped the scales at a whopping 196 and 198 pounds. Before drying out, the ivory most certainly would have been the heaviest ever taken in Kenya.

When Winston Guest, now back in the United States, heard about this giant elephant, which very likely belonged to him, he promptly dispatched one of his representatives to Kenya to claim the ivory. But the envoy was sent to Africa by ship, which was a four-week trip. In the meantime the government had confiscated the ivory. The magnificent tusks were sold at a government ivory auction in Mombasa, but by an unlucky twist of fate, the new owner of the ivory carved up the tusks before Guest's envoy arrived to claim them.[19]

❖

ALFRED VANDERBILT was among the ultra-rich American sportsmen of his day who made the long journey to Africa to hunt trophy-size elephant with Bror. On Vanderbilt's first safari Blixen elected to hunt in some of his favorite thornscrub country around Voi. The hunters caught sight of a big tusker, which they tracked day after day, never catching up to it. Blixen and Vanderbilt hunted that one elephant for two and a half months, but as Bror wrote, "We wore out many boots, smashed up an aeroplane and three cars, but all to no purpose. We did not see even the tip of the elephant's tail. Vanderbilt was a thoroughly good fellow, but nonetheless I expected dismissal from day to day." Bror continued, "I have no doubt that he saw the honest endeavors I was making, but he must have thought that he might be able to get hold of a luckier safari leader."

One afternoon the two men were chatting in camp, and Blix expected the moment had arrived when Vanderbilt would tell him he would like to try another white hunter. Vanderbilt said, "Look here, Bror, suppose if I come back next year? What do you think is the longest time I can have to spend to get a big elephant?"

Bror replied, a little shamefacedly, "Two months ought to be enough."

"Let's say three months to be on the safe side," said Vanderbilt nodding. "And you can be sure I'll come. This is the first time I've been after anything that money can't buy, and these two and a half months have been the best fun I've ever had."[20]

Shortly after Vanderbilt's departure Bror's next elephant safari well illustrated the vagaries of trophy elephant hunting. His succeeding safari clients were also "repeats," and old friends—an Englishman, the Honorable Captain Freddie E. Guest, and his daughter, Diana (no relation to American safari clients, Raymond and Winston Guest). In a single week's hunting at Voi Freddie Guest's safari shot four elephant carrying remarkably heavy ivory averaging 116 pounds each. Bror ruefully observed, "The Goddess of Sport is certainly capricious."[21]

Bror's incredible record of four-hundred-plus pounders during the course of a single elephant safari would stand until long after Blixen's death; indeed, until after the Second World War.

The premier white hunters generally conceded the most difficult, the most physically demanding, time-consuming, and exciting hunting of all was the pursuit of a really big tusker—an old elephant carrying

Bror Blixen (left) and
Philip Percival.

ivory in excess of one hundred pounds per side, the magical "one hundred pounder." Moreover, in Blixen's day he was competing with top-drawer no-nonsense professionals, some of them former full-time ivory hunters. Blixen was closely watched—and judged—in the critical eyes of his colleagues and competitors. Yet he was readily accepted for his determination and prowess by these discerning peers. Blixen was comfortably competing in this department with the much longer established big boys in the ivory-hunting business, Judd, Black, Hoey, and Pearson.

Eric Rundgren, who was a leading white hunter in the fifties and sixties, maintains that the way a hunter was judged in those days was not only by the overall quality of the trophies he produced for a client, but by the quality and size of trophy ivory, and in his view, Blixen came up trumps in both categories, especially so in the matter of classy ivory. Rundgren's was no mean accolade, even if fellow Swede Bror Blixen was his godfather, as well as one of his father's former partners in the failed Blixen coffee plantation.

RUNDGREN REMEMBERED Blixen well. "He was always in good humor, enthusiastic and prepared to attempt any scheme. His personality captivated people. My father used to say he could talk anybody into anything. A picture that is clear in my mind is of the first time my father took me into the Norfolk Hotel in Nairobi, and our finding Blixen there surrounded by about a dozen admiring fans, most of them women, whom he had just treated to lunch. I clearly remember thinking that this was really the only life for me. What profession had more glamour, could offer such opportunities, and was more fun? It made no difference, later, when Blixen came to our home to borrow money for a passage to Sweden, and my father remarked after he left that there went a man who in twenty-odd years must have made two hundred thousand pounds out of hunting and now literally didn't have a cent."[22]

Blixen continued to operate safaris in Kenya, Uganda, and Tanganyika until 1938, when he abruptly called it quits. Romulus Kleen was on Blixen's last safari in Africa. "We made a track along the Voi River," Romulus told me, "over to Msambweni. Blix made me promise that neither of us was to shoot an elephant under 120 pounds. He got rather annoyed when I bagged one 105 and 108 pounds, but forgave me in the end!"[23]

In the same year that Blix quit hunting, the adventurous Eva Dickson, who had become Bror's third wife and who had made a number of daring long-distance automobile journeys, was tragically killed in a car crash on a trip to Baghdad. Bror's second wife, Cockie Birkbeck, then living in South Africa, was surprised to read her own obituary in a leading Johannesburg newspaper. The newspaper muddled up the two Baronesses von Blixen. The editor, on learning of the mistake, rang Cockie to apologize. "Don't mention it," Cockie responded, "I'm returning all my bills marked Deceased." The editor insisted that a correction be published in any words Cockie cared to chose. "*Any words?*" Certainly, the editor confirmed. Cockie dictated the correction: "Mrs. Hoogterp wishes it to be known that she has not yet been screwed in her coffin."[24]

BLIX EVENTUALLY got married again in Sweden, where he had happily settled for good among friends and family. By a cruel twist of fate, Blix, who had often laughed at death as he faced dangerous game at close quarters; a man who had cheerfully flown numerous low-level aerial reconnaissances in rough air over trackless country; a man who had made eight trips as a passenger in small single-engined aircraft from East Africa to England; a man who had crossed the Sahara Desert six times in two-wheel-drive touring cars, would in the end strangely meet the same fate as his wife, Eva Dickson. In 1946 Bror was killed in a car crash in Sweden on an icy road.

The thoughts of Bror's first wife, Karen, even in old age, back in Denmark, were never far from the often idyllic days of her African past. On a wall to one side of Karen's desk in her study was a framed map of her African farm and the Ngong hills, with a photograph of Denys Finch Hatton and a few letters of his kept on her desk. Every night she went to her study to look at them and then faced in the direction of Africa. In her will she left one hundred shillings to each of the Africans from her farm.[25] Despite her great love for Denys Finch Hatton, Karen Blixen once said, "If I should wish anything back of my life, it would be to go on safari once again with Bror."[26] Much acclaimed around the world for her beautiful writing,* Karen Blixen died at her home in Denmark on September 7, 1962.

The remarkable part of Bror Blixen's life that he shared with Karen was portrayed in the film *Out of Africa*, in which Blixen's role was taken by Klaus Maria Brandauer, Karen was played by Meryl Streep, and Robert Redford starred as Denys Finch Hatton.

---

*In 1954 Ernest Hemingway mentioned Karen Blixen as a suitable candidate for the Nobel Prize for Literature, but it was not awarded to her.

15.

THE ROYAL SAFARIS

The first member of the Royal House to journey to East Africa was the Duke of Connaught, who made two visits before the First World War. It was not until 1924 that the Duke and Duchess of York (later King George VI and Queen Elizabeth, the Queen Mother) went on a safari to Kenya headed by a small coterie of white hunters made up of Alan Black, Sydney Waller, Pat Ayre, and Andy Anderson, assisted by Bud Cottar, eldest son of Bwana Charles. The safari was outfitted by Safariland Ltd. Both the Duke and Duchess were avid hunters. "She was a fine hunter," Pat Ayre recalled. "Deer-stalking in the Highlands of Scotland enabled her to become a very capable shot." The Duke got a big lion, trophy rhino, buffalo, and, according to Ayre, "One of the best leopards I have ever seen."[1]

A few years later, in 1928, another royal safari was the talk of Nairobi. In that year it was Edward, Prince of Wales (later King Edward VIII before abdicating to marry American divorcée Wallis Simpson), who was the royal visitor. On his tour the prince was accompanied by his brother, Henry, the Duke of Gloucester. The Honorable Denys Finch Hatton, an old Etonian with the right accent and British social connections, was the white hunter nominally in charge of arrangements for the prince's safari. At that early stage in his career, Finch Hatton had only been a professional hunter for about three years, and wisely decided he was in need of additional expertise for such important clients. His first choice as white hunter, the venerable J. A. Hunter, was committed to another safari. Finch Hatton was able to secure the services of veteran white hunters Andy Anderson, Pat Ayre, and, in Tanganyika, Bror Blixen and famed war hero and game warden Monty Moore, V.C. To look after the prince's brother, the Duke of Gloucester,

Finch Hatton selected the masterly Alan Black. Black in turn was backed up by Sydney Waller, a first-class pioneer hunter.

The Prince of Wales and the Duke of Gloucester hunted the plains northeast of Mount Kilimanjaro. The camp set up for the prince's safari was overshadowed by the towering plum-pudding snowcap of Mount Kilimanjaro. Queen Victoria, grandmother of the royal brothers, had given Africa's tallest mountain to the German Kaiser on his birthday. Kaiser Wilhelm had no snowcapped mountain in all his colonial territory of German East Africa, while British East African territory encompassed Mount Kenya, Mount Elgon, and, in Uganda, the picturesque Ruwenzoris, or Mountains of the Moon, as well as Kilimanjaro. Cartographers of the day merely had to make a zig and a zag to exclude Kilimanjaro from Kenya, and place it in German territory (now Tanzania) to formalize the gift.

When the Prince of Wales left the safari to resume official duties of his royal tour the Duke of Gloucester remained to hunt in what is now Tsavo national park, but was then known as the Serengeti Plains in Kenya (although not remotely connected with the more famous Serengeti Plains in Tanzania). One of the lengthy bush tracks Black cut from Mbuyuni (Ostrich) railway station to the village of Ziwani (Spring Water) is still known as the Prince of Wales Road.

In the course of his African hunt the Duke of Gloucester became involved with safari aviatrix Beryl Markham, who later visited him in England. Beryl's estranged husband, the wealthy Mansfield Markham, squirmed with embarrassment, even threatening to cite the prince in his divorce case. After the affair Beryl and Prince Henry apparently remained good friends.

WHILE IN East Africa the Prince of Wales made a safari to Uganda during which he hunted elephant with two reformed but famous ivory poachers: Captain J. D. Salmon, who by then was Uganda's chief game warden, and Pete Pearson, who, except for a taste for champagne, led a spartan life. Salmon, known as Samaki (Swahili for fish) because of his surname, had previously conducted safaris with the king and queen of England on their 1924–1925 visits to East Africa when they were still the Duke and Duchess of York.

In Uganda the Prince of Wales and his party sailed up Lake Albert aboard the comfortable lake steamer *Lugard* to enter the Victoria Nile.

From the deck of the *Lugard* the prince viewed numerous crocodiles, hippo, elephant, buffalo, and Uganda kob. One evening the steamer dropped anchor below the stunning spectacle of Murchison Falls, where a narrow granite pass tightly compresses the river Nile before it tumbles 180 feet into a swirling cauldron, alive with giant crocodiles. At dinner that night the prince asked Salmon how many elephant he had shot. Salmon replied, "Sir, you might as well ask a dentist how many teeth he has pulled!"[2]

Some days later the prince and his hunters were on the tracks of a big solitary bull elephant. When they caught up with the animal, it came straight for them. Instead of seeing the elephant's rear end, the hunting party had a close-up frontal view of a very angry, fast-moving tusker. Pete Pearson grabbed the prince and threw him to one side out of danger, but straight into the heart of a thornbush. Pearson and Samaki Salmon fired together. The elephant stopped its headlong charge and crumpled exactly twelve feet from where His Highness lay sprawled in the thorn thicket.

AT BABATI, warden Monty Moore awaited the royal party. Moore had scouted out both buffalo and rhino, but the Prince of Wales wanted a lion, and for the moment nothing else would do. Having only two days to produce results, Blixen immediately set about positioning lion "kills" or baits near a wide spot in the road called Kwakuchinja (To Kill). It happened that a lion struck the Kwakuchinja bait the first night, but did not stay around to meet his pursuers.

Determined that the Prince of Wales would have his trophy, Blixen got down to business. He immediately got more baits and placed four zebra carcasses, each one separated by some distance and placed for approach, wind, and cover, all in a position to attract lion. When he cautiously visited the kills at dawn the next day, he was gratified to find two lions on each one of his four zebra baits, making a total of *eight* lions. It was a measure of his success as a lion baiter, as well as proof of the prodigious lion population in Tanganyika.

Blixen returned to fetch the prince and Finch Hatton at Babati. Back at the first lion bait, Bror positioned Finch Hatton and the prince, accompanied by two of the prince's armed equerries and his adjutant, who was armed with a shotgun, as well as cool war hero, warden Monty Moore, at the most likely spot. Blixen had arranged to hire a number of

African beaters to assist with the hunt, but none showed up. As Blixen had no beaters he elected to become a one-man beating party himself, although, as he freely admitted, "I do not like hunting lions in long grass!"

A quote of what happened next is taken from notes kept by the Prince of Wales, which later became a book transcribed by one of his secretaries, Patrick R. Chalmers, in *Sport and Travel in East Africa*. Chalmers wrote:

> Blixen (whose attitude towards lions is that of the prophet Daniel) decided to be the sole beater. He had not gone far when a lion appeared at the edge of the covert. It turned rapidly and re-entered the bush. "Shoo," said Blixen, not to be denied, "Shoo," and he clapped his hands. Out bounded the lion.
>
> He really looked rather fine. Broadside on, he galloped across the front. H.R.H. was shooting with a .350 double-barrel Express. . . . With the first barrel he missed cleanly and cleverly. A little rattled at that, he took more time for his second shot. The left-hand barrel was fired at the lion when he was 140 yards away. The grass was tallish, and the big, yellow beast went bounding through it in great leaps. It was a difficult shot because of the grass, and a long one. But it was a lucky one also, for it knocked the lion over. H.R.H. reloaded and ran up to where it lay.[3]

The lion thereupon got up and made off, but stopped suddenly and wheeled about. Before the lion could get going again, the prince gave him both barrels in the chest, and the lion fell over dead. It was an old lion in good condition. The prince was so tickled with Blixen's performance and with his lion that he asked Blixen if he could come back for some more hunting as soon as he had finished his official duties at Dar es Salaam. "Certainly, Your Royal Highness!" Blixen replied.

Upon the prince's return from Dar es Salaam, Blixen moved the safari camp to Singu Estates. He enlisted the aid of the powerful Mbulu chief, Michaeli, who offered him five hundred warriors as beaters for the prince's hunt. The prince entertained a group of local farmers at a tented reception hosted by Blixen. At the time there was anxiety over the poor health of Edward's father, and before the hunt could begin, a telegram arrived from Buckingham Palace informing the prince it would be necessary for him to return to London at once.

BROR'S WIFE Cockie later related various anecdotes to Elspeth Huxley about the prince's safari. According to Cockie, even when the prince was on safari his attention was easily diverted by female company. At Dodoma, a dusty Tanganyika town between Arusha and Dar es Salaam, the prince disappeared into the night with the wife of a junior official, then turned up several hours late for a formal dinner. Rumor had it that in Nairobi the future king, after sharing champagne with two young typists, had danced on the tables of Government House. After Cockie admired an ice-making machine that the prince had brought to Africa for his safari, a similar machine arrived at Babati a few months later with the compliments of the Prince of Wales.[4]

THE PRINCE of Wales returned to East Africa in January 1930 to hunt elephant with Denys Finch Hatton and Bror Blixen. The hunters met the prince's special train at an isolated station called Maungu, a prime location for elephant seventy miles from the Kenya coast.

Blixen and Finch Hatton were an unlikely pair of hunting partners by anybody's reckoning. At the time Finch Hatton was having an affair with Bror's first wife, Karen, while also involved with Bror's safari pilot, Beryl Markham, with whom Blixen also had a brief fling. Finch Hatton was almost certainly more cerebral than Bror, yet Blixen possessed an uncanny hunting instinct that put him at the forefront of his profession. Strange bedfellows they may have been, but by all accounts they remained good friends.

With the Prince of Wales in their safari car, the two white hunters drove along tortuous old elephant roads that wound through thickets of *commiphora* trees until they reached the well-used water hole at the foot of Kasigau Hill, a famous location for heavy tuskers, about thirty miles south of Maungu. This entire region of Kenya was second home to Blixen and Finch Hatton, both of whom knew it intimately from numerous elephant hunting safaris. Until recent times (less than twenty years ago) it remained as some of the finest elephant country in Africa.

Kasigau Hill was a big and surprising disappointment, and well illustrated the uncertainties of elephant hunting. It is one of the reasons people hunt elephant. This time the hunters drew a total blank, as they did at Kilibasi Hill, another famous elephant spot. Days later the party returned to the royal train waiting at Maungu station, and set off for Voi, where they shunted onto the main line to Moshi (Smoke) in Tanganyika. Finch Hatton had arranged for trackers to scout the region in advance between Maktau station and Lake Jipe, and for porters to meet the train at Maktau. Near Maktau the waiting trackers excitedly reported fresh spoor of a single large bull elephant, and the hunters immediately set off in pursuit on foot. It was to be a long walk, and says much in favor of the prince, who rose mightily in the estimation of Denys and Bror.

The prince was excited at the prospect of catching up with a really big trophy tusker, and may have overexerted himself to start out. Thinking they had a chance to close quickly with the elephant, the hunters set a crackling pace covering ten miles in just over two hours despite the intense heat. Bror figured the elephant would most likely pull up during the hottest time of the day and seek shade for a few hours' siesta. With that in mind the hunters took an hour off themselves: finding a little shade they rested and enjoyed a snack lunch, before taking up the spoor again. Bror later thought that indulgent break may have cost them the chance of closing with the elephant that day. The spoor never meandered, never wavered. It ran south toward Tanganyika straight as an arrow. Bror was puzzled, for the elephant never paused to rest. On he went, and the hunters did likewise, sticking to the spoor at a fast walk to keep up with their perspiring trackers. The pace and the heat were terrific. Blixen carefully watched the prince from the corner of his eye, but the little man showed no emotion and no signs of collapse. Blixen wrote, "Finch Hatton and I, of course, are trained cross-country walkers and I knew by experience that H.R.H. had remarkable powers of physical endurance, but he had no opportunity of training himself in this particular kind of walking. Nothing in his expression showed he was tired, that the blisters on his feet burned like fire—he did not give a sign of feeling inclined to call a halt."[5]

The hunters only pulled up when it got too dark to continue. They quickly pitched a cheerless little pup tent on the drafty, wide-open plain for the prince. They ate cold bully beef and beans from tins the porters carried, and turned in early without the comfort of a shower, or even enough water to soak their aching feet. Finch Hatton and Blixen slept in blankets on the ground in the open, and were ready to leave as soon as it was light enough to see. Blixen noted that the prince could have surrounded himself with all sorts of luxuries and comfort, but he didn't.

When the hunters started out the next morning there was considerable optimism, for the elephant's spoor looked fresher than it had on the previous day. Blixen wrote, "The volcanic soil burned our feet; there was no merciful shade within reach; every step caused us horrible pain. But on we went."

Twelve hours later, just before sunset, the hunters thought they were really close to their quarry at last. "The spoor positively smelt of him," Blixen noted. They had covered over forty miles on the tracks, yet they had not had so much as a glimpse of the elephant. "Our feet were in a deplorable state," Blixen wrote. "We should get the old fellow next day!" As darkness closed in the exhausted hunters slept where they fell in as cheerless a spot as the previous night.

The next day was like the one before, except "our feet almost refused to do service. Our pace had to be reduced, but not only on account of our feet—our provisions began to run short; we had to content ourselves to half rations, and that too reduced our strength." Still, on they went, hour after grueling hour, with the blazing sun pounding them.

On the fourth day, Blixen wrote, "It did not look as if any of us three would be able to put on his boots!" But they did, and, trudging in the mind-bending heat during the hottest time of the day near 2 P.M., Finch Hatton suddenly became aware of the elephant. The others paused breathlessly, while Finch Hatton crept forward into dense brush and was able to establish it was the elephant they had been tracking. "He was as big as a house," Blixen wrote, "and with tusks which must weigh nearly four hundred pounds [two hundred pounds each tusk]."

The hunters crept closer into the bushy thickets. The prince had to use a peephole in the bush to make his shot, but just as he was ready to fire a disaster occurred. In his very own style, Blixen wrote, "Some cursed dry twig had taken care to place itself under the Prince's foot; the twig snapped, the elephant listened for a quarter-second with ears spread wide, and then there was a crashing among the bushes—the beast set off at a rate of forty miles an hour and was gone before we could count three."[6]

THE FOOTSORE safari returned to Nairobi on the royal train, then repacked and headed in cars for Kajiado, south of Nairobi in Masailand, where the prince wanted to obtain big game photographs. The prince's party, along with Bror and Denys, was joined by Kenya's chief game warden Archie Ritchie, old lion hunter Lord Delamere, and Kajiado district commissioner Clarence Buxton.

Near Kajiado the prince was suddenly charged by a rhino as he photographed. Finch Hatton's and Ritchie's rifles rang out simultaneously, dropping the rhino a mere six feet from the prince. Even with the rhino almost on top of him, H.R.H. never moved, Blixen noted with astonishment.

A traditional Masai lion hunt was arranged for the benefit of the prince so that he could photograph the Masai in action, hunting lion with only their native spears.

The prince was keen to visit Fort Portal in western Uganda because of its location at the base of the fabled Mountains of the Moon, the Ruwenzori. The edge of the steep Bundibugyo escarpment near Fort Portal affords a spectacular vista across the hills of the eastern Congo to the Ituri forest, home of the pygmies. The Prince of Wales was determined to stand upon this escarpment and experience for himself one of the world's great views.

The royal safari had sailed south from the tiny port of Butiaba on Lake Albert to the Semliki Valley, a true wonderland of big and small game. Semliki abuts the northern slopes of the Mountains of the Moon. As the royal party prepared to set out across the valley, Uganda's chief game warden Samaki Salmon breezily informed the prince that it was only a day's trek in the cool mountain air to reach Fort Portal. "We shall be in by sundown," Salmon declared. Just then the prince spied a bottle of whiskey, and picking it up he was about to hand it to one of his bearers to pack in his kit when Salmon said a little contemptuously, "We won't want that; there's enough whiskey at Fort Portal to float a frigate and we shall be there by dinnertime!"

Perhaps with foresight, the prince announced firmly that if they *did* want his whiskey they would want it very badly indeed. Ignoring Salmon, he said, "Here, boy, catch hold!" and tossed the bottle to his bearer, who grabbed it and packed it in his rucksack.

The royal safari started out walking amid herds of thousands of Uganda kob, big herds of buffalo, and scattered herds of Jackson's hartebeest as they crossed the golden grass floor of the Semliki Valley. The hunters trudged five miles and then began the ascent of the formidable Bundibugyo escarpment at the valley's southern end, where the foothills of the Mountains of the Moon rise in a near vertical bluish haze. The hunters followed a dim game trail that led them into dense forests, then finally disappeared entirely. Still, the party led by Salmon pushed on, struggling in the undergrowth. Soon raindrops began to fall.

Samaki Salmon swore softly. It turned out he had not been on this trail in five years, and in the intervening period the trail had turned to bush. Nobody said anything. Hour after hour the Prince of Wales tramped along in the wake of Uganda's chief game warden with mounting misgivings.

When the safari reached a mist-enshrouded hill somewhere above the escarpment, Salmon stopped. "We're lost," he announced to his astonished and slightly disconcerted royal party. The rain came down harder. They were in uninhabited country, but trudged on until it grew dark, windy, and cold. The rain did not let up, and now they were in a sea of eight-foot-tall elephant grass. Further travel in the pitch dark was impossible. A small circle was cleared in the tall grass, and with the African bearers and the prince's two aides the exhausted hunters prepared for a long night. The rain settled in to a steady downpour. At an altitude of five thousand feet the night was very cold. The safari carried no food, no blankets, no tents, no rain gear. Just then a lion roared nearby. Out loud His Highness cheerfully recalled numerous man-eating lion incidents on the Uganda Railway from Patterson's *Man-Eaters of Tsavo*, relating them from memory. The lion roared again, and again, and the rain became a steady, chilling deluge. Nobody slept. All thoughts were of food and dry clothes.

The prince took it well. He called his bearer and produced his bottle of whiskey to be shared. Sitting in the dark in the rain, without a light or fire, the men passed the whiskey bottle around. Without it, things would have been a lot less cheerful.

When a gray dawn broke, the royal party was ready to push on into the long wet grass. Samaki Salmon and the prince eventually climbed a small hill and fired shots into the air. Presently they heard an answering gunshot in the distance. Fifteen hours overdue, the royal visitor and his highly embarrassed hunter were guided into Fort Portal by a series of gunshots.[7]

16

TRAILBLAZERS OF THE TWENTIES

Of Bwana Charles Cottar's three sons, the middle boy, Mike, was the most talented of all and among the most gifted hunters of his era. His safari clients included some of the wealthiest and most famous men and women in the world. Perhaps his most loyal client was American multimillionaire, Woolworth "Wooly" Donahue, of Woolworths chain store fame, along with his hunting companion and beefy bodyguard, an American named "Babe" White. During a safari in Tanganyika Mike and Donahue had stood on the eastern shores of Lake Victoria, the vast body of water bordered by three East African countries, at a town called Musoma. It suddenly occurred to Mike that a ferry between Musoma and Kinesi village across the bay, a distance of some two miles, would save at least fifty-five miles of godawful road around Mara Bay. He conjectured to Woolworth that a ferry service might be an interesting and profitable business venture.

The enterprising Wooly agreed, and had an even better idea. What if they had a boat specially built so that it could carry a full safari crew and provisions for a month or more, and with sufficient range to cross the second-largest lake in the world. Why, if they had such a boat then the two of them would be able to use it to hunt in all sorts of virgin country around Lake Victoria, not only in Kenya and Tanganyika but in Uganda as well!

The following year Wooly was as good as his word. He shipped the *Gray Goose*, a sleek, roomy, motorized cabin cruiser, from the United States to Mombasa, and from there, on a special flatbed railway car, all the way to Kisumu on the eastern shores of Lake Victoria. The *Gray Goose* was luxurious by any standard. She was fitted out with a carpeted salon, cushioned chairs, bunk beds, shower baths, and a kitchen.

The *Gray Goose* was Wooly's gift to Mike Cottar in gratitude for their successful safaris together. It was not the first gift Mike had received from grateful clients. He had been presented with everything from cars to rifles, cameras to binoculars.[1] The *Gray Goose* allowed the hunters to get into rugged territory, much of it never hunted before. They made trips to the western shores of Victoria to what is now the Biharamulo Game Reserve in a successful search for East African sable antelope in its northernmost habitats. In the region's *miombo** forests they discovered big herds of elephant, Lichtenstein's hartebeest, topi, and southern reedbuck. On open floodplains near the shore black rhino were common, and it was a paradise for lion and leopard. Cottar and Wooly hunted extensively before sailing north to explore the Sese islands where they went after the hard-to-hunt sitatunga, an aquatic antelope found in island swamps.

In August 1926, Martin and Osa Johnson had obtained rare footage of African spearmen hunting lions. White hunters Philip Percival and Pat Ayre had been in charge of that Johnson safari, and they had imported forty Lumbwa spearmen to the Serengeti from their domain in Kenya's western highlands.

One of Mike Cottar's clients, Paul L. Hoefler, wanted to make his own film of Nandi lion hunters. Cottar sought the assistance of a young Nandi chief named Oliatorio. Fifteen Nandi warriors from Kenya's western highlands were transported to Cottar's Serengeti camp at Banagi Hill. Mike soon found a pride of lions, then, using his car as a photographic platform, prepared Hoefler for action. One of the Nandi warriors nonchalantly strolled within twenty-five feet of an angry cat. This was too much for the big lion. With a loud roar it charged straight for the warrior, who stood unflinchingly as the lion rushed him. Dropping on one knee behind a heavy buffalo-hide shield, the spearman had his weapon poised to strike as the big cat hit his shield, throwing him to the ground beneath it.

Then the lion ferociously attacked the shield. In seconds two more Nandi spearmen drove their spears into the attacking lion as the rest of the Nandi rushed in with spears. The dead lion quickly resembled a pincushion. The youth who had received the charge came out of the encounter with only a few scratches, a hole in his shield where the lion

---

*Miombo, *Brachystegia pterocarpus*, is dry savannah forest covering 21 percent of Tanzania.

Nandi hunters wearing lion-mane headdresses.

had lodged a claw, and a buckled spear. The Nandi immediately named him Ngutuny Siiya (Lion's Claw). Hoefler thought they should have named him Lion Heart, for the African's bravery amazed the American.

The Cottar brothers, Hoefler, and his cameraman Austin soon went on another Nandi lion hunt. This time the near-naked Nandi warriors came toward four lions, their polished spears glistening in the sun, their red-ochered buffalo-hide shields held before them like Roman gladiators. The first lion decided to escape. He made a dash for an opening in the Nandi line, and although half a dozen spears were thrown at him, he got away unscathed. But the Nandi had no intention of letting the lion get away. They took off after the big cat in a foot race.

The lion ran for two hundred yards, then turned to face its tormentors. The Nandi fanned out to encircle him. As they did so the lion charged, making for a tight-knit group of three warriors. The nearest warrior threw his spear with tremendous force, but the lion came on and knocked him flat. Another warrior released his spear, which passed through the lion, and it immediately turned to bite at the spear. Then the downed warrior sprang to his feet, drawing his short *simi* sword. Even before he could use it two companions hurled their spears into the lion, killing it. Mike and Hoefler filmed the sequence.

Nandi lion spearmen are surely among the bravest men on earth, yet they show respect for the vanquished in mortal combat. Traditionally the Nandi lift a fallen lion from the place where it died and carry the animal a short distance, where they gently lay down the lion. In moving the lion from the place where he died they are paying tribute to a noble enemy. Then the warriors softly chant a victory song extolling the ferocity of their foe, who has killed their cattle but died an honorable death in battle.[2]

During the filming of this sequence one of Mike's African crew lost a prized tobacco pouch. He insisted on going back to look for it, even though Mike and his brother Bud had carried out a careful search. The African never returned to camp. His remains were discovered by Cottar's trackers three days later. He had been killed by a lion.

ONE OF Mike Cottar's regular hunting companions was Donald Ker. The Ker family had been drawn to Africa by the exotic tales of a family friend, an elephant hunter known as Uncle. His accounts of the good life in the British colony made such an impression that in 1911 the Ker family sailed from Southampton, England, with high expectations. Their first home was in Groganville outside Nairobi, where wild animals roamed and only five other houses existed, one of which belonged to the Cottar family. It was here that Donald Ker made the acquaintance of Mike Cottar, who was the same age but seemingly much older than his years. The Kers later moved thirty miles to a coffee plantation near Thika, where Donald's neighbor and schoolmate was Elspeth Huxley, who found fame as the author of *The Flame Trees of Thika*.

Donald shot his first lion on the plains at Stony Athi when he was fourteen. Two years later Mike Cottar invited him on an elephant hunt. Donald and Mike drove to Meru in a car resurrected by Mike, who was a wizard mechanic, for the Model T had seen brutal service with Mike's father. At Meru, a village on the northern slopes of Mount Kenya, they left the car and hired four Meru porters to assist them on a foot safari headed for the Tana River. During the march Mike became ill with blackwater fever. Donald Ker wrote:

Two gunbearers, Syd Coulson, and his cousin, Mike Cottar (right), in Masailand.

This tropical fever only inflicts one who has had malaria a great number of times, and is usually brought on by over-doses of quinine whose action causes blood to congeal in the kidneys, and turns the urine the color of port wine (hence the name, blackwater). It is generally regarded as being about ninety per cent fatal.[3]

In less than one hour from the time he began to sicken, Mike Cottar was unconscious. Ker abandoned their meager supplies and Mike's heavy rifle. He got the four porters to carry Mike on an improvised stretcher for the daunting fifty-mile uphill hike over Mount Kenya's foothills back to Meru. During this marathon Mike Cottar occasionally regained consciousness, and Ker managed to hydrate him with small sips of water. After a blistering march the exhausted men settled on a rocky plain for the first night's sleep. Cottar was unconscious, and Ker thought he might die. During the night a rhino passed between Ker and Cottar's stretcher, and the thunder of the animal's hooves awoke the slumbering porters. Ker took the opportunity of urging the porters to carry the stretcher in case the rhino paid them a return visit. The party struggled on in the moonlight, but it was slow going. By the second night the porters were too exhausted to continue. The following night they reached Meru, where a kindly Indian doctor administered champagne in large doses to Mike. In those days it was thought that only champagne, and plenty of it, was the cure for blackwater, as it was supposed to efficiently flush the kidneys. Ker nursed Cottar in a grass *banda* (hut) for the next ten days at Meru.[4] Over the years Mike Cottar miraculously survived seven bouts of blackwater fever. Yet it was blackwater that enlarged Mike's spleen and would one day contribute to his untimely death.

One month later Donald and Mike were back in the desert country, this time at the forbidding Lorian swamp, which was, Ker recalled, "Four 'Ford' days from Nairobi." At that time Lorian had grass over ten feet tall, and its reeds and thickets were home to great numbers of big game. The hunters immediately found huge herds of elephant but saw nothing with big ivory. One day they followed seven bull elephants into the depths of the swamp in waist-deep water. Without warning the wind changed, and the elephants got the hunters' scent. One bull swung about and promptly charged. Donald and Mike fired simultaneously, dropping the bull at a range of fifteen paces. The waves set up by the fall of the six-ton beast knocked Donald off his feet. Ker later said this terrifying incident gave him a new respect for dangerous game.[5]

A Somali man arrived in camp one day to say his brother had just been attacked by a hippo and was dying. The Somali youth had been herding cattle near the Tana River when a bull hippo inexplicably rushed from the water and killed a heifer. The Somali tried to drive off the hippo and was promptly attacked and bitten in the stomach. Cottar found some permanganate of potash crystals, the only medicine they had, which they carried for snake bites. The Somali boy's intestines were hanging out in great bloodied white streamers. Mike cleaned the wounds and poked the intestines back into the man's stomach. Then he sewed up the wound with needle and cotton. It looked like a hopeless case, and the man was carried to his village to die. One year later Cottar and Ker returned to Lorian and found the same youth completely recovered, although with a very jagged scar, and still herding his cattle.[6] In gratitude, the boy's father offered gifts to Donald and Mike, including a camel each, as well as his own daughters. But neither man was then much interested in women, and even less so in livestock.[7]

ON A VISIT to the United States in 1936 Donald Ker stepped into a storm of controversy when he unwittingly exploded the myth surrounding one of the most famous names in the annals of big game hunting. Ruli Carpenter, chairman of the board of the DuPont Company, was planning an African safari to collect specimens for the Academy of Natural Sciences of Philadelphia. Carpenter had sent Ker a first-class passage on the next sailing of the S.S. *Berengeria*.

"So the first thing I did," Donald said, "was to switch to second class so I could use the difference for spending money! . . . At that time a white hunter arriving in the USA was a celebrity and Mr. Carpenter notified the press of my arrival, so there were a lot of people at the dock at New York to meet me. The press bombarded me with questions about East Africa—the game, safaris, the war in Abyssinia—and then one of them asked if I'd met Frank Buck in Africa. This was when his *Bring 'Em Back Alive* films were popular. I replied that Frank Buck has never been in Africa. All his pictures were taken in enclosures in India."[8]

Next morning at breakfast, Carpenter, with a laugh, handed him a Philadelphia newspaper. "Well, Don," Carpenter said, "I guess you've really fixed yourself!"

"There was a headline, and big article about this white hunter from East Africa exposing Frank Buck and saying he'd never been in Africa! Oh, my God!" Donald said.

Three weeks later Donald was a guest of the Explorers Club in New York. "One of my hosts said, 'Don, come over here, I want you to meet Frank Buck.' I just wanted to crawl under the rug!"

"Well," Frank Buck said, "so you're the little bastard who said I'd never been in Africa! You're right, of course, but I'm a showman and uh, well, uh, you know how it is about publicity. Come on, I'll buy you a drink!"[9]

ALTHOUGH STILL in his twenties, Donald Ker, like Mike Cottar, had more safari business than he could handle. Ker owed this demand to a series of highly successful museum collecting expeditions, and those with Edgar Monsanto Queeney, president of Monsanto Company, whose wide-ranging movie safaris made Donald famous. Thus it was that Ker gave safaris to a tough, likeable twenty-one-year-old named Bunny Allen.

Frank "Bunny" M. Allen soon became an icon in the hunting world. His family were English Gypsys in the Thames Valley, and he grew up with Romany stag and pheasant poachers who made frequent forays into royal preserves, including Windsor Forest. As a youth Allen also took up boxing and was sparring partner for some of the best heavyweight professionals in the country, among them champions like Georges Carpentier and Joe Beckett, who trained at Covent Garden. Bunny's two older brothers had gone to Kenya, and he followed them in 1927.

Bunny Allen recalled, "A few days later I met a ready friend at Nanyuki. He took me under his wing, put a double Rigby .470 into my hands and asked me to drive the buffalo out of his wheatfields. As a net result of this beginning I met the chief game warden, Archie Ritchie, and got game control work." Tough Nanyuki white hunter Raymond Hook, who specialized in high-altitude safaris with strong pack animals called zebroids, which he bred by crossing donkeys and zebras, took a liking to young Allen. Bunny learned a great deal about outfitting from Hook, whose chosen territory included Mount Kenya's rugged moorlands. Over this period Allen met two Africans who taught him just about everything he ever knew about African hunting, and both became lifelong friends and partners. One of these men was a small tracker named Tabei Arap Tilmet. It was only with close questioning that Allen, who had quickly learned Swahili, discovered the tracker's name was Tabei. Arap means "son of" and Tilmet was his father's name. The other tracker was Kikunya. Allen discovered this was not his real name either, but a nickname the Kikuyu had given him. His real name was Memasabom Arap Meteget. Both were from the Kipsigis tribe of western Kenya. Kikunya had been a gunbearer for Ralph Medcalfe, nephew of ivory hunter Karamoja Bell.

Allen gained most of his early experience in the Mount Kenya and Embu country, and often accompanied Bill Ryan on buffalo and elephant control work. A couple of close shaves on control work convinced Allen that his double .470 Rigby had saved him. "I like those two quick shots which can mean the difference between you or the animal being cold meat."

It was a leopard that gave Bunny his most permanent scars, including the trademark gash across the bridge of his boxer's nose. At the time Bunny was hunting with a Texan woman called Una in the Voi area. Bunny climbed a rocky hill in hopes of spotting a buffalo. Instead he found a big leopard on a ledge, and sent his gunbearer back down the hill to find Una. She duly arrived, and Bunny pointed out the leopard, which was unaware of the hunters as it lay on a ledge surrounded by boulders.

It was an easy shot and Una fired, hitting the big cat in the gut. Bunny urgently whispered, "Shoot again!" Una did but missed another easy shot and the bullet whined off a rock. Then the leopard disappeared among boulders.

Bunny sent his client back to the safety of the car with his gunbearer Tabei, who was to return with a shotgun for Bunny. Without waiting for Tabei's return, Allen went after the leopard alone:

> As I searched for him he came for me. It was almost a repeat of a former client named Nick Vandescut's leopard, coming from a greater height, and throwing me down on solid rock. As he came off the ledge I fired, and certainly hit him somewhere, yet it was an unaimed shot from the hip, probably into the guts. As he landed on me he gave my prominent nose a swipe with one great paw. Then he lay on me and started to chew my arm, his huge amber eyes locked with mine, not more than ten inches distant. I felt no pain. At such times I am sure one's senses are dulled. In fact all I can remember vividly is the beauty of that leopard's eyes.
>
> He rather appeared to slip his mouth around to the back of my head and neck and I felt one paw on the top of my head. Before I could even think of what to do next, the leopard left me. I was on my feet pretty fast—aware of no pain—and then, much to my relief, Tabei appeared with my shotgun.[10]

Tabei and a very bloodied Bunny Allen soon caught up with the leopard, which Bunny surprised. He swiftly dispatched the cat with a load of buckshot. Allen then realized he was more seriously hurt than he had first thought. His arms, legs, and face were mauled, and he had been severely bitten on the backside and could not sit or drive. Tabei drove him to a tiny hospital at Voi for initial treatment, and then on to Nairobi, two hundred miles away, for an extended hospital stay.

17.

As soon as he first set foot on African soil, Syd Downey was totally entranced, not only by the continent's birds, animals, and splendid scenery, but also by the wide-open spaces and the way of life it offered. He was to leave briefly only three times in the next fifty-nine years. In 1924 when Syd was nineteen his British parents had left their home in Argentina and immigrated to Kenya. The family purchased a coffee plantation known as Misarara Estate in the high country at Limuru, northwest of Nairobi. As a young outdoorsman in South America, Downey had spent his time exploring the rolling Argentine pampas. Once in Kenya he spent every weekend hunting and exploring the countryside.

Syd's first extended African safari was to the fabled Mara River in Kenya's south Masailand early in 1927. In those days that part of Masai country, which later came to be known as the Masai Mara, was little traveled by Europeans. Only a few daring pioneer hunters, such as George Outram, Bill Judd, and R. J. Cunninghame, had penetrated or traversed the region since 1905.

The giant wonderland of game along Kenya's southwestern border with Tanzania was once known to white hunters as the Mara Triangle, its western boundary running north along the spine of the Isuria escarpment from the Tanzania border to its apex beyond the old Mara bridge, then southeast to the northern fork of the Talek River, and from there southeast to 7,400-foot-high Masele Hill on the Tanzania border.

The base of the Triangle was the international boundary between the two countries. It was a vast reservoir of game unsullied by highways save for two dirt ribbons that passed for roads, both of which ran on divergent courses south of the Masai town of Narok. One road went to another Masai town at Loliondo in Tanzania, then on to Ngorongoro Crater, while the other took various courses south to the Serengeti. Old Bwana Cottar's track went as far as his favorite camp on the Barakitabu stream crossing. American white hunters Al Klein and Leslie Simpson had continued Cottar's track to Kuka Hill across the border on the Serengeti proper, and set up their respective camps in what was then Tanganyika.

THE HUGE numbers of plains animals resident in the Triangle are annually augmented when the Serengeti migration wheels north from its line of march to Lake Victoria, spilling into the Triangle between June and September each year. When the entire Triangle was open to hunting it was a vast region more than double the territory within what is now the Masai Mara game reserve's present 580 square miles.*

Nomadic inhabitants named the region Mara, a Masai adjective that loosely means "mosaic" or "manifold" and refers to the area's myriad forms of landscape—rolling hill country extending to savannah grassland, broken with bushy thickets and scattered woodland.

The spear-wielding Masai cattlemen wear brilliant red togas that mark them from great distances. After the rains a short pink-russet grass known to hunters as rose or red oat grass *(Themeda triandra)* competes with wild flowers to enhance the beauty of the plains.

Wherever Syd found or made crossings at *dongas* (gullies) or streams, he was careful to approach the crossings from a different direction so that his wheel marks would not become obvious. White hunters were experts at keeping rich game country unmarked and inaccessible to others. Their clandestine behavior stemmed from a powerful proprietary instinct, one that is easy to understand considering how much time and effort was involved in finding little-known hunting grounds.

As Downey became familiar with Masailand, he chose a campsite at Egalok, the spot in Kenya where the Masai Mara tourist lodge known as Keekorok now stands. Recalling Egalok when it was his hunting camp, Downey said the rarest living thing in the Mara was another human

---

*Controlled hunting areas required special permits from the game department that gave one party of no more than two hunting clients exclusive use of the area for a limited time, usually two weeks.

Masai in Masailand.

being.[1] Only occasionally would he cut the track of another hunter—usually that of Philip Percival, who at the time worked for Safariland.

Despite the great difficulty of getting into the Mara, Syd Downey hunted there often. The main "road" between the turnoff on the Nairobi–Lake Naivasha road and the Masai town of Narok, sixty miles away, was a nightmare of powdered volcanic dust and broken lava boulders. In the pre–World War II days there was no road south of Narok village. From the Uaso Nyiro River, ten miles south of Narok, Downey made a track to Maji Moto (Hot Water Springs) on the Loita Plains, and then farther south to join up with Bwana Cottar's near transparent track to Barakitabu.*

---

*Two Swahili words, *bara* (road) and *kitabu* or *tabu* (hardship or difficulty), are linked to form the name Barakitabu.

Maybe a handful of white hunters had taken a similar route to Barakitabu. Syd usually made his way cross-country to the Talek and Mara rivers, then south to the Longajaniet-Meareu, more commonly known as the Sand River, on the Kenya-Tanganyika border. It was many years later before his carefully crafted route to Egalok became the main highway to the Mara. Syd regarded this part of Masailand as the finest all-around hunting country in the world.

Downey explored the roadless terrain with two African men, both of whom were his constant companions. One, Gichuri, was a burly Kikuyu with great physical strength and a keen mind. He was the often expressionless majordomo and remained with Syd throughout his hunting days. The other, a slim Kamba tracker named Mwangea, whose front teeth were filed to sharp points, then a common custom among the meat-eating Kamba bow hunters, was Syd's hunting tutor and tracker. From him Syd learned how to find and keep his way in trackless bush, where to find water, and how to use the wind when hunting. He also learned invaluable facts about animal and bird behavior.

Downey regarded the years from 1926–1929 as his critical fledgling time as a hunter. He later commented, "When you begin hunting you go through three stages. You start by thinking you know everything, but of course you know nothing. The second stage is when you realize you don't know anything at all. And the third stage is when you have learned a bit, but realize you will never know it all!"[2]

Syd officially began his career as white hunter when he joined Leslie Tarlton's Safariland. Of all the old-timers, Philip Percival made the greatest impression on Downey. After he was fully licensed as a white hunter, Downey would often ask himself in a difficult or sticky situation, "What would Phil have done under these circumstances?"[3]

Gaining experience with dangerous game in Downey's largely self-taught fashion was a risky business. Syd had his share of "scrapes," as he called them, with big game, but he put them down to inexperience or overconfidence, or both. One of Downey's scrapes occurred when he was hunting with a pal named C. H. J. Wood, who wounded a buffalo. The winged buffalo made off at high speed. Syd fired a single shot at it with a magazine rifle, and the buffalo tumbled into a gully. Both men thought it was dead. But as the hunters neared the buffalo it got up and went for them, putting a horn tip through Downey's trouser pocket and ripping the pants off him. Wood stood his ground and fired, dropping the buffalo as it spun around to go after Downey again.[4]

⟡

ANOTHER SCRAPE occurred when Downey was on safari with his friend Eddie Grafton, a handsome young English hunter and a rising star at Safariland. Syd and Eddie were on safari at another of Syd's favorite spots, Hell's Gate, then a pristine volcanic gorge near Lake Naivasha in the Great Rift Valley between the Akira Plains and Lake Naivasha. It was the haunt of numerous buffalo, lion, and leopard, as well as lesser game, such as bushbuck, impala, klipspringer, and reed-buck. The region is patched with clumps of blue-stemmed *leleshwa* bush, gleaming shards of shiny black obsidian, and matte-black volcanic rock. Geyserlike natural steam jets stud the area, and above and nearby lammergeiers nest on the tall, sheer red cliffs on one face of the canyon.

The two were following buffalo in the bowels of the gorge when they suddenly found themselves in the path of a stampede as hundreds of buffalo rushed at them from a break in the canyon's walls. The drumming of hooves was magnified and added to the drama. There was nothing to do but shoot their way out—or be horned and trampled to death. Downey later told how Grafton reacted with lightning reflexes, "as though the juggernauts coming at him were clay pigeons. Grafton aimed, fired and dropped the leading buffalo on his nose, collapsing the buffalo only a few feet away."[5] The rest of the herd veered around the fallen animal, and the hunters escaped unhurt.

Eddie Grafton was a fine marksman, but his skills did not save him on a subsequent buffalo hunt at Hell's Gate. On that occasion Eddie and a companion, Sheila Herne, returned to the same place where Grafton had been with Downey. This time Grafton fired a single round at a big horned solo buffalo, which immediately fell to his shot. But this time the buffalo did not stay down. The enormous beast was back on its feet in a jiffy as it swarmed into *leleshwa* thickets.

Grafton must have felt comfortable with his shot, and probably thought the buffalo had gone down for good once it was in the brush. At any rate, Eddie and his D'robo tracker got onto the blood spoor right away, leaving Sheila to wait beneath a tall shade tree. After awhile Sheila heard two shots fired in quick succession far down in the canyon, and she fully expected to see Grafton return at any moment. Instead, Grafton's shaken D'robo tracker arrived to report that Eddie had been killed by the buffalo, and the enraged animal was standing over his body. Sheila and the unarmed tracker drove to a sisal plantation near Lake Naivasha, which was managed by her brother-in-law, my uncle John Douglas. Douglas was an immensely powerful man who despite having only one arm routinely hunted buffalo at Hell's Gate using a .500 double-barreled rifle.

Douglas returned to the gorge with Sheila and the tracker where Grafton presented a horrific sight, having taken a horn through the face and been killed instantly. The buffalo was nowhere to be seen. From the tracker Douglas learned that Grafton had failed to stop the buffalo's charge. Eddie had been tossed high in the air, and when he landed on his back the buffalo charged the fallen man, its horn tip piercing Grafton's face.

Following the blood spoor, Douglas did not have far to go before he caught up with the buffalo. When the huge black beast whirled to face him, Douglas shot it through the brain. Grafton's first shot had been a touch low in front of the shoulder. His second shot was also too low and close to the first, while the third shot with his .470 double rifle was fired at point-blank range. The solid bullet passed through the buffalo's cheek, then barely raked the outer side of its rib cage.[6] Syd Downey felt the death of his friend Eddie Grafton keenly. It seemed unbelievable that such an experienced hunter, who was also such a fine shot, should lose his life to a buffalo.

DURING THE years Syd Downey was hunting for Safariland, Donald Ker was conducting safaris for the Nairobi outfitters and gunsmiths Shaw and Hunter Ltd. There was no special friendship between the two men; on the contrary, their early relationship was marked by a feud that arose over a seemingly trivial incident.

Since Syd Downey's earliest safaris into the Masai Mara, he had held strong proprietary convictions about the sole occupancy of a hunting area by a single party. He considered his campsites and hunting tracks to be sacrosanct. In 1936 Ker and his safari party arrived at a campsite that Ker considered *his*, on the Rupingazi River in Meru district, and found Syd Downey already in residence. Ker moved to a campsite eight miles away between the Rupingazi and Nyamindi rivers, but the two crossed swords when both safaris ended up stalking the same herd of buffalo. In those days the country was wide open and there were no hunting "blocks" demarcated, nor were there limits or restrictions on who hunted where. There was, however, a gentleman's agreement in the fraternity that one party did not encroach on another's turf if a safari was already in the area.

Ker's idea of safari hunting etiquette was just as firm as Syd Downey's, and in his mind he had been wronged. Back in Nairobi, Donald Ker took the matter seriously enough to complain to the two-year-old East African Professional Hunter's Association, suggesting Downey had been guilty of encroaching "due to a certain amount of ignorance regarding hunting etiquette." The Hunter's Association reviewed the transgression, and white hunter Andrew Fowle, assigned to arbitrate the Ker versus Downey case, ruled: "Downey, admitted by both parties, was on the ground first, and therefore any new party, in his own interests alone, should move right out." However, Fowle added, "The complainant was in the wrong in camping on another man's ground." Fowle pointed out that the only possible exception to this unwritten rule would be in the case of a white hunter following an elephant that took him into country being used by another safari. Then the elephant hunter "was quite within his rights to continue his hunt."[7] Such was the early code of the bush.

In the end this storm blew over before it jeopardized a most valuable friendship. Years later, after World War II when there were more safaris in the field, both Donald and Syd would lend their full support to proposals for a hunting block system granting hunters sole use of an area by booking it and paying a fee.

AS TIME progressed, Donald and Syd had occasion to hunt together many times, often in the Masai Mara. Ker later described how they constructed a secret and removable pontoon across the Mara River to give them entry into new country:

> When Syd and I used to hunt in the Mara in the early days we were frustrated by not finding a good crossing over the river. There was thick forest on the other side, but we heard from the Wanderobo [tribe] of wonderful country beyond and of course we were eager to get there.
>
> I estimated that it would take nineteen 44-gallon [U.S. 50 gallon] drums to keep a one-ton safari car afloat. So we took down drums, bolts, wire, rope and everything we needed and spent three days making a pontoon. We tossed a coin to see who would have the honor of driving the first car across the Mara, and Syd

won the toss. But at the other side, when he accelerated to get up the bank, the pontoon shot out to the rear and the car went down into five feet of water, with nothing but the radiator cap showing! So much for my mathematical calculations!

Syd came up gurgling and then we had to get the car out of the river. We took turns holding our noses and going down and jacking it up with a huge Tanganyika jack while one of us stood on the bank with a rifle, ready to shoot anything that looked like a crocodile.[8]

On a later safari Syd took the indefatigable author Negley Farson to the Triangle but was careful to first obtain the writer's assurance that he would never reveal its location. Farson had obviously been made aware of the extreme precautions taken by Syd and Donald to protect their hallowed ground, for he later wrote:

We came to the edge of the Rift. It was filled with clouds which seemed to flow like great rivers below us. I could sense the space, and get some idea of the descent by the pitch of the gradient that lay ahead of us. Our aneroid here registered 7,000 feet. We were taking this instrument along because the country we were going to shoot in had never been shot over until 1928, and Downey wanted to map some of the rivers and ridges in it. It was characteristic of him that he should have spent a couple of years planning how to get into the country, and that, having found, or made drifts across several rivers to get into it, he should keep it to himself. He asked me to do likewise. At first I thought his attitude rather precious. But now, having seen the unmolested game in that inaccessible triangle, I feel as anxious as he for its preservation; I shall merely call the place where we began to hunt "a river in Kenya."[9]

Parts of the Masai Mara at that time harbored numerous tsetse flies, the vector of trypanosomiasis, commonly known as sleeping sickness. The fly's sharp sting is similar to that of an African honey bee, but the discomfort is usually of shorter duration. The benefits of the tsetse were enough to make most hunters disregard the danger, for areas infested with tsetse precluded most human settlement and game therefore was always abundant. Wildlife is immune to the tsetse-borne disease, but domestic stock is not.

Syd Downey with a record-class buffalo.

Ironically, the insect nearly cost the life of Syd Downey. Although it was not known for certain, it is most likely that Downey was fly-bitten in the Mara. He had been on safari there, hunting with a client by the name of Colonel Brandeis for several weeks, when he came down with a 104-degree fever. By the time the disease became apparent, Syd was camped far away on the Tana River, hunting elephant with another client, Count Ahlefeldt-Bille, the chief game warden of Denmark, and the Tana region's game warden, George Adamson, of *Born Free* fame.

Fortunately for Syd, Stan Lawrence-Brown, at that time himself a white hunter working for Syd and Donald Ker, was camped nearby. Stan got an aircraft sent to Garissa, and Syd was flown to Nairobi, where he was saved with a cure recently developed by the British army.[10]

The Danish warden persuaded Syd to return with him to Denmark to recover fully. Later Ahlefeldt-Bille wrote, "Perhaps a safari in the wind, cold, and snow of the north prolonged his life."[11]

Over the years the Mara Triangle remained Downey's favorite hunting turf. He obtained many record trophies there. On another safari with Count Ahlefeldt-Bille, Syd found the world's record impala for his friend. Those horns measured an amazing 36⅛ inches long, with a horn tip to horn tip measurement of 33¾ inches. That record has never been beaten.

18

WARDENS, LIONS, AND SNAKES

In East Africa big game hunters and game wardens often enjoyed a strangely symbiotic relationship, for their shared concerns created a mutual dependency. The livelihood of both professions was dependent upon the continued existence and abundance of wildlife in Africa. Even more important perhaps was their shared passion for Africa and their love of life in the bush. Both groups were entrusted with the burden of responsibility for game and habitat preservation. In the commonality of interests, it was not unnatural or unusual for white hunters to become game wardens, or for game wardens to become white hunters.

Several white hunters became famous wardens, and one of the most respected of these became the savior of the largest game reserve in the world, C. J. P. Ionides, whose Greek surname (pronounced *eye-on-ee-dees*) belied a British upbringing. As a youth in England he had been enthralled when reading the hunting exploits of Frederick Courtney Selous. After army service in India, Ionides, known as Iodine in Africa, wangled a transfer to the 6th Battalion of the King's African Rifles. In 1926 he was posted to the British administrative capital of Dar es Salaam, Tanganyika. At the time Dar es Salaam was a small, humid seaport boasting a British club, a couple of hotels, the best of which was the New Africa, along with half a dozen shady bars. Seeing no future in peacetime soldiering, Iodine resigned from the army to become a full-time ivory hunter.

Iodine made a number of long-range ivory poaching raids in the Belgian Congo and the Portuguese territory of Mozambique. In Tanganyika he went straight, for the most part, and purchased elephant licenses; after a long sojourn in the bush he would return to his base at Dar to re-equip. Iodine found that he could make a passable living out of ivory hunting: "You could walk into your bank with a pair of elephant tusks and lodge them to your account as you would a cheque."[1]

At Dar Iodine ran into a white hunter named Ken McDougall, who talked Iodine into becoming a professional white hunter. Iodine writes:

> I was immediately attracted by his diabolically criminal-looking face. He was drunk and had embarked upon a diatribe directed against his erstwhile trusted house servant, who apparently had deserted him the night before. McDougall's favorite African mistress was due to produce what he believed was his child. The baby arrived and McDougall had taken one look at it to realize why the trusted servant had left in such a hurry.[2]

Aware McDougall was a hopeless drunk, Ionides still went into partnership with him in a safari venture based at the up-country town of Arusha, in the belief that outside of towns McDougall "was a very fine hunter, besides being a good naturalist." But booze also made McDougall fighting drunk, a trait that hardly sat well with safari clients. Inevitably the partnership ended.

IODINE'S OLD army friend, Jock Minnery, had became game ranger at Arusha, and another of his friends, Monty Moore, was warden of the Serengeti. Iodine badly wanted to join the Game Department, something that was not easy to do in those days. "Coming from an admitted poacher," Iodine wrote, "this may sound like an American gangster saying that what he really wanted to do was be a cop. But I had primarily gone into professional poaching to gain experience in hunting as well as to be able to survive as a hunter. Having learnt all the tricks I would be invaluable to the department, as indefatigable in the pursuit of poachers as I had been in the pursuit of poaching. Only a slight mental readjustment was required, of outlook and intention."[3]

With the help of his friends Ionides became an assistant game ranger in 1933, beginning with the slim salary of £40 per month. During the 1930s the Tanganyika Game Department had just six European game rangers headed by chief game warden Philip Teare, and 120 African game scouts. This tiny staff was supposed to control all matters concerning wild game in Tanganyika Territory, which consisted of 362,688 square miles. As a new recruit Ionides was sent to Kilwa, a small but ancient coastal port 180 miles south of Dar es Salaam. At

Kilwa he set about policing his range with a vengeance. In line with his new duties Ionides engaged in elephant control operations on a large scale in aid of "crop protection."

Ionides focused on the massive tract of remote country known as the Selous Game Reserve, named by the British in 1922 in honor of Ionides' boyhood hero. The Selous, in the southeast section of the country, contained a huge reservoir of big game that had been protected by the Germans as far back as 1905. After World War I, administration of Tanganyika passed to the British who put in place the Tanganyika Game Department to regulate activities connected with wildlife, hunting, and game reserves.

The greater part of the Selous region is wooded forest called *miombo*, interspersed with pockets of *terminalia** woodland, broken by baobabs and borassus palms. Seasonal sand rivers flow during the rains over broad black-cotton soil floodplains. The whole region is webbed with mighty and hardly known river systems that include the Kilombero, Rufiji, Great Ruaha, Luwegu, and Mbarangandu.

The Selous game reserve varies in altitude between 900 and 2,000 feet above sea level, and offers a prodigious variety of wildlife, including lion, leopard, buffalo, rhino, elephant, crocodile, hippo, southern impala, Nyasaland "blue" wildebeest, greater kudu, sable, common and red forest duiker, common waterbuck, both southern and Bohor reedbuck, bushbuck, klipspringer, wart hog, Burchell's zebra, and Sharp's grysbok. Ionides became their warden.

Iodine felt that a game reserve should be ecologically large enough to be self-sufficient while also being exempt from human settlement. This was a tall order even at that time. Then fate intervened in the form of a serious outbreak of deadly sleeping sickness affecting humans residing in areas Ionides had long hoped to include in the reserve. The fleeing native population settled far away from their former lands in an area free of tsetse flies. In 1936 Ionides managed to bring the newly vacated land into the reserve.

DURING IONIDES' tenure in the Selous his experience as a white hunter was often called upon to deal with man-eating lion and leopard. As warden he was supposed to protect the inhabitants residing beyond

---

*Terminalia has numerous varieties, named for an end terminal point, e.g., a dense grouping of leaves at the end of a twig.

the boundaries of the reserve, who were often terrorized by both predators. Until Iodine's arrival this dangerous work had been left to
unskilled game scouts who killed more people than lions.

In order to get fast reports of man-eaters Iodine set up a first-rate network using village drummers. One man-eating lion was notorious
because it had been killing people for two years. A prosperous peanut
farmer left his village on a short business trip, leaving his flighty young
wife at home. "That same evening," Iodine wrote, "she was visited by
her lover who took her into an open, shed-like construction with a grass
roof and no walls. They were actually copulating when the lion suddenly appeared, picked the man off the woman, and dragged him into
the bushes and ate him. The woman had been mauled a bit and had to
be taken to hospital, and of course the husband was credited with being
a very bad wizard who had the lion for a slave."[4]

Ionides and his game scouts tracked the man-eater for four days, but
it always eluded them. On the fifth day of spooring, they caught up with
the lion late in the afternoon, and Iodine shot it. After that Ionides
hunted many man-eaters, always in hopes of catching up with them in
the late afternoon when they were more likely to lie up in the heat for a
siesta. He learned that most man-eating lions moved about a lot, sometimes lying up for a while, then moving to another spot, perhaps where
there was better shade, sometimes changing position during the course
of a day as many as six or seven times. On several occasions he found
his quarry *behind* him. In his twenty-three years in the Game Department, Ionides shot over forty lions, the majority of which were
man-eaters, while the remainder were stock raiders.

Tall, scrawny, and bony, with a suntanned face and a shock of prema-
turely gray hair, Iodine looked meek enough, but he held strong opinions and could speak with biting force and clarity. Although he was
well educated he chose to live a solitary and frugal existence far from
civilization in the African bush. Guests noted that his house at remote
Newala in Tanganyika had neither curtains nor carpets, or even a refrigerator. Iodine never wore a watch, had no radio, jacket, or tie, and never
wore socks. He maintained that while his servants had some of these
items, he could see no reason for any of them. His main pleasures at
Newala were a pair of wind-up gramophones and a small selection of
classical music, along with his hobbies—snakes and reading. He wrote
copious notes with an old-fashioned "ink-dipping" steel-nibbed pen.
His spartan habits included a strange diet, usually potatoes, gravy, and
boiled cubes of goat meat. Sometimes he would eat rice or boiled yams.

He refused to touch vegetables or fruit. But he smoked cigarettes, and very infrequently drank gin and water without ice. His daily mainstay was coffee with lots of sugar.

Aside from his great fame as a warden, Iodine also gained international recognition as a herpetologist. He once waded into a river to capture a large and deadly Storm's water cobra who eluded his home-made "grabstick." Iodine finally caught the snake by the neck with his bare hands. In 1958 at Nairobi's Coryndon Museum he presented the unusual specimen safely writhing in a hemp sack.

During his adventurous life Ionides wore many hats: hunter, poacher, game protector, game collector, author, soldier, scholar, solo eccentric, and, most of all, colorful character. His lasting accomplishment was the creation of the Selous Game Reserve, which he designed as a viable *hunting* reserve, a place where safari clients could hunt virgin country under strictly controlled conditions. In excess of 20,000 square miles, the Selous is the greatest and largest self-sustaining hunting preserve in the world, for which Ionides was dubbed "Father of the Selous."

TANGANYIKA'S "Iodine" Ionides, the failed white hunter turned game warden, had a friend and contemporary in Kenya named George Adamson. Like Iodine, Adamson was a white hunter destined to follow a path similar to the one taken by his friend. Unlike Iodine, George was a moderately successful white hunter, although George would become a warden famous not for snakes but for lions.

During the course of his early safari career mild-mannered Adamson had been fascinated with lions. He studied the big cats endlessly in the wilds. He hunted them remorselessly with safari clients, went after man-eaters and cattle raiders as a warden, and finally he raised numbers of orphaned or abandoned lion cubs.

George never cared much for money or luxury, but he was passionate about his desire to live in the bush among wild animals. In 1938 he became a Kenya game warden with a salary of £30 per month (then about $80).

Adamson's modest base consisted of several thatched huts near the town of Isiolo, at that time little more than a dusty Somali village in the thornscrub country of the Northern Frontier District in central Kenya. As game warden it was George's job to patrol a vast region of deserts and

Samburu warriors.

mountains inhabited by a spectacular variety of animals, as well as scattered nomadic tribes, among them Somali, Samburu, Turkana, and Rendile. His patrols were mostly foot safaris lasting weeks or months in rugged, roadless terrain, accompanied only by a few armed African game department scouts and a dozen donkeys used as pack animals. During one of these patrols near the Mathews range of mountains, George was met by a deputation of spear-wielding Samburu tribesmen. They complained about lions that were raiding cattle *bomas*, and more recently had taken up man-eating as well. George agreed to help the Samburu, and for their part the warriors promised to report news of lions.[5]

Several days later, as George waited in camp for news, he was enjoying breakfast when he was astonished to hear one of his pack donkeys braying, and the sound mixed with the angry trumpets of an elephant. Moments later the terrified donkey raced past with a big elephant chasing after it. The two animals disappeared as they ran through the thorns. Adamson saw no reason to interrupt his breakfast, until he looked up and saw a Samburu warrior sauntering along in the direction the elephant had taken. Before George could warn the man, the elephant rushed out of the brush trumpeting in fury as the Samburu took to his heels. The elephant chased after the Samburu with a vengeance and, like the fleet-footed donkey, the man also got away. As the day wore on, George grew bored waiting in camp for information. He strolled into the brush and soon ran into a lioness. Reasoning the area could only hold a certain number of lions, he thought she was bound to be among the raiders. George swiftly fired a shot at her, and taking the bullet the lion rolled over, then dived into a thicket before he could shoot again. Knowing the lion was hit and very likely still close by, George carefully circled the brush, but he could not find any lion tracks leading out. He climbed a tree hoping for a better view; then he thought she might be dead. Descending the tree, George lobbed stones into the brush, but nothing stirred. At this point he decided to return to camp and come back with his game scouts for a thorough search.

As Adamson walked away he heard a growl, and when he whirled he saw the lioness just as she launched a charge. George hastily fired, but the lion came on. He worked the rifle bolt to eject the spent shell, but the shell jammed in the breech. By then the big cat had reached Adamson, and in a flash she knocked him down, biting his arms and a thigh. The two wrestled in the dust with the lion tearing at George with her teeth and claws until Adamson passed out.[6]

When Adamson regained consciousness he could not see the lion. Yet instinct warned him she might be watching, and any activity would surely provoke another attack. George remained still for what seemed an age. Yet he knew he had to do something soon, because he was losing blood. Gingerly crawling forward George got a hand on his rifle and ejected the buckled shell. Armed again he staggered toward camp, but as waves of nausea swept over him he was forced to sit down. Close to blacking out from loss of blood, George fired a couple of shots in the air at intervals, hoping his game scouts might come looking for him. Instead, one of the D'robo poachers George had arrested earlier during his patrol, and who was now part of George's safari, appeared out of the brush. He instructed the D'robo to return to camp and fetch the men, water, and his folding camp cot to use as a stretcher. Once his scouts had carried him to camp Adamson wrote a note to his friend, the district commissioner at Maralal, one hundred and twenty miles away. Then he sent a D'robo game scout named Lodogia off with the scrap of paper. Fearing gangrene, Adamson knew his only chance was to keep his fearsome wounds clean. He instructed his men to wash the wounds with a solution of Epsom salts and water every four hours, no matter how much he objected as the liquid burned into his raw flesh. George's men found a few sulfa tablets in a first-aid box, and he dosed himself with these.[7]

That night, staring into the blackness, George saw the shadow of an elephant as it rushed at his tent. One of his men, Benua Jawali, had been keeping an eye on George, and now he helped George up and handed him a loaded rifle. Adamson steadied the rifle against the tent's center pole and rapidly fired a shot at the advancing shadow. The elephant continued its rush but veered past the tent. The next day the huge beast was found dead from a heart shot nearby. It was the same crazed elephant that had chased the donkey and the Samburu man.[8]

Adamson lay in camp for six agonizing days. The game scout, Lodogia, had raced on foot to the outpost at Maralal, and made the daunting run in a remarkable five days. This incredible feat of endurance had taken Lodogia through harsh thorn desert full of big game, and then he had to make a series of steep and rocky climbs across mountainous country rising three thousand feet.

Six days after the mauling, the district commissioner arrived in camp with his truck. His effort in reaching Adamson was also an exercise in endurance, for he left as soon as he received George's note and drove all night. There were virtually no roads in the area at the time, and much of the journey was navigated across country. The D.C. was surprised to find George still alive. He had contacted the Royal Air Force in Nairobi and asked for help before he left Maralal. The R.A.F. flew Adamson to Nairobi hospital, where he made a painful recovery.[9]

IN 1943 George met Joy Balley, the strong-willed Austrian wife of a Swiss botanist working at Nairobi's Coryndon Museum. Kenyan society believes that it was Joy who set her sights on the soft-spoken George, and once she had made up her mind he would be *her* trophy, he hadn't a prayer. The couple was married in Nairobi in 1944.

A number of movie and television films were made about George and his big cats, but it was his wife's books, especially *Born Free*, that caught the imagination of animal lovers. Adamson, the ex–white hunter, would remain on the Kenya conservation scene until both he and Joy were brutally murdered in separate incidents in January 1980 and August 1989.

By and large African safaris of the 1930s were still leisurely affairs. Over the years certain refinements had been added, and safaris were now a good deal more comfortable than those of earlier times. Days in the bush routinely began with a wake-up call before dawn. Morning tea was served in the client's sleeping tent by a *khanzu*-clad waiter. Tea was followed by a hearty breakfast served in a special mess tent by uniformed staff. Thus prepared to face the rigors of the hunt, the safari party would set out on foot, horse, camel, or, more commonly, motorized transport.

After a morning's hunt there would be the prospect of a picnic lunch in the bush, often served on fine china. Specially built wooden safari chop boxes might contain cold guinea fowl or sliced game meat, cheeses, fresh baked bread, along with delicacies like ham, sausage, or pâté from provisioners in Nairobi, or even as far away as Fortnum and Mason's in London. A selection of fine wines, or at least hot tea or coffee, might be considered appropriate. After lunch a siesta beneath a shade tree was in order, until hunting resumed in the cool of the afternoon, usually after three o'clock. The hunters normally returned to camp at nightfall or just after dark for hors d'oeuvres and a drink around the campfire, then a hot canvas tub or showers awaited them, before tucking in to a multicourse formal dinner served by candlelight or pressure lanterns.

Providing the necessary safari accoutrements in a primitive environment required organizational skills and careful planning. The sophisticated international clientele now trekking in and out of East Africa had high expectations. A white hunter was supposed to provide a luxurious, once-in-a-lifetime hunting experience. At the same time he was also expected to be fully professional in his approach to the business of hunting, as he was for the safety and well-being of his clients. The pace of a safari as well as camp transfers were made entirely at the discretion of the white hunter, who had to gauge game movements, weather, and local conditions, as well as his client's inclinations.

PROFESSIONAL safaris were altered forever by the standard use of cars. The passing of the old days was much lamented by some of the earlier, sometimes more adventurous hunters. The great ivory hunter "Karamoja" Bell gave up his African safaris after returning to Kenya with two friends between the world wars. Bell, who had journeyed on foot into some of the wildest areas in Africa, was unable to accept the changes that motor vehicles had brought to his beloved continent. The single, narrow dirt road running through the vastness of his beloved Karamoja region in Uganda seemed like blasphemy to Bell, who had crisscrossed the wild and unknown district many times on foot. Bell settled at his Coriemoille estate in the Scottish Highlands and never returned to Africa.

White hunters were aware of the same dangers of civilization that had so disturbed Bell, yet hunting territories were still plentiful in the thirties, including newly discovered regions now accessible to hunters in specially built safari cars that cut tracks into remote, unmarked country. New roads meant more hunters and less wildland. Professional hunters felt it was time to take steps to ensure the protection of the unique wildlife and habitat of their country.

On a blustery morning at the start of the monsoon rains on April 12, 1934, a group of white hunters met at the Norfolk Hotel in Nairobi.* They were there to create a historic organization called the East African Professional Hunter's Association, known by its acronym EAPHA. Its motto: *Nec timor nec temeritas*—Neither fear nor foolhardiness. It would prove to be the most respected society of its sort in the world, and in time spawned several international hunting and conservation organizations. Within a few years of that first EAPHA meeting, East Africa was to have the most stringent game laws in the world.

---

*The meeting was jointly chaired by Nairobi lawyer A. Dacre-Shaw and Lord Bertram Cranworth. Philip Percival, Leslie Tarlton, Al Klein, Major G. H. "Andy" Anderson, Jack Lucy, Sydney Waller, Pat Ayre, George R. Runton, O. M. Rees, Andrew Fowle, Donald Ker, Vivian Ward, and A. T. A. Ritchie, Kenya's chief game warden, were present.

The Norfolk Hotel, Nairobi.

It was the hunters who succeeded in obtaining passage of a raft of new regulations, everything from the banning of night shooting to the use of dogs for hunting and protection for females of almost all species. All game was protected within five hundred yards of a water hole or salt lick. Bow hunting by sportsmen was outlawed and shooting from within two hundred yards of a vehicle was unlawful. The sale or trading of game meat was forbidden.

The EAPHA's constitution was drafted with a view to conservation. The hunters pressed Kenya's chief game warden, Archie Ritchie, for many new regulations, including one that read, "Only one lion should be hunted per license holder in the Southern Masai Reserve." Certain regions, including the Masai reserve, were made off-limits to motorized safaris. Proposals were advanced for the creation of partial and total game reserves that would later become national parks. It was suggested that a radius of thirty miles around Marsabit Mountain should be included in the Northern Game Reserve.

Many years later, in the early 1970s, several countries formed their own hunters' associations based on the EAPHA's constitution, but none matched the extraordinarily high requirements necessary for fully licensed membership in the EAPHA. The Association's members,

although few in number, began to wield considerable influence on the country's game policies. Syd Downey and Donald Ker vigorously lobbied for the establishment of a national park that would include the entire Masai Mara Triangle, easily the richest game area in Kenya. Chief game warden Ritchie enthusiastically supported the proposal. Syd and Donald also began lobbying for a game reserve on the Serengeti Plains in Tanganyika.

TANGANYIKA GAME WARDEN Monty Moore had been in charge of the Serengeti range long before it became a national park. In 1935 he was allowed to create a special 600-square-mile lion reserve. His signboards around Banagi Hill and the Seronera River proclaimed, "If you see lion—try shouting not shooting." But the EAPHA's members continued to agitate for more protection, and in 1937 His Majesty's government announced its intention of instituting a national park on the Serengeti.

Before the Serengeti achieved national park status, it was policed by a first-rate group of wardens that included John Blower (later Uganda's chief game warden) and several former white hunters turned wardens, beginning with a Tanganyika white hunter named Major Ray Hewlett. Later, when the Serengeti became a park, the first park wardens were Myles Turner and Gordon Poolman, both leading Kenya hunters. Years later Turner was joined by P. A. G. "Sandy" Field, an experienced administrator, honorary EAPHA member, and keen ivory hunter. All these extraordinary men were in the mold of another hunter turned game warden, Kenya's great conservationist and founder of its national parks, Mervyn Cowie.

It was only a few short years after the formation of the East African Professional Hunter's Association that the Second World War broke out in Europe, and African territories once again found themselves on opposite sides of a global conflict. At the outbreak of hostilities, the British in Kenya were surprised to discover that the Italian armies resident in Abyssinia and Somalia were fully trained and well equipped for battle, while their own force in East Africa was struggling into being. The Italians had the means to attack the British in Kenya, and it was felt that their own security interests would dictate that they do so.[1]

Although there were fewer than thirty white hunters in existence at the time, as in the First World War they played an important part in the

East African campaign during the Second World War. The hunters immediately volunteered and most went to units that fought in Somalia and Ethiopia, while some served in Burma and North Africa. White hunter Bill Ryan was with General Cunningham's forces as they advanced north from Kenya to rout the Italians from Mogadiscio. Ryan, the green-eyed Irishman who was master of both six-gun and elephant rifle, was made commandant of the central police station at Mogadishu. His freewheeling administrative style and gregarious personality baffled the warlike Somalis, ever keen to imagine an insult, or start a fight. Ryan recalled: "In Mog, bombs, shootings and knifings were the order of the day. The Somalis had a lot of abandoned Italian ordnance and carbines, and they were up to every dirty trick in the book."

Bill had the best intelligence network in the country, for he organized Somali prostitutes into a first-rate spy system. Ryan was next given command of a roving police unit, whose guerilla fighters were mostly Somalis. Ryan, who spoke eight languages including Somali and Italian, led his band behind enemy lines in a series of lightning raids using fast horses and camels. One time Bill had to shoot one of his own wounded men because he could not evacuate him, and the man refused to fall into the hands of the Abyssinians while alive. Both Somali *shifta* (bandits) and Abyssinians delighted in genital mutilation of prisoners and gave no quarter to their POWs.

Major Douglas Collins, who would gain fame after the war in the safari business, was sent to the loneliest places on earth with a unit of native Somali Gendarmerie. He lived a life of constant attack and counterattack against *shifta* for most of the war, and for a period after it. Few men could have withstood what Collins endured for such a long period without relief.

White hunter R. L. "Dickie" Crofton was killed in a firefight in Abyssinia, while Carl Nurk was shot down by machine-gun fire leading Abyssinian irregulars in a frontal attack on dug-in Italian positions. Nurk won a posthumous Military Cross for outstanding gallantry.

Donald Ker was a scout in the celebrated East African Reconnaissance Squadron, known as "The Reccies." Syd Downey went to Intelligence, then to the 2nd Ethiopian Battalion at Khartoum, Sudan. He joined a secret mission planned by General Orde Wingate, and accompanied Abyssinian Emperor Haile Selassie on his triumphant return from Khartoum to Ethiopia. The emperor's return was a rugged trek across unforgiving terrain during which the caravan's camels died like

flies.[2] In a scene that could have come out of Evelyn Waugh's *Black Mischief*, Downey and the royal entourage neared a rendezvous with the emperor's followers, and the local soldiery became wildly excited. For the occasion of the return of their "Lion of Judah,"* the Abyssinians had brought out Selassie's grand old limousine. One enthusiastic supporter threw a hand grenade. In no time there was a colossal grass fire and the emperor's precious luxury motor vehicle was burned to a cinder.

Downey led missions behind enemy lines with cutthroat Abyssinian irregulars backed by a few trained WaKamba soldiers from Kenya. Syd once set an ambush beside a remote road in the mountains of Ethiopia. Two WaKamba armed with .303 rifles lay beside him as he set up a Vickers machine gun. His plan was to ambush small convoys as they approached a bridge. Downey heard a convoy coming, but he did not know the Italians were evacuating a force of seven thousand with mechanized transport. In Syd's view was six hundred yards of straight road. He saw an Italian officer looking down the road, as though expecting an ambush. Then three armored cars swept into view. Downey's guerillas had only one antitank gun, but it was too late to withdraw. His men were supposed to wait for the enemy vehicles to get within one hundred yards' range before commencing their attack. But the Abyssinians opened up with small arms too soon. The armored cars immediately returned fire spraying bullets everywhere.

Downey hunched over his Vickers and fired into the advancing vehicles, but after a short burst the gun jammed solid. The two Africans with Syd started firing their .303 rifles, which attracted enemy fire. The entire area was swarming with Italians, and a group of forty made a rush at Downey's position, firing as they came. Downey drew his pistol and returned fire, which quickly cleared the enemy off the road. One of Downey's WaKamba soldiers was shot dead, while the other crawled to a new position. Grenades were lobbed as bullets whipped leaves off the branches around Syd, who was by then out of pistol ammunition.

While all this was going on a wounded Italian officer came stumbling

---

*Haile Selassie was Ethiopia's 225th emperor in a line extending three thousand years from King Solomon and the Queen of Sheba. He was ousted in a Marxist coup in 1974 and imprisoned. Ethiopian dictator Mengistu Haile Mariam's "Red Terror" regime killed thousands, and in 1975 the emperor was murdered—smothered as he slept—and buried beneath a toilet. The Marxist government was overthrown in 1991, and Haile Selassie is now buried in the Royal Mausoleum in Addis Ababa.

down the road. When he saw Syd he threw up his hands in surrender, shouting, then collapsed beside Syd. The Italian was badly wounded and Syd shifted the man's Sam Browne belt, which was rubbing against a gaping abdominal wound. At that moment a gun barrel was rammed into Syd's back. Downey thought his end had come, but the wounded Italian shouted not to shoot. The Italians stripped Downey of everything he had as booty—his watch, military insignia, hat, and belt. Downey helped carry the wounded Italian to the road. Hostile troops milled about Syd in a threatening manner, but the officer waved them off. Downey's savior was lifted onto a truck as he thanked Syd for helping him. He gave Downey his watch as a memento, and Downey kept it all his life.

The Italians asked Syd if there was another ambush or mines in the road. Downey would not say, but noted that his captors put a marked Red Cross ambulance at the front of the column. Downey was taken to major Italian strongholds at Dambacha, then to Dessie. On arrival he was struck in the face with a whip, splitting his nose, lips, and breaking teeth. Downey told his attacker that in England they would think it very cowardly to do a thing like that. His assailant backed off and an Italian officer apologized.[3] The fortified town of Dessie, thought impregnable by the Italians, was later stormed and taken by just sixteen Allied troops.[4]

IN THE VANGUARD of the Allied armies advancing toward Addis Ababa was Tom Murray Smith, who as a decorated World War I veteran had been permitted to enlist his safari gunbearer, Manda, to serve with him in an infantry battalion. Murray could hardly believe his eyes when he spotted Philip Percival in a truck with *his* famous gunbearer, Kiti. Kiti, Manda, Philip, and Murray had a hearty reunion on the spot.

The Ethiopian capital of Addis Ababa fell to the British in April 1941, and Donald Ker's armored reccie car accompanied Colonel John Pemberton to take the Italian surrender. Ker recalled:

> We set up Officer's Clubs, and several brothels were commandeered for the purpose. I was in the Officer's Club when in walked Syd Downey! He was the first British prisoner taken by the Italians, and had been treated brutally. Anyway, there Syd was in the brothel turned Officer's Club in Addis, and several other Kenya

hunters turned up. We danced with the whores and had a whale of a party.[5]

After the fall of Addis Ababa there were enough hunters in the capital to hold a meeting of the East African Professional Hunter's Association at the Governor's Palace. Philip Percival presided with a committee made up of Tom Murray Smith, Pat Ayre, Pip Beverly, and Vivian Ward. A month later another meeting was held at the posh White Eagle Hotel, followed by a boisterous party enlivened with captured enemy booze.

Donald Ker and Syd Downey discussed their plans for after the war. Downey said he would return to Safariland, but Ker insisted, "No, you're not, Syd. You and I are going into partnership. We're going to start our own company!" The war continued four more bloody years, but afterward Ker and Downey Safaris became the most prestigious safari company in modern history. Much to Syd's discomfort, Donald Ker liked to say around campfires that the idea for the firm originated in an Addis Ababa brothel.[6]

20.

After the Second World War safari hunting changed dramatically. The world was already moving at a faster pace. The days when safari clients would arrive from North America or Europe by boat and then embark on an African hunting safari of several months' duration were mostly in the past. Now a more hurried traveler could fly from Europe on a Sunderland flying boat, and arrive in Nairobi in just three or four days. Such lumbering but comfortable aircraft regularly made the trip down the Nile south to Lake Victoria, then onward to Lake Naivasha in Kenya's Great Rift Valley, with only brief stops at remote outposts for fuel and rest.

Advancements in air travel were matched by innovations in ground transport. For better or worse, the continent's abundant wildlife was now more accessible than ever. The first four-wheel-drive vehicles had arrived in East Africa during World War II and it was not long before a few surplus vehicles found their way into private hands.

Meanwhile roomy "shooting brake" vehicles became widely used as hunters converted two-wheel-drive British Austin, Bedford, and Commer pickups or sedan cars into safari vehicles. Shooting brakes, as station wagons or estate cars were then known in England, were further refined in Africa to suit local conditions by Nairobi-based Indian craftsmen. Typically these cars had all but the front mudguards, hood, and windshield removed. The body and roof were replaced with wood, and sometimes covered with a thin sheet of galvanized metal. There were no windows or doors. Instead roll-down canvas curtains were buttoned to the roof in case of bad weather. These cars were heavy and comfortable in good weather and allowed quick and silent exits as no shooting was permitted from vehicles. The new safari cars had padded roof turrets allowing passengers to stand for observation or photography. Both front and back bench seats were removable, a convenience that provided cushioned benches for al fresco picnics in the bush. Toolboxes and sometimes extra fuel tanks were fitted beneath the seats, and vertical gunracks* were mounted between the front and rear seats.

The hunters' real preference was for the larger and stronger American-built Chevrolet, International, Hudson, and GMC vehicles, which were far more comfortable and had higher ground clearance, yet they were almost impossible to obtain after the war.

A company called Safariland Ltd. had become the best-known hunting outfitters in the world soon after the British East Africa Protectorate (known simply as B.E.A.) changed its status and name to Kenya Colony back in 1920. The firm rose from the ashes of its predecessor, the once illustrious Newland and Tarlton, which had been dissolved in 1919. Safariland inherited N&T's most glamorous names in the hunting world, including those of Leslie Tarlton himself, Alan Tarlton, R. J. Cunninghame, Alan Black, Bill Judd, Arthur Hoey, George Outram, Sydney Waller, Philip Percival, Al Klein, Jack Lucy, Pat Ayre, J. A. Hunter, and Wally King.[†]

The company's first managing director was Paul Whetham, who on one occasion was anxiously asked by a prospective client, "What sort of men do you employ as white hunters?" Whetham replied, "Well, we've got all sorts. There are only two of them in town at present—one is an ex–railway guard, and the other's the son of an earl. Both are tops, take your choice!"[1] Louis Woodruff was the former, the Honorable Denys Finch Hatton, the younger son of the Earl of Winchilsea, the latter.

IN 1946 the leader of the world's Ismaeli Islamic sect decided to visit Africa, and it was to Leslie Tarlton's Safariland Ltd. he entrusted the

---

*Military gunracks consisted of a spring lock to clamp the rifle's barrel in a steel canister that was hard on guns, and harder to open quickly. A Pakistani hunter, Mohammed "Bali" Iqbal, designed a lightweight aluminum clamp, which was manufactured by Nairobi gunsmiths, Wali Mohamed and Company, and used by most hunters.

†Between 1921 and 1938 Safariland employed hunters Alastair Gibbs, Jerry Dalton, Vivian Ward, Bror Blixen, Bror Kuhle, Ture Rundgren, Owen Rees, Ben Fourie, G. H. "Jack" Riddell, Jock Rattray, Louis Woodruff, H. Malewsky, Colonel W. V. D. Dickenson, Sydney Waller, Syd Downey, Andy Anderson, Tom Murray Smith, and, much later on, Denys Finch Hatton. Carl Nurk, M.C., and R. L. Crofton were killed in Ethiopia during World War II. Safariland's post–World War II directors included C. G. MacArthur, a former game warden, and Jim Corbett, author and tiger hunter from India. After World War II among the new Safariland hunters were Eddie Grafton, Mike Button, Fred Poolman, John Pitcairn-Holmes, Frank Bowman, and Bill Jenvey.

arrangements. Tarlton put Andy Anderson in charge of the safari, and assigned Vivian Ward as camp manager. In the remoteness of a bush camp the white hunters set up a special telegraph office to ensure that the Aga Khan was in touch with his far-flung followers and business interests. For the occasion Safariland erected an enormous camp covering five acres. Trainee hunters built a 2,500-yard airstrip by hand, then kept the landing area clear of wild game so that successive planeloads of luxury supplies and visiting dignitaries could arrive unimpeded. The Aga Khan had originally set out with sixteen guests, but the list was augmented as various acquaintances arrived in camp. Once, 44 unexpected visitors showed up for lunch, and sat down to a sumptuous meal.[2]

WHITE HUNTERS were sometimes drawn from the ranks of those recently arrived in Kenya fresh from distant battlefronts. Among them was an energetic Australian named Bill Jenvey, who had ended the war with a boxful of campaign medals and the rank of Flying Officer. It was Jenvey's good fortune to approach Safariland's Tom Murray Smith on the street in Nairobi. So anxious was Jenvey to get a chance at fulfilling his life's ambition that the former Australian jackeroo offered to work for no pay. Jenvey recalled: "Murray hired me on the spot with a salary of £11 [$32] per month."

Murray Smith's next safari was scheduled to travel to Kenya's fabled Tana River for a specialized elephant hunt, and he offered his young trainee from Australia the opportunity to accompany him. The safari convoy left Nairobi heading north to Thika, then turned northeast onto a narrow and dusty dirt road. As they drove on across the washboard the heat intensified, and the rolling hills and grasslands soon gave way to a flat and arid panorama of iron-gray thorn brush. At first Jenvey was dismayed by the empty desert landscape. "I thought it unlikely to find elephants in the dry scrub country we passed through before reaching the river—it seemed to provide little for them to eat. But I was on a steep learning curve."

On the way Murray Smith stopped to pick up his "elephant man," a favorite African tracker and hunting partner named Mwalimu Manza. Mwalimu was a steady-eyed, stately fellow who was an expert on big elephants along the Tana River. The name Mwalimu means "teacher" in Swahili, an appellation that proved prophetic, for in time Murray Smith's gentlemanly tracker came to impart much of what he knew about elephants to Bill Jenvey.

The great Borana elephant tracker,
Mwalimu Manza.

On that safari Murray Smith was assisted by a second hunter, Kenya-
born Fred Poolman. Poolman was the eldest of a trio of brothers, all of
whom were hunters from the highland district of Naro Moru. Jenvey's
first assignment was the ignominious job of repairing Murray's broken-
down car, an essential mechanical skill required of fledgling white
hunters.

Murray Smith's safari clients were three Americans. Each had come
to the Tana River to hunt for an exceptional trophy elephant—a *hundred pounder*. Early one morning Bill Jenvey joined Murray Smith and
his client as they walked parallel to the Tana searching for fresh spoor.
It was on this hunt that Jenvey witnessed Mwalimu's uncanny ele-
phant-tracking abilities. Mwalimu had picked up the spoor of a huge
bull headed away from the river, going back out to the desert. The
tracker quickly set out on the spoor, leading the hunters toward the
scorching sands and desert thorn scrub known as the *borani*. Murray
Smith paused briefly to advise Jenvey and the perspiring client that
they could expect a long, hot walk ahead unless the bull changed its
course and turned back into the leafy riverine forest. According to Bill
Jenvey, Mwalimu stopped and turned to Murray and said:

> "I know this elephant, Bwana. He's no good, only one tusk." Mur-
> ray told the tracker to leave the spoor and look for others. The
> client objected strongly. He shouted, "How could anyone in this
> wilderness come across an elephant track and say the animal had
> only one tusk? What is really happening is this son-of-a-bitch of a

tracker doesn't want to go out into the desert—the lazy bastard wants to hunt in the cool of the forest."

Old Murray then said to Mwalimu in Swahili, "We have to teach this fellow a lesson. Show us this one tusker!" In blistering heat we tracked for four long hours far out into the *borani*— through the *luggas*, or dry sand rivers, leading to the Tana. Finally Mwalimu quietly announced, "We'll leave this *donga* [gully] now, Bwana. The elephant is not far away. He will be resting under a big tree in the *donga* over there." Mwalimu pointed across the wind. If we were to stay on the tracks of the bull it would get our scent. Mwalimu was about to leave the tracks and circle so the wind came our way.

Murray informed the sweat-soaked client, "We'll be looking at the *one tusker* in about ten minutes. Because of the wind we are leaving the tracks and circling."

Climbing out of the *donga* we crested a ridge from which the change in the *donga*'s course could be seen. But just where to cut back to it? Mwalimu knew exactly. Some minutes passed before he slowed, nodded, and pointed to the top of a large acacia tree which had come in view below us. Its lush foliage indicated underground water, and this was where Mwalimu expected the bull to be, taking into account the age of the tracks, the distance we had travelled and the time of day. Our final approach confirmed his skill. Resting in the shade was a 75-pound *one tusker*. A chastened client had a sharp lesson.[3]

On that safari Mwalimu ended up finding *three* hundred pounders. Not long after their pursuit of the one-tusked elephant, Jenvey saw his first hundred pounder, actually a 122 pounder. Tana River game warden Jack Bonham was astonished at the monster-sized tusks. He was "surprised," Jenvey remembered, "that such outstanding specimens were still available."[4] Later on when the safari had moved camp to the Uaso Nyiro River, the redoubtable Mwalimu found a 115 pounder, and soon after a 118 pounder.

In time Bill Jenvey was to be considered among the best of the ivory hunters. He obtained a record-class elephant with ivory weighing an amazing 148 and 146 pounds for a client named Gurnee Munn Jr. from Palm Beach, Florida. On the same safari he led Munn to the third world-record leopard in Kenya. The leopard had a length of 10 feet ⅜ inches, and weighed 225 pounds. Jenvey capped this by finding an excellent tro-

The northern Uaso Nyiro River where Mwalimu found his 115-pound elephant tusk.

phy Cape buffalo with horns measuring 49⅞ inches for the same client.

During his long career Jenvey was to hunt with many of the old-timers, but it was from Tom Murray Smith that he learned most of the tricks of the trade. "Murray was always adamant," Jenvey said, "that clients developed a sportsmanlike conception of wildlife and hunting." Bill greatly admired his mentor, especially his strict adherence to principles laid down by the East African Professional Hunter's Association, of which Murray Smith was then president. When Tom Murray Smith retired, it was Bill who inherited his two gunbearers. Jenvey stayed with Safariland during its peak glory years, when its white hunters were among the best in Africa.*

*After the Second World War a number of fine young men joined Safariland's old-guard hunters. Among them were Mark Howard-Williams, David Sheldrick, Roy Home, Bob Foster, Bunny Ray, Tony Henley, Geoff Lawrence-Brown, Mohammed "Bali" Iqbal, Owen McCallum, Douglas Collins, Ken Jespersen, Barry Roberts, Jackie Blacklaws, Walter Jones, Harold Prowse, and Count Rudi Van der Stegen.

During the war the vast repository of big game in Kenya's Mara Triangle had been undisturbed. In the course of a forty-five-day survey in the Triangle, Syd Downey and Donald Ker saw 250 lions.[1] After this reconnaissance the hunters were more aware than ever of the importance of preserving the unique natural state and balance of East Africa's wildlife. Back in Nairobi both hunters argued with British authorities that lions should at least be partially protected, and their hunting strictly regulated.

Ker and Downey Safaris began modestly enough with an office in Ker's house in Nairobi. It was not long before Donald and Syd's burgeoning careers as white hunters required them to spend unfettered months in bush camps. Wisely, they joined forces with a successful Nairobi businessman, Jack Block, who had taken more than a passing interest in their safari activities.

Jack Block and his family owned Block Hotels, which included the Norfolk and New Stanley, both of them catering to an international safari clientele. It seemed that all parties could benefit from a business relationship. Thereafter Block Hotels took over administration of Ker and Downey and provided the company with offices in their hotels, and later in a smart Block building in the center of town.

At its inception, Ker and Downey had only three qualified white hunters—Syd, Donald, and their only full-time employee, Frank Ernest Bowman, a quiet-spoken Australian who had seen intense wartime action in Abyssinia. Each of the three received the grand sum of £150 ($420) per month, but only when they were actually on safari with clients. Morris Smith, a former police officer who had lived in bush outposts for years, turned professional and hunted mostly with Syd. He

Harry Selby (left) and author Robert Ruark, 1957.

eventually went to the Game Department to manage the "Ivory Room" in Mombasa, where tusks and rhino horns confiscated from poachers or shot on government "cropping" operations, as well as "found" ivory, were sold at Smith's auctions.

As the postwar demand for safaris grew, more hunters joined Donald and Syd, among them Harry Selby. Selby had cut his teeth as an apprentice hunter with Philip Percival. It was not long before Harry's life changed forever. In 1953, at the age of twenty-eight, he was selected to take American author Robert Ruark on safari. The combination of Ruark and Selby was fortuitous in every way. Their safari was immortalized in Ruark's best-selling book, *Horn of the Hunter*, published in 1954. Overnight Harry became the most famous white hunter in the world. Selby's name was synonymous with everything that a first-rate professional hunter should be. He was seen as the epitome of the modest, no-nonsense, clean-cut man of action that he really was. What's more, his colleagues thought as much of him as Ruark did, even though Selby was often subjected to more than his share of "great white hunter" wisecracks from fraternity pals.

Robert Ruark did not hunt exclusively with Selby. Once when Harry was ill Ruark hunted with Frank Bowman, whom he christened his "Professor." Ruark wanted an East African greater kudu so badly he could taste it, having failed to bag one on two previous trips. He got his kudu with Frank. The two men hit it off in a big way, and Frank, always the perfect gentleman, was able to hold his own around the campfire with a thirsty Ruark after a long day's *bundu* bashing. Bowman constantly looked for new, difficult country where others were unlikely to venture. He safaried to the remotest parts of the mighty Rufiji and Ruaha rivers in Tanganyika, which in those times was virtually unknown *bundu*.

DONALD KER led two lengthy and prestigious expeditions with Edgar Monsanto Queeny for the American Museum of Natural History, during which a number of remarkable documentary films were produced. Queeny was chairman of the board of Monsanto Chemical Company and a director of American Airlines. He was also founder of Ducks Unlimited, which was started in Arkansas as a means of conserving migrating ducks. Queeny had donated 12,000 acres of rice fields to provide alternative feeding for ducks when natural foods were in short supply. Edgar wrote to Donald and said he was prepared to spend three or four months to get photographs of *Indicator indicator*, the elusive little honeyguide bird used for centuries by local D'robo tribesmen to locate honey. Acting as guide, a chattering *Indicator indicator* will typically approach a D'robo, attract his attention, and lead him to a beehive so that a fire can be built to smoke out the bees. When the African removes the honeycomb, the wax and the grubs are left for the bird. Local superstition says that any person who fails to remember his obligation to *Indicator indicator* will next time be led to a snake or other suitable punishment.

Queeny's Museum of Natural History party arrived in East Africa from the United States in grand style. Among other things, they brought with them their own aircraft, a DC3 named *Flagship Nairobi*. Queeny was incredulous when Donald Ker was able to lead the safari straight to its objective. Once in the Mara Triangle Donald had recognized what to him was the familiar chirp of the honeyguide bird, *Indicator indicator*. The safari caravan was halted and Donald simply picked up a dead log and began to beat on a tree in the manner of D'robo honey hunters. Playing the tribesman's part in the symbiotic relation-

Donald Ker on safari in the mid-1930s.

ship, Ker was able to provide the Museum of Natural History with all the pictures they wanted. Donald modestly recalled, "We built a film around the bird and the Wanderobo [hunters] showing how they depended on each other."[2]

Queeny wanted to record the sound of lions chewing as they fed. To set the stage, they put out the remains of a wildebeest. That night at dinner as the soundtrack was played back, lions in the bush surrounding the camp began grunting in response to what they mistook for genuine sounds of a kill. Later, Queeny played the lion recordings to a pride of big cats. Donald recalled:

> The pride of lion, consisting of two lions, five lionesses and four cubs, had been observed feeding on a zebra. As soon as the record started, the lionesses left the kill. The lions roared a challenge and ran toward where they thought another lion was roaring, and disappeared. Then Queeny played a recording of hyenas, and the lionesses immediately took the cubs deep into a thicket.
>
> Then we saw the two lions returning, so I drove up and Jack

184 // WHITE HUNTERS

[a cameraman] started the record. The lions roared and came straight toward us and roared again and were ready for a battle royal. Their lower jaws were chattering with excitement and they really looked scary, and then they ran off looking for the challenger.[3]

To Ker's knowledge lion recordings had never yet been played back to wild lions, and he realized how this could be misused in hunting. Back in Nairobi Ker immediately went to the Game Department to plead for a change in the game laws forbidding the use of recordings to call game. The law was quickly amended.[4] It was typical of Ker, who was at the time a professional hunter himself, that he would remain uncompromised on the matter.

Queeny went to incredible lengths to get unusual footage. At Mzima Springs he used a diving bell to obtain the first underwater films of hippo. In Uganda he wanted photographs of a pocket of northern white rhino that lived near the Sudan border. He enlisted help from Peter Molloy,* the British game warden at Juba. White rhino frequented a twenty-one-mile corridor west of the Nile, and Molloy had a ferry constructed for Queeny at Khartoum, so that Ker's huge safari could get over the Nile at Nimule. In Sudan documentaries of the Dinka and Latuko tribes resulted in Queeny's dramatic movie, *Pagan Sudan*.

Both Donald and Syd were already leaning toward photographic safaris. Neither had ever been much interested in shooting. The chase—the hunt itself—was all that really mattered to them.

Of Downey British author Negly Farson observed:

He loved animals; he did not want to see them shot out; he had made it his life's work to study their mentality; yet the technique of the chase—say, a stalk—made him tremble like a pointer.[5]

There was something distinctly unpleasant about shooting these innocent buck [topi] for bait. I did not like it. Neither did Downey. You could see that he had a distaste for the job. For all his years as a leading white hunter Downey never acquired a taste for killing. He was a true hunter, rather than a killer—perhaps the finest example of the species.[6]

---

*Peter and Yvonne Molloy's knowledge of Sudan was unrivaled. After Sudanese independence in 1954, Peter became the first director of Tanganyika national parks.

◇

SYD DOWNEY had simple tastes in most things, except his love for what was then regarded as expensive American vehicles, particularly for Buick sedans and the International hunting trucks he exclusively used. Certainly his taste in rifles was conservative in the extreme. His favorite was an old-fashioned Winchester .30/.06, which he used for most nondangerous soft-skinned game. For dangerous game he was wedded to a .470 double rifle. Both rifles, Downey insisted, "did the job, besides, ammunition for both was obtainable at a reasonable price."

Aside from his strong personal convictions as a conservationist-hunter, Downey was realist enough to know that his expertise with big game gave him a fine entrée to the world of Hollywood's moviemakers. It was Donald and Syd's good fortune that their new company was already operating when Hollywood was eager to exploit Africa's film potential. Sundry producers and directors, newly attired in custom-tailored safari suits, turned up at Nairobi to scout film locations. A production company was preparing to film Hemingway's classic tale "The Short Happy Life of Francis Macomber." Neither Ker nor Downey fitted the Hollywood mold of macho, muscle-bound, rednecked, gunslinging heroes white hunters were supposed to be, but Ker and Downey won a contract to outfit the production company.

A reconnaissance for the filming of Hemingway's story gave Syd and Donald an opportunity to return to the Mara Triangle so that film locations could be checked out. Downey abandoned his old, prewar hunting track, and cut a new track following a southwesterly direction to Subatai hill, and that modest hunter's track was so well engineered it later became Kenya's main highway to both the Masai Mara game reserve (formerly the hunting area known as the Mara Triangle) and Tanzania.

The moviemakers, United Artists, under the direction of Zoltan Korda, gave Hemingway's story a new title, *The Macomber Affair*. The stars were Gregory Peck, Robert Preston, Joan Bennett, Reginald Denny, Carl Harbord, and Jean Gillie. The film proved to be a box-office hit and renewed interest in safaris to a level not known since Theodore Roosevelt's 1909 safari. Not coincidentally, a great deal of the movie was shot in the Mara region so loved by Syd and Donald.

K&D Safaris, as they were by then known, attracted a potpourri of personalities on their roster of white hunters.* The mixed bag ranged from big, booming, boisterous Eric Rundgren, all the way down to the small, wiry, quick-witted Scotsman, John Cook. K&D's Bill Ryan was an experienced hunter who began his career by taking on a man-eating lion when he was fourteen years old. He was a meat hunter for his father's sawmill workers in the Aberdare Mountains before he was fifteen. Bill had been shot in the elbow as a youth during a rhino hunt, and although his arm was in a "fixed" position at the elbow, the handicap did nothing to slow him or his ability with a double rifle. Bill was the most sought-after hunter at K&D, and the most popular man in the fraternity.

IN A LONG but low-key career Downey's greatest triumph was winning the Oscar of African hunting, the Shaw and Hunter trophy, *twice*—first for a 54¾-inch East African greater kudu taken by his client Scott W. Hayes in 1956. He won again in 1959 with a 14¼-inch giant forest hog shot by François Edmond-Blanc on the Aberdares. Ironically, within a few years both Syd and Donald would hang up their guns to become outspoken advocates for game conservation. Thereafter they concentrated on custom photographic safaris or museum collecting expeditions.

---

*K&D's regular hunters included Bill Ryan, Tony Henley, George Barrington, Harry Selby, John Dugmore, John Sutton, John Cook, John Sullivan, Kris Aschan, Tony Archer, Peter Becker, Fred Bartlett, Don Bousefield, Eric Rundgren, Alan North, Terry Mathews, John Kingsley-Heath, and, later, Mike Webley, John Fletcher, Tony Seth-Smith, David Williams, and David Mead. The first manager was Ronnie Stevens and the directors were Jack Block and Sol Rabb.

22

HEROES OF THE SILVER SCREEN

The professional hunters had Papa Hemingway to thank in large part for the spotlight of world attention thrust upon them in the free-wheeling postwar years in Africa. The Great White Hunter became Hollywood's latest hero. Aspiring amateur hunters from all over the world clamored for a taste of Hemingway's feats with big game. To fulfill their dreams and follow in Ernest's footsteps, adventurers booked passage to East Africa.

Hollywood depended on the expertise of the safari fraternity to make African movies. While some hunters scoffed at the overblown melodramatic hoopla of it all, most good-naturedly participated whenever they could. For one thing it was good business. For another, it expanded their frontiers beyond mere hunting. The glamorizing and dramatizing of the white hunter's life was in full swing—and a good time was being had by all.

Just as *The Macomber Affair* had been a financial and publicity windfall for Ker and Downey Safaris, the movie *King Solomon's Mines* brought welcome capital to the newest of three major safari firms. Hunter David Lunan, who had the bearing of a tall, dark, and handsome movie actor, and his partner, Stan Lawrence-Brown, had recently registered Lawrence-Brown and Lunan Safaris Ltd. The firm's name had a nice ring to it, but the two partners were almost always broke. Wartime military pay had never made anybody rich, and Stan and Dave were in the same financial straits as other postwar hunters.

Stan Lawrence-Brown, born in India of British parents, had grown up in Kenya, and had worked for Ker and Downey before going into partnership with David Lunan. To the Africans Stan was known as Bwana Korongo (Mr. Roan Antelope) because of his broad, heavy shoulders, a build that to the humorous Africans likened him to the sturdy outline of the world's second-largest antelope.

David Lunan's boyhood neighbor had been Leslie Tarlton, the founder of Kenya's first safari company. Tarlton had taken Lunan and his brother on duck shoots, and kept the boys spellbound with tales of adventure as he taught them about hunting. As a result Lunan followed in Tarlton's footsteps.

The partners had great aspirations, but were held back by humble pocketbooks. In the end it was the financial windfall from two record-class elephants that enabled Lawrence-Brown and Lunan to join the professional ranks as outfitters. The two had purchased elephant licenses in Tanganyika in hopes of getting ivory heavy enough to pay for start-up expenses. With a modest fly-camp they hunted in south Masailand, where they soon found many hundreds of elephant, but no giant bulls carrying big ivory. After three weeks' hunting they were running low on supplies, and almost in despair, when they came upon the tracks of two big bulls near the Masai village of Kibaya. Stan and Dave spoored the bulls all day. Late that afternoon they caught up with the elephants in dense bush. Neither man could believe their good luck. Stan shot the first bull carrying tusks weighing 135 and 132 pounds. Dave immediately shot the second bull with tusks of 129 and 126 pounds.[1] From the sale of the ivory Stan and Dave had enough money to purchase rudimentary safari equipment, and Lawrence-Brown and Lunan Safaris was launched.

The biggest obstacle for hunters was finding vehicles. For years after the war new cars were almost impossible to obtain in Africa. As luck would have it, Dave found four four-wheel-drive Dodge Power Wagons at a military disposal. The vehicles had seen rough service in the Abyssinian campaign, and all were fitted out as water tankers. The two hunters went to an Indian Sikh named Partap Singh, a coach builder in Nairobi. Singh replaced the water tanks with wooden shooting-brake bodies and the vehicles gleamed like brand-new, custom-built safari cars.

When the partners got word MGM was about to make *King Solomon's Mines* starring Deborah Kerr and Stewart Granger, the two hunters found the producer and landed a contract to take out a film unit consisting of twenty-four clients. The filming was to begin in three weeks' time, and after getting a substantial deposit they managed to buy enough equipment to outfit the safari.[2]

David Lunan, cofounder of Lawrence Brown and Lunan Safaris and later founder of White Hunters (Africa) Ltd., as well as Gregory Peck's stand-in for *The Snows of Kilimanjaro.*

The dramatic opening scene of *King Solomon's Mines* shows a bull elephant rushing toward the cameras in a genuine full-out charge, which is abruptly stopped by a bullet from Stan that hits the elephant between the eyes. The elephant goes down, poleaxed in a cloud of dust. At that moment the cameras cut to Stewart Granger portraying the hero Allan Quatermain. Granger is shown in profile as he fires a double rifle, and then the camera switches back to the downed elephant.

English Gypsy hunter Bunny Allen was also on the *Solomon's* set and witnessed the elephant charge. He thought Stan had pulled off a spectacular shot in dropping the elephant, for had it not been shot it would very likely have killed a cameraman. The relieved movie crews and actors sat upon the fallen elephant and posed for photographs. Then everybody went back to camp, and a crew was sent to get the ivory. But the elephant was nowhere to be found. It had simply vanished. Stan's "perfect shot" had not been so perfect after all, even though it looked great to all who had seen the animal knocked cold.

Stan's bullet had passed close to the brain—close enough to stun the animal. When it recovered the elephant hightailed it out of the country. Stan, Bunny Allen, and a team of trackers spoored the elephant for days.

But they never caught up with it, for by then the elephant was fully recovered. An aircraft was hired for the search, but the elephant was never found. Following that incident Stan advised, "Always put an insurance shot into dangerous game." After the *Solomon's* debacle it was advice he fervently practiced himself.

With the advent of Hollywood in Africa hunters' salaries shot up. Stan recalled, "We paid good hunters 250 quid [pounds] per month on *Solomon's*. Before that hunters could be had for between £100 and £200."[3] There had never been any cap on hunters' salaries, even before the war. Top-notch men did demand higher salaries, which they usually got, especially for risky or daring performances around dangerous game.

The considerable proceeds from *King Solomon's Mines* set up Lawrence-Brown and Lunan's new company, giving them an immediate jump-start. "It was money for jam," Stan gleefully commented. The resulting publicity attracted the attention of other major American moviemakers. Dave and Stan outfitted Twentieth-Century Fox's film unit for Hemingway's *The Snows of Kilimanjaro*, starring Gregory Peck, Susan Hayward, and Ava Gardner. This time Dave Lunan was hired not as a white hunter but as Gregory Peck's double. Even so, during filming Lunan had to shoot a charging rhino that nearly hammered crew members.[4] Soon afterward Lunan was "scalped" by a leopard, whose dewclaw somehow trepanned Dave; his scalp was ripped off, hanging over his face by a thread of skin.

JUST AS Stan Lawrence-Brown and David Lunan could claim their safari company had been built with ivory foundations, Bunny Allen could say the same of his home. Allen had also made a reputation as an outfitter to Hollywood's moguls. Bunny wrote:

> After the war I needed money to build a house on my farm at Burguret. Off I went to the Tana River. For four days I walked the proverbial butt off with nary the sign of an elephant. Then elephants started coming to the river. In ten days I had three hundred pounders in the bag. The first two had tusks 115 and 110 pounds, and the second was 125 and 121. The third gave a classic cavalry charge from 80–90 yards and went down from a classic brain shot at 30 yards. His tusks were 154–148. My house on the Burguret River was built with ivory foundations![5]

◇

METRO-GOLDWYN-Mayer and the director of *Mogambo*, John Ford, had already made an agreement with Safariland Ltd. to outfit their production, but the filmmakers told Allen they wanted him to make all arrangements. Safariland was more than happy to oblige, with the understanding that Bunny would use their hunters and equipment. Allen hired Safariland professional hunters, among them old-timer Tom Murray Smith. Ava Gardner was one of the glamorous stars on location with Bunny, and although she was aware of Hollywood's extravagances, she wrote:

> We flew into Nairobi, Kenya and joined up with the fifty-plus trucks that were going to take us to Uganda, the film's primary location seven hundred miles away.
>
> The whole damn trip was what the publicists like to call the greatest safari of modern times, and I wasn't about to argue. Not only did it take eight genuine white hunters to get us in gear, but once we settled, our encampment was three hundred tents strong. And if you think those were just for sleeping, think again. My God, we had tents for every little thing you could think of: dining tents, wardrobe tents with electric irons, a rec room tent with darts for Brits and table tennis for the Yanks, even a hospital tent complete with X-ray machine, and a jail tent in case anybody got too rowdy.
>
> They built an eighteen-hundred-yard airstrip in the middle of the jungle in a whirlwind five days. Every day, supplies and mail were flown in from Nairobi on sturdy old DC 3s, and exposed film stock, carefully packed in dry ice, would be flown out.[6]

The script called for gorilla scenes, which were shot in French Equatorial Africa. MGM put their faith in an American animal expert named Yakima Canutt, who took off from the set in search of lowland gorillas. At a place called Ewo, assisted by French game wardens, Canutt obtained outstanding gorilla footage. No apes were injured, but they did discover an old male dying of leprosy, a disease never before suspected in these animals.[7] Hunter Murray Smith and stars Clark Gable, Ava Gardner, and Grace Kelly never saw any of the gorilla sequences actually filmed. They were 1,500 miles away on the Kagera River.

During the four-month film shoot all the *Mogambo* white hunters

Bunny Allen with Ava Gardner and Clark Gable during filming of *Mogambo*.

were wowed by sexy, approachable Ava Gardner. Tom Murray Smith became friendly with Grace Kelly, whom he did not think deserved her glacial reputation. The biggest hit of all was Clark Gable, who liked to go over to the white hunters' tents after filming and have a drink with them. "He was simply splendid," Bunny says. Gable fancied a lion-skin cap Murray wore, and Murray gave it to him. Gable had smuggled in a pearl-handled .38 revolver, which he presented to Murray as a memento. "Gable was a passable rifle shot," Murray said, "but much better with a shotgun. He was a sportsman with no trace of the exhibitionist in his makeup." Grace Kelly liked to join Murray and Clark on hunting trips to get away from the set whenever she could. They took off on short safaris around the Uganda camp, where all sorts of game was plentiful. Recalling his days with Grace Kelly, Murray said, "She was a complete charmer. Quiet, unassuming, and beautiful manners."[8] The standards of the day assured the utmost discretion on the part of the white hunters, and the *Mogambo* stars knew it. On the set Grace Kelly fell in love with Clark Gable, who had recently been divorced from his British wife, Lady Sylvia Ashley. The Gable-Kelly romance flourished during filming, despite their thirty-year age difference. When Frank Sinatra visited Ava Gardner in camp, the sounds of sexual shenanigans coming from their tent were tactfully ignored by the safari crews.

During one hunt with Murray Smith, Clark spotted a giant python, which he shot. Knowing that Grace admired the skin, Clark gave her the eighteen-foot-long python skin, which she later had made into a suitcase. Grace Kelly never forgot her safari with Murray Smith, even after she became Princess Grace of Monaco, and she always sent him a note with her annual Christmas card.

23.

LUNAN'S WHITE HUNTERS

David Lunan, who had acted as Gregory Peck's stand-in during the filming of *The Snows of Kilimanjaro*, amicably parted company with his partner Stan Lawrence-Brown during the early 1950s, and the Nairobi outfitting firm of Lawrence-Brown and Lunan was closed down. In 1954 Lunan founded White Hunters (Africa) Ltd., and began anew to assemble a top-notch group of professional hunters.

The popular Lunan had no difficulty in attracting some of the best hunting talent in Kenya, and a number of established hunters defected from his competitors, Safariland and Ker and Downey. Dave had long envisaged a cooperative-style company that would permit white hunters to buy ownership shares. Lunan's business strategy, coupled with the high esteem with which he was regarded by colleagues, was a powerful draw. He would guide the fortunes of White Hunters (Africa) Ltd. as its chairman for the next twenty years.*

Dave Lunan's first codirectors were Tony Dyer and John Lawrence. Lawrence was a gravel-voiced former Kenya national park warden. Dyer had learned the ropes as apprentice to Donald Ker. He was so keen that he worked for the first two years at Ker and Downey without salary. Dyer went on to hunt professionally for fourteen years, but remained involved with the East African Professional Hunter's Association and became its president in 1964.

---

*The firm's partner-hunters were Tony Henley, Bob Foster, Glen Cottar, Owen McCallum, Walter Jones, Bill Morkel, Jackie Blacklaws, Bunny Ray, Rene Babault, Edgar DeBono, Sten Cedergren, Tony Seth-Smith. The firm was managed by Douglas Brett, Robert Caulfield, and, ultimately, Mrs. Peg Pearson.

Edgar DeBono with captured poacher's wire snares.

UNTIL 1956 there were only six safari companies in Kenya: Ikram Hassan's family-owned outfit, African Hunting Safaris, based in Mombasa, and in Nairobi Safariland, the largest firm, was in competition with Ker and Downey, Lawrence-Brown Safaris, and Lunan's White Hunters (Africa) Ltd. The one solo outfitter making a name for himself was Edgar DeBono, whose Big Game Hunting Ltd. had a small office down the road from Safariland on Gulzaar Street. Big Game Hunting Ltd. consisted of Edgar and his raven-haired English girlfriend, Marjorie Gutteridge, along with sixteen exceptional African safari hands.

DeBono spoke English with a strong Italian accent. He was fluent in Italian, German, French, Spanish, Arabic, Amharic, and Swahili, along with a dozen African dialects. Edgar was a pleasant-looking man, five foot eight inches tall, well built, dark-haired and brown-eyed, with the swarthy skin of a southern Italian. In fact he was not Italian, but Maltese. Edgar had been a professional hunter in Eritrea before the war, where he was badly mauled by a leopard. During the war Edgar was a decorated British intelligence agent in the Mideast. With the war over DeBono was on a safari in Sudan, where he landed a job as game warden. Three years later Edgar was nearly killed by a crop-raiding buffalo that refused to die, despite having taken four shots in the heart region. DeBono was flown to a hospital in Kenya, and while recuperating he fell in love with the country, as well as with Marjorie. He hunted on several safaris with J. A. Hunter and the two became lifelong friends. J.A. said Edgar was the best double-barreled rifle shot he had ever met. Indeed, while Edgar owned a battery of rifles, he very seldom used anything except his .500 Holland double, no matter what type of game he was hunting. DeBono decided to go it alone in the safari business in 1953, when he and Marjorie formed Big Game Hunting Ltd. DeBono ran a tight ship, and the firm was an immediate success, attracting important clients such as German industrialists Dr. von Opel and Dr. Heinz Nordhoff, then president of Volkswagen Corporation, and Dutch entrepreneur Ben Pon. In June 1956 Lunan's partner, John Lawrence, persuaded DeBono to come aboard White Hunters (Africa) Ltd. as a company director.

A BRAWNY hunter named Tony Henley left Ker and Downey and joined Dave's outfit in 1957. At thirty years of age Henley was a big man, over six feet and weighing 220 solid pounds. He was fair-haired, blue-eyed, and had a persuasive personality. White Hunters (Africa) Ltd. considered themselves fortunate in signing him on, for he brought with him important repeat clients including the Duke of Grafton, Michael Martell (of the French Martell brandy family), and the Marquis del Merito.

Henley had previously been a Uganda game warden for five years. In Ankole one lion had killed forty-six Africans over a period of eighteen months, and Henley was sent to deal with it. By plotting the location of each kill he concluded the lion had a regular beat midway between the towns of Masaka in Buganda Kingdom and Mbarara in Ankole Kingdom. He felt sure the man-eater would return to selected points sooner or later, so, acting on his own catlike instinct and a hunch, he selected the most likely spot. Henley's patience and theory worked, for he nailed the man-eater without incident.

Henley did not have the good fortune to avoid bodily contact with a lion. It happened on a safari when he and a client were following a herd of elephant among which he had spotted a decent tusker. Suddenly they came upon a very big lion. Henley quickly asked the client, who was using a .375 Holland & Holland rifle, which of the two trophies he wanted. The answer was a lion. From there events moved quickly, as Tony related:

> The first shot missed but the lion did not move. The next shot hit him low, and he jumped up and disappeared behind an anthill. I caught a glimpse of him going like hell when he emerged from behind the anthill, and gave him a quick shot for good measure, but hit him too far back. He disappeared into thick bush.
>
> Suddenly there was a terrific growl and the wounded fellow came at me from behind a small bush. I fired, but the bullet had no effect. I clearly remember the great yellow eyes fixed on me before the lion knocked the rifle out of my hand, dug his claws into my back, and bit me between the shoulders. Fortunately his teeth did not penetrate me as deeply as they might have, because I was wearing several layers of thick clothing, including a wonderful heavy green sweater knitted by my mother-in-law. I fell under the animal's weight and in doing so put my right arm up to protect my neck. Fortunately, he let go of my shoulder, taking my arm in his vice-like jaws and sinking his great fangs into my biceps and forearm. I tried to reach my sheath knife with my left hand, but he had me in a very firm grip and every time I struggled he lifted me up and shook me like a rat. I realized I had no hope of getting my knife out. My only hope was to pretend to be dead, so I said to myself, "One, two, three," and let everything go limp.
>
> It worked. He stopped biting and just lay on top of me, breathing heavily. I then reckoned that if I could remain still he would either die on top of me or get up and walk away. How long I had been in this position I do not know, maybe ten minutes or more, when to my horror I saw my Land Rover approaching, being driven very slowly with several people brandishing rifles in the back.[1]

Two of Henley's friends had recently been shot and killed while being mauled by lion, and he was understandably anxious:

> So when the car stopped some thirty yards away, I said as loud as I dared, "Only shoot him in the head." His head, although close to mine, was the highest point and the most vital if the bullet hit

the brain. After watching two rifles pointing in my direction for what seemed like an eternity, there was a loud bang and I felt the concussion of the bullet. By good fortune and a very well placed shot fired by Dr. Pastorek, the 7-mm bullet passed through the center of the lion's brain, killing him instantly.[2]

Although badly hurt, Henley insisted on taking the trophy lion with them. In Henley's party was an elderly doctor, who cleaned him up before he was flown to a hospital.

ONE OF THE most unlikely hunters to team up with Lunan's outfit was an irrepressible American named Walter Jones. A native of Alabama, Wally arrived at Dave's offices in 1957, already a licensed hunter.[3] Wally's presence in Africa seemed as though it had originated out of a fictional comedy. At the age of sixteen Wally had gone to a movie house in Mobile, Alabama, to see the film of Hemingway's *The Macomber Affair*. The hero who stood in for Gregory Peck in the animal scenes was David Lunan. That movie had done it for Jones. "When I came out of that little old theater," Walter said, "I *knew* that was all I wanted to be—a white hunter in Africa." At the time it seemed to everybody but Walter that he was in the throes of a most improbable Walter Mitty fantasy.

Jones spent the next four years dreaming of Africa while he served in the United States Marine Corps. His determination only strengthened with the passage of time. As soon as he was released from service, Wally wrote to every white hunter whose name he could find in sporting publications, such as *Field and Stream* and *Outdoor Life*. Only one man, Safariland's veteran Murray Smith, answered Walter's letter. "Mr. Tee," as Walter called Tom Murray Smith, advised, "There is no point just writing about becoming a white hunter. If you really want to become one, you will have to come out here and get a job. That's the only way you'll know if you can make it!" That was all Wally needed to hear.

When Walter's father caught wind of his son's far-fetched African scheme, he warned, "Good luck, but when you're ready to come home I'm not giving you a penny." Wally never doubted that he would succeed. With a few personal belongings in his kit bag Wally boarded a Robin Line ship bound for Africa and his destination, Mombasa. When he arrived months later at the sweltering seaport, Wally purchased a second-class train ticket for Nairobi, and boarded the Lunatic Express.

Rocking through the African night, the small-town southerner was dumbfounded by the luxury of the train's dining car. He was amazed at the sight of fresh-cut carnations and chrysanthemums in wall-mounted crystal vases and starched white tableclothes with place settings laid out in Old World colonial fashion. At his left hand were three forks of different sizes, one for fish, one for the main meat course, and one for dessert. On the right side of his plate were three knives, a crescent-shaped fish knife, a steak knife, and a butter knife. Above his plate of soup were a soup spoon, a dessert spoon, and a coffee spoon. Recalling his discomfort about all the cutlery, Wally, in his drawling speech, remembered, "Hee-yell, I didn't know what to do with all that silverware! So I watched the other diners and I just did what they did!"

The next day, in Nairobi, Wally followed his dream to the New Stanley Hotel, where he rented a room. Jones was twenty-four years old and he had $150 to his name and all Africa at his feet. But when he sought out his correspondent "Mr. Tee" at Safariland's office, he was disappointed. He learned Murray Smith was on safari, and Safariland had no job to offer. It was suggested he try a white hunter named Bunny Allen, then putting together a movie safari for MGM's *Mogambo*. Recalling that meeting, Wally says, "That is one *damn* nice man, that Bunny Allen." Allen's job interview with former Marine Walter Jones went like this, according to Wally:

> Allen: Are you a good mechanic?
> Jones: No, Sir!
> Allen: Do you know anything about cars?
> Jones: No, Sir!
> Allen: Do you know anything about electricity or generators?
> Jones: No, Sir. I don't know a *damn* thing about electricity, Sir!
> Allen: Well, we are going to have a lot of people to feed on this trip. Have you done much hunting?
> Jones: No, Sir! All I've shot is one rabbit and one squirrel. Sir!
> Allen: O.K. You're hired.

Jones had arrived at exactly the right time. Bunny was desperate for help with the management of a large camp. Allen paid Wally the whopping salary of £50 ($143) per month, a fortune to Wally at the time. Room and full board, which included three full meals with all courses, plus early morning and afternoon tea at the New Stanley, Wally recalls, "was only 19 shillings per day [less than $3 per day] and that was in one of the best hotels in the country!" But he did not stay at the hotel long. A local jack-of-all-trades, Bobby Cade, who was working on the *Mogambo* set, lived near Nairobi's then airport, Eastleigh, where he was building the entire set for *Mogambo* in sections. Wally hung his hat at Cade's home.

After *Mogambo* was completed Wally got work as a "stooge" trainee to gain experience. With a relaxed style and natural ability, Wally made friends in the safari business easily. He fulfilled part of his dream when he hunted with his mentor, Tom Murray Smith.

Eventually Wally Jones became part of Lunan's White Hunters (Africa) Ltd., and ended up a ranking professional, working with Gregory Peck's stand-in—just like in the famous movie he had seen in faraway Alabama so long ago, and which had launched Wally on his unlikely quest to Darkest Africa.

24

THE TANGANYIKA HUNTERS

The former colony of German East Africa was renamed Tanganyika Territory after the First World War, in 1918. Tanganyika held some of the greatest concentrations of big game in Africa, and Arusha became an important center for safaris. The town, situated near Mount Kilimanjaro on the northern plains, was much smaller in area and population than Nairobi, but there were certain similarities. Both were colorful towns. Both were located in the cool highland regions of their respective countries, and both were known for their fun-loving citizenry. Not far from Arusha were vast wheat- and grain-farming areas on the slopes of Kilimanjaro, Africa's tallest mountain. While Nairobi rapidly grew into a large cosmopolitan city, Arusha remained a small hunting and farming community but with the same Wild West flavor as its Kenya counterpart. While the settlers around Nairobi were primarily of English descent, Arusha had more of an international flavor. Even at its zenith of prosperity in the late 1950s, Arusha was never a large town, having a total population of less than 8,000, including about 1,000 white settlers of all nationalities, many of them not actually resident in the immediate township, but on outlying ranches.

While Kenya had its Masai Mara, Tanganyika held the Serengeti. While Kenya had its famed deserts in the Northern Frontier, Tanganyika had Ngorongoro Crater, one of the wonders of the world, as well as Lake Manyara, which was also alive with big game. In addition Tanganyika had the largest game reserve in the world, the Selous.

BRITISH EAST Africa had always attracted the lion's share of celebrity tourist hunters. Some of the early visitors stayed on and made enormous contributions to development. After German East became Tanganyika, one of its most significant investors was Kenyon Painter, an Ohio entrepreneur who first came to Arusha on a safari in 1907. He bought 11,000 acres of land outside town and developed the region's premier coffee estate. He gave the town its first post office, built a church, a hospital, and then an advanced coffee research center at a place called Tengeru, sixteen miles from Arusha. Painter invested eleven million dollars in and around Arusha. His single-story New Arusha Hotel was one of the region's most noted landmarks and was headquarters for the Tanganyika Tours and Safaris company.

STAN LAWRENCE-BROWN, Dave Lunan's former partner, had set up shop at Arusha in 1957. Lawrence-Brown Safaris (Tanganyika) Ltd.'s main competitor was Russell Bowker Douglas, who owned Tanganyika Tours and Safaris Ltd. Among hunters Russell's firm was affectionately known as Tanganyika Whores and Shauris Ltd. (*shauri* is Swahili for "ruckus" or "problem"). The firm's letterhead proudly announced, "By Appointment to H.R.H. Prince Bernhard of the Netherlands." Prince Bernhard, or P.B., as he is popularly known in the hunting fraternity, went on four hunting safaris with Douglas. Russell recalled, "P.B. was one of the finest sportsmen I ever met. He liked to take photographs, and would only shoot if an outstanding trophy was found. He actually shoots very little, but he *loves* safaris!"[1]

Russell was a well-liked fixture in the Tanganyika hunting community. He was as much at home with royalty as he was with rednecks. Russell's firm was staffed with a fine team of young professionals.[*]

Russell shot his first leopard on the family's Kedong Valley ranch before he was a teenager while covered by his father's rifle. He was hired as an elephant-control officer in Uganda, earning £10 per month from the Game Department. Later he turned professional and took his first month-long safari into the Semliki Valley. His profit from that safari was £10 (then worth $7). In 1937 Russell transferred to the Kenya Game Department as elephant-control officer. He once tracked a crop-raiding herd into a dense patch of woodland where visibility was reduced to a few yards. As he gained on the herd a bull spun around to face him, and

---

[*]T.T. & S. Ltd.'s hunters: Bob Foster (for a time), John Fletcher, Anton Allen, Nicky Blunt, Pat Hemingway, Jackie Carlyon, Neil Millar, David Williams, Don Rundgren, Mike Dove, and Chris "Tiger" Lyon.

Douglas shot it. Then all hell broke loose. Another elephant was suddenly above him and Russell fired into its throat. The elephant collapsed, but as it fell it brought down a tree that pinned Russell to the
ground. His gunbearer eventually freed him after fetching an ax, but
Russell was laid up in bed for weeks with massive bruising, a broken
arm, wrist, and nine busted ribs. Russell never lost his respect for elephant. It was a sentiment ardently shared by his friendly rival, Stan
Lawrence-Brown. Both Tanganyika hunters considered elephant by far
the most dangerous of the Big Five.

Russell built a major tourist destination with construction of the
Lake Manyara Hotel, which has a marvelous view overlooking the
Great Rift Valley. In Arusha, Russell's safari office was in the lobby of
the New Arusha Hotel. In those days, in front of the hotel there was
a sign:

THIS SPOT IS
EXACTLY HALF WAY BETWEEN THE CAPE AND CAIRO
AND THE EXACT CENTER OF
KENYA, UGANDA, AND TANGANYIKA

Russell's partner, George Dove, sported an enormous waxed mustache as his trademark. Dove was a pleasant, hardworking man with his
heart in the right place. George, and his son Mike, built two important
tourist lodges, Kimba camp at Ngorongoro Crater, and Ndutu lodge on
the southern border of the Serengeti national park.*

One of Russell's hunters was Jackie Carlyon, who hailed from
Cornwall, England. He was a nephew of fiery soldier Colonel Richard
Meinertzhagen. Carlyon, who had private means, came to Africa as a
mining engineer, but got a job stooging for a license with George Dove
and Russell Douglas. Carlyon was one of the most likeable of men, and
one of the few "gun nuts" in the hunting community. He constantly
experimented with heavy-caliber weapons, and was an acknowledged
ballistics expert. He was also an outstanding shot with heavy rifles,
despite his rather puny stature. In 1962 Carlyon's promising career was
snuffed out in a car crash, when he was killed with his gunbearer driving from Arusha to Nairobi.

---

*After Tanzania's independence there were a number of deportations of whites from the
country. Because of this uncertainty George and his family settled in Australia.

◇

STAN LAWRENCE-BROWN had his office in the Safari Hotel one hundred yards up the street from his rival, Russell Douglas. The Safari Hotel was newer, and probably fancier than the New Arusha, but it did not have the trout river frontage, lovely grounds, or the Old World charm of its rival. The Safari was a four-story rectangular box built of stone and concrete, and in its time the interior was comfortably appointed with lofty rooms. Even today, while the Safari has sunk into obscurity with the advent of newer hotels, one cannot help but notice that this large hotel has all its plumbing on the exterior of the structure, a result of an oversight by the contractors, who had forgotten to include plumbing. The hotel was owned by two aristocratic English sisters, Gladys and Margot Rydon. Both women owned prosperous coffee estates. Gladys lived in a magnificent mansion overlooking a mysterious crater lake called Duluti, seven miles east of Arusha. Margot's son, David, was killed by a buffalo near Arusha in 1964.

The Safari Hotel was masterfully managed for the Rydons by a pale-skinned Englishman named Ben Benbow. Benbow was a professional hotelier down to his manicured fingertips and slicked-down hair. He was the only man in Arusha who always wore a suit and tie. Among his dusty, khaki-clad safari clientele, he stood out like a catwalk mannequin in the Ituri forest. Rotund, jovial, and present when guests registered, day or night, Benbow was on a first-name basis with every white hunter as well as with celebrity actors such as Robert Taylor, John Wayne, and Hardy Kruger. The walls around the huge copper bar at the Safari were decorated with framed and signed photographs of white hunters with their clients and trophies.

Stan Lawrence-Brown wasted no time in recruiting lieutenants. He had brought with him from Kenya a young and talented hunter named David Ommanney. Ommanney had worked for both Stan and Dave Lunan during their partnership, having begun his apprenticeship with them in 1952. At Arusha Jacky Hamman came on board, followed in 1957 by hunters George Six, Derrick Dunn, Brian Herne, Nick Swan, and, in 1960 a very good Kenya hunter, Mike Hissey, and Stan's brother, Geoff. On a casual basis Stan hired Douglas Collins, Lars Figgenshou, and, for a time, Greg Hemingway (youngest son of Ernest). *

---

*Lawrence-Brown also employed casual hunters and "stooges" Arthur Squiers, Bob Robertson, Royce Buckle, Bruno Crone, Jon Hall, and store manager Dave Turner-Dauncey.

Greg's older brother, Patrick Hemingway, was a hunter with Russell's Whores and Shauris, just down the road.

By any measure Stan Lawrence-Brown was one of the leading hunters of his day. He was an extremely good rifle shot, particularly with his Holland and Holland .470 double ejector. Back when Lawrence-Brown and Lunan began their hunting venture, their first major safari clients had been Marje and Donald Hopkins of Spokane, Washington. Don Hopkins was a very wealthy man and codeveloper of several different rifles known as O.K.H.s.* The first Hopkins safari was a three-month trip in Kenya and Tanganyika. Both Marje and Don became grand safari aficionados, whose hunts often lasted six months, and sometimes much longer. At first both Marje and Don hunted with Stan, but as husband and wife became more competitive, subsequent hunts were arranged separately to keep the peace.

After his first trip Hopkins became fascinated with elephant hunting. He made a record eleven safaris averaging nine months apiece in search of an elephant (thought to be mythical by his hunters) with tusks weighing 150 pounds each. Stan was always nominally his white hunter, although a second, and sometimes a third hunter, was engaged at the same time. During the course of a Hopkins safari, Stan was often away, back in Arusha or Nairobi, and whoever was second hunter took over the show with Hopkins. I once hunted with Don for seven months, during which time Stan came and went, sometimes remaining away for a month at a time.

In pursuit of big elephant, Stan Lawrence-Brown had miraculously survived two maulings, though neither occurred on a Hopkins safari. Not surprisingly, he regarded elephant with some caution, although he liked to be within at least thirty yards range before allowing a client to shoot. The first of Stan's elephant attacks occurred near the Tana River village of Saka, when Stan was hunting with a client named Francois Sommer, a demanding Frenchman.

Stan and Sommer forded the Tana at Saka, wading from sandbar to

---

*These rifles were known by the initials of their joint American developers: Charles O'Neil (a gunsmith), Elmer Keith (a gun editor), and Don Hopkins. The .426 O.K.H. was a souped-up version of the Westley Richards .425, while the .285 O.K.H. Wildcat was developed for sheep hunting. It was made by necking the .30/.06 case to 7mm. The .333 O.K.H. was a .30/.06 cartridge necked up to take .333 bullets used by the .333 Jeffrey rifle, and the .333 Belted is a short Magnum case for the same cartridge. Hopkins used the .333 Belted with success in Africa. The trio developed a version of the .470, known as the .475 O.K.H. in magazine form. Only one white hunter, Reggie Destro, converted to .475 O.K.H.

sandbar despite the crocodile population, and then entered the dense riverine jungle. Stan's trackers picked up the fresh spoor of three elephant bulls. In a short time they caught up with the bulls in acacia forest, and although they could not see the animals, they could hear the crack of branches as the elephant moved about feeding. Stan crept nearer followed by his client, and at a range of twenty yards the foliage parted to reveal a big elephant, its trunk held suspiciously high testing for alien scent. In a second the elephant dropped its trunk and charged the offensive human odor, smashing down bushes in its path.

Stan threw up his .470 and fired the first barrel, but the elephant came on as if nothing had happened. Sommer apparently fired a shot, too. As Stan's second barrel roared, the elephant grabbed for Stan with its trunk. He was knocked aside by the elephant's trunk, and instead of grabbing him it snatched Stan's wide-brimmed Borsalino hat off his head, flinging it violently to the ground. For some reason the elephant broke off the attack and crashed away, leaving a shaken and bruised Stan. Stan's gunbearer Mohammed and Tana River tracker Mwalimu Manza, who were unarmed, had somehow dodged the enraged elephant.

With Mwalimu's help Stan, despite a dozen broken ribs and severe bruising caused by the elephant's trunk, followed the spoor for weeks, but never caught up with the animal. Stan said there was no blood spoor and he was certain the elephant recovered from those head shots. Even after he had quit spooring the elephant Stan engaged extra Tana River trackers—led by legendary Borana tracker Gholo—to assist Mwalimu with the search, but even these experts were never able to catch up with the elephant, despite Stan's promise of a hefty bonus.

Stan said he never could figure out why the elephant had not finished him off when it had the chance. He concluded that his hat had saved his life when the elephant's attack was distracted by it. Stan Lawrence-Brown did not consider himself superstitious, but after that incident he wore a wide-brimmed Borsalino hat with a khaki *pugree** hatband. The Borsalino was his trademark, and he was rarely seen without it. Almost everybody in Stan's employ wore a similar hat and *pugree*.

Every now and then one reads fanciful accounts that mention "disappearing" African bearers who vanish when danger threatens. Nobody is

---

Pugree is an Indian word for turban, but when used as a hatband it resembles a pleated scarf worn around the crown of the hat.

denying that occasionally bearers disappear, and who can blame them for a quick retreat if their bwanas fail to knock down charging animals? Bearers are usually unarmed. In the experience of most professionals it is often the bearers who are the bravest of the brave. Many hunters, including Stan Lawrence-Brown, owed their lives to their bearers.

During his second mauling by an elephant, Stan's life was saved by the quick action of his gunbearer, a small Masai D'robo tracker named Longolla Lakiti. Subsequent to Sommer's safari, Stan was hunting with clients in Tanganyika's south Masailand. He and two clients, a husband and wife, found the spoor of four bulls that had crossed the sandy road during the night. Several miles of tracking brought them within earshot of the elephants, which were spread out and feeding in open brush. Beside a large baobab tree Stan left his lady client with her gunbearer, the nervous, strung-out Mohammed, who had been with Stan during the Saka elephant attack.

Stan, client, and tracker Longolla inched forward to inspect the bulls in turn. The first tusker broke out of a bush twenty yards from the hunters, and they saw his ivory, which Stan judged to be seventy pounds a side. They let him go, and worked their way toward another elephant feeding in a thicket fifty yards farther on. They got to within thirty yards of the elephant, which suddenly charged. The elephant's head broke out of the brush ten yards from Stan. He fired for a frontal brain shot with his .470, but the elephant grabbed Stan in its trunk, whirled him aloft, and tried to skewer him onto a tusk. Stan put his arm around a tusk in a desperate armlock, holding on with all his might to prevent being hauled onto a tusk and impaled. Meantime, Longolla grabbed Stan's rifle out of the dust, pressed it against the side of the elephant's head, and fired the second barrel. The elephant collapsed with a brain shot but with the unfortunate Stan still gripped by its trunk. Longolla* had saved Stan's life, but the fall injured Stan's back and he suffered from back pain for the rest of his life.

Stan Lawrence-Brown had many fine professional hunters associated with his firm in Arusha, but perhaps the best all-around hunter was David Ommanney. Dave was born in Jalgaon, India, in 1931, the son of a British policeman in the Indian Colonial Civil Service who settled his family in Nanyuki, Kenya. As a schoolboy Dave had been befriended by

---

*A few months after this attack, Longolla Lakiti went to work for me, and remained in my service for twenty-four years.

David Ommanney, 1957.

the famous tiger hunter from India, Jim Corbett, then in retirement at the small town of Nyeri in the foothills of the Aberdare Mountains. Corbett's influence helped prompt Ommanney to become a white hunter.

"There were only three safari outfitting organizations operating in Nairobi at the beginning of the fifties," Dave recalled. "Safariland, Ker and Downey, and Lawrence-Brown and Lunan." Dave started with a visit to Safariland. The manager, Wally King, was not encouraging. Dave made his way to Ker and Downey's office where he met Donald Ker. Ker took one look at Ommanney and said, "Ker and Downey would never employ anyone who wore shorts!"[2] In 1952 Ommanney was hired by Lawrence-Brown and Lunan Safaris as a "stooge." There was hardly any money, and Stan worked him to the bone. But Ommanney does not resent the hardships, the brutal training, and long hours. He stuck out his stooging job with teeth gritted, although perhaps 98 percent of would-be hunters with stars in their eyes dropped out. The trainee's backyard university was fixing cars, meeting and greeting clients, tracking animals, scouting on reccies, skinning game, or standing in line at some bureaucratic counter getting interminable permits. There was always a rush to get the next safari on the road and get a shady, scenic campsite located, cleared, tents pitched, kerosene refrigerator and lamps working before the white hunter bwanas and clients arrived half a day later expecting hot showers, hors d'oeuvres, and a five-course dinner on the table. Bored to distraction sorting and packing supplies, or being jumped on for some petty fault, being eternally broke, tired, sore, bug-bitten, and belittled was not everybody's cup of tea. In those days only men who really meant to make a full-time career out of hunting would put up with the hardships. The years that were required to qualify for an unrestricted professional hunter's license constituted a most serious business, and Ommanney winces at the recollection of it.

Once he was qualified Ommanney never looked back. One of his clients, Russell Wailes, dreamed of bagging a "gray ghost," the elusive East African greater kudu. Ommanney put Wailes on to the tenth-largest specimen ever taken, with horns measuring 56½ inches. A triumphant Ommanney could only smile at the East African Professional Hunter's Association's swank dinner presentation when he won the Hunter of the Year Award in 1958. Donald Ker congratulated Ommanney warmly on his winning trophy. Ommanney has a dry, witty humor, and nobody is spared, not even Donald Ker. He never let Donald forget his "short pants" remark when he was turned down for a stooging job with Ker and Downey. Ommanney's face became familiar to every American hunter, for he was named Winchester's "Man in Africa" and graced the covers of numerous sporting magazines.

The following year Dave Ommanney bit the dust hard. It happened in the Burungu area of northern Tanganyika, not far from a cluster of hills known as the Pyramids because of their uncanny resemblance to the real thing. Ommanney was "on loan" to Safariland Ltd. for a client named Baron Boeselager. In January 1959 Boeselager wounded a leopard near the Pyramids. Ommanney had followed Boeselager's leopard, and when it attacked he fired at it with his shotgun. The leopard took the full charge of Dave's buckshot, but continued the attack, severely mauling Ommanney:

> I was being chewed by a big male [leopard]. My gunbearer, Salim
> Ali, who had my .470, came to my aid, and jumped on both the
> leopard and myself and pushed the leopard away. He also tried to
> knife it, but he had one of Harold's skinning knives,* with a

---

*Just before this attack I accompanied Ommanney on safari with his clients Harold and Alma Dugdale of St. Joseph, Missouri.

curved blade, and it did little damage. Salim was certain the cat was mortally wounded, either by his knife or by me when it came for me. Anyway, to cut a short story shorter, after I left for Arusha hospital [75 miles away] Salim and Mutia, my other gunbearer, went back to look for the leopard. It was in the same patch of grass that we had left him in. The leopard jumped on Salim and chewed him up. Mutia shot at it with my .30/.06 severing the last six inches of its tail.

The leopard retreated into the grass whilst the gunbearers retreated to camp, half a mile away, leaving the cat the victor on the battlefield. Safariland sent down Theo Potgeiter [a white hunter], who at that time was employed by Selby and Holmberg Safaris. Strangely enough Potgeiter found the leopard still in the same place. It went for Theo, who was armed with my shotgun. He missed the first barrel, and clobbered it with the second. The leopard still came on, now on three legs. Theo was bending the barrels of my shotgun on the leopard's head when the client, Baron Boeselager, shot and killed it.[3]

Ommanney was not amused that his favorite bird gun had been wrecked, even less so when he saw his bloodied gunbearers, particularly Salim Ali. Salim's face was badly marked up by the leopard's claws, one dewclaw gouge running deeply across his forehead, just missing an eye, and continuing across his nose and cheek. Salim was bitten on the hands and arms. Ommanney had a chunk torn out of his arm and shoulder, and was badly clawed as well. The incident forever convinced him that "shotguns are for shooting birds."

Ommanney says his heavy rifle was always a double. He makes no pretense of having selected such and such a rifle because of some weighty conclusion based on vast experience or profound ballistic knowledge. "I used a .470 mainly because I had one," Ommanney states. "If I'd had a .475, .475 No. 2, .500/.465 I would have used that. I just happened to get into a .470 Rigby with twenty-four-inch barrels. For light stuff I used a .30/.06. My God, I used that rifle for years and years! But also a .260 Winchester and .300 Winchester. My favorite all-rounder is a .375 H&H with a scope. To my mind the Winchester pre-'64 model 70 action is the best, and I was never paid to say that!"

25.

THE MOTH AND THE FLAME

One of Stan Lawrence-Brown's partners was a South African named Jacky Hamman, whose family had settled in Tanganyika before the Second World War. Like many families in remote areas of Tanganyika, the Hammans depended on hunting for food. Jacky Hamman was most noted for three qualities he had in abundance—his sense of humor, his outstanding ability with a huge .577 double rifle, and his utter fearlessness.

Jacky was popular with safari cronies as well as with the fairer sex, and he was always in demand on infrequent visits to town. On one occasion a pretty Arusha lass whom Jacky had been romancing managed to extract a marriage proposal from him. His paramour even persuaded him to withdraw his meager savings from the bank in order to purchase an engagement ring. On the way to the gem shop in Arusha Jacky had time to reconsider. He changed course, and instead headed to the *boma*, the old German administrative fort. Instead of an engagement ring, Hamman purchased an elephant license. Licenses were nonrefundable, and with his money spent Jacky hightailed it out of town.[1]

Hamman had always used his .577 rifle with deadly effect, despite his small physique, for he weighed only 110 pounds and stood a mere five foot two on tiptoes. At thirty years of age Jacky was the least imposing-looking of the white hunters. He had thinning fair hair and water-blue eyes, and his pale countenance was kept that way because, like Stan Lawrence-Brown, he always wore a wide-brimmed Borsalino hat. Hamman was a Boer who had only learned to speak English during the Second World War, when he served in Abyssinia with a South African Armored Car Brigade. But his English was good despite his heavily clipped Afrikaans accent. Supremely confident in his own

Buffalo beneath the Great Rift Valley escarpment, 1955.

abilities, Hamman's favorite saying was that no animal was any match for an armed man.

Jacky gauged his clients carefully, and those he figured liked close encounters or who could stand up to the moment of truth without blinking he would take along when he went after wounded dangerous game. One client who witnessed Jacky's delight in close shaves was Peter Hirsch. Their hunting camp was south of Lake Manyara on a farm owned by a Greek named Marianakis. The Marianakis family hoped Hamman would help them get rid of elephant and buffalo that were tearing up their plantation. Late on the first evening, Hamman had seen hundreds of buffalo, but the next day they could not find any. There had been rain, and the grass was head-high. Hamman and his client hunted in the long grass, and as the men climbed a small knoll, Hirsch saw a buffalo bull standing on a little mound eyeing them.

The buffalo was one hundred yards off, a range regarded by Hamman as a long-distance shot for this species. He thought there was little chance of getting closer without being observed, so he told his client to shoot. Hirsch raised up and fired, but the buffalo did not go down. Instead it lurched off the hillock, and suddenly many buffalo exploded in all directions from the tall grass. Hirsch managed to get off a second shot as his buffalo tore away toward the forest. He had the satisfaction of seeing his shot bring the great beast down. When the hunters reached the spot where the buffalo should have been, there was no sign of it. Hamman and his men made a nerve-wracking four-hour search but came up empty-handed. Gloomily the hunters marched five miles back to camp in darkness. Their spirits were hardly revived there when the wind suddenly rose and a ferocious thunderstorm rolled in. The gale blew down all the tents, save one. Hirsch was trapped beneath his tent as he struggled to keep a pressure lantern from setting fire to the canvas. The men spent a damp and restless night, and next morning Jacky insisted they return to search for the buffalo. Starting from the beginning, they retraced the buffalo's water-logged tracks until Jacky's gun-bearer, Hassani, triumphantly found the dead buffalo. But as they approached the dead animal, another big buffalo barreled off into taller reeds. Hirsch wrote:

"Take him," screamed Jacky, and I fired both barrels in rapid succession. We heard the buffalo go down. Then we heard him get up. "Look out," yelled Jacky, "he's coming for you."

I opened the breech and inserted two solids and snapped the action closed. As I pushed forward on the safety I noticed that the top lever was not completely over and I opened the gun and tried to close it again. It wouldn't lock properly. Jacky was now by my side as I fumbled to get the rifle working. He practically danced up and down in his anxiety to get me into action. I withdrew the cartridge in the right barrel and threw it away. Just as I did so the head of the buffalo burst from the heavy grass.

Without thinking I snapped the action closed. This time there was a satisfying click and, unconsciously remembering to pull the back trigger, I took a snap shot at the buffalo as it loomed, black and menacing, in front of me. The bullet hit the buffalo in the nose, went on through his brain, and came out at the back of his neck. Down he went with a crash, and as he expired he gave a long, low, mournful bellow. I felt I had had it. I turned to Jacky, somewhat nettled. "Why the hell didn't you shoot?" I demanded angrily.

An innocent look came over Jacky's face. "You're paying for the thrills," he said, "you ought to get them. Besides, if he had gotten any closer I'd have helped you out."[2]

Hamman conducted a safari to his favorite place in central Tanganyika, known as the Yaida Valley. One morning Hamman and his client made a stalk on a big salt and pepper–maned lion. As the hunters crept forward a black mamba raised itself from the grass and struck Jacky in the thigh. Within seconds his leg ballooned to twice its normal size, turned beef red, and Jacky knew he was in bad trouble. He sat down, sending his gunbearer rushing back to the hunting car for his Fitzsimmons snakebite serum. Meantime the trophy lion, which had been feeding on a kill, looked up. Seeing the hunters it bounded away. Jacky rigged a makeshift tourniquet with a belt in hopes of slowing the venom. When the gunbearer returned with the special mamba serum, Jacky injected himself twice, once into the snakebite, and once in the upper arm, hoping to get the serum into his heart before the venom got there. Miraculously Jacky survived the snakebite. He was very sick for a long time, and in town he relied on the advice of his friend Dr. George Six, whose wide-ranging interests included herpetology.

A month after his encounter with the mamba Jacky could be seen hobbling around Arusha on a stick with a swollen blue-black leg. Like a snake does, Jacky's leg had sloughed off all the skin. George Six was of the opinion Hamman would have died within half an hour from the deadly neurotoxic venom but for the fact that the snake's fangs had to penetrate the tough khaki material of Jacky's short pants, where most of the venom had been expended when the snake struck. Six added that the gods had been with Jacky, because had he been struck in a major vein or artery there would have been no hope for him. Six said mambas sometimes strike several times with great rapidity. Luckily for Hamman, this snake had struck only once.

DR. GEORGE SIX, a London physician, was an unlikely member of Tanganyika's hunting community. He had come to Africa not with the intention of practicing medicine, but to purchase a farm. Six and his English wife, Mary (née Bell), the daughter of a judge, rented a house outside Arusha. George soon made the acquaintance of Jacky Hamman at Arusha's government administration building, known as the *boma*,* where Hamman was purchasing game licenses for one of his safaris.

The suave and sophisticated George Six was Hamman's diametric

---

Boma is Swahili for "corral."

opposite in every way—in physique, temperament, education, intellect, and background—yet the two became firm friends.

Once settled in Arusha Dr. Six opened a gun shop next door to the Safari Hotel where Lawrence-Brown Safaris, Jacky Hamman's outfit, was located. He then purchased two thousand acres in Tanganyika's densely wooded Kiru Valley, south of Lake Manyara. The farm was virgin bushland and lay close beside the wall of the Great Rift Valley, only a few miles from Magara, where Bror and Cockie von Blixen had once lived at Singu Estates. George's acreage was in tsetse fly country and useless for domestic animals because of the deadly tsetse-borne disease, trypanosomiasis. In such regions in Tanzania there is an almost total absence of human settlements due to tsetse flies, but nearly always there is an unusual abundance of wildlife, and the Kiru Valley was no exception. In the 1950s it was chock-full of game, particularly elephant, rhino, and buffalo, and provided plenty of sport for the hunting enthusiast.

When George Six decided to take up hunting as a full-time occupation, Jacky Hamman helped him get the experience he needed to qualify for a professional hunter's license. It was Jacky who told Stan about George and what a great asset he would be to Stan's outfit. When Lawrence-Brown met George he agreed with Jacky's assessment. The relationship proved beneficial—Six invested in Stan's firm, and in 1956 he became a director and one-third shareholder of Lawrence-Brown Safaris.

George eagerly took up big game hunting and Hamman was his mentor. Between professional safaris the pair hunted elephant together in every corner of Tanganyika. Jacky's influence was apparent with George's choice of a heavy rifle. Unlike Jacky, George was big, powerfully built, and strong, but like Jacky he exclusively used a .577 Manton box-lock double rifle.

Hamman, the experienced hunter, returned George's admiration. "That George is something else," Jacky liked to say. "He can tell you about removing an appendix, fixing a diesel injector, give the Latin name for some kind of mud fish, or you can ask him about the muzzle velocity of *anything*, and he can damn well tell you right now."

ALTHOUGH George Six had long ago given up his urban existence in favor of a wanderer's life of adventure, he maintained excellent contacts in Europe, especially in the French and German movie communities. Although George was of mixed English-French parentage, he spoke the King's English, as well as fluent French, Spanish, Swahili, and German.

One of George Six's numerous international acquaintances was the controversial German filmmaker Leni Riefenstahl. Leni had been one of the women admired by Adolf Hitler, and she was also Germany's most famous movie actress, having won acclaim for performances in *The Blue Light* and *The Holy Mountain*. Riefenstahl made the admired *Olympia* about the 1936 Berlin Olympics for Hitler, and that is where she first met George Six. In his varied career, George had participated in the 1936 Berlin Olympics as a member of the British swimming team. During subsequent travels Six had taken up photography, first as a hobby, later as a profession. While on assignment as a *Life* magazine photographer in the Red Sea and the Gulf of Aqaba, he worked with pioneer underwater photographer Hans Haas.

In 1956 George became reacquainted with Leni Riefenstahl when she asked him to help her make a full-length documentary film about the slave trade in East Africa. George invited me to join him on the Riefenstahl safari, which lasted over seven months and traveled through Kenya, Uganda, and the Belgian Congo. Leni's movie was called *Schwarz Fracht*, or *Black Cargo*.

For some reason during a preliminary survey of Kenya before filming was to begin, Riefenstahl was driving George's specially built, wooden-bodied, shooting-brake Willys Jeep. The heavy car went into a fast skid on a rough stretch of graveled road leading to the Tana River near Garissa Bridge, rolled down an embankment, and came to rest upside down. Luckily for Leni, George was aboard, because in the accident she suffered a concussion and a deep gash to the head. She was also badly bruised and had sprained her neck. George suffered a broken kneecap and a broken wrist. From his medicine chest in the car, George washed and stitched Leni's head wound. In those days safaris did not have radio telephones. Instead, a Nairobi radio station would broadcast messages to white hunters listening out in the bush after the regular BBC world news broadcast each evening. In an emergency it was necessary to find an administrative outpost and hope that it had radio contact with Nairobi.

On the remote Tana River road traffic was scarce, but fortunately for Leni a police Land Rover happened to be passing George's crashed Jeep, and the police inspector drove Six and Riefenstahl into the Somali township of Garissa. At that time there was no flying doctor service, but the police radioed headquarters in Nairobi. My uncle, Norris Kirkham, of the Kenya Police Air Wing, was sent to rescue Leni and George. After a stay at Nairobi Hospital Leni returned to Germany before resuming her safari with us. She came back wearing a neck brace, accompanied by a number of German cameramen and technicians, along with her assistant, the gracious Hanni (Isle) Lanske.* Leni Riefenstahl's† film *Black Cargo* contained excellent wildlife footage, but it was generally regarded as a flop at the box office.

IT WAS NOT to be a lion, leopard, buffalo, or black mamba that killed zestful Jacky Hamman in the prime of his life. In January 1958, David Ommanney, the gifted star at Lawrence-Brown Safaris, was sharing a hunting camp with Hamman and Geoff Lawrence-Brown, Stan's younger brother.

Jacky, like many South African hunters, had a tremendous love of antique guns, exposed-hammer firearms in particular. Before his safari with Ommanney, Jacky had purchased a new Land Rover pickup truck from which he had removed both doors in order to give himself and his clients quick and silent exit when hunting.

Jacky and his client went out guinea fowl hunting in the Mto-wa-Mbu (Mosquito River) area in northern Tanganyika. Hamman, the quick-shot artist, known to be a stickler for gun safety, was driving his doorless car with his hammer shotgun *loaded*, its butt resting on the car's floorboard beside his feet, its barrel cradled in the crook of his arm. Driving cross-country the vehicle hit a bump and the shotgun's butt slid across the floorboard and out of the car, but as it did so one of the shotgun's hammers hit the edge of the floor. Hamman took the full shotgun blast at almost point-blank range, and the charge struck just beneath his ear. It was David Ommanney who transported

---

*In December 1994 Hanni Lanske, then living in Austria, said of her friend Leni Riefenstahl, "She is in remarkable condition for her ninety-two years and still enjoys film and diving travels."

†Leni Riefenstahl told me in 1994 that she was on her way to Papua, New Guinea, to make an underwater documentary. She took up underwater photography in her mid-seventies. Leni photographed the last wild tribes in Sudan, and wrote two best-sellers on the subject. Her memoir, *Leni Riefenstahl*, was published in 1993.

Jacky's body back to Arusha where Jacky's widow, Betty, and his two young children lived.

George Six remained in Arusha for some years after the death of his good friend. Besides his chosen career as white hunter, Six kept up his other remarkably varied interests. The former physician obtained a contract to supply live venomous snakes to American research groups. As dense bush was cleared on his Kiru Valley coffee plantation, enormous anthills were uncovered. George had a tractor driver knock down the anthills with a bulldozer. This usually revealed an amazing number of snakes living in these abandoned cement-hard anthills. Once the 'dozer blade leveled the anthill, George would dash into the rubble and catch snakes. He often held the snakes with a forked "catching" stick, then grabbed them in his bare hands, holding them behind the neck, then by the tail. He would hold the snake at arm's length with the reptile's head facing the ground. Some days the catch would total as many as thirty venomous snakes, everything from boomslangs* to black mambas and puff adders. George carefully catalogued the snakes, then placed them in fine wire-mesh cages for shipment.

While Six assisted with safaris for Stan Lawrence-Brown, his farm was managed by a salty old Australian named Bill Aherne. The plantation was regarded as a model, especially as George had ingeniously built gravity-fed irrigation canals that stretched for miles. Six was to suffer a terrible accident on the farm when his leg was crushed while he worked beneath a crawler tractor. The accident forced him to quit professional hunting. When Tanganyika became Tanzania, the newly independent government nationalized all the farms and most private businesses. George, who had put every cent he had into his Kiru Valley coffee farm, lost everything, and shortly afterward Mary, his wife, died of a heart attack. Later, the new Tanzania government persuaded George to design game-viewing lodges on the western Serengeti Plains. One was built at Seronera, the other at Lobo, both major tourist destinations.

George moved into a seafront home at Oyster Bay, near Tanzania's capital of Dar es Salaam, where he opened a design office. Tanzania has always been short of European women, much less those who were

---

*A large greenish arboreal venomous snake, *Dispholidus typus* from Afrikaans words *boom*, meaning tree, and *slang*, meaning snake. It is also known as the Common Tree Snake, grows to five feet and more, and is found throughout Africa south of the Sahara.

members of the intelligentsia. George was fortunate to meet his second wife, an Ohio-born Irish-American named Marty Lanning, through a magazine for members of the Mensa Society. In 1980 the excesses of Tanzania's radical socialist government became too much, even for tolerant George Six. With one suitcase, George left to settle in America, where he became a designer of aquatic gardens for the city of Raleigh, North Carolina.

One of the most experienced of Tanganyika's old-time hunters was a mild-looking man of medium height with dark brooding eyes and thinning hair named Clary Palmer-Wilson. The son of a Uganda Railway engineer, Clary was born in Nairobi in 1907. At the age of fourteen he shot his first elephant under the direction of Tanganyika ivory hunter, Basil Reel. As a young man Clary hunted elephant almost full time:

> I hunted with anyone I could persuade to buy a license and only took ten percent of the value of the tusks for myself. I just wanted the experience for I could not get any experienced trackers or gun-bearers to hunt with one so young. I took out Arabs, Somalis, anybody I could find, and because I owned a Jeffrey .400 double, I oozed confidence, which gave most of them a feeling of security.[1]

Long after the advent of motor cars, Clary hunted almost exclusively on foot in Tanganyika. He always carried specially made, lightweight leather shoes with thin leather soles. Clary would slip them on when he was about to make his final approach on an elephant. It was a trick he had learned from Basil Reel. "You could move in those shoes without making a sound. If I did not have those shoes with me," Clary said, "I went in for the final stalk barefoot."

Although Palmer-Wilson got his first professional hunter's license in 1926, he much preferred to hunt on his own account. Clary was so engrossed in the pursuit of big ivory that he only occasionally agreed to act as a white hunter during his early days; after 1938, however, he found himself much in demand to lead client safaris. As an ivory hunter

Clary lost track of the number of elephant taken after he had shot two hundred. "There is no point in sheer numbers," he insisted. "It's the *hunting* that is important." Yet his skills attracted many notable clients, including King Ferdinand of Bulgaria.

During a long career Clary survived a murder attempt made by a tribesman he had once arrested for poaching. The poacher had tried to poison him, but Clary's bush-craft rivaled that of the African's. Clary knew a primitive plant that was the poison's antidote and was able to concoct a remedy. He later survived several bouts of blackwater fever, a deadly form of malaria. In Clary's day the only cure for malaria was quinine, although too much quinine could have serious side effects. If the malaria was sufficiently advanced, and quinine had been administered in large doses without apparent benefit, local bush lore had it that the only chance for survival was a megadose of dry champagne to flush the kidneys. During a safari Clary Palmer-Wilson was struck down with blackwater fever and was certain he was about to die. With the recent poisoning incident in his mind, he wrote a note to British authorities to tell them his death (if it occurred) was in no way to be considered the fault of his African crew. Clary then persuaded his men to force two bottles of champagne down his throat. He passed out and remained in a coma for two days, but in the end Clary's men had no need for exoneration.[2]

Palmer-Wilson was one of the true elephant aficionados. He would never say how many hundred pounders he had shot, but his modesty did not fool any of the old-timers. He was known to be one of the greatest and most dedicated of that small band of ivory hunters who lived on the Ivory Trail. Perhaps Clary's most notable hunt was the search for a famous elephant known as the "Crown Prince." The Crown Prince was supposedly the same elephant unsuccessfully hunted by the Prince of Wales during his safari with Bror Blixen and Denys Finch Hatton in 1928. The elusive Crown Prince and his giant pair of tusks attracted the best hunters of the day, including two noted Boer ivory hunters, Martinus Nel and P. J. Pretorius, both of whom spent much time and effort on their respective hunts. The Crown Prince was sought by other well-known ivory hunters, including George Rushby, Basil Reel, and Eric Rundgren. But of all these talented hunters Clary Palmer-Wilson was undoubtedly the most single-minded in his pursuit of the Crown Prince.

Clary hunted the Crown Prince continually *for eight years*. One day in Tanganyika's south Masailand, Clary finally caught up with his quarry. On that day he had tracked the Crown Prince for eleven straight hours, and he was afraid nightfall would overtake him before he came up with the elephant. He had been on the tracks since first light, and had been led across the crocodile-infested Ruvu River, then through miles and miles of countless thickets of heavy brush. In a near fever-pitch of excitement, Clary knew that at last he might get a fair shake at the Crown Prince. He had been obsessed with this mighty elephant, dreamed of his magnificent ivory, discussed him, anticipated him, and followed countless tips and leads, and yet while he had been close to his quarry several times over the years, it seemed that something critical had always happened at the last minute to disrupt the hunt, just as it had with Blixen and Finch Hatton.

Twice in the past it had seemed certain Clary would meet up with the great elephant, but the wind had shifted and both times the Crown Prince bolted without Clary ever getting a glimpse of him. Another time a bushbuck had barked in alarm when Clary was within several hundred yards of the elephant and that had spooked him. One time a pesky honeyguide, *Indicator indicator*, simply would not give up chattering above Clary, trying to get him to open a beehive so the little bird could feast on the grubs, and that had been enough warning for the Crown Prince, who knew the chattering bird indicated the presence of man. "I reckon I was within one hundred yards of the Crown Prince that time," Clary said ruefully. "But by God that elephant was clued-up. When I found where he had been feeding and he must have heard that wretched bird, he turned about and took off at a dead run and never stopped, no matter that the brush was so thick you could not see ten yards ahead of you. But I knew his signs as no other man did. I stayed with him for weeks, sleeping on his tracks, drinking in mudholes he had fouled, eating whatever I could find, for my two bearers carried only a little rice, but I never caught him."[3]

Now eleven hours into the present hunt, Clary became more vigilant and increased his pace as, pouring with perspiration, he relentlessly tracked the Crown Prince amid spiked sansevieria and wait-a-bit thorns. The wind held in a soft, warm breeze. There were no birds, no sounds at all. Clary caught the sickly sweet-sweat scent of elephant, and now he felt a surge of excitement as he quickly slipped on his special leather shoes. Then he lay down on the ground listening. He could still smell the Crown Prince, but he could not see him. Clary slithered beneath the undergrowth, leaving his two bearers behind to avoid any additional noise. Crawling, crouching when he could, doubled up, stopping to listen, his eyes remained glued to the faint spoor on the baked black-cotton soil.

Clary continued to stop every now and then to lie on the ground and listen, as he watched carefully for a sign of the Crown Prince's great feet in the gloom of the evening. At last Clary had crawled within fifteen yards of the giant elephant. But as Clary raised up to shoot, the elephant turned momentarily, his ears outspread, suspicious. At that moment Clary fired, dropping his quarry instantly with a side brain shot. The record-class tusks weighed 159 and 143 pounds each, a gigantic elephant whose ivory, while enormous, was far lighter than it had appeared. For Clary it was the end of an impassioned and all-consuming quest, something quite inexplicable to any but a small band of die-hard elephant hunters.

Palmer-Wilson's skill with elephant was matched by his experience with Cape buffalo. "I shot over three hundred buffalo," Clary said, "most of them on my own, without the help of native trackers." Palmer-Wilson enjoyed solo hunting, preferring to use African trackers and gunbearers only when he had overseas clients. Trekking through the African bush by himself, often after dark, Clary learned to navigate by the stars and claimed he was never lost.

In Tanganyika in 1946 Clary created controversy in the professional hunting community because he had obtained the world record buffalo, a cow with a remarkable spread (greatest outside width of horns) of 64 inches. After a huge hullabaloo generated by several professional hunters, Rowland Ward's *Records of Big Game* withdrew his entry from their list, stating a cow buffalo should not be included in the records. Clary told me he thought much of the trouble was professional jealousy. Even though the outcry died down for a while, a number of Clary's friends in the safari business considered Rowland Ward's action so unjust they rose to Clary's defense. Clary himself was above it and refused to get into the discussion. Rowland Ward recanted and reinstated Clary's buffalo in their *Records of Big Game*, where it remains to this day as the outright world record.

Clary Palmer-Wilson's record buffalo was an unexpected trophy. A wealthy Mexican client, Manuel Manterola, had brought with him on safari an interpreter and photographer named Manuel Hernandez Cabrera. Manterola had not allowed this photographer to use a gun to hunt anything. At the end of the safari Cabrera asked Palmer-Wilson to take him out for a few days, even though he was not a rich man and could not pay the usual safari fees. Clary was sympathetic and agreed to take him out for a short hunt.

Cabrera was apparently an indifferent marksman. He wounded a bull buffalo out of a herd of six animals, and when a second shot was offered he fired and hit the wrong buffalo, killing it instantly. Clary was understandably upset by this performance. He went after Cabrera's first buffalo alone and finished it off. With the hunt over, Clary's men were packing tents and equipment when Cabrera begged him for one last chance to film more buffalo. Clary took him into the forest where they came upon a herd of four hundred buffalo. Clary recounted what happened next:

> I said to Cabrera, "Stop the camera. That's the world record buffalo!" I grabbed my .375 and ran right into that herd of 400 buffalo, and dropped the world record with one shot. I ran back to Cabrera, handed him the rifle, and told him to fire a couple of shots well above the herd. When the dust settled, there sat the record buffalo with the herd disappearing into the forest. I took Cabrera up and he put the finishing shot into the buffalo. If I had allowed him even one shot into that herd he would have wounded several animals![4]

After Cabrera left the country Clary was hounded by the press wanting a story about the record buffalo. The animal was a very old cow rather than a bull, and its incredible horn length seemed unbelievable. Clary was questioned closely by colleagues, and he told them exactly what had happened. Later he said, "Several hunters (both professional and amateur) had seen that big buffalo and tried to get it, but nobody had ever succeeded, including Prince Windisch-Graetz (a resident of Kenya) and a grandson of Emperor Franz Joseph of Austria, who hunted that buffalo for three years without getting a shot at it. Every hunter would have given his eye-teeth to get that trophy!"[5]

27

THE ENEMY WITHIN

In 1947 an aristocratic Polish couple joined the safari community in Tanganyika. Laddy Wincza and his wife, Ada, had left their native Poland after the war and set out for Africa to make a new life. They purchased land in the Usambara Mountains near the once busy and thriving German settlement formerly known as Wilhelmstahl (now Lushoto).* Soon after their arrival the unlikely refugees were befriended by Clary Palmer-Wilson. Clary took an immediate liking to the spirited Winczas, and they to him; the three were to remain lifelong friends and hunting companions. Like others with disparate backgrounds in Tanganyika, the couple fitted easily into the multinational expatriate community in that part of Africa.

Captain Wladislaw "Laddy" Wincza's wealthy Polish family's Norman origins were documented back to the fourteenth century. He met his future wife at the University of Vilnius, Poland, where both gained law degrees. Ada's background was similar to Laddy's. Her family had owned vast estates in Poland and Lithuania for over four hundred years. She was Poland's gold medalist rifle shot in college competitions, and, as the country's youngest accredited journalist, she covered the Berlin Olympics in 1936.

The couple was married after Laddy Wincza enlisted in a Polish cavalry regiment as war loomed with Germany.

It is not hard for those who knew Laddy Wincza to believe an incredible story related by Count Franz "Ferry" Meran, who asserted that during the war Laddy was one of the very few survivors of a horseback

---

*Lushoto is now a grimy, crumbling village. The only signs of its once glorious past are the sturdy stone-rag (uncut stone) buildings erected by German colonists.

charge against an advancing German Panzer division as machine guns blazed, cutting down most of Laddy's fellow cavalrymen.

AFTER THE WAR the Winczas' wealth was lost to the communists, but their spirit remained intact. At Lushoto the Winczas built a home on their farm aided only by unskilled labor. Ada then started a pork factory, which flourished with the name Ada's Food Products; she was soon raising more than three thousand pigs commercially and had the largest pork factory in East Africa. Laddy won his professional hunter's license in 1954 after six years' apprenticeship, mostly with Palmer-Wilson. The Winczas' fluency in six languages gave them a head start with European clients.

When Tanganyika became independent in 1961, the Winczas were caught in the wave of nationalization. Just as they had lost everything in Europe, they once again saw their property—this time hard-earned—seized by a socialist government. Laddy and Ada packed what they could into safari vehicles and, with their daughter Eve, headed across the border to Nairobi. Clary Palmer-Wilson would not leave with them, and for the moment neither would Meran. Clary insisted Tanzania was his home and he could not imagine a life anywhere else.

In Kenya, Laddy and Ada Wincza began anew once more. They had long ago made friends in the Kenya hunting community, and their firm, Hunters and Guides, was a success from the start. They hired two full-time hunters, the volatile Kenyan Ian MacDonald and Englishman Steve Smith.

Ian MacDonald had a reputation as the most unpredictable and mercurial member of the hunting fraternity. He was short in stature, both cocky and cocksure, and without regard for his own safety. He stood five feet two inches, was dark-haired and brown-eyed, and although on first acquaintance he looked nondescript, he was in fact a fiery dynamo truly exhilarated by extreme danger. More than anything else Ian got his "high" on high risk.

Laddy and Ada Wincza saw something in MacDonald that many others could not see. They had hunted with Ian and considered him a first-rate bushman. For this ability they took him on, even though his ferocious temper gave them cause for concern. "Ian had an extremely complex nature," the Winczas wrote. "He was a romantic. He loved and appreciated music. He wanted to prove to everybody that he was a he-man, although nobody ever doubted it. He had a subconscious death wish. He was tossed by a buffalo, nearly killed by a lion, and mangled by a leopard. He seemed to provoke animals to charge him. Ian grew to be a very difficult man to get on with and he only felt at ease, and did not show off, in the company of primitive [sic] peoples."[1]

Almost certainly Laddy and Ada are the only people who took the trouble to analyze the gunpowder in Ian MacDonald. They tried to steer clear of MacDonald's nitroglycerine fuse and make use of his better qualities, namely, his great talents as a hunter.

Ian MacDonald had been born at Kenya's Kikambala beach in 1924. Kikambala was a densely jungled region sixteen miles north of Mombasa, lying in a true stronghold of big game between two wide and deep tidal creeks, called Mtwapa and Kilifi. His family built a successful beachcomber hotel in what was then an isolated region. The original MacDonald place consisted of a series of palm-thatched bungalows built with hand-cut coral blocks. It had a restaurant offering exquisite seafood dishes, prawn curries, crab, and lobster served with mangos, paw-paw, and passion fruit. Famous up-country white hunters routinely vacationed there with their families.

There was no doubting Ian MacDonald's natural bush skills, which were highly developed as a child at Kikambala beach. Ian spent his days hunting with Giriama tribesmen, who more or less adopted him. The immense hardwood forests around Kilifi were then teeming with elephant, buffalo, and leopard, and also with an astonishing variety of venomous snakes. By the time he was ten years old, Ian knew the African methods of manufacturing deadly *acokanthera* poison for arrows,* as well as fish poisons.

Ian would often disappear into the coastal forests with his African friends without the permission of his parents, sometimes for weeks at a time, armed only with a sheath knife, bow and arrows, and wearing a

---

*Arrow poisons are derived from three botanical genera: *Acokanthera*, *Strophanthus*, and *Urginea*. The poison is made with thin slices cut from the tree and boiled in water until a sticky black goo is produced. One arrowhead packed with *acokanthera* may have enough poison to kill twenty-five adult humans when absorbed into the bloodstream. Some hunting tribes, such as the Giriama and Liangulu, test the poison by making a small cut in the arm above the elbow to allow a trickle of blood to run to the wrist. Poison is touched on the blood at the wrist. If the poison is good it rapidly coagulates the blood. The bloodied poison is scraped off the arm before it gets to the incision. The flesh of animals killed with *acokanthera* poison can be eaten, except for the area around the arrow wound. There is no known antidote for *acokanthera* poisoning.

pair of short pants. He went barefoot and shirtless and lived just as his tribal friends did—on honey, small antelope, forest berries, and roots. He thought nothing of spending the night in the hollow of a baobab tree or drinking as the Giriama hunters did from elephant-fouled water holes. Ian's family were so concerned about him they sent him to a boarding school in Scotland, where he remained until the outbreak of World War II. As part of the British army, Ian went to the jungles of Burma where he fought in the campaign against the Japanese.

After the war MacDonald returned to Kenya and joined the Kenya police, then was promoted commandant of police at Kajiado, a small outpost in Masailand, where his affinity for the Masai made him extremely popular with the tribe. In 1959 Ian decided to become a white hunter. He apprenticed with Clary Palmer-Wilson and qualified for his unrestricted license. As a hunter for the Winczas it was soon apparent that MacDonald often attracted a certain type of client equally keen on thrills.

Despite Ian's combustible persona, his African safari crews worshipped him, but gave him the name Bwana Kabangi. *Bhang* or *bhangi* is Swahili for marijuana, and to them it seemed his hyperactivity was similar to one who is under the influence of *bhang*. Yet Ian's manic reputation as Bwana Kabangi did not worry him a bit. Perversely, he seemed to relish the non compos mentis allusion his nickname suggested. As if to confirm the assessment, Bwana Kabangi began to drink excessively whenever he was between safaris in Nairobi.

On safari Ian was a hard worker and mostly stayed sober, but his highly erratic temperament made him a difficult companion for the unwary tourist. His adoring African safari crew tactfully learned to abide his turbocharged tantrums. They appreciated his great generosity toward them, as well as his amazing command of their assorted languages. The Africans never tired of Ian's endless, often childish pranks. To them he could be screamingly funny. They simply loved the easily crazed confusion he somehow created, and the chaos of all that followed of which he alone was king.

MacDonald was more responsive to Africans than he was to other Europeans. His own gunbearer, a fearless, exceptionally gifted Liangulu hunter named Singi, had more than once refused to continue a hunt when MacDonald became too extreme, too seemingly suicidal, even for brave Singi's tolerant tastes. Such was MacDonald's respect and affection for the African that their relationship was not damaged in these instances. Singi's bravery was unquestioned and the two worked together for many years. Each hunter was mindful that his life often depended on the skill and reactions of the other.

On one safari in particular, MacDonald and Singi had a bad encounter with a huge leopard that the Masai called Shetani (Devil). MacDonald's Masai friends in the Loliondo area of Tanganyika had told him about Shetani, a big and cunning leopard that frequently killed Masai goats and sheep. Ian baited the leopard, setting a decomposing gazelle carcass in a tree beside a brushy ravine. The hunters did not have long to wait before Shetani hit their bait. So it was that a wary Shetani arrived at the end of the day when the wind rose, and darkness crept across the chilly plains. MacDonald and his client were waiting for Shetani in a blind near the bait tree. The leopard crept into the branches as the sun's last red rays sank behind the Olosha hills. There was not a moment to lose before total darkness set in. Ian's client lined up on the leopard, holding the shadowy form in his cross hairs. It was an indistinct target, but he fired anyway. With a grunt Shetani dropped from the tree, lightly wounded.

MacDonald knew from the way the huge cat reacted after the shot that he had big trouble on his hands. The angry leopard would already be in near impenetrable bush on a very dark night. It was no place to risk a client's neck, and as for his own, well . . . MacDonald did not have a flashlight handy, so he asked Singi to escort the shaken client back to camp and return with a Tilley kerosene lantern. MacDonald sat alone in the darkness listening to the night sounds in the hope that he might be able to detect the leopard's whereabouts. His ears were tuned for the sounds or movements of other animals, such as the rustle of a disturbed bushbuck, the beat of a startled owl's wings, or the shriek of a bush baby. But there was nothing save the dull throb of crickets.

Why Ian MacDonald had no flashlight, even back in camp that night, remains a mystery. He had every reason to believe the leopard was only lightly wounded, and therefore would be full of fight. It was characteristic of Ian that he was so disrespectful of danger to himself, he cared little for rational procedures. But it was almost beyond comprehension that he would be crazy enough to go after a lightly wounded leopard with a loudly hissing kerosene-fueled pressure lantern. The lantern, designed for use as a camp fixture, would not only illuminate the trail but Ian and Singi as well. In this situation a prudent man might postpone the hunt until daybreak in order to even up the chances of getting off a shot before the leopard attacked.

MacDonald loaded his shotgun with SSG buckshot, and with Singi carrying the lantern the two began slowly following a thin, blood-flecked spoor from the base of the bait tree into dense underbrush. The leopard waited until MacDonald and Singi had followed the blood trail into the thickest part of the gully. Ian only became aware of the leopard as it rushed him in a throaty growling charge. From a range of six feet Ian saw the blur as Shetani raced forward close to the ground. MacDonald had been expecting the onslaught, but even so he was surprised by the swiftness of the attack. Ian snapped off his first load of SSG, which hit the leopard in the right front leg. The leopard did not even break stride, but it missed the agile Singi, who was on his hands and knees holding the lantern to see the blood spoor, with Ian crouched beside him. Singi and the light went one way, and the lamp's glass and mantle broke. The lantern now gave off a dull orange glow.

The big cat immediately went for Ian's throat. Ian was wearing a leather flying jacket that gave some protection. The leopard had Ian down in a flash. But MacDonald fought back immediately. He swore and cussed and attacked the growling cat with his bare hands, grabbing it by the throat as Shetani's jaws locked on his forearm. MacDonald was battling the ultimate mangling machine. He was outweighed, out-maneuvered, and almost overpowered. Somehow he got the cat in an armlock stranglehold, hoping to choke it, but the cat went berserk and broke free, sinking its fangs into Ian's arm through the leather jacket, then rapidly biting the other arm. Shetani attacked MacDonald's flailing legs. As the battle raged Ian punched the leopard and the two thrashed about in a bloody melee. A shredded dewclaw from Ian's first shotgun blast had exposed the leopard's tendon like a grappling hook. The claw hooked into the white of MacDonald's left eye. Just then Singi recovered his *panga* (machete). With the broad-bladed *panga* Singi whacked the leopard across its back as it pummeled MacDonald. Even in death the leopard's claw remained gouged in Ian's eye. But that was not the only injury MacDonald suffered. He was ripped, sliced, mauled, and bitten. Fearful of further damage to Ian's eye, Singi, with the help of a Zippo lighter, cut the leopard's tendon, leaving the dewclaw in Ian's eye socket. Then he helped Ian, who was barely able to walk. The pressure lantern still hissed and gave off a weak glow, but it was useless as a light. As the two men struggled through the undergrowth MacDonald reportedly managed a hoarse victory laugh. They reached the hunting car in total darkness. Singi did not drive, so somehow MacDonald managed to drive himself back to camp. In camp Ian radioed his Irish wife,

Conchita, in Nairobi asking for an aircraft to pick him up next day. Then he lay down with a stiff whiskey while his camp headman carefully washed his dreadful wounds with near neat Dettol disinfectant. At Nairobi Hospital surgeons removed the leopard's claw from Ian's eye and patched up his numerous wounds. Miraculously Ian's sight was not lost in the injured eye. Swathed in bandages and wearing an eye patch, MacDonald was hunting again in less than a month.[2]

THE WINCZAS wished MacDonald well when he decided to go it alone with his own outfit, which he called Big Game Safaris, but competition was tough. Despite his skills as a hunter, he was only moderately successful.

Six months after his encounter with Shetani in 1967, Bwana Kabangi would again be blatantly tempting the Grim Reaper. Ian had learned to fly, and had made enough money to buy a single-engine aircraft. It was not long before he was winging his way on solo flights all over game country. One day MacDonald was returning alone from a private billfishing trip to his boyhood haunts at Kikambala beach. Ian flew west along the Athi River to Glen Cottar's Tsavo Tsafaris tourist camp, halfway between Mombasa and Nairobi.

Glen Cottar, grandson of old Bwana Charles Cottar and a good friend of Ian's, made him welcome. Cottar said he and his wife, Pat, pressed Ian to stay the night as their guest, but MacDonald was impatient to go on to Nairobi after lunch. He was in unusually good form, the Cottars said, making funny wisecracks and enjoying the meal.

Ian took off from Cottar's dirt airstrip beside the camp and, circling, zoomed low along the river, his wheels just inches above the water as he waved to the Cottars before he climbed away into the afternoon sun. MacDonald set a course parallel to the Mombasa-Nairobi road. He buzzed old J. A. Hunter's lodge at Kiboko, banked and roared low on another pass, pulling up with his propeller just feet above the acacia trees. Guests spilled out of the lodge to watch MacDonald as he turned and dived at the lawn beside the lily pond J.A. had dammed in the Kiboko River. He was so close to the ground that stunned tourists could see Ian's grinning face. Then MacDonald leveled out, flying at full throttle across the red-dirt flats studded with six-foot-tall antheaps.

Uganda white hunter Erik Andersen had taken delivery of a new Land Rover in Mombasa, and he was "running the car in," keeping the speedometer below 40 mph on the long return drive to Kampala. Andersen watched in amazement as Ian's aircraft skimmed above herds of wildebeest and zebra on the Soysambu plain, between Emali and Sultan Hamud railway stations. At the time Andersen thought, "That plane's flying far too low." It was also flying too close to the main highway. Near a straight stretch of road Ian's aircraft spun into the ground, exploding in a fireball. Bwana Kabangi was killed instantly. The wreckage burned ten yards from the highway.[3]

The Africans had always insisted Kabangi was a real *dume*, Swahili for "fearless macho male." Ian's widow, Conchita MacDonald, commissioned a bronze statue of a buffalo that she donated to the East African Professional Hunter's Association. Known as the MacDonald Trophy, it was awarded annually to the hunter who obtained the best buffalo for a client. MacDonald admired the bravery and ferocity of a buffalo above all animals. They were qualities he himself possessed in abundance.

28.

THE HASSANS OF MOMBASA

In the days when Ikram Hassan became a professional hunter just before the Second World War, only a handful of the legendary white hunters of Africa were from a race other than white European. But among this small collection of hunters were a few men of brown complexion, meaning of Asian (East Indian or Pakistani) heritage who made the grade and became full-fledged "white hunters" in colonial East Africa. Ikram's father, Dr. Syed Gulam Hassan Shah, had been a pioneering veterinary surgeon who arrived in British East Africa in 1905. His veterinary job entailed extensive foot safaris into distant parts of the colony, and he would return to his family with vivid stories of adventure and encounters with big game animals. Despite the fact that their father abhorred killing under any circumstances, Ikram and his two brothers grew up obsessed with the sport of hunting.

When the Hassans settled into a new home in Mombasa, Ikram became a long-distance swimmer and runner, and spent a lot of time hunting with a family friend, an old ivory hunter named Iftakhar Shah. During one of these hunts Ikram's middle brother, Mahmoud, was badly gored by a buffalo. Mahmoud went on to become a noted elephant hunter. As the youngest son, Ikram shocked his parents when they discovered he daily swam across the mouth of Mombasa's old dhow harbor from Fort Jesus on Mombasa island to the coral reef on the northern mainland at English Point, a distance of over half a mile each way. The harbor's mouth often has strong tidal currents, as well as the occasional shark and barracuda. Ikram's father wanted his sons to "get a profession." As soon as Ikram graduated from Mombasa's Alidina Visram High School, he studied at Kabete College to become a veterinarian, but quit after two years to form a safari company.

Ikram Hassan and
trophy black-maned
lion.

In those days Asians sometimes endured racial slights at the hands
of low-echelon British officials in Kenya. Ikram Hassan, for one, could
never be goaded into reacting to lowly white permit-writers. He was the
picture of patience, poise, and culture. Among all in the hunting fraternity he established a reputation as the perfect gentleman, a man who
inspired trust.

In 1947 Ikram's firm, African Hunting Safaris, advertised "Poor
Man's Safaris." He kept his prices 30 percent below any competitor,
saying he would rather hunt than be rich, and if that meant being com-
petitively priced, he would manage it somehow. Ikram's safaris were a
family enterprise, with his wife, Dr. Bilquis Hassan (whom he married
in 1954), a practicing physician, and his handsome sister Razia, a
prominent Muslim social worker, helping out from their splendid
Moorish compound at Mombasa's Tudor Creek. Ikram's safari crew
matched the best in the business, and included two Duruma tribesmen
from the Taita hills named Simba and Rurumu, and Setili, a former
Liangulu ivory poacher. In support was a Giriama hunter named Karisa,
and Zui, a fabulous Kamba tracker. Hassan's African hunters and camp
staff remained with him for life.

Although Ikram kept his safari firm small—he was its only professional employee—he occasionally hired hunters when the need arose.
Hassan's closest friend in the fraternity was Mohammed "Bali" Iqbal,
who was one of the few other successful Asian professionals of the
day. Bali, unlike Hassan, had worked for large safari companies in the

past. But like Hassan, he specialized in big ivory and frequented the same coastal areas Hassan used.

Outwardly Ikram and Bali's differences were profound. Ikram resembled a retiring, abstemious monk, and was in fact a faithful practicing Muslim. He was tall, reed slim, soft-spoken, thoughtful, well-read, and displayed a serious disposition. New acquaintances never suspected his real vocation in life was that of professional hunter. Bali, the black sheep of a prosperous Nairobi trading family, was a most flamboyant character, bespectacled, unkempt and overweight, and known for his raucous laugh. He was a lover of loud jokes—"This place is just like Wimbledon—all balls and rackets!"—jazz, good food, beautiful women, fast cars, racehorses, and fine hunting rifles, together with an unabashed fondness for what he called "good hooch"—Johnnie Walker Black Label being his drink of choice. As a gregarious companion and skillful ivory hunter he was exceedingly popular among his white hunter peers. Yet Ikram and Bali,* both of Pakistani origin, shared an all-consuming love of elephants and elephant hunting, and both maintained some of the best safari camps in Africa.

JUST ABOUT EVERY safari Hassan conducted, and there were a great many of them spanning a forty-five-year career, ended happily. Ikram liked to say that he had never been charged by any animal unless it had been bothered in some way. Even then, he gave the animal the benefit of doubt. "Any animal will charge and attack if it is provoked or is startled," he told one client, "or if a female with young feels threatened." He preached caution, skillful hunting, and good shooting, and went to infinite lengths to make certain no animal was wounded. He liked to stalk close, and wanted his clients to fire from a dead rest when possible.

ONE DAY Ikram was scouting game for a client when he encountered a single cow buffalo in the Maktau hunting area. The buffalo immediately rushed him without provocation. Ikram fired his Mauser 9.3 x 62

---

*Mohammed "Bali" Iqbal was gored by a buffalo at Kibwezi, Kenya, in 1974 and died from complications shortly afterward.

rifle as the buffalo hit him. Stunned by the attack he came to as the buffalo stood over him goring his thighs. In his diary Hassan wrote:

> I noticed that the tips of her horns were very curved, and she could not get them into me. This gave me a world of confidence that no matter what happened I would live. Failing to get the tips of her horns in or under me, it smashed me with its massive head, and trod on me with its hooves. Every time that it tried to crush me I would slither forward and lessen the pressure.
>
> God knows how long it kept on. Suddenly I noticed that I was not being crushed or trampled. So I turned and saw the buffalo standing a few yards off, looking the other way. I thought to myself that, having thought she had killed me, she was now looking for my gunbearer.

The buffalo staggered a few paces, blood on its nostrils. Hassan saw his Mauser lying between himself and the buffalo. Gingerly he reached for it, crawling slowly. The buffalo was five paces away, still looking in the other direction:

> I was sure that it was just feigning disinterest in me so I should make a move. But I had the consolation that it could not do more damage than it already had done. After what seemed ages I at last got my hand on the gun and, getting on my knee, worked the bolt rapidly, but before I could fire the buff tottered and fell over. I got up and put a bullet in the animal's neck and sat down on its shoulder to take stock of my injuries. There were no broken bones, but my whole body was sore from the beating.
>
> By this time the trackers rolled up with big grins on their faces and exclamations of rejoicing that I was still alive. To them it was a big joke. They laughed and imitated the charge of the buffalo. On examination it turned out that some hunter had previously wounded the buffalo in the rump with a small rifle, and failed to get it.[1]

Hassan's nose was broken and bleeding, two teeth were knocked out, and his body pulverized. He was far more seriously hurt than he first thought, for he had bruised kidneys and internal bleeding, which put him in the hospital.

Between client safaris, Ikram and his brothers hunted elephant for themselves. During one elephant hunt Ikram tracked a huge elephant and got it. The tusks weighed 146 and 144 pounds, and the ivory had an 18½-inch circumference at the lip, with the longest tusk 8 feet and 11 inches in length. On the way back to his car fifteen miles away Ikram recalled:

> We ran into Major Kinloch, the administrative officer from Kilifi.* He came to say hello and congratulate me. On meeting him, I found that he had an elephant license, so we went after the big herd, which were still in the vicinity. We followed and as luck would have it we found a second big elephant. The ivory of this elephant came out at 133 and 131½ pounds. The Major can never forget our first proper meeting! That was his best trophy, and it was one of the most unexpected and pleasant little hunts I have had.[2]

The Hassan brothers had been converted to big-bore rifles over the years. Ikram would no longer consider hunting dangerous game with anything smaller than a .470 double rifle. For many years Mahmoud favored a magazine rifle, the powerful .505 Gibbs, but after a bad experience with an elephant he lost confidence in it, gave it away, and stuck to his Belgian-made Rahillon .416 magazine rifle.

One day in 1953 a young English friend of Hassan's, John, who had become interested in big game hunting, begged to be allowed to accompany Ikram the next time he went on safari:

> He came into my office at tea time. He was fond of yarning, and he liked to avail himself of my books and hunting magazines. I mentioned that I was going off elephant hunting for about ten days. John asked if he could come along, as he was terribly keen on hunting a buffalo. I agreed to take him along and help him get a buff. We camped at the foot of Mount Kilimanjaro. John made himself useful around camp and I was rather pleased I had brought him along.

The hunters reconnoitered the country for several days to monitor elephant movements. They also found lots of fresh buffalo spoor:

---

*Major Bruce Kinloch, M.C., 3rd Ghurka Rifles, was chief game warden of Uganda, and later Tanzania and Malawi, and author of *The Shamba Raiders*.

We decided to have a go at them, and we were away at dawn to the plains where the buffalo got down from the hills at night. I advised John to use one of the big elephant guns that I had instead of the .375 that he owned. He was very emphatic about the capability of his small weapon and said that he felt more at home with it than he would with a new weapon. That was in his favor, so I let him use the rifle.

We walked along an elephant road towards the hills in the hope of cutting fresh buffalo signs. Having gone for an hour we came across a herd of buffalo feeding across our front. It was open scattered bush country, and we started stalking to a fallen tree twenty yards away. What we did not at first notice was the herd was spread out and a couple of buffs were to our right. We were in plain sight of them, as they were looking at us curiously. I pointed out a trophy buff to John. He took careful aim and we heard the bullet *thump*, as the buff took off. We followed a bit and found it was a stomach shot. It so happened that at the split second John pressed the trigger the buff had moved. Now there was nothing to do but to follow the buff. I was in the lead with one tracker, and John followed about ten yards behind with the other. We had gone about a mile and had passed through some pretty close-knit bush but the buff had gone through at a gallop, and then across an open plain.

At the end of the plain we came to a patch of grass about two feet high, with a small bush or two. It did not look enough to hide even an antelope. When we were about four paces from a bush, much to our surprise looking at us with his nose held high was the buffalo. I raised my .470 and fired straight at the buff's nose. The bullet threw it back and down. It was up in a split second and in the same moment galloped off and disappeared in the brush. We had been surprised because we expected to find the buff hiding in thick brush, not the scanty cover it had chosen. As the buff was disappearing, John hit the animal again. We started to track, and signs became more hopeful as the buff slowed to a brisk walk instead of a gallop. Another twenty minutes and we heard a commotion in front of us. We rushed up and found three lions scattering to one side and the buff disappearing at a gallop farther along. As we were watching another two lions walked out of the bush, stretched, yawned, and leisurely followed the first two lions, who had by now stopped. The buffalo had blundered onto the sleeping lions and the surprise was mutual, with either party taking off in different directions.

The heat was terrible by now. We set off tracking for two more hours, until we came to a small hill with the tracks going up into the thickets. I felt that the buff would not be going far now, and I warned John to be cautious. Near the top of the hill we noticed a black lump in some bushes twenty yards away. The tracker who was looking down at the tracks started to move on and I touched him on the shoulder and indicated the black mass. He stepped lightly behind me confirming my doubt that the black mass was the buffalo. John had also stopped behind me, and I pointed at the black mass with my chin, wanting him to be ready. Being new to the bush and in the excitement he said, "You sure?" At the question the buff was up. As it got on its feet I fired at its shoulder as it stood quarter-facing us. John also fired simultaneously. The buff charged. There was a thin patch of bush in front of me, and for a moment the buff was out of view. It came into view three paces away, and I again fired my last bullet into its neck. To my amazement the buff did not drop and in those few seconds I knew that I had had it as I did not have time to load. Its head went down to hook me on its horns. As it did I dived to the side avoiding the swing of the horns. I missed the horns but the shoulder of the buff caught me and sent me spinning, knocking the gun out of my hands.

As I fell I noticed a small tree two yards away, but it was only six inches in diameter. I quickly crawled behind the tree on my hands and knees with the thought of avoiding the horns. As I turned the buff also spun around and faced me. I noticed that its lower jaw was hanging down. It was a bloody savage sight, with fierce snorts and broken jaw the buff was wheezing with blood bubbling out of its nose. So I knew it was hit in the lungs as well.

Then the thought flashed that unless John did something my chances seemed pretty slim. Then the stillness was broken by a shot from John. At the shot the buff turned and went after him. As it turned I stood up and noticed John tearing off with the buff after him. I quickly picked up my gun, reloaded, and was running after them. I could not fire as John was always in the way. So I yelled at him to run to one side or lie down so I could fire. I have never seen anyone run so very fast in my life before or since, but then John had a jolly good incentive behind him. When the buff got near him it swiped him with its horns, but John was just one jump ahead of him. The horns touched him and tore his shirt off. Again in desperation I yelled at him to run to one side or lie down. In the second jump that buff tore the backside of his trousers with another swipe. In full stride John swung around a tree. It was a dry tree, and the buff's horns could not avoid it so it hit the tree, which to my amazement came down and knocked John off balance. The buff closed up with the lead it had got by swinging around the tree, and before he could completely get in stride again, the buff caught John and swung him up into the air. In the same second he was up in the air and above the treetops. As he went up I shot into the buff's behind. The bullet travelled all the way up the body. John fell and the buff fell on him.

I yelled at John not to try to get up as that was the safest place. In a moment the buff was up and tried to hook John with its horns. I fired right away at the neck. Again to my amazement the neck was not broken, but the buff jumped towards me and stood facing me. I opened my gun without taking my eyes off him as I was trying to reload from my belt, and at the same time I was backing away.

When I was reloaded, I slowly got on my knee and took deliberate aim. In those few seconds, John had crawled up and took off and disappeared. That was a relief, and the thought flashed that he was not badly hurt after all. The buff turned and started looking for John. Not finding him it started jogging away. This time I aimed at the root of the tail and fired. The shot at last knocked it over and the buff gave its death bellow. Just the same I went to one side and put another shot in the head.

After some time John ambled up in rags, holding his side. His stomach had been torn near the hip. Fortunately the horn had gone in and caught near the hipbone in a curve and had only punctured the stomach wall. We skinned the buff head and brought John back. In a few weeks he was nearly good as new but a wiser sportsman. Now he wanted to carry the heaviest weapon he could get his hands on!

On examination we found that the buff had shots in the shoulder, lungs, badly raking shots, and its neck vertebrae was completely smashed to the extent that the [spinal] cord was visible, but somehow it still held together. Theoretically the very first shot which broke its jaw, smashed part of the neckbone, and went into the body should have killed it. In practice it is always otherwise. That is why hunting is such a fascinating sport.[3]

29

AFRICAN ODYSSEY

In Tanganyika during the 1950s one of the most intriguing reputations belonged to a hunter whom few in the fraternity had actually encountered face to face. He was a true nomad, an elusive rolling stone. Jorge Alves DeLima Filho is a Brazilian, a man possessed of both leading-man good looks and Latin charm. The erudite DeLima is as polished as a prize pistol. He stands well over six feet tall, with dark eyes and a broad mustache. His imposing physical appearance and chiseled features are softened by a ready smile and eager enthusiasm. A cosmopolitan world traveler, Jorge speaks English with only a trace of an accent. In conversation he can slip seamlessly into Italian, French, Spanish, or Portuguese. His adventurous years in the heart and vitals of Africa have also left him fluent in more than a dozen African dialects.

DeLima roamed the whole of Africa, incessantly on the move, unable to settle down or stay in one place for long. Jorge mostly preferred to hunt alone. The man genuinely lived to hunt, and he would rather do that than eat or sleep, drink or flirt. His flirtations at that time were mostly with the great continent, Mother Africa herself, the true love of his life.

DeLima traveled with a couple of battered safari vehicles, carrying with him only the barest essential equipment and several trusted African safari hands. Neither distance nor time meant anything to him. Jorge hunted all of East Africa, North Africa's deserts, Sudan and its mighty sudd swamps, all of Central Africa, most of West Africa, and all of South Africa. And in between he explored Mozambique and Angola, and the Rhodesias as well. He hunted Bechuanaland long before it became Botswana, and long before any of the Kenya hunters moved there and made it a fashionable place to hunt.

There has never been a hunter anywhere in Africa at any time who

Jorge DeLima with a Barotseland lion.

has even come close to matching his exploits in so many different territories, although there may be two or three who lay dubious claim to
such enterprises. DeLima did not merely visit a country or area for a
few days or weeks, so that he might include it on his résumé—indeed,
he was often there for months at a time, or in some cases years, until he
knew the place thoroughly, scouring the remotest corners on foot,
dugout, or with his old hunting car.

DeLima made a living exclusively out of hunting. With his fine education, aristocratic appearance, and patrician manners, DeLima mixed
easily with the upper strata of European and American society. Yet in
those days he rarely accepted client safaris. He made his way mostly by
selling the ivory he hunted in the days when that could, with some
ingenuity, still be done legally.

GEORGE, as he was known to the primarily English-speaking hunters
of East Africa, was thirty years old in 1956. That year he once again
turned up in Arusha, this time with a couple of lion skins he had shot in
Barotseland.* They were the most magnificent black-maned specimens
his colleagues had ever seen.

---

*Barotseland formed the most westerly section of then Northern Rhodesia (now Zambia)
that was bounded by the Cuando (Kwando) and Zambezi rivers on the south and by

At the Safari Hotel where he often stayed, DeLima liked to meet up with old friends. One evening he produced a battered Michelin map of Africa and pointed out the places where he had most recently found big elephant. "Here, and here, and here is a good place. I got a big one here!" he said pointing to a spot in Angola, and to another in the Congolese rain forests several thousand miles to the north. He once asked, "Why don't you come with me?" I wished that I could, but I had commitments with the safari company that employed me. I've had regrets ever since. DeLima's modest and plainspoken accounts of his life in unexplored terrain were enough to stir the soul of any adventurer:

> I disembarked in Africa for the first time, in what was known as French Equatorial Africa, in 1946. The capital, Bangui, was just a large village, and hyenas and leopards stalked freely in the town, and good tuskers could be shot not more than thirty miles from what is today the capital of a country.
>
> This colony was then made up of various areas which today are countries, such as Central African Republic, Gabon, Chad, Middle Congo, etc. In Moyen Congo I did a lot of shooting sometimes just myself, sometimes with clients. There was lots of game, forest elephant, the *cyclotis* type, dwarf buffalo, bongo, forest pig etc. All these could be hunted along the Bayanga-Sanga River, an area of tremendous heat, insect life, and very dense forests with lots of pygmies. In those times you could take out hunting licenses in the name of European residents, and shoot a lot of elephant on their behalf. I moved from Bangassou onwards on foot and shot for more than six months in the area of Obo-Yubo that embraced three different territories at that time— French Equatorial Africa, Belgian Congo, and the Anglo-Egyptian Sudan. I shot exclusively for ivory, and just a few animals for the pot. I got about eighty tusks and a good number carrying 70 kilos [150 pounds] of ivory on both tusks. I shot some lion for sport which rarely had a fair mane and were not of very outstanding size. Leopards were common and many were bagged off elephant carcasses.
>
> The tusks and skins were mostly sold in Bangui to the Arabs which took them to be sold in Nigeria. Around Bangui, off season,

---

Portuguese territory on the north and west. There were no European settlements in Barotseland. Mongu was the main station, and Lealui the residence of the Barotse chief.

we used to shoot many buffalo, and also there were good elephant in the area with very decent tusks, and the meat [buffalo and elephant] was bought by the D.C.'s for feeding the natives. From Bangui, today's capital of Central African Republic, we used to cross the Ubangi Chari River into the Belgian Congo where elephants were extremely numerous. In the late forties I shot for ivory in Angola. I once sent two lorries into Kenya with heavy ivory in 1955. Dear old Johnny Raw of Rowland Ward sold these tusks.

I went to Mozambique where I shot a lot of buffalo for the Sewa Sugar Company near Beira. It was not uncommon to meet herds of over six hundred animals in the plains of Marromen. These herds were so compact that they could hardly go faster than a slow gallop and one could easily on foot kill more than three or four buffalo a day. Lions were plentiful and you could meet them in the plains without having the necessity to resort to baits.

I shot in many parts of Mozambique, making for six months my headquarters at the junction of the Lugenda and Rovuma rivers, being the border between Mozambique and Tanganyika.

I hunted a lot in the Semliki Valley, also in the Lake Albert–Lake Edward regions [in Uganda] and in the vicinity of Beni and Bunia [in the Belgian Congo] where elephants were abundant as flies.

The enormous flat plains around Mungo [in Angola] were a true paradise for lion (splendid manes), kudu found in large herds on the plains, buffalo, and colossal herds of red lechwe.

The largest elephant I shot in body size, with front footprints reaching 60 cms. [23½ inches], could be encountered in this part of Africa. The tusks were short and heavy. Though I have shot elephant and made a good average, the heaviest I got in Angola was 44 and 46 kilos [96.8 and 101.2 pounds]. I obtained very beautiful and long tusks in the Bunia [Congo]. They were long, and six feet in length was not rare, but rarely have I shot anything over 25 kilos [55 pounds] in that area.

As far as rhino is concerned the best horns I and my clients shot came from southern Angola. With patience horns of between 60 and 75 cms. [29¼ inches] were not difficult to find, and very thick and heavy ones.

Because of the low temperature in the area during the dry

season around my camp near Mavinga, one could meet with splendid large lions, some with magnificent manes, and leopards were plentiful and were large with brilliant coats.

In French Africa, as well as in the sand areas of Angola and northern Mozambique, most hunting and moving around had to be done on foot in the forties.[1]

BY THE 1950S DeLima found that new regulations forced changes in his nomadic lifestyle. Jorge explained, "In the early fifties I abandoned ivory shooting because of the limitations and severe restrictions on elephant hunting, and commenced the so-called hunting safaris with clients, mostly from Brazil and Italy." The altered modus operandi meant DeLima now traveled with modern vehicles and luxurious equipment, and was subject to the whims of clients and time restraints. The biggest sacrifice was the loss of freedom to go places as the spirit moved him. George recalled:

Our area, the Mavinga Concession, was in the southwest part of Angola, and we also took our safaris into Barotseland across the river. We used to cross our vehicles on very crude rafts. In my last year in Africa I had two partners, Baron von Alvensleben and M. de Abreu, with a large outfit in Mozambique, Mozambique Safariland, which attracted famous sportsmen from all over the world. I used to take clients into Angola who were looking for good sable, lion, and rhino, and then fly to Mozambique with the same clients for good buffalo, nyala, and also elephant.[2]

For Jorge Alves DeLima Filho it had been a long, adventurous, and mostly happy love affair with the great continent. But the end, when it did come, was quick, costly, emotionally devastating, and violent, too. The affair still rankles deeply. George wrote:

Though away from Africa it brings me a lot of emotion and profound frustration when these lands are mentioned, where, if you still remember, I had an association with Stan Lawrence-Brown in Tanganyika. I established myself with a vast hunting concession in Angola. I operated there until the end of 1969, when just five days after my leaving the base camp in Mavinga, the camp was attacked by terrorists who killed most of my servants, destroyed all of my camp, and set all my vehicles on fire, the loss being total. I knew that the end of the Africa I had known had arrived. It was useless to try to recuperate things for a fresh start. When we are young we know that old age will come, and Africa was the same thing, one day it would vanish, but 40–50 years ago it was such a remote possibility that we all clinged to "her" without thinking that in a future not so far from then, things would take such a course so melancholic and sad and depressive in such a short period of time. Occasionally, very rarely indeed, I have seen on TV, Nairobi with all these modern buildings and the sight shocks me. I would never return to this Africa. I do desire to keep until I am gone the old image of it.

Since I left Africa, though I have had two very happy marriages, to tell you the truth, I have never recuperated myself, and a state of sadness and fixed residence of Africa is in my soul, and I feel no great enthusiasm towards life as I used to enjoy before. The various and different stages through which Africa passed before can only be properly understood by men who have had the privilege to lead that marvelous life with desirable emotions and a sensation of well-being.

Although I lost all material things I worked so hard to obtain with the terrorist attack to my camp, I left my *soul* in Africa and *joie de vivre*.[3]

30

THE MESSAGE OF MAU MAU

During the early 1950s safari activities in Kenya were interrupted as the country was gripped by the political and social unrest that was to escalate into the Mau Mau rebellion. As the first rumblings for independence were heard in the British East African possessions of Kenya, Uganda, and Tanzania, the territories all experienced incidents of social tensions among their African inhabitants. Of the triad states it was only in Kenya that the political currents intensified into sustained violence. The Mau Mau Emergency, as it came to be referred to by the local citizenry, would touch the lives and businesses of everybody living in Kenya during those tumultuous years.

The origins and strengths of the uprising lay within the Kikuyu tribe of central Kenya. The Mau Mau movement began as a secret and subversive political society whose main objective was to liberate Kenya from colonial rule. Among the British East African territories, Kenya had been designated a Crown Colony, and unlike Uganda and Tanganyika, European settlement was actively encouraged by the Colonial Office in London. Kenya had always been most favored for European (white or non-African) settlement because it was thought to have a more favorable highland climate, better suited to the European. By the early 1950s, 57,700 Europeans of all nationalities and 151,000 East Indians and Pakistanis lived among 5,902,000 Africans in Kenya.

Kenya's lush highlands north and west of Nairobi were referred to as the White Highlands because they formed a strong nucleus of white settlement, almost all of it spread over a vast area in the form of big agricultural enterprises, which occupied the most desirable farmland.

The Kikuyu are the country's largest and most powerful tribe. Historically they had inhabited many of the highland areas later so productively farmed by Kenya's European settlers. A progressive and agricultural people, the Kikuyu were determined to regain possession of their country's fertile farmland and to exercise control over their own destiny, using whatever means necessary. The Mau Mau called themselves freedom fighters. The British government branded them as nothing less than terrorists.

As the Mau Mau movement gathered momentum, African unrest spread both in the city and in the countryside. Insurgent gangs adopted increasingly violent and bloody tactics in their campaign to accelerate the departure of the British government and the European settler population. In hit-and-run guerilla attacks, the elusive Mau Mau would strike in the night, brutally attacking isolated settlers in rural farmhouses. Armed gangs committed unspeakable atrocities upon human beings, including children. Domestic farm livestock and household pets suffered savage mutilations. The Mau Mau had a clear message to deliver: Kenya belonged to the Africans, and they would wage a war of terror until Kenya was a free country. The British, for their part, made it equally clear that they would take all necessary steps to maintain security and enforce law and order.

On October 20, 1952, the British government proclaimed a state of emergency in Kenya. Seemingly overnight, barbed-wire barricades appeared throughout the city to protect sensitive and strategic areas. Armed sentries were posted to patrol police stations, law courts, and the radio broadcasting station in Nairobi. Every European resident of military age was called up to serve in either the Kenya Regiment (KENREG), the Kenya Police Reserve (KPR), the General Service Unit (GSU), or one of the other more specialized security force units. Not even those in important civilian jobs were spared.

Former hunter turned game warden Colonel Mervyn Cowie, founder and director of Kenya's national parks, was appointed by the British government to a new position known as Director of European Manpower in the fight against the Mau Mau. At the same time Cowie tried to keep an eye on the national parks he had created, but his new job was also extremely demanding. In certain areas, a dawn to dusk curfew was imposed on African residents. Mau Mau suspects were rounded up and detained at camps dotted around the country where they were screened and interrogated for Mau Mau activities. In a short time one camp alone, located at Manyani on the Mombasa road, held eighteen thousand Mau Mau prisoners.

◇

THROUGHOUT the latter months of 1952 and early 1953 the Mau Mau took the offensive with a series of deadly attacks on isolated European farmhouses as well as African villages thought to be loyal to the colonial government. The first spate of brutal murders of settler families galvanized Kenya, because the victims were known for their selfless kindness toward Africans.

Eric Bowker was a fifty-year-old retired British army officer who lived alone and farmed in a remote part of the highlands. Bowker's employees later said he was greatly admired and respected. Bowker was unusual in that unlike almost every settler in Kenya he kept no firearms. It turned out that some of his farmhands were Mau Mau, and on October 28, 1952, they stormed his house and slashed his two Kikuyu house servants to death with *pangas* (machetes). Bowker was taking a bath at the time and the gang chopped him to pieces in the bathtub.

The elderly Meiklejohns farmed wheat in the highlands near Thomson's Falls. Kindly Commander Ian "Jock" Meiklejohn had retired from the Royal Navy. His wife was a retired physician who operated a free medical clinic for Africans on their farm, as well as a free school and other benevolent services. In November 1952 a gang of five Mau Mau that included their own house servant burst into the Meiklejohns' house and slashed them with *pangas* as they sat at dinner. The couple were terribly mutilated and left for dead. After the gang ransacked the house and departed, Mrs. Meiklejohn thought her husband was dead, but somehow she made it to her car and, bleeding profusely, drove ten miles to Thomson's Falls police station where she collapsed. When police arrived at the farm they found Jock Meiklejohn trying to assemble a shotgun, although he was mortally slashed. He died next day in the hospital, although his wife survived. The director of manpower, Mervyn Cowie, wasted no time in organizing a band of white hunters and game wardens that successfully tracked down Meiklejohn's murderers and shot them.

The violence was by no means directed only at white settlers. Four days after the Meiklejohn attack, Tom Mbotela, a moderate Nairobi city councilman who had once been vice president of the Kenya African Union (KAU), was murdered. Mbotela had left the KAU after it was dominated by Jomo Kenyatta and his more revolutionary-minded group, for he felt the organization had become too extreme for his tastes. Tom Mbotela had recently survived two assassination attempts, but the third succeeded. The councillor was jumped by a gang in a Nairobi street as he walked home after a council meeting without his usual bodyguard. Tom was stabbed in the neck, and his arms were slashed off.

Another British settler family, Roger and Dr. Esme Ruck, lived on a remote farm on the Kinangop, a vast moorland reminiscent of the Scottish Highlands, lying west of the Aberdare Mountains. The Rucks were young, attractive, and well liked, particularly by the Kikuyu tribe, whom they had befriended. At Christmas they distributed toys to Kikuyu children, and Dr. Ruck, like Dr. Meiklejohn, had a free medical clinic for Africans on her farm.

On January 24, 1953, a Mau Mau gang waited in ambush on the verandah of the Rucks' lonely farmhouse. A horse groom, Mbogo, and a tractor driver, Gitahi, called out to Roger Ruck that they had captured a stranger. Ruck went outside to see what was happening and was cut down by the gang waiting for him on his verandah. Esme Ruck grabbed a shotgun and stepped outside to help her fallen husband, and she was immediately cut down. The gang found the Rucks' six-year-old son hiding under a bed. They dragged the terrified child out and slashed him with *pangas*.

More than any other event in the early days of the Mau Mau, the Ruck murders ignited supremely hostile sentiments among white settlers. There was outrage that the Mau Mau had murdered another family known for their affinity with Africans, and because six-year-old Michael Ruck had been brutally dismembered. Three days after the murders fifteen hundred armed and angry settlers marched on Government House in Nairobi making vociferous demands for the government to deal with the Mau Mau and wipe them out. The police had got wind of the demonstration, and police units as well as a guard of King's African Rifles were posted at the gates to Government House. The settlers were in no mood to be detained and swept past the guard and up the 300-yard driveway. The commissioner of police, M. S. O'Rorke, and a cordon of brave white police officers with arms linked held them back at the steps leading to the main doors. The well-armed settlers gave vent to their frustration with a shouting match denouncing the governor and the government's inability to handle the crisis.

The governor, Sir Evelyn Baring, who was unpopular with settlers at the best of times, refused to grant them an audience or hear their grievances. Just the same, Baring could hardly ignore the settlers' discontent. He well knew there were hotheads among them, and anything might happen. Outspoken criticism of the government was a tradition in colonial Kenya. But it most often came from a small fringe of up-country "extremists." Most white up-country farmers were known for three things—their incredibly generous hospitality, their quick tempers, and their even quicker trigger fingers. But it was not lost on Baring that this demonstration had been staged by normally much better behaved Nairobi citizens.

The next day British Major-General W. R. N. "Looney" Hinde (so nicknamed because it was said in battle his courage was that of a madman) arrived from Cyprus to take charge of the military. Hinde had been a Desert Rat who had fought Rommel, and he proved to be immensely popular with Kenya settlers.

DURING THE bitter offensives launched by the Mau Mau they were sometimes unpleasantly surprised. Mrs. Kitty Hesselberger and Mrs. Raynes Simpson owned a farm near Nyeri. The two women knew they were perceived as easy Mau Mau targets and prepared themselves accordingly. Both were excellent shots with pistol, rifle, or shotgun, and they practiced routines in the event of an attack and also had searchlights along with a siren mounted on the roof of their house. Both women were surprisingly alert and always faced the door at meals. As a matter of habit Kitty kept her pistol drawn and close to hand on the arm of her sofa as they listened to the evening news on a radio. One night, both women noticed the house servant seemed nervous, and Raynes Simpson positioned herself on another sofa facing the door. Kitty asked the house servant what was wrong, and at that moment the Mau Mau came crashing through the door. Raynes Simpson dropped the leader with a shot to the head as he rushed her with a *panga*. A second man almost reached Kitty as Raynes hit him, then fired again, unfortunately missing the man as he fell, but killing their only ally, a boxer dog. By then Kitty, a good bird hunter, had brought her shotgun into the battle and opened up on the gang as they clambered to get out of the house, followed by a hail of lead. The final tally was three dead Mau Mau, and from the prolific blood trail at least one was winged and got away.

◇

WHITE HUNTERS of military age were among able-bodied men called up to serve in the security forces of the colony. Most were forced to put safaris on hold for the duration of the Emergency. Some of the older hunters continued to lead safaris, although travel through much of the country became difficult or impossible.

The graphic horrors of the Mau Mau rebellion in Africa soon appeared in newspaper headlines around the world, and came to personify the savage peril of the Dark Continent. Vivid accounts of murders and mayhem in Kenya made dramatic and portentous reading, even for sophisticated international sportsmen. The most intrepid outdoorsmen, accustomed to facing life-threatening charges from lion and elephant, thought twice before tangling with the fearsome Mau Mau.

Almost every male and female European resident over the age of sixteen openly wore holstered handguns around the clock, both in towns and in rural areas. Men who usually dressed in bush jackets, safari shirts, and wide-brimmed terai bush hats now wore military camouflage or khaki uniforms topped by berets. The British wasted little time in displaying their military might. Overseas troops appeared on the streets of downtown Nairobi. The military presence was meant to be visible, and Sir Evelyn Baring conducted his inspections of newly arrived British and Scottish regiments during parades on Delamere Avenue in the center of Kenya's capital.* Shiny black prison trucks known as Black Marias became a familiar sight on the roadways as suspected terrorists were transported to interrogation facilities in the Nairobi suburb of Langata.

British troops that arrived in Africa sometimes had scant preparation for the guerilla war being waged high in the difficult terrain of Kenya's cold upland forests. One of the first battalions of five hundred men to arrive in Kenya was the Lancashire Fusiliers, which had been trained to fight in the Sahara Desert and came equipped for that climate and

---

*British regiments in Kenya in full battalion strength were: 1st Battalion, The Black Watch, Cameron Highlanders, Devonshire Regiment, Inniskilling Fusiliers, King's Shropshire Light Infantry, Royal Irish Fusiliers, Royal Northumberland Fusiliers, King's Own Yorkshire Light Infantry, Gloucestershire Regiment, 39th Corps Engineer Regiment, The Buffs, and The Rifle Brigade. They fought alongside units of the King's African Rifles, including the 6th and 26th Tanganyika Battalions K.A.R., 4th Uganda Battalion K.A.R., and 3rd, 5th, and 23rd Kenya Battalions K.A.R., supported by the East African Armored Car Squadron (the Reccies).

topography. Old Kenya settler-soldiers fired scathing verbal broadsides at this unfortunate unit, which became notorious for its inefficiency and mostly poor officer structure.* Even seasoned British regiments flown in from Malaya had little relevant experience, and their tropical jungle dress was quite unsuitable for the frigid Kenya highlands.

The Kenya Regiment worked closely with the Kenya Police Reserve and its Tracker Dog Sections. This regiment was a proud local militia with a history and reputation for valor, but was mostly commanded by English officers seconded from crack British regiments such as the Coldstream Guards. The Reg, as it was known, was made up of four hundred settlers, white hunters, game wardens, and local businessmen, most of whom knew the country and spoke Swahili. Some Kenya troops were attached to British forces in the role of guides, trackers, and advisers.

SHORTLY AFTER declaration of the Mau Mau Emergency, authority for the control of civilian arms was vested in the police. The old Central Arms Registry, which controlled the licensing of guns, was replaced by the Central Firearms Bureau (CFB) in November 1953. The new bureau was zealous in the extreme and staffed by chair-bound British officers, virtually none of whom could have held down the most mundane job in the real world. Hunters as well as ordinary citizens were forced to license guns and use police-approved gun safes. A firearms officer was empowered to arbitrarily deny or issue gun permits as he saw fit, and this authority was sometimes greatly abused. The death penalty was introduced for illegal possession of weapons or ammunition. The first death sentences were carried out when a KAR corporal and a Kikuyu cook were hanged for allegedly selling ammunition to terrorists.

It soon became apparent the Mau Mau had been stockpiling weapons for some time in preparation for an armed uprising. Back in 1950 a theft of 32,000 rounds of .22 ammunition had occurred at Gilgil Depot, a regional firearms depository of the British government. A month later 40,000 rounds disappeared.

On March 26, 1953, a Mau Mau gang of forty under the command of self-styled "General" Dedan Kimathi pulled off the most spectacular gun raid to date. They brazenly drove up to the Naivasha police station

---

*In World War I during the Gallipoli landings at W Beach, at great cost the Lancashire Fusiliers won a record six Victoria Crosses for outstanding bravery.

in two trucks, overpowered the guard, and stole 47 weapons, including automatics, and 3,780 rounds of ammunition as they released African prisoners. In the process they killed one prisoner and three African policemen, beheading one of them. The Mau Mau had been armed with only three rifles and three grenades, along with knives and *pangas*. The same night another Mau Mau gang attacked a small Kikuyu village called Lari. The Lari Massacre, as it became known, shocked Kenyans of all races by its sheer brutality. Lari was a village inhabited only by Kikuyu, yet over one hundred defenseless men, women, and children were butchered by members of their own tribe. The victims were decapitated, disemboweled, mutilated, and pregnant women had their stomachs slit open. Domestic animals including cattle were hamstrung, often with the back legs chopped off.

The armed struggle between the British government and Mau Mau insurgents became increasingly deadly as the confrontation escalated into a knock-down, no-holds-barred bloody bush war. The Mau Mau were resourceful fighters. What they couldn't steal, they manufactured with whatever limited materials were available to them. From their crude camps deep inside the forests, the Mau Mau constructed homemade weapons, usually consisting of a piece of iron pipe attached to a rough wooden stock. The bolt was a sharpened door bolt held back by a spring, or sometimes even by rubber bands. The cartridge was wedged into the barrel and a primitive trigger arrangement released the sharpened bolt. Such weapons were often as dangerous to the shooter, or anyone nearby, as they were to the intended victim.*

THE HIGH-ALTITUDE forests of Kenya's central highlands were the primary sanctuary of the Mau Mau movement, but the Mau Mau did not reside only within such secluded hideouts. Many insurgents lived and worked openly among the Europeans by day. A number of sympathizers held domestic positions as cooks, house servants, or gardeners and resided undetected in their employer's household compound. During the dark of night the gangs would assemble to strike with no warning. By first morning light the Mau Mau would disperse, dissolving back into the refuge of the forests or fading into the anonymous crowds of African townships.

---

*Thirty-six hundred homemade Mau Mau weapons were recovered, according to the British government's official Corfield Report.

Not all Kikuyu by any means accepted murder and terrorism as the method of securing reforms. Many of those known as "loyal" Kikuyu were steadfastly against the terror and brutality of the gangs, but those who attempted to remain apart from the conflict were sometimes forcibly recruited into Mau Mau and made to undergo loathsome "oathing" ceremonies. Among the often deeply superstitious Africans, the administration of powerful secret oaths, bolstered by threats of violence, was enough to induce practically any act of complicity or violence against whites or even against nonconforming fellow Kikuyu or other tribes. Some of the most heinous crimes were committed against those Europeans who outwardly appeared to have the best of relations with the Kikuyu. Indeed, some of the earliest targets were selfless missionaries living in isolated areas whose sole reason for being in Africa was to provide health and educational assistance to the African people. Mau Mau retribution was always brutal, and often random and senseless.

The secrecy and covert nature of the Mau Mau fostered an atmosphere of suspicion between Kenya's diverse racial groups. For the first time Europeans looked upon Africans with uncertainty, even fear. The loyalty of most Africans in general, and Kikuyu in particular, became suspect.

IN NAIROBI the face of the enemy, sometimes real, often imagined, was seen everywhere in the multitude of passing faces. Security forces who were charged with singling out Mau Mau among hundreds of thousands of ordinary law-abiding citizens in Kenya's capital city often had little to go on other than their instinctive feelings. In such instances the local forces who knew the ways of Africa and Africans, and could converse in African dialects, held a distinct advantage over their British counterparts.

On one occasion a well-armed gang of five murderous thugs had been wreaking havoc among residents of a Nairobi suburb. White hunter Bryan Coleman was among the security forces called together on a stormy evening at the Muthaiga police station to hear a detailed briefing about the terrorists. Like everybody in the armed forces at that time, Coleman wore a revolver and usually also carried a Sten or Patchett submachine gun as well. When he later went off duty that night, Coleman hurriedly discarded his khaki police tunic and short pants for civilian clothes, and mounted his Harley-Davidson motorcycle as he headed for home. Because of the cold rain, he happened to be wearing the full-length navy wool greatcoat of the Kenya police.

Coleman had not traveled far in the darkness when he saw a Ford Zephyr car with five African men in it. His sixth sense kicked in, and he leapt into action. "I instinctively knew it was *them*," Bryan later commented. "I don't know how I knew, but I just *knew*." He swung his big motorcycle into a U-turn and roared after the Ford. In the heavy downpour Coleman drew alongside the Ford, and reached for the Smith & Wesson .38 that was usually holstered at his thigh. The .38 was not there. Coleman froze. It was then that he recalled unstrapping his Sam Browne belt and revolver holster as he changed clothes. His Sten gun had also been left behind. As he roared along in tandem with the speeding Ford, Bryan could see the faces of the armed Mau Mau. It was too late to back off, so Coleman reached over and smashed his fist against the suspects' car window, signaling with all the ferocity he could muster for the vehicle to pull over. For better or worse, they did.

Coleman's sharp instincts, developed during other types of pursuit, had been correct. The occupants of the car were the same dangerous terrorists who had been the subject of the police briefing. Coleman later recalled, "I kept one hand under my greatcoat, as if I was holding a gun. I told them to drive to Muthaiga police station, and I would ride along beside them. I said if there was any monkey business I would shoot the lot of them." To his amazement the gangsters, perhaps awed at his command of the Kikuyu language, or perhaps because they figured the lone motorcyclist must have some angle or reinforcements they did not know about, promptly went with him, docilely marching into the police station with their hands above their heads.

"It was unbelievable," Bryan said, relieved, "because they were armed to the teeth with automatic weapons." In retrospect Coleman chuckled as he recalled the episode. "And that little affair was the *only* time anybody in the police commended me for *anything*!"

LONG-STANDING relations and friendships between blacks and whites in Kenya were often poisoned by the hate of Mau Mau. Individuals of different races who had lived in harmony for years now found themselves pressured to join one camp or the other. White hunter Mike Hissey was one of those astonished to find that one of his most trusted African employees was a Mau Mau. In the 1950s, his experience was all too common. For Hissey and others, the failure to detect a sympathizer could have deadly consequences.

Mike Hissey was originally from England and had been drawn to Kenya by his love of hunting. He worked diligently to carve a flourishing wheat and cattle farm out of virgin bush on the slopes of Mount Elgon in western Kenya, 250 miles from Nairobi. The area was full of elephant and buffalo, and provided a challenging life for a hunter. Hissey had great affection for Africa and for its indigenous peoples. Although his region was not heavily infiltrated by Mau Mau, Mike, as a loyal resident, joined the Kenya Police Reserve to aid government forces in restoring security. Ironically, it was the absolute trust Hissey placed in his African employees that nearly cost his life and the lives of his family. Looking back on those times Mike recalled:

> We only had one Kikuyu working on the farm and he was my head mechanic. His name was Wilfred Kamau. One day a truck-load of police arrived at the farm and picked up Wilfred and eight tractor drivers and took them off to Kitale for questioning. The eight drivers were from assorted tribes, like Jaluo, Kitosh, and Kipsigis. I met the CID [Criminal Investigation Department] chief and he told me that both my family and myself were very lucky because we were due to be murdered the following Friday night. Wilfred was the local Mau Mau Oath Administrator and Treasurer.
>
> But Wilfred was also lucky, because two weeks after his arrest a law was passed to hang all Oath Givers. Instead he was sentenced to life imprisonment and sent to an island off Kisumu [in Lake Victoria]. The tractor drivers were given seven years in jail.[1]

Hissey had always had a friendly relationship with Wilfred, the Mau Mau oather, just as he had with all his employees. The Africans fondly called him Bwana Hiss because they seemed unable to pronounce Hissey. Mike went to the police cells to visit and question Wilfred. To Mike's surprise Wilfred matter-of-factly admitted that Mike, his wife, and children *had* been targeted for murder. With no apparent rancor, Wilfred agreed that only the police raid had foiled the bloodthirsty scheme.

The message of Mau Mau had been delivered. No one in Kenya was safe.

31

HEARTS OF DARKNESS

The headquarters and main refuge for Mau Mau operations lay within Kenya's own hearts of darkness, well hidden beneath the shadowy forest cover of the Aberdare Mountains and Mount Kenya. White hunters found themselves much in demand for service in fighting units. Those with specialized knowledge of the highlands were called upon to head tracker teams. These teams patrolled at altitudes between 5,000 and sometimes above 10,000 feet in lichen-festooned forests, often in freezing rain and mist. Their survival skills in hostile terrain often exceeded that of the Mau Mau themselves. Professional hunters often brought with them their African trackers and gunbearers, some of whom were loyal Kikuyu or Kikuyu D'robo. These trackers provided invaluable assistance in deciphering the faintest of clues found on the sodden, leaf-covered jungle pathways.

Ker and Downey's Bill Ryan and his famous peacetime tracker, a Turkana tribesman named Konduki, also worked together during the Emergency. Bill, who grew up among the Laikipia D'robo hunters and spoke eight languages, including faultless Kikuyu, was posted as an adviser and interpreter to British troops. One day Bill and Konduki were driving in a Land Rover along a forest track and, rounding a tight corner in the jungle, came to a crude roadblock. As their vehicle came to a halt, the two men simultaneously realized they had been set up for an ambush. Both immediately threw open the car's doors and dived into brush beside the road, fully expecting a hail of automatic fire to rip into the car. Nothing happened. There was no fire, and no sound.

A few days later Bill was interrogating captured Mau Mau thought to have set the ambush. In Kikuyu he asked them why they had not shot

Bill Ryan and famous tracker Konduki, after escaping a Mau Mau ambush.

him. Their reply was, "God said—better not. We don't kill our friends, white or black!"[1]

Bill Ryan and Konduki were sometimes attached to tracker teams, for in addition to tracking Mau Mau gangs, teams were often sent to recover stolen livestock. Ryan and Konduki were in their element at this type of work.

No. 1 tracker team was led by white hunter Peter Becker, who once engaged a gang of twelve Mau Mau in a running battle near Nyeri. In the exchange of fire Peter killed nine terrorists. Over one ten-day period before Christmas 1954, Peter and his men hunted down and shot seventeen gangsters. Tracker teams typically had a Land Rover, two African trackers, five or six African soldiers, and a tracker dog. By the end of 1954 there were five tracker teams commanded by hunters, as three more teams were formed.[2]

Becker had enlisted in the Kenya police reserve four hours after the state of emergency was declared with the firm belief the crisis would be over in two weeks. "Four years later I knew better!" Peter lamented. Becker had spent his boyhood on a ranch in the Aberdare foothills, not far from Treetops, a game-viewing lodge built in a giant *mugumu*, or fig tree, overlooking a water hole and salt lick.

The last few hundred yards to Treetops is approached through the forest on foot, and tourists are always escorted by an armed hunter. An elephant once attacked a female tourist, but was shot by hunter Ken Levett and fell dead within inches of the terrified woman.

Peter Becker's friend, Indian tiger hunter and author Jim Corbett, left his home among the adoring villagers of Kaladhungi, India, and settled in Nyeri. He was a regular at Treetops and in 1952 he escorted Princess Elizabeth through the forest. Elizabeth, the Duke of Edinburgh, and Lady Pamela Mountbatten spent the night game viewing at Treetops with the aid of floodlights. During Elizabeth's stay her father, the King of England, died, and she became the British monarch.

Treetops was built by Nyeri coffee farmers Alfred and Avis Sheldrick (parents of former white hunter, game warden David Sheldrick), whose business partner was killed by a rhino. Their crude tree platform was enlarged into a proper treehouse by Outspan hotelier Eric Sherbrooke-Walker after his guest, Tsar Ferdinand of Bulgaria, almost trod on a sleeping rhino while chasing butterflies. Just before Princess Elizabeth went to Treetops, Prince Philip played polo at Nyeri Polo Club. Shortly afterward the Mau Mau burned the clubhouse to the ground, and they also torched Treetops in 1954.*

BIG GAME hunting skills were often called upon during patrols. The highland forests were not only the refuge of armed and desperate gangs, but they also harbored enormous reserves of wildlife. Dangerous big game was just one more hazard facing security forces carrying out mountain patrols. For this reason some white hunters carried sporting weapons loaded with solid bullets in addition to their light submachine guns.

Of the Big Five trophies of lion, leopard, elephant, rhino, and buffalo, all were found within the forests. In more peaceful days the two mountains and the surrounding plains were a hunter's paradise. The Aberdare Mountains are home to many animals, including bushbuck, waterbuck, wart hog, the elusive eastern bongo, and giant forest hog. Lion and eland could be found high in the moorlands.

Over this period a great many of the unfortunate wild animals inhabiting the forests were wounded by shrapnel during aerial bombing attacks carried out by the Royal Air Force flying aged Harvard and Lincoln bombers.† Game was also hit during mortar and artillery barrages,

---

*Treetops was rebuilt as a double-storied tree lodge.
    †Aerial bombing caused few Mau Mau casualties. Mau Mau confidence soared when RAF pilots were caught in downdrafts and crashed four Harvards in quick succession.

or caught in the crossfire of Bren and heavy machine-gun fire during shoot-outs between British ground troops and heavily armed Mau Mau gangs. Those animals injured by stray bullets could be relied upon to have a temper and disposition to match. Many a stealthy patrol was suddenly charged by a wounded rhino, elephant, or buffalo. In such cases the only remedy was to stand your ground and shoot it out.

IT WAS ONLY natural that Peter Becker's friends, the Poolman brothers Gordon, Fred, and Henry, would be singled out to lead specialized tracking patrols. Whereas Peter Becker had lived close to Nyeri, the Poolman family farm lay on the shoulders of Mount Kenya. The Poolmans were unassuming individuals, big in stature, but easygoing by nature. They had learned to hunt as children with the Kikuyu D'robo in the forests surrounding their farm. Like the D'robo they could mimic the call of a rhino and called the dangerous beasts for fun. True children of Africa, they spoke fluent Swahili and Kikuyu.

The Poolmans and their widowed mother, Eva, epitomized the resourceful, hardworking type of early Kenya pioneers. With the sweat of their collective brows they had carved a successful farm out of virgin bush a few miles from Naro Moru, a ramshackle village beside the railway line on the western slopes of Mount Kenya. The Naro Moru country is just south of the equator and boasts some of the most beautiful farming land in the world. The grasslands on the Poolman place held plains game such as lion, Thomson's gazelle, hartebeest, zebra, eland, and wart hog. The family pretty well lived off the land, with the brothers providing game meat and the farm providing cereals, corn, vegetables, fruit, dairy products, eggs, and poultry. Mrs. Poolman was a no-nonsense woman who could ride and shoot with the best of them. She could skin a buck, bake a loaf of bread, fix the ignition on a truck, weld an axle, or tongue-lash an errant laborer, all with equal dexterity.

HUNTING WAS not then regarded by any of the Poolmans as sport, but rather as a necessity. Lion and leopard were constantly after the cattle or sheep, chickens, and dogs, and hyenas were always anxious to snaffle a newborn calf. Like others in the area they found buffalo and elephant "control" hunts to be an integral part of successful wheat farming. As hunters the three Poolmans had developed skills comparable to first-rate African trackers.

At six foot two inches, Gordon Poolman was taller than his brothers and had striking tawny-colored eyes. As the leader of a Mau Mau tracking team, Gordon cut a fine figure as he patrolled the glittering green jungles and bamboo forests of the Aberdares in search of enemy hideouts, a cocked Sten gun always at the ready. Patrols such as those Gordon led often went on for days, with his soldiers existing on meager rations and spending their nights wrapped in soggy blankets. Tracks of numerous buffalo, giant forest hog, bongo, bushbuck, leopard, rhino, and elephant crisscrossed every which way, but the narrow trails where sunlight barely reached were sometimes speckled with human spoor as well as animal spoor, and at any moment deadly gunfire might erupt from the leafy canopies.

When not battling Mau Mau and big game in the forests, Gordon and other troops were headquartered at the nearest town of any importance. Nyeri was formerly a peaceful little settlement on the slopes of the Aberdares. Prior to Mau Mau times it was known to the world as the home of three hotels, the White Rhino, the Outspan, and Treetops. Now, as both British and Kenya troops gathered at Nyeri to carry out strategic assaults against Mau Mau, Nyeri was transformed overnight into a quasi-military settlement.

Nyeri also became something of a forces recreation center for boisterous troops returning from forays into the forest. The White Rhino Hotel was a meeting place where all ranks could gather for a drink and let off steam. The colonial-style inn had a rollicking bar that was filled day and night with off-duty soldiers celebrating a safe return from one patrol and fortifying themselves for the next. It was commonly said of the White Rhino's rooms that the walls were so thin one could hear one's neighbor "change her mind." Another pun insisted, "The White Rhino charged on sight."

Without much malice Kenya troops referred to British soldiers as pongos, pommies, or poms for short, an appellation borrowed from Australian slang, thought to be an acronym for Prisoners of Her Majesty. In return, British troops readily identified the local lads by their "Kenya colonial" or "Kenya cowboy" accent, a distinctive, slightly clipped version of British pronunciation. *"Kenya born and Kenya bred,"* the poms would drunkenly chortle, *"Strong in the arm and soft in the 'ead . . ."*

A natural rivalry grew up between the fighting troops, although more often than not any real animosity between the cowboys and the poms was buried in bar singsongs of regimental verses. Most of the troops were armed with service revolvers, six-guns, or automatic pistols and sometimes lightweight Patchett, Sterling, or Sten submachine guns, even during off-duty hours. Handguns in open quick-draw holsters were worn with bravado on the dance floor by pom and cowboy civilians of both sexes who joined in the nightly festivities. Despite the hardware, barroom fistfights remained just that, and were not apt to go further.

White hunter Gordon Poolman was one Kenya cowboy who had a memorable Hollywood-style showdown with a pom. In Gordon's case the public confrontation was to have lifelong repercussions. The brawny Gordon was a quiet teetotaler who never looked for trouble, but who could easily handle himself in the tightest corner. While serving in the Aberdares, he had secretly been enamored of an English lady called Connie (a pom, no less) who ran the bar at the White Rhino. Being far too shy to ask for a date, Gordon would sip a lemonade and silently gaze at the unsuspecting object of his affections as she chatted with soldiers at the bar.

Connie was a homely blonde, blue-eyed Cockney born, as she liked to say, "wivin' the sound of Beau Bells" in the heart of London. She wore bottle-bottom-lens spectacles and was known for her quiet good humor and the sharp wit for which Cockneys are famous. Connie cheerfully took in stride the romantic passes made by homesick soldiers, whether they be poms or cowboys. One day in 1954 Gordon Poolman, still clad in the camouflage fatigues of a jungle warrior, entered the White Rhino bar. On that particular day a pom soldier who'd had a few drinks made more than a pass at Connie. When the buffoon grabbed her, Connie struggled. As the situation progressed, Gordon Poolman could watch in silence no longer. In true Gary Cooper fashion Gordon stepped forward, grabbed the lout, pulled him off Connie, and hauled off a whopping knockout punch. The pom was floored. Generally such happenings led to ferocious free-for-alls, but this time there was stunned silence. The pom soldier was still lying on the floor, and the damsel was no longer in distress. Ice-cool Gordon Poolman defiantly stood his ground in a sea of Sam Brownes, khaki uniforms, and submachine guns. But nobody dared to mix it up with him. Eventually Gordon jerked the dazed pom off the floor, propped him on a bar stool, and gallantly bought him a drink. Then he shook hands with the dazed soldier and strode manfully out of the barroom, too modest to seek praise from the heroine. But Connie was impressed. The Hollywood script rolled on, and Gordon the big Kenya cowboy ultimately married his leading lady.

32.

THE BAMBOO BADLANDS

Fred Bartlett was another white hunter who made his home in the highlands of Kenya and who, like his friends Peter Becker and the Poolman brothers, was among that group of hunters considered to be specialists in what the British referred to as the Bamboo Badlands of Mount Kenya and the Aberdares. Bartlett's quiet demeanor belied his bold methods of hunting dangerous game in thick bush, and he was known to relish close encounters.

Bartlett, a big, dark-haired man with a square forthright jaw, looks like what he is—a man of honor. Fred's word is his bond. He is a man above reproach, yet his cool gray eyes hide a sense of mischief and low-key humor. A fellow white hunter, John Fletcher, who hunted buffalo with Bartlett on Mount Kenya, recalled with admiration that "Fred was one of the quickest shots with a double rifle, and that came from his buffalo-control work."[1] Bartlett had certainly shot more buffalo than almost anybody by the time he packed it in with the Game Department to become a white hunter. On control work he had shot 500 buffalo, about 100 elephant, as well as 20 lion and the same number of leopard.[2]

Fred Bartlett's brother-in-law and partner, Don Bousfield, had the fair-haired and blue-eyed face of a choirboy and a soul of devilish mischief. Don thrived on the excitement of big game hunting, and he could find humor in any situation, no matter how perilous. Bousfield had previously been a crocodile hunter at Lake Rukwa, in Tanganyika, before he became a professional hunter for Ker and Downey.

Fred and Don led a tracker team stationed in Bartlett's home country, near Timau, a farming region at 8,000 feet on the northwestern slopes of Mount Kenya. Fred faced terrorists with the same confrontational head-on approach that he used for big game. In retrospect, the fact that Bartlett or Bousfield survived the Mau Mau was a mystery to both of them. "We had a lot of successes," Fred later commented with typical understatement. Bousfield was struck by more than one terrorist bullet. Bartlett recalled two narrow escapes:

> The first occasion was when he [Don Bousfield] was chasing a terrorist who disappeared behind a big tree. As Don got up to where he had seen the Mau Mau last, the terrorist stepped out and fired a short burst from a Sten gun, and two bullets hit Don in the chest. The impact of the bullets knocked him down. The terrorist then fired a short burst at the tracker with Don, but missed. The Mau Mau then ran off. Don came to a short while later as the rest of the patrol ran up. When he got to his feet he was asked if he was all right. He said he was, and then saw blood running onto his boots. He then passed out, and was taken to a hospital where he spent a couple of weeks. The doctor told him that the maps he had folded into a tight wad deflected the bullets, saving his life.
>
> Later while tracking a large gang high up Mount Kenya, Don, my brother, Albert, and I, along with the rest of the tracker team, were ambushed by the gang. Don was walking just a couple of yards ahead of me when a bullet fired from a cliff on our right hit Don's pack, and the impact knocked him down. He fell behind an outcrop of rock, and then several bullets hit the rocks he had fallen behind. I dived behind the same rocks for protection. We returned fire, and after awhile managed to shoot two of the gang before they made off. The bullet hitting Don's pack had just missed his neck.
>
> I always used an Italian Beretta submachine gun which I found very good and accurate up to 100 yards. But on occasions I carried my .30/.06 rifle loaded with armor-piercing bullets in case I was charged in the bamboo by rhino, buffalo, or elephant—as many of these animals were wounded by the security forces with shrapnel. On one occasion I shot a rhino at point-blank range to save our party. This happened in bamboo when I was leading. The rhino got to his feet. I crouched down hoping it would go away from me. The rest of the party crowded up behind me to see what I was looking at. The rhino suddenly charged. My first shot hit it in the chest, which turned it, and my second took him in the side and put him down. Had I not shot it, he would have gone over all of us.[3]

◇

MIKE PRETTEJOHN, a handsome man who might easily have been sent to Africa by central casting to portray the role of white hunter, grew up in the shadow of the Aberdares. Prettejohn was a district officer with the Kikuyu Home Guard. These units were almost exclusively made up of Kikuyu tribesmen and were usually led by young colonials like Prettejohn who had developed a good rapport with the tribe. Mike's unit was given the task of organizing the "villagization" of the local populace, and providing Home Guard units for protection.*

The Mau Mau attacked countless fellow Africans suspected of having sympathies with the colonial government. Some of their own Kikuyu chiefs, such as the powerful and respected senior chief Waruhiu, were their targets. Waruhiu was ambushed by a lone gunman, Chicago-style in broad daylight in his Hudson car, just seven miles from Nairobi. Two weeks later Kikuyu Chief Nderi was murdered at Nyeri.[4] The horrific confrontation escalated and ripped Kenya apart, setting black against black, and settlers of all nationalities as well as the British government into a prolonged guerilla war.

Mike Prettejohn was given command of a unit of Kikuyu Home Guard, whom he trained:

> The Home Guard Posts were built with a moat that was filled with *panjis* [spiked stakes] set along the bottom of the moat, and a bullet-proof wall with extended turrets at two opposite corners so that one could shoot down the length of each wall at any assailant. At night the drawbridge was pulled up and the villagers were under strict curfew. Anyone found beyond the village bounds at night was shot on sight.[5]

In their efforts to put down the Mau Mau rebellion, the British assigned some conscripted Kenya Regiment individuals to form clandestine "pseudo" Mau Mau units to infiltrate and destroy real Mau Mau strongholds in the heart of the forests. This exceedingly dangerous work involved white undercover agents disguising themselves as

---

*The Home Guard was raised in response to Mau Mau attacks against their own people. Hunters in the Kikuyu Home Guard were Finn Aagaard, Guy Catchpole (later killed by a buffalo), game warden Dave McCabe, M.C., and Mike Higginson, secretary of the East African Professional Hunter's Association.

"black" Mau Mau gangsters. The idea of employing pseudo-terrorists for counterinsurgency work was not new to the British, for they had successfully developed similar tactics during uprisings in Palestine and Malaya. However, in Kenya the use of pseudos was considered one of the most improbable and perilous of concepts.

It happened that one former hunter, who was a game warden at Tsavo, turned out to have experience with covert pseudo-type work in Kenya. The British became aware of this unexpected expertise when twenty-three-year-old Bill Woodley was called up to serve in the Kenya Regiment. Woodley, a gregarious and enterprising Kenyan, had been raised on the Athi Plains outside Nairobi, and spoke fluent Swahili and Kikuyu. A fine hunter, tracker, and bushman even before he left the Prince of Wales school, Bill hunted elephant in the Portuguese colony of Mozambique with Colonel "Tiger" Mariott, a Tsavo national park warden. By the time he turned eighteen, Woodley had shot ninety elephant. Although he remained an ardent supporter of the white hunter fraternity, he thereafter turned his attentions toward conservation. When he became a game warden in 1948, Woodley had enlisted pseudo–elephant poachers, most of whom were formerly *real* elephant poachers before being arrested by Woodley and his colleague, Peter Jenkins, during anti-poaching operations in the eight thousand square miles that comprise Tsavo national park.

Woodley's methods were simple enough. In the course of his job as warden he arrested poachers from hunting tribes, usually from the WaLiangulu, WaGiriama, and WaKamba. After his prisoners had served their time in jail, Woodley would offer the best of them positions as game scouts employed by national parks. Working together with the former poachers he was able to develop a mutual respect and enlist the tribesmen in his cause. His "set a thief to catch a thief" modus paid dividends and earned Woodley kudos for his extremely effective anti-poaching methods. Woodley was confident the same tactics would work against the Mau Mau.

Serving first in the Kenya Regiment, Bill was transferred as a platoon sergeant to the 26th King's African Rifles, based in what was known as Location 8 in the Fort Hall district of the Kikuyu reserve. There Woodley investigated Mau Mau murders. It occurred to him that some of his best trackers at Tsavo were former Liangulu elephant poachers, and now in the highlands of Kenya he and his men were often stymied when they were unable to follow the tracks of a murder gang over difficult jungle terrain. Woodley suggested that some of the Liangulu trackers employed as game rangers at Tsavo could be useful on the Aberdares. With permission from his peacetime boss, the national parks' director, Mervyn Cowie, who was now also director of manpower, Bill went to Tsavo and came back with two Liangulu hunters named Hekuta Simba and Galo-Galo Guyu. At first he had to pay them out of his own pocket, as British army regulations did not yet cater to trackers. Bill armed one of the trackers with an old .303 magazine rifle, and the other was armed only with his bow and arrows.[6]

It was not long before another murder occurred near Fort Hall. This time an Indian trader had been killed by the Mau Mau, and Bill and his men were hot on the trail. They surprised and arrested the entire gang with murder weapons and loot. Within weeks Bill and his men repeated their success and caught the murderers of two more men. Then, at a place called Ol Kalou, twenty miles north of Gilgil, on Christmas Day 1953, an old farmer named Charles Hamilton Fergusson and his neighbor, Richard Bingley, were slain as they shared Christmas dinner. Bingley's hand was cut off before he could fire a shot with his revolver.

Woodley and his men tracked the murder gang to the Ngobit River. Closing in silently on the terrorists they opened fire, killing four Mau Mau and wounding one.[7] They found Fergusson's articles and clothing on the dead Mau Mau.

Taking previously proven concepts of "turning" hard-core Liangulu and Kamba poachers into efficient national park rangers at Tsavo was a feat Bill Woodley thought he could duplicate by turning hard-core Mau Mau into first-rate pseudo-terrorists. Woodley said that the pseudo idea in Kenya was thought of first by a white farmer named Steve Bothma who was fluent in Kikuyu. Woodley and Bothma were given the green light to form a pseudo-terrorist group using captured Mau Mau. The British army brass were highly skeptical, to say the least.

It was not long before Bill's military superiors were astonished that Woodley could so readily turn hard-core Mau Mau gangsters against their own and induce them to lead pseudo units against former comrades. The brown-haired, brown-eyed Woodley, himself disguised as a Mau Mau, with plaited wig, blackened face, and wearing the ragged garb of a forest gangster, personally led the first pseudo gang against the insurgents. On this historic pseudo raid Bill was accompanied by Steve Bothma and a Kikuyu soldier named Gibson Wambugu. As a result of the ensuing close-quarter gunfight Wambugu was decorated for outstanding gallantry.[8]

Bill Woodley's continued pseudo successes were such that eventually all companies of the Kenya Regiment were operating pseudo units, often with white hunters. The Kenya police soon imitated these methods and formed "special force teams." The white pseudos blackened their faces using a variety of methods, including stove polish and greasepaint. Some pseudos even clouded the whites of their eyes with weak solutions of iodine (not to be recommended) and wore ragged clothes, matted corn-row wigs, and tattered greatcoats against daytime chill and freezing nights, as well as to hide their submachine guns. The filthy, battered greatcoats had pockets sewn into the liners for dried food, ammunition clips, hand grenades, knives, and handguns.

Woodley's friend, white hunter Mike Prettejohn, recalled:

> Our Home Guard reorganized into pseudo Mau Mau gangs. This became a hunt of a different kind—far more exciting and infinitely more dangerous. For those Kikuyu known as "loyals," who joined us in the hunt against their own people, the stakes were even higher. It was a very brave decision, for if caught they risked hideous deaths, and their families victimized and usually brutally killed.[9]

One incident after a pseudo gang made contact with the Mau Mau well illustrates the dangers from even a tiny slip. A pseudo had to leave a smoky hut swarming with heavily armed real Mau Mau to urinate. He was lucky not to have been detected because he had forgotten to "black up" the exposed part of his anatomy. The pseudo was fined three days' pay for his negligence.[10]

Pseudo gangs had not only the Mau Mau to fear, but the security forces as well. If pseudos unexpectedly ran into security forces they could expect to be in for a hot time. More than one pseudo unit was shot up by British or other troops or attacked by the Kikuyu Home Guard with arrows, spears, and buckshot.

Pseudo counterinsurgency groups usually numbered four to six men, two or three of whom might be "reformed" Mau Mau, or simply black African security force members or safari trackers. Numbers of black pseudos had been recruited from martial tribes like the Masai, Turkana, Nandi, and Kamba. The rest of the party was made up of one or more white pseudos. These groups used a variety of methods to make contact with real Mau Mau, and once they had done so it remained for them to convince the terrorists they were genuine. It was dangerous work and casualties were high. Once among a gang of terrorists the pseudos, upon a prearranged signal, opened fire at point-blank range with submachine guns and sometimes lobbed grenades.

The desperately hunted Mau Mau lived a very hard existence. They seldom washed, and their long dreadlocked hair was unkempt. This disheveled appearance was alarming to British troops, but not to the Kenya cowboys or pseudos, who knew the Mau Mau plaited their hair not to look intimidating, but for the practical purpose of lice-catching.

The Mau Mau said they could "smell" the security forces, as indeed they easily could—soap, tobacco, even the traces of alcohol or starched clothes were alien odors in the great forests. The white hunters and cowboys, for their part, could smell the Mau Mau, who reeked with an assortment of odors, not the least of which was rancid fat (to ward off insects) and smoke. For this reason all pseudos crouched around smoky cooking fires to acquire the right "aroma."

MYLES TURNER was no stranger to highland Kenya, where he had been raised in Nanyuki, then hunted as a control officer and survived two buffalo attacks. He had became a white hunter in 1949, when there were only about twenty-five qualified hunters in East Africa. He was seconded to the Kenya police during the Mau Mau period:

> Where once I used to hunt buffalo and rhino, it now became my job to help the Security Forces in their fight against a few thousand well-armed hard-core terrorists who had withdrawn into Kenya's forest vastness under the leadership of Dedan Kimathi,* the scar-faced, self-styled "Marshall" of the Land Freedom Army, Stanley Mathenge, General China, and others.
>
> It is impossible to imagine more difficult country to work in. The cedar forests, choked with heavy undergrowth, riddled with huge gullies and ravines, full of caves and mountain streams and

---

*Dedan Kimathi was captured after a long quest by Kenyan Ian Henderson. Kimathi was sentenced to death "for unlawful possession of a weapon" and hanged on February 18, 1957.

miles of dense bamboo, made this terrain a guerilla fighter's paradise, and a pursuer's nightmare. In the end, however, Mau Mau was defeated, the forest gangs rounded up, and life returned to normal, although Kenya would never be the same again.[11]

The Mau Mau insurrection was finally over,* and for those who had faith and remained in Kenya, things got better as peace brought prosperity, as well as a boom in the safari business.

---

*The Kenya Regiment suffered the highest casualties with 63 men killed. Other units combined suffered 104 fatalities and 1,582 wounded, against a total of 11,503 terrorists killed. Wounded and captured Mau Mau totaled 1,035.

33

OUT OF THE FOREST,
INTO THE BUSH

After the Mau Mau rebellion ended, Kenya's economy needed the important safari tourist trade more than ever, and the colony went all out to accommodate overseas visitors. Travel restrictions were lifted, and once again white hunters and their clients were free to roam the full reaches of East Africa. Border crossings between Kenya, Uganda, and Tanganyika remained a simple business, a mere formality. Although game licenses and regulations varied slightly in each of the triad states, a common currency and a common set of customs regulations facilitated free-ranging safaris.

The price of a full-blown hunting safari had hardly changed and cost one client with one white hunter between $60 and $93 per day (depending on the outfitter), excluding game licenses. Licenses in Kenya, including 2 elephant permits, 1 lion, 1 leopard, 1 rhino, and a good selection of supplementary licenses for game such as roan and kudu, as well as a bird license, totaled about $1,120.* Few safari companies would accept a hunt shorter than thirty days. Most brochures advertised a fixed rate for hunts of thirty, forty-five, and sixty days.

Peter Becker, who for several years led tracker teams into the gloomy shadows of highland forests, was among those liberated to return to the bright sunlight of wide-open bush country. Before the Mau Mau rebellion Peter's mentor in the safari business had been Mark Howard-Williams, one of the most enigmatic personalities ever to grace the East

---

*By comparison, a twenty-eight-day hunting safari in Tanzania for one client and one white hunter currently costs $44,000, plus air charters (at least $12,600) and trophy fees (from $28,000 and up, depending on which species are hunted).

African hunting scene, a daredevil whose career was short, controversial, and in the end tragic.

The debonair Howard-Williams had emerged as a white hunter in the 1940s. During the years of the Second World War, when Peter was still a youngster, Mark had served as a lieutenant in a British Armored Car division and often called in at the Becker farmhouse on Mount Kenya. The arrival of his revered hero was always a much anticipated event, although as time passed, it dawned on Peter that Howard-Williams probably had other reasons to visit. Becker later reflected good-naturedly on those days and mused, "I think he quite fancied my eighteen-year-old sister!"

Becker's first rifle, a .256 Italian carbine, had been captured by Mark during his time on the Abyssinian battlefront. The friendship endured as Howard-Williams became a white hunter with an elite safari clientele that included the Aga Khan and author John Gunter. In 1947 when Peter graduated from the Prince of Wales School in Nairobi he persuaded the hunter to take him on as a trainee. On his first trip, Becker recalled, "The client was a Swiss watchmaker, and Mark made me the camp manager. As you can imagine I was on Planet 7!"[1]

Becker's darkly handsome patron looked like what every young boy imagined Tarzan would look like if he wore a wide-brimmed Borsalino hat. Peter characterized him as a mixture of two legendary hunters, "B.A. [Bunny Allen, for courtly manner, and his luck with women] and E.R. [Eric Rundgren, for his hunting prowess]." Old-timer Fergus McBain agreed, commenting, "He was as wild as they come and I think probably the greatest hunter-womanizer that I have known, and that is saying a lot!" For a few years Howard-Williams's star burned brightly in the tight-knit white hunter fraternity. He was a charming playboy whose propensity for wine, women, and dangerous big game was reckless, though not uncommon in the safari world. His colorful reputation and his rash bravado only enhanced his charismatic appeal. When Howard-Williams's hunting car was sighted in the distant hunting regions he frequented, tribesmen greeted him as they would a chieftain, rushing forward to shake his hand.

Between safaris Becker often shared evenings with Mark at the New Stanley Long Bar or Torr's Hotel, the favored watering holes patronized by Nairobi's hunters. As a witness to the acceleration of wild-man antics, which ultimately eroded a fine reputation, Peter was sadly aware of his inability to come between Mark and his demons of destruction. As suddenly as he had risen to the heights of his profession,

Howard-Williams flamed out. At the age of thirty-one he was found shot dead at the Salisbury Hotel on the edge of town. Becker recalled that the fateful day came at the end of a long drinking spree when Mark had been challenged to a game of Russian roulette. One time too often he played with fire; Howard-Williams took the dare, and it cost his life.* Becker was convinced that had Howard-Williams lived, his name would be as highly regarded today as those of legendary prewar hunters Bror Blixen and Alan Black.[2]

Peter Becker became a hunter with the Nairobi firm of Ker and Downey for five years, until he felt the time was right to open his own independent company of Peter Becker Safaris.

Mike Prettejohn, the ex–Kikuyu Home Guard commander and another one-time denizen of the Bamboo Badlands, also founded his own safari company in peacetime:

> After the Emergency was over I bought a cattle ranch near my old home between Mount Kenya and the Aberdare Mountains on which I still have the good fortune to live. It was a rough bit of country and better for wild animals than cattle. I had a hefty loan to repay and so started hunting professionally, which I did from the ranch and from my old haunts, but I soon realized that hunting territory familiar to myself was *very* different to guiding others in thick bush. Although forest hunting was the most dangerous, it was also the most rewarding. We did, however, bag many magnificent trophies with buffalo seldom under 46 inches, and many at 48. Similarly, there was a good number of rhino trophy records with 36-inch-plus horns as well as the much prized bongo. Two of our bongo topped the record book. My old school friend Peter Becker joined me in a partnership, as he had a cattle ranch nearby, and we pooled our resources.[3]

Prettejohn is widely regarded as a bongo specialist. Hunting the eastern variety of bongo calls for an exacting combination of stamina, dedication, and experience. The elusive five-hundred-pound animal is one

---

*As in many frontier towns innuendo and outright lies bury facts when tragedy occurs; such was the case with Mark's death. Recently a former Kenya resident now living in America, whom I've never met, called and claimed to have known Mark Howard-Williams. He said Mark was in bed with the wife of a British army sergeant when he was shot to death by the woman's husband. But that is only one of many stories that circulated.

Mike Prettejohn on the Aberdares with a record (33⅛ inch) eastern bongo.

of the most difficult to hunt because of its shy nature, highly developed senses, and because it inhabits the bamboo forest zone on the Aberdares, as well as the Cherangani Mountains in western Kenya.

Few clients were prepared to forsake all other hunting and invest a month or more in the strenuous physical effort necessary for a bongo hunt. One of Mike's clients, Martin Anderson, shot a bongo with horns 33⅛ inches, winning Mike the Shaw and Hunter Trophy in 1962. Even in the heyday of bongo hunting in the sixties, few bongo were actually taken. In 1960 thirty bongo licenses were issued, yet only two bongo were actually shot. Over the next four years 171 bongo licenses were sold for a total of only 20 bongo trophies actually taken.[4] Bongo hunting aside, Mike Prettejohn had his fair share of mishaps:

> A buffalo had recently killed a woman and had previously claimed other victims. We tracked him into a heavily wooded *donga* [gully] where he was resting up for the afternoon. When we came on him the client wounded him, and I was unable to get a shot off before he disappeared into the brush. We followed and put him up three times that day without seeing him. When it was too dark to continue tracking we returned to camp.
>
> The following day we were back on his spoor, and we found

where he had lain up for the night, but had moved on. As we debated our next move the bushes beside us exploded. I hastily got in position to shoot before he disappeared again. I did not think fight was his intention. Then with a sinking feeling of *déjà vu*, I was confronted head-on with a speeding black mass, nose forward and horns locked back. I instinctively loosed off a shot but to no avail. Before I could get off another shot the buffalo was on me, knocking me over backwards and, without trampling me, passed right over the top. There was hardly time to be grateful for the end of this bout when he wheeled round and came for me again with his head and horns lowered. Luckily for me he was an old bull with a heavy boss and stub-ended horns which made it difficult for him to hook into me. I clung onto his head and horns anchoring my legs around his neck, and hoped to God that the client or my gunbearer would hurry up and get it all over with. The buffalo, realizing that he could not hook me, dragged me along the ground before kneeling on me to pummel my chest into the ground with his boss. Thinking I was a goner, there was a loud report, and my ears rang. Although the pressure on my chest was released instantly, I found myself unable to move, pinned beneath the dead weight of the buffalo. It took six men to roll him off me. Surprisingly, no bones were broken, but there was severe bruising, punctures, grazes and cuts. Suffice to say all extremely painful but nothing compared to the lavish infusion of iodine that followed. I ran a high temperature first night back in camp and was given a shot of penicillin by one of my safari crew who was accustomed to taking on an odd variety of chores in the bush. Later on I discovered I was probably suffering from lead poisoning, but at the time I had no idea about this!

For months my right leg gave me a lot of pain and at times I was unable to use it at all. Eventually a large bruise developed on my behind, and the pain subsided. A doctor suggested this colorful lump was due to internal bruising and gave me external medicine to rub on it, but the more I rubbed the larger the bruise became! Finally a solid but moveable lump came up, and I no longer felt any pain.

Some time later I was on safari with a doctor from Denmark, and he proposed, while he sewed up a deep cut on my cheek, and without benefit of anesthetic, to remove the offending object from my backside. I politely declined. The cut on my cheek resulted from a very close shave from a bullet fired from behind while hunting an elephant we encountered at close quarters. What struck my cheek must have been a piece of cartridge wadding, but whatever it was, had it been half an inch further to the left that would have been final for me.

When I returned from that safari my own doctor admitted there was indeed something more than a bruise on my behind, and he gave me a local anesthetic. As he peered into the hole he had made and poised with a pair of tweezers, he commented that the object he saw in me appeared to be gold-plated! With more determined probing he produced a perfect .458 bullet. This was exactly one year after the buffalo incident.

When we came to reconstruct that particular buffalo encounter, it was recalled that my gunbearer's shot had been fired at the buffalo from behind. The .458 bullet travelled through the buffalo, then through its neck and lodged itself in my leg, which at the time was wrapped around the buffalo's neck. By the time the bullet reached me it was luckily well spent. The terrible pain had been caused by the bullet as it worked its way out via my sciatic nerve![5]

AFTER THE Mau Mau Emergency was over, Myles Turner also resumed his hunting in the Kenya highlands. In 1955 he rejoined Ker and Downey Safaris, and later won the Shaw and Hunter trophy for a record lesser kudu with horns 35¾ inches, taken by his client, Prince Abdorezza Pahlavi of Iran. That year Myles married Kay Tubb, a secretary in Ker and Downey's office. At the height of his safari career, thirty-four-year-old Turner abruptly quit hunting to become warden of the Serengeti national park, with a meager salary of £75 per month, less than one-third of what he earned hunting. In November 1956 Myles and Kay moved to Banagi Hill and a decrepit old house once occupied by the first warden, also a former white hunter named Major Ray Hewlett.*

---

*In 1933 Royal Flying Corp fighter pilot and former white hunter Ray Hewlett became warden of the Serengeti and pushed for national park status, which was not gazetted until 1950.

GORDON POOLMAN also went to the Serengeti, as assistant warden to Myles. He and his Cockney bride, Connie (formerly of the White Rhino Hotel), lived in thatched rondavels (round huts) beside the Seronera River, twelve miles from the Turners at Banagi Hill. The two couples were the only Europeans within a radius of 110 miles.

In those days the Serengeti's 5,600 square miles was virtually unknown except to a handful of hunters and game wardens. Myles Turner became synonymous with the Serengeti over the next sixteen years. Some time after Myles resigned from the Serengeti to take up another park appointment, Queen Elizabeth II made him a Member of the British Empire (MBE) in recognition of his services to wildlife.

BILL WOODLEY, whose pseudo operations had contributed greatly to the defeat of the Mau Mau in the Aberdares, never returned to safari hunting. Bill was awarded the Military Cross for gallantry in action. He returned to national parks as warden of Kenya's mountain parks, based at Mweiga on the eastern slopes of the Aberdares. It was familiar territory that had so recently been the haunt of Mau Mau gangs.

In a highly controversial move Woodley offered employment to some former Mau Mau enemies, who repaid his bold initiative with their loyalty and trust. The ex-Mau Mau game rangers became the most elite mountain anti-poaching units in Kenya. In peacetime Woodley's right-hand man and closest confidant at Mweiga was none other than one of the most senior Mau Mau commanders, S. K. Muhangia. Another group of ex-Mau Mau fighters was trained with Woodley in Austria to form mountain rescue teams to assist distressed climbers on Mount Kenya.

34.

THE MAHARAJAH OF MAYHEM

The Africans called him Mchangi. *Mchangi* are the tiny colored beads used by some tribes to embellish necklaces, belts, and wrist ornaments. Terry Mathews, who had hunted with Mchangi Rundgren, explained the reason for the nickname. "If *mchangi* are dropped on the floor, you may think you have picked them all up, but for days afterwards you are still treading on them. To the Africans, Eric was just like that—here, there and everywhere!"[1]

The nickname did not bother Eric Rundgren; in fact, very little bothered him. He unhesitantly trampled on anybody if he felt like it, and not necessarily for good reason, or any reason at all. Mchangi be damned, the fallen would pop like grapes beneath his feet. Rundgren entertained no fear of social suicide.

Mchangi made no attempt to rein in his explosive nature, totally aware that each bombshell only served to boost his bad-guy mystique. He cynically gazed out at the world from heavily hooded Nordic blue eyes. Reddish-haired and fair-skinned, Rundgren had a square jaw with lips that could as easily snarl as smile. In his prime he was well muscled and big boned, standing just under six feet in his socks, and weighing in at around 225 pounds. For his size Rundgren moved easily on the balls of his feet, his shoulders hunched like a prizefighter, often with a cigarette in his pudgy fist.

At the height of his volcanic career as a white hunter in the mid-fifties and sixties, Eric Rundgren was the most controversial professional of his day. People loved him or hated him, and there were plenty of white hunters, clients, game wardens, colonial administrators, and the general public in both camps. Even his supporters in the hunting world acknowledged Rundgren was not exactly a member of the cultural elite. Rundgren's long-suffering employer was Ker and Downey Safaris. Ruth Hales (later Bill Woodley's wife), a vivacious woman who worked in the outfitter's Nairobi office, often had to run interference for Eric, and she became adept at smoothing ruffled client's feathers.

One arriving client, a prominent New Yorker, opened his briefcase at Nairobi airport to show Rundgren a new pair of expensive Zeiss binoculars, which he had just purchased for his safari. No doubt he anticipated Eric's approval for having selected such a fine piece of essential equipment. Rundgren held the binoculars in his big fist—pretended to study them—held them at arm's length, as might a connoisseur viewing an objet d'art. He put them to his eyes, focused on a distant lightbulb, and did not say a word. Instead, he removed a large folding knife from his pocket and carefully carved his initials, *ER*, into the binocular tubes. Handing the binoculars back to the stunned client, Rundgren drawled, "Well, I suppose you can use them during the course of the safari, but remember they're mine at the end of the hunt!" The unfortunate client was too dumbfounded to react. It was gross intimidation at its most unsubtle; unmistakably Mchangi in his bully-boy mode. Even his peers wondered aloud how Rundgren got away with some of his antics, or why any of his clients would tolerate the way he came on so strongly with them.

Eric Rundgren was certainly the most experienced hunter of all time. He had shot more dangerous game than anybody else on earth. Rundgren never boasted about that; it is simply a fact. As a hunter Rundgren packed testosterone in his cartridge belt. Nothing would deter him during a chase. Fellow hunter Terry Mathews recalled, "He had no respect for his cars, for his clients, his equipment, or those who worked for him. If he wanted something, he went after it. Sometimes he would travel on all through the night. Anything that got in his way, he just drove over it—thornbushes, potholes, rocks, rivers, gullies, he only had one objective in mind and that was to get good results."[2]

Eric came by his extraordinary hunting instincts naturally. His godfather had been another bad boy, the popular Baron Bror von Blixen-Finecke. Eric's father, Ture Vladimir Rundgren, a native of Odensvi, Sweden, had been among the early Kenya white hunters, and along with Blixen had steered young Eric into a life of hunting.

Before Eric was sixteen his father took him on his first professional hunting safari where he met pioneer hunters Leslie Tarlton and Alastair Gibbs. The safari was an extravagant expedition arranged for a famous Norwegian Antarctic explorer, and young Eric marveled at the luxury of the safari—rivers of champagne, caviar, Danish hams, even pâté de foie gras served on silver platters around the campfire.

Later, while he was employed by the government forestry department, Rundgren also helped out at the Kenya Game Department, then headed by Archie Ritchie, and he shot buffalo, elephant, and lion on control work around the Aberdares. One of Rundgren's early projects involved capturing wildlife to help stock a private game sanctuary owned by the Prud'hommes, who were keen amateur hunters. Gabriel Prud'homme was an impecunious Frenchman and fancied himself a ladies' man. His claim to fortune was his marriage to a wealthy American heiress named Rhoda, who had built a magnificent mansion above Nanyuki, on the slopes of Mount Kenya. The Prud'hommes and the impressive wildlife sanctuary they created around their home was much admired, and far ahead of its time. The sanctuary and the Prud'homme mansion were known as Mawingo (Swahili for "clouds") and both were eventually sold to Block Hotels. The estate became the Mawingo Hotel, which in turn evolved into the now famous Mount Kenya Safari Club.

During wartime Rundgren was drafted into the 11th Indian Division, British army, and saw service in Abyssinia. It was not long before he was chafing at the strictures and routines of military life. Eric took action of his own. He wrote to Kenya's chief game warden, Archie Ritchie, reminding him of their Mount Kenya hunting days and magnanimously offering his *immediate* services to the Game Department. Whatever the finer points of his argument the letter was effective, for in 1944 Ritchie was motivated to use his considerable pull.

Even before hostilities ended a triumphant Rundgren became a warden, where he secured a posting back to his old hunting grounds at Nanyuki. Rundgren had a large pair of boots to fill—his predecessor in the Nanyuki range was none other than the much storied J. A. Hunter.

On one occasion Rundgren was instructed by Ritchie to shoot five hundred crop-raiding buffalo on Mount Kenya. There was no doubt the entire region was overrun with the offending marauders, but even Rundgren was shocked by the scope of his assignment. Five *hundred* buffalo! It was difficult and strenuous enough, not to say dangerous, to kill just *one* buffalo. Most of the buffalo living on Mount Kenya had already been harassed by farmers, hunters, and tribesmen trying to move them away from their crops. As a result, when the wary buffalo

Eric Rundgren at the height of his volcanic career, 1958.

made nighttime crop raids they retired before dawn to the safety of the forests where it was treacherous to follow.

To meet the challenge Rundgren developed a specialized dog pack, which became his most important tool for buffalo control. The chances of escaping death or permanent injury from continuous buffalo hunting in thick forests, day after day, is slim at best. Rundgren was tossed, horned, and savaged on seven different occasions by buffalo. As a result he suffered recurring back and hip problems, and massive horn wounds in his legs bothered him all his life.

During one pursuit a wounded buffalo charged, slammed hard into Rundgren, and tossed him over a riverbank. He landed in the gravel stream, but held on to his .450 double rifle. Above him on the bank was the buffalo looking down at him. Lying in the shallow river Rundgren shot the buff in the throat and it collapsed.

By the time Rundgren had personally shot over three thousand buffalo he had no taste left for control work. This staggering number of buffalo taken on behalf of the government is a greater number than any one man has ever shot. Rundgren was not proud of these statistics, and he avoided discussing it. But the fact remains that it is a record. Yet hordes of buffalo continued to come from Mount Kenya's forests to wipe out entire fields of wheat and barley, despite his control efforts. During Eric's tempestuous time as a warden, his hands had been full, not just with buffalo and irate farmers. Huge herds of elephant raided plantations and grainfields and wiped them out overnight. It was intensive, stressful hunting the duration and extent of which may not have been equaled by another human being. Rundgren's area also had large numbers of lions that constantly raided cattle, and occasionally humans. Along with the lion problem, leopard were forever after sheep and goats. Lion were prolific in Rundgren's 7,000-square-mile range and were the bane of every rancher's existence. There had been a population explosion of lion, notably in Laikipia district, and Rundgren once again received orders from the Game Department in Nairobi to "shoot a couple of hundred lion." In just seven years of mixed control hunting Rundgren personally shot 434 lion, easily another record, if one's counting.

CHIEF GAME warden Ritchie's prima donna was an ace hunter, but not the perfect game warden. As a control officer there was simply nobody to touch him, and Mchangi knew it. But as a representative of the Kenya Game Department he was unpredictable, volatile, and to many people he was nothing but a lout, both rude and irresponsible. His explosive personality, his loathing for paperwork, and his often abrupt manner in dealing with "nitpickers" and "bahstuds," whether colleagues or ranchers, did not endear him to everyone. Late in 1952, at the age of thirty-four, Rundgren resigned from the Game Department during a heated argument with a colleague.

Jack Block, then chairman of Ker and Downey, offered Rundgren a job with a salary of £150 per month. Rundgren wanted £250.[3] Block told him he was not paying his best hunters that much. Rising to his feet Eric angrily growled that he'd get it elsewhere. And he did. Safariland was Ker and Downey's main rival, and manager Douglas Brett hastily agreed to Rundgren's terms. There was apparently no concern on Brett's part over the fact that Eric had never conducted a single professional safari. In those days any ex–game department warden was automatically issued a professional license if he wanted it.

As it happened his first safari nearly cost Rundgren his life twice over. In turn he was mauled by a leopard and charged by an elephant. Despite his unrivaled experience with dangerous game, this first safari was something of a rude awakening for the Maharajah of Mayhem.

Years later Rundgren grudgingly conceded that "hunting for yourself with only your own hide and that of your bearers to watch out for is one thing, but hunting with nincompoops is another kettle of fish." He was beginning to understand that a white hunter's lot was nothing like it was cracked up to be.

Rundgren's trip for Safariland was conducted in company with salted white hunters Myles Turner, on loan from Ker and Downey, Safariland's Jackie Blacklaws (who later died of sleeping sickness), and Barry Roberts. The clients were six prominent Mexicans whose camp was sited in Masailand. Rundgren quickly had a big tom leopard feeding on a bait. At their request Rundgren's two clients wished to shoot at the leopard together. This was an unusual arrangement at the best of times, and as Rundgren was to discover not a very wise one. He may have consented to this silly request because he was anxious to please on his first professional safari. He would never permit it again.

The hunters did not have long to wait in their blind. The leopard silently appeared in the tree, standing on the branch above the bait. The big cat offered an easy shot as it stood motionless. It should have been a certain thing at twenty yards, from a dead rest while concealed in a blind. Rundgren gave the agreed signal to shoot. Both rifles roared.

To Rundgren's surprise the leopard did not fall dead. Instead it coughed and leapt off the branch, hitting the dirt with a grunt as it streaked across a patch of open ground to be swallowed in a brushy *donga*. Rundgren fetched his car, which was parked some distance away, and drove back to collect his clients from the blind, where he had ordered them to remain. Eric simply could not believe how anybody could miss such an easy target.

Rundgren looked around for blood spoor and found none, then he sent his porter, a man named Nymai, up the tree to see if there was any blood or bullet hole in the tree. Nymai found no blood, but he did find where one bullet had buried itself in the branch upon which the leopard had been standing. It was anyone's guess where the other bullet went. The mess made Rundgren uneasy. Most white hunters might have let it go at that. No blood, no wounded leopard. Just the same, Rundgren thought he would have a quick look around before it got too dark.

Eric was without a proper gunbearer that day, accompanied only by Nymai, whose usual job was to fetch firewood and keep the camp clean. Rundgren went to check the gully where the leopard had disappeared. The leopard suddenly broke cover with a grunt and went after the hapless Nymai. The porter ran like a hare, with the leopard after him and about to pull him down, when Rundgren snapped off two hasty shots from his double rifle.

One shot crumpled the leopard momentarily, but the shot was too far back of the shoulder. The leopard recovered instantly, whirled, and ignoring Nymai instead went for Rundgren, who had not had time to reload. Eric swung the empty rifle at the leopard's head, but the cat's rush knocked him flat. The enraged cat immediately went to work.

Man and beast rolled in mortal combat as Rundgren's blood flowed. Instead of playing dead, Eric fought back with his great brawn. It was a costly decision, for hunters know that the damage in such an engagement might be minimized by not counterattacking. But it simply was not in Rundgren's nature to take a defensive posture to protect head and neck. It is impossible to imagine the speed and ferocity of a leopard's attack unless one has witnessed it.

Rundgren tried to strangle the leopard. This is akin to wrestling a chain saw that has run amok. The leopard bit and scratched and ripped as Eric desperately tried to hang on. A claw hooked Rundgren's ear and almost tore it off his head, then the leopard broke Rundgren's grip, biting his arm and breaking the bone, then attacking wrists and fingers, scalp, and shoulders. In the blood-soaked battle Rundgren kicked, swore, and fought back as the big cat shredded him. With a grip on the leopard's throat Eric thought he felt the cat weaken, and he hoped his efforts, coupled with the bullet damage from his .475 Jeffrey, were taking their toll. Rundgren knew that even if he did break off the fight and try to get away, the leopard would probably go after him and get a fang hold on *his* throat. He was damned if he did, and damned if he didn't. Then a rifle boomed close to Eric's head, and the leopard went limp. In the absence of a trained gunbearer one of the Mexican clients had rushed in and fired a shot, killing the leopard.

In those days safaris did not carry radio telephones. Jackie Blacklaws, one of the hunters in camp, drove to the Masai village of Narok, found the only telephone in town, and called for an aircraft. A member of the Mexican party was a skilled doctor, and he worked on Eric's wounds late into the night.

At Nairobi next day Dr. Gerald Neville attended Rundgren, who was fearful of gangrene. Recently a white hunter named Roy McAlpine-Leny had been gored by a buffalo and not received medical attention for a day. Gangrene set in and his leg was amputated, but it was already too late. Roy had died of septicemia. Roy's fate was not lost on Rundgren.

Fergus McBain, a former Kenyan now living in Australia, and a self-proclaimed white hunter groupie, recalled his visit to Rundgren's hospital bed that stormy day:

> At the time I was working as a lowly grip for Metro-Goldwyn-Mayer, who were making *King Solomon's Mines*. News came through to the film unit that Eric was in very poor shape. Stewart Granger had a great admiration for him, and immediately called a halt to filming, much to the fury of Compton Bennett, the director, and commandeered an MGM car. Knowing that I knew Eric, he asked if I would like to go along too. We were the first visitors, apart from Pat, Eric's wife, to see him in hospital. Eric was unconscious, the color of putty, and making heavy weather of breathing. He reinforced my notion of his indestructibility.[4]

After two weeks Rundgren left the hospital, but he was not fit to hunt. His clients begged him to rejoin the safari because they wanted outstanding ivory and believed he was the best man to help them find it. Rundgren agreed, provided they paid for a nurse to accompany him to change dressings. The request amused Rundgren no end. What hunter had ever had a nurse on safari just to look after him!

Rundgren's clients hunted with the other professionals while Eric's trackers prowled the Tana's riverine forests in search of elephant. The trackers reported a bull elephant, which Rundgren inspected but dismissed as it only had forty-pound tusks. When they heard Rundgren's low ivory estimate the clients insisted on seeing the animal themselves. Myles Turner led the clients into dense *m'swaki* thickets to show them Rundgren's elephant, while Eric wisely waited farther back.

Myles found the elephant at a range of twenty yards, when it immediately charged. Turner fired two .470 rounds hoping for a last-ditch frontal brain shot. He missed the brain, but a bullet was so close to it that the elephant swerved aside, just missing Turner as it crashed out of the brush headed straight for the tree where Rundgren waited. Eric was unarmed, because his hands were heavily bandaged. He ducked behind the bole of the tree as the elephant rushed past a few feet away. The incident shook up Rundgren because he was powerless to do anything about it.

Myles left his clients behind with Rundgren and went after the elephant with his trackers. Turner remained on the elephant's spoor for three days until they caught up with it, and Myles killed it.

When Rundgren's account of the leopard mauling became widely known in Kenya after the Mexican safari, his story was fiercely disputed by his clients. The clients were the Pasquel family, and the famous physician with them was Dr. Agundis. It was Dr. Agundis, according to Pablo Bush Romero, a frequent safari client, who had saved Eric's life *twice*—"First by killing the leopard, and again by giving Rundgren highly skilful medical care without which Eric would have died."[5]

FOLLOWING his experiences on the Mexican safari Rundgren upgraded his arsenal and armed himself with a .577 Westley Richards double. He also put his salary dispute with Jack Block behind him and joined prestigious Ker and Downey Safaris. About this time Eric sold his Naro Moru farm, which he had purchased when he left the Game Department, making a hefty profit of £10,000 (about $28,000) on the deal, at that time a handsome sum. Soon afterward he was informed he had neglected to pay tax on the sale, which when paid off left the miffed Rundgren with only £600 ($1,680) in his pocket.[6]

During his career Rundgren found some outstanding trophy ivory for clients as well as for himself. While on an African version of a bushman's holiday Rundgren and a friend came upon the largest elephant he had ever seen. He first glimpsed the giant tusker, a 178 pounder, not far from where Bror Blixen, Denys Finch Hatton, and the Prince of Wales had lost their trophy elephant thirty years before, at a spot close to the Kenya-Tanganyika border. Eric followed the tusker for two days and nights without food, drinking only from fouled water holes. In broken thornbush and lava-strewn country the elephant crossed into Tanganyika. Rundgren caught up with it and shot it. Not surprisingly a record elephant like this caused a great deal of interest. Somehow word got out the elephant was shot in Tanganyika, not Kenya. The allegation immediately brought both the Kenya and the Tanganyika game departments into the act, and the situation, as often with Rundgren, became heated. Jerry Swynnerton, then Tanganyika's chief game warden, was so hot about it he personally went in search of the elephant carcass to inspect it. Had the ivory from this safari not been so spectacular, and the hunter been almost anybody but Rundgren, the whole matter may have been resolved with far less hoo-ha and publicity.

Because of the proximity of the Tsavo national park to the region in which Rundgren had been hunting, John Alexander, a warden at Tsavo and the only qualified surveyor in the employ of any wildlife agency, was asked to verify the unmarked international boundary to confirm that Rundgren's elephant had indeed crossed into Tanganyika. John Alexander was most reluctant about this particular duty, but unhappily he had to confirm the truth. "Rundgren," John said, "*had* crossed over and the elephant *was* shot in Tanganyika, about one and a half miles inside the country."[7] Rundgren never again spoke to Alexander, even after John quit as a park's warden to become a white hunter.

Rundgren thought the best thing was to get rid of the evidence.[8] In those days most tusks were cut into sections for easy packing by ivory dealers for export. Rundgren's ivory was taken to an Asian dealer, who, rightly fearing the giant tusks were illegitimate, lost no time in sawing them into pieces. That did not save Rundgren from being prosecuted. In the end the money he had made from the ivory went to legal fees, and he was stung with a big fine. Many thought him lucky to get off so lightly. Critics said he should at the very least have had his professional license suspended for a couple of years, charging that with his experience he knew perfectly well he had crossed the frontier and had tried to cover up the crime.

ALTHOUGH Rundgren had once been a game warden few subjects got him so worked up. He intensely disliked the "nitpicking, chinless Pongos (Englishmen)," such as the hapless John Alexander, yet warmly admired the likes of a few locals like Tsavo's Bill Woodley (who happened to be a close friend and colleague of Alexander's). Another pet peeve was the subject of *instant* white hunters. Unless a hunter had suffered, *really suffered*, a long and hungry apprenticeship, or, as in his own unusual case, they had done extensive hunting themselves, Rundgren loudly scoffed at their potential. Without justification some of these well-qualified individuals were dismissed by the Maharajah of Mayhem as mere "bahstuds."

One hunter so maligned was Erik Andersen, a likeable and competent Danish hunter from Uganda. Andersen, a soft-spoken, well-mannered fellow, also happened to be big and extremely tough. There were parallels in the lives of the two white hunters: both were of Scandinavian origin; both entered professional hunting somewhat late in life; both had done a tremendous amount of hunting before turning professional in their mid-thirties; and, finally, both shared the same first name. While Rundgren was easily aroused to anger, Andersen was slow, but if provoked he was a formidable opponent.

Erik Andersen had operated drilling rigs in the back of beyond for many years, isolated places such as Karamoja and central Tanganyika, where he had hunted on a daily basis before turning professional in 1963. Yet Rundgren, upon meeting Erik Andersen at the New Stanley Long Bar for the first time, referred to him as "another bloody *instant* white hunter," a remark that drew Andersen's immediate response. Andersen quietly suggested Rundgren "step outside, and repeat the remark." Fortunately perhaps for Rundgren, he snorted, backed down, and quickly moved away. No doubt the encounter would have been a battle royal, but if it *had* come to that, most white hunters who knew both men would have put their money on Andersen. After that Erik Andersen never failed to steam with anger at the mere mention of Rundgren's name. "He's nothing but a small-town bully,"[9] Andersen maintained, "and I'm ashamed he's one of my Scandinavian countrymen."*

John Sutton, a leading Ker and Downey hunter, also stood up to Rundgren. While the two were traveling in a convoy across the Serengeti Plains to establish a joint camp, Sutton's Land Rover broke down—not an uncommon occurrence because safari cars take a terrible beating. Sutton got out his tool box, raised the hood, and went to work. Rundgren pulled up with his clients and began tormenting Sutton. "Hurry up, you bahstud! You're holding up the whole bloody safari!" Sutton was pouring perspiration and up to his armpits in grease. Instead of offering help, Rundgren heckled, making cracks about Sutton's ancestry and mechanical skills. Finally Sutton, a small wiry man, sprang from beneath the car with a wrench in his fist. "One more crack, and by God I'll knock your head off!" Sutton says Rundgren backed away. "I knew how to handle Eric. Lots of young hunters did not. He walked all over them. They were intimidated by him, and he got a kick out of it."[10]

THERE WOULD always be sportsmen who would come to Africa to hunt with Rundgren—for his daredevil tactics and incredible hunting

---

*Eric's father, Ture Vladimir Rundgren, was Swedish, but his mother, Elizabeth (née Roberts), was Irish. Eric was born in England, at Berwick-upon-Tweed, on June 26, 1918, and arrived in Kenya when he was seven months old.

ability. One loyal client said, "At least he was a *great* bad ass! You never knew what he would do next. Every moment was a surprise!"[11]

Rundgren's view of clients was summed up in a remark he made after he had a drink or two under his belt, "Safari is not bad, it's the bloody clients that spoil the show." His grumbling fooled nobody, least of all Rundgren himself. He knew very well his clients had made him, and he knew which side his bread was buttered on. In 1964 Rundgren left Kenya for Bechuanaland (now Botswana), where he started his own outfit, although he returned to East Africa for safaris from time to time.

Rundgren will be remembered for many things, not least because he helped a good number of young hunters in the early stages of their careers. Back in 1952 one of those young hunters was Mike Prettejohn, who accompanied Rundgren on a private rhino hunt on Mount Kenya. During the hunt Rundgren got the fifth–world record rhino. Prettejohn commented, "Eric had the instincts of a wild animal, and could outwit them all. He was a brilliant bushman, and gave me invaluable experience and advice that no one will ever have the opportunity to repeat."[12] Rundgren was never as sagacious as Sutton, never as diplomatic as Selby, but he was, as fellow hunter Bill Ryan said so long ago, "a bloody fine hunter. A legend in his own time."

35

A TALE OF TWO HUNTERS

Of all the young hunters who passed under the critical gaze of Eric Rundgren, the crusty veteran judged Kenyan Tony Archer to be apart from the rest. "Tony possesses a greater natural gift for hunting than any man I know," Rundgren declared after a safari with Archer in Mozambique. Acting on his own advice, Rundgren made a strong recommendation to Syd Downey and Donald Ker that Archer would be an asset to the firm.

Tony Archer qualified for a professional license in 1957. The following year he took one of Bror Blixen's former American clients, Raymond Guest, on an extended hunt along the Nile in Sudan. Guest was so pleased he returned for another safari with Archer in 1959, this time in Kenya.

Though well into his sixties, Guest had long dreamed of hunting a hundred pounder, the trophy of all trophies. Raymond's brother, Winston, had hunted ivory a generation earlier with Bror Blixen. According to Tony Archer, Raymond disapproved of brother Winston's use of aircraft (piloted by Beryl Markham) to search for a hundred-pound elephant and insisted his own hunt should be conducted entirely on foot.

Raymond's safari commenced from a camp near Mutha Hill, in the dry thorn scrub of Ukambani district. Archer's trackers found big spoor early one morning, and Tony, Raymond, and their men began tracking the bull, which was traveling in a herd. By noon the hunters closed on the herd and Archer easily identified the trophy tusker. The men could not move in for the kill because the big bull was continuously surrounded by other elephants. Archer decided to wait until evening when the herd would begin to move again.

That evening, having made a careful approach to within a range of thirty yards from the "big one," Guest was about to shoot when the wind changed and the herd immediately took off. Guest realized he could not run after the elephant, and turning to Tony, he asked, "Can you get it?" Tony raced after the elephant and caught up half a mile farther on. Tony angled in close and dropped the big bull, as he had been asked to do. When Archer got back to his client, Guest shook his hand and said, "Congratulations! It's what I would have liked to have done all my life at your age. Can I make you a present of the tusks?"

Guest's offer was extremely generous, but it also created a dilemma for Archer. Tony demurred, not certain how ethical it was to accept a client's trophy. Three days later, with incredible luck and effort, Archer found a second hundred pounder. Guest shot the magnificent trophy, and the ivory weighed an impressive 117 and 118 pounds.

Yet Archer, struggling with the correctness of Guest's generosity, had still not accepted Guest's present, and it was not until after the safari that Tony consulted Syd Downey about the issue. Downey saw nothing wrong with it, and urged Archer to accept. Archer sold the tusks for $2,000, then a princely sum. Guest returned with his son for yet another safari with Archer, this time to Kosti, in Sudan.[1]

TONY ARCHER'S good name was often heard around campfires. In 1959 he accompanied hunters John Sutton and Terry Mathews with a trio of Americans: Hollywood actor William Holden, Chicago oilman Ray Ryan, and businessman Carl Hirschmann. During the course of the safari it happened that Ray Ryan suffered an injury above his eye caused when the recoil of his rifle scope gashed him in the eyebrow. This minor injury resulted in the safari heading for the Mawingo Hotel at Nanyuki to rest up for a few days. Ray Ryan and Bill Holden were at once enchanted with Mawingo and its postcard setting at the base of Mount Kenya.

As soon as the safari returned to Nairobi, Ray Ryan went to Ker and Downey's chairman, Jack Block, and offered to buy the Mawingo. Block immediately replied that he could have it for £50,000 ($140,000), in those days an outlandish sum in Africa. Block was surprised when Ryan said, "Done!"

The Mawingo Hotel was renamed the Mount Kenya Safari Club and was immediately successful. Tony Archer recalled that Jack Block liked to tell a story against himself after the sale of Mawingo to Ryan and Holden for £50,000.

Bill Holden was in the elevator at Nairobi's New Stanley Hotel with Jack Block. Block said, "Let me tell you a story. After the sale (of the Mawingo) was clinched I said to my father (Kenya hotel pioneer, Abraham Block):

> "What would you say if I told you I'd sold Mawingo for £25,000?"
> My father replied: "I'd say, well, yes, not bad."
> I said: "And what would you say if I told you I'd sold it for
> £40,000?"
> Dad answered, "You're learning son."
> I said triumphantly, "I sold it for £50,000."

Bill Holden, who had listened to this without interruption, said coolly: "Just for your information, Jack, we were prepared to go to seventy-five thousand."[2]

HOLLYWOOD actor Robert Stack is a man of action. At age nineteen he held two world skeet-shooting records and was on the University of Southern California's polo team. Stack was also the top-ranked West Coast speedboat racer in 1940–1941 and saw action in World War II as a navy lieutenant. When Stack went on safari to Kenya he made a fine pairing with Tony Archer. Stack was in Africa with war hero General Joe Foss, who holds the Congressional Medal of Honor for shooting down Japanese Zero fighters in World War II. The two men were to star in a segment for ABC's *The American Sportsman* television series. Stack later wrote:

> Tony Archer looked like a young Van Johnson, and was a dedicated naturalist and conservationist. He had also killed his first elephant, a rogue that was laying waste to the surrounding farms, at age thirteen. He was a tough taskmaster. I spent many hours with this strange, quiet young man, and like to think I became his friend. He was another of Africa's contradictions, a professional hunter dedicated to the preservation of the country's wildlife.[3]

In Robert Stack's book, *Straight Shooting,* he portrayed his white hunter as one with singular determination: "My job is to get you close

Hollywood actor Robert Stack and Tony Archer.

to the animals," Archer announced tersely. "Yours is to do your part well."

Archer and white hunter Bill Ryan went with Stack and Foss to the Nairobi safari clothiers, Ahmed Brothers. Stack wrote, "I had nearly chosen an outfit which looked like the one Stewart Granger wore in *King Solomon's Mines*, when Tony led me to the opposite end of the store."

"Get cracking, Bob," he said. "No more playing tourist. It's time to get you outfitted." Later Stack says he did manage to wangle a large Borsalino hat. "But when I was about to add a leopard-skin hat band, Tony put his foot down."

"I'd be afraid to be in the same camp with you wearing that bloody leopard band," he grumbled.[4]

After hunting big stuff at close quarters with Tony Archer and observing the other Ker and Downey hunters in camp, who included Bill Ryan, Terry Mathews, and David Ommanney, Stack observed:

> These hunters were just like the boat racers, motorcycle nuts, stunt men, and bullfighters I grew up with. Here was something I understood. The accents may have been different, but they had one thing in common: They were out of their skulls.[5]

Tony Archer's closest friend in the safari business was his gun-bearer, a famous Liangulu elephant hunter and former poacher named Abakuna Gumunde. Abakuna shot over two hundred elephant with his bow and arrows—a remarkable feat when one considers most of his poaching was in and around Tsavo national park when it was well patrolled by the likes of Bill Woodley, Peter Jenkins, and David Sheldrick. The risk of being caught by this formidable trio and jailed was extremely high, and in the end even the great Abakuna Gumunde was arrested. When Abakuna was released from jail he met Tony Archer, who hired him on the spot. In a short time Abakuna became Tony's right-hand man, friend, confidant, and a member of the Archer family. He accompanied Tony on hunting safaris all over Africa, and even to Nepal and India.

Some of Archer's famous clients included Prince Bernhard of the Netherlands, Jack Heinz and his son (of the 57 Varieties), Robert Kleberg of the King Ranch in Texas, and Senator Lloyd Bentsen. A leading ornithologist, Archer has conducted numerous museum safaris as well as the Machris-Knudsen Expedition for the Los Angeles County Museum, the Smithsonian, and the Royal Ontario Museum of Canada with the Winnifred Carter Expedition, among others.[6]

JOHN FLETCHER, like Tony Archer, trained in part under Eric Rundgren, and regarded Rundgren as a mentor, although Fletcher started his career in Tanganyika with Russell Bowker-Douglas. Fletcher is the temperamental opposite of Tony Archer, but the two hunters became good friends. Archer's serious and conservative persona was strangely compatible with Fletcher's extroverted nature. Tall, blond, and ruggedly handsome, Fletcher was born in Edinburgh in 1933.

Eric Rundgren instigated Fletcher's relocation from Tanganyika to Ker and Downey. Rundgren took Fletcher on elephant-control work between professional safaris, hunting in coastal forest where the shooting was often done at a range of ten yards or less. Rundgren led John into some of the hairiest scrapes imaginable, but John acknowledges he would never have been able to gain that much experience with anybody else.

Fletcher was on safari with fellow Ker and Downey hunter John Sutton and a party of clients in Masailand when one of Sutton's clients wounded a leopard. Sutton followed the cat, but the leopard quickly got him down and gave him a good mauling, then abandoned the attack. A bloodied John Sutton was carried into camp. Bloodied or not, Sutton had not lost his dry sense of humor. "Sutton," Fletcher said, "was *really* enjoying the moment, for he had a wicked grin on his face, knowing *I* had to go after the winged leopard."

Dogma demands that every effort is made to follow and shoot a wounded animal, not only because it will pose a danger for others who may come across it, but more particularly for humanitarian reasons. Game Department law makes it mandatory that wounded game be dispatched.

Fletcher had radioed Nairobi for an aircraft. While they waited for the plane to arrive, Sutton cheerfully volunteered, "My gunbearers will show you where we last saw the leopard!" Having bandaged and cleaned up Sutton's wounds, Fletcher got him on his way to the "flying doctor's" plane.

Few hunters are keen to clean up after another. There are many variables following somebody else's dangerous game; the condition of the animal, the location of the first shot, the thickness of the brush, and the remaining amount of daylight are all crucial factors. The hunter asks himself: Will the leopard go for me right away, or will it drag me into dense brush before it attacks? Will it come low in a short-range frontal attack, or will it let me pass and then ambush me from behind? How badly hurt is it, and how fast will it come? Has it stiffened? And finally, just how big is this beast?

Fletcher shouldered his shotgun realizing he was likely to have a hot time of it. As always, the question of the accompanying client was a difficult one to address. This time was no different than it usually is, for the client said he wanted to come along. Most clients have no idea or will not accept the reality of the dangers presented by wounded big game. Few hunters want clients with them in such situations, for they can be a liability or worse. Fletcher reluctantly agreed to let his client accompany him, at least for the first part of the hunt. As the hunters approached the spot where the leopard had caught Sutton, an old Masai man suddenly appeared and offered to help.

"I have a very good dog," the Masai explained to Fletcher. "It can go into the brush and flush out the leopard for you." John demurred, preferring to do the thing his way, but the Masai man was so insistent, John agreed to give him a few shillings and let his dog have a go at it. With some misgivings, the hunters waited while the man went off to fetch his dog.

"The dog arrived with the Masai," according to Fletcher, "a big, brown, flea-bitten mongrel." The hunters crept into the first thicket and were immediately met by a growl from the leopard somewhere ahead in the underbrush. The Masai urged his dog to go in after the leopard. The hunters stood about while the dog gingerly sniffed around the brush and finally with some trepidation entered it. For a while nothing happened. Then all hell broke loose as the leopard gave a snarl followed by agitated grunts that quickly rose in volume. Obviously the leopard was charging, and by the sounds coming from the brush it was headed straight for the hunting party.

"At that moment," Fletcher said, "instead of a ferocious leopard breaking out of the brush, out came the big brown mongrel, yelping and fleeing for its life. It was going like hell across some open ground. My client was so itchy fingered he snapped off two shots at the running dog, thinking it was the bloody leopard. Fortunately he missed the dog by a wide margin. Still, the dog immediately got an extra spurt of speed, for not only did it think the maddened leopard was after it, but now two heavy-caliber bullets whistled past throwing up big spurts of dust. The dog redoubled its efforts, accelerating until it went over the horizon."[7]

There was no more short-cutting the situation. Fletcher left his trigger-happy client behind, and went in ready for action, inching his way into the undergrowth and expecting a charge at his next breath. His eyes checked darkened shadows, every piece of mottled shade, every tuft of grass. There was a speckle of dried blood, another, and another. Then no blood. No clear marks on the leaf mold. He got to his knees to examine the spoor, and to look beneath the brush. There was nothing but the hum of sweat flies after the moisture on his forehead. Suddenly the hunt ended in anticlimax. Instead of a crazed leopard, Fletcher found the carcass of a very large dead cat.

ON ANOTHER safari Fletcher's client was the famous Mexican bull-fighter Gaston Santos. "He was a great shot," Fletcher said, "and being a bullfighter he had very fast reflexes. He was also as good with a rifle as he was with a shotgun."

Early one cold morning Fletcher and Santos closed with a big buffalo on the Ololol escarpment above the Mara River, in Kenya's Hunting Block 60. John Fletcher recalled:

> The stalk was quite easy, and we crawled to within forty yards of the buffalo. Gaston's bullet took him behind the shoulder, too far

back, too high, and into the lung area. A lethal shot usually, but it takes time to have effect. Gaston's bullet spun the buffalo around. He fired his second shot as the buffalo was taking off, raking him in the hindquarters, but it did not slow him up. In seconds he had vanished into a gully nearby, and all we had was a frothy blood trail to follow, a sure sign of a lung shot. I could tell he was not going very far.

Soon I heard him moving ahead of us, and I put my tracker, Sangau, up a tree to see if there was any sign of him. Sangau could not see the buffalo, but we could hear his rasped breathing, and I knew it was just a matter of time. I decided to move in and dispatch him as quickly as possible. Gaston and I edged into the thicket very slowly following the blood trail, with the sounds of the buffalo breathing ahead of us. I was just creeping around a patch of tall grass, when there—just twenty paces away—was the buffalo, with his legs just showing in the undergrowth, and his head down watching us. At this moment I slowly stepped aside to give Gaston a clear shot. But I was fully expecting the buffalo to go for us at any second.

Gaston was right behind me, and I motioned for him to shoot. Gaston, kneeling down for the shot, fired. The buffalo immediately went for us, smashing down the bush as he came. At that moment it was very obvious the buffalo was coming for me. I threw up my .500 double and fired both barrels straight into the middle of his chest, but he still came on as if nothing had happened. I realized there was not enough time to reload, and I was about to be hooked by those nasty horns. I was wedged against a tree, desperately trying to jam two more shells into my double, when I heard Gaston fire again from somewhere on my right. The buffalo crashed on its chin right at my feet, stone dead.

"How's that for a client?" Gaston said, grinning, "Let's see if your hands are shaking?" Of course they were a bit. It had been a close call, but I tried not to show it too much. Gaston was a great one for the *macho* bit, and thrived on this sort of excitement. It had been a brilliant snapshot, with hardly enough time for him to get the rifle to his shoulder. Very lucky for me to have someone like him along, otherwise things could have turned out a lot different.[8]

36.

THE WANDERINGS OF AN
OFFICER AND A GENTLEMAN

Even among such a disparate group of adventurers as the white hunter fraternity there were a few men universally regarded as "characters," people who were vastly different from their colleagues in one way or another, and occasionally in a great many ways. Such a person is Douglas Tatham Collins, also known as Ponsumby, or more usually as plain old Shagbag Collins. He was one of the least likely to stride across Africa's plains as a white hunter of considerable renown.

Dougie's first African destination was the ancient Land of Punt, more usually known as Somaliland, where so many of the old-time safari hunters at the end of the last century had trudged the burning wastes amid fierce maneless desert lions and the hot-eyed, quick-tempered Somalis around the Horn of Africa. During the Second World War Collins had led a unit of the Somali Gendarmerie, recruited by the British after the Italians were driven from Somaliland by General Cunningham's forces advancing from Kenya. To fill the Italian vacuum the country was administered by the British, and Collins was posted to the hinterlands, known as the Furtherest Shag. Collins, a self-proclaimed "true romantic," had been happily isolated for years in some of the most hostile environments the African continent could dish up. Lesser men had been driven to madness, drink, depravity, and, not infrequently, suicide. But Collins had not only survived in the bloody company of endless *shifta* (bandit) battles, *fitinas* (intrigues), and firefights, he had flourished. Yet it was mostly a wretched life of camel and foot patrols under a searing sun, of relentless attacks and counterattacks, great deprivation, thirst, and danger. Not least of all was the fearful isolation, where even radios were unobtainable. Out of

Douglas Collins and client, Armando Conde, Tanganyika, 1957.

that long desert sojourn came Dougie's best-selling book, *A Tear for Somalia*. His literary inclinations set him far apart from most of his colleagues in Africa.

At unexpected moments today Douglas will burst forth in resonant tones with stanza and verse from a suddenly remembered poem, and his everyday discourse is sprinkled with references, many of them originating from academic tomes absorbed long ago in England. He retains expressions picked up in the Furtherest Shag, and his speech is peppered with Gendarmerie slang: *wompo* (booze), bangsticks (rifles), crumpet and dingbats (women), squeakers (children), griff (news), and so on.

Collins dreaded a peacetime post or transfer to cooler climates, but his prayers were answered and he was sent to Wajir, an isolated *Beau Geste*–style fort in the Furtherest Shag of northern Kenya. It was a familiar harsh desertscape occupied by big game and nomadic Somalis. Like Somalia, Wajir was a hotbed of ongoing Somali *shifta* activity. Dougie's off-duty time between skirmishes in the Northern Frontier was spent on hunting trips, sometimes alone with a tracker or sometimes in the company of his friends, Isiolo game warden George Adamson and Tana River warden Jack Bonham. At some point over this period Collins decided he would become a white hunter. His well-documented hunting experiences gave him entrée into the tight-knit Kenya safari fraternity, ever wary of outsiders. Yet Dougie was not the screen image of a tall, dark, and handsome hero of Hollywood legend, bristling with muscles and mystique. He is well spoken, well read, fair-haired, pink-skinned, and trim but tough, a former officer whose determination to make a career as a white hunter commenced in 1956.

Collins joined Safariland Ltd., where he had the good fortune to hunt with old-guard white hunters Philip Percival and J. A. Hunter. Then Dougie founded his own firm, Kenya Safaris Ltd. Even after he had become a fixture in hunting circles, some old-time white hunters did not know what to make of the man they referred to as Shagbag or Ponsumby. The Africans had less trouble identifying him, and nicknamed him simply Bwana D.C. (Mister District Commissioner) or Bwana Major, both previous ranks Collins had held. Dougie's peers were convinced from the start that Douglas was far too much of an English toff (for "toffee nose") for most clients, especially the Americans. "He's too bloody attached to his class prejudices to give them up," it was said. But the fact is that neither rank nor title mattered to Douglas, and despite his Britishness, he was totally mindless of class, color, and religion. In any contest the sentimental Collins would always champion the underdog. With self-deprecating good humor he pointedly referred to his own ancestral tribe, the English, as Pongos, or as the Inglezi. What was important to Dougie was style.

To the amazement of the New Stanley Hotel's Long Bar contingent, who forecast that Shagbag's white hunting enterprises were doomed to failure, and that "Shagbag couldn't arrange a piss-up in a brewery," Collins's new safari company did well. The quality of Dougie's big game trophies could not be denied, and Collins good-naturedly shrugged off the gibes.

As for the Africans he worked with, Collins's years of living in the bush among primitive tribesmen had made him an astute judge of the African character. The safari crew he assembled was first-rate. Although organization was never Dougie's strong point, he expected the best from his men, and they hardly ever disappointed him. The most important man among his staff was a small, bony Kamba tribesman named Buno, who was all heart, skill, and forbearance. The wizened little gunbearer would be Collins's shadow through thick and thin for the rest of his hunting days.

There was no denying that fate on occasion did give Shagbag Collins a hand. During one safari hunt in northern Tanganyika's Loliondo area, Collins had just led his client, international businessman Wally Heinze, the chairman of Playtex, then known for the revolutionary "Living Bra," into a herd of six hundred buffalo. Collins believed in leg-work and relished long, unhurried treks on foot, and his clients soon realized he was no car hunter. On a trek with Heinze, hunter and client inspected the massive buffalo herd, when all of a sudden two enormous bulls began to battle. The clash of their mighty horns, boss on boss, and the sounds of anguished bellowing as the two titans did their best to gore each other were deafening. Collins stood back and timed the strug-gle, as might a referee in a boxing match. From the moment he and Heinze came upon the scene, Dougie reckoned it took fifteen minutes before one of the beasts slipped on wet grass and went down. Instantly the other bull took advantage of his fallen foe and rammed a horn tip into its side.

"Blood and intestines ballooned," Collins wrote, "and the mortally wounded bull tried to break off the fight, as it staggered in our direction. The younger animal watched the bleeding old bull for a few moments, and then walked slowly back to rejoin the herd." Collins and Heinze watched the dying bull, its head hung low. "Do him a favor and shoot him," Collins whispered. Wally Heinze obliged, killing the buffalo with a single merciful shot. The horns of the trophy bull had a record-class spread of 54 inches.[1]

DOUGIE HAD always been a heroic presence to Somalis in both Kenya and Somalia, and especially so to one named Abdi Rascid Shermarke. It seemed that fate really did protect Douglas Tatham Collins, or it may have been his Somali amber love beads. It happened that Somalia was now independent of both the British and the Italians (if not the Ethiopi-ans) and the country's new president was none other than Dougie's for-mer office clerk in Somalia, Abdi Rascid Shermarke.*

In the universal manner of Somalis, Shermarke had never forgotten his former boss, the fearless, exceptionally just English major, fondly

---

*Abdi Rascid Shermarke, born in 1917, came from Somalia's Mijjertein province. He was an official in both the Italian and British administrations and a committee member of the Somali Youth League (SYL).

known to the Somalis as Abdi Malek (The Bastard), who had befriended him when he was a lowly worker so long ago, and who had sympathized with the Somali Youth League's aim of independence for a Greater Somalia. Collins at that time was on a safari along the Tana River with American celebrity photographer Peter Beard. The Somali president tracked Collins down and left a message for Abdi Malek at Yusuf Abdulgani's *duka* store at the Kenyan desert town of Garissa. Dougie was invited to come to Somalia and hunt anything, anywhere he wanted. President Shermarke also asked Collins to move permanently to Somalia and assist him in opening up tourism in general, and hunting in particular.

Collins traveled to Somalia, taking with him his trusted gunbearer, Buno. He was feted by the president, put up in splendid style at the Croce del Sud Hotel (the Southern Cross) at Mogadishu, and a large banquet was arranged in his honor at Afgoi, where he had been posted with his Gendarmerie in 1941. Collins was impressed by the generosity and sincerity of his Somali friends, and particularly so by the president.

Shermarke's government made two handsome old Arab-style villas on the seashore at the Somali town of Kismayu available for Dougie's use. Collins had been there to inspect them, and he was greatly impressed. He said to me, "Come with me. You can have one villa, and I'll have the other. We've been given spacious storehouses. The hunting is fantastic. There are big elephant about, and many local species you can't get elsewhere—Pelzeln's gazelle, Speke's gazelle, Soemmering's gazelle, dibatag [or Clarke's gazelle], beria antelope, and so on. Lion are thick on the ground." I said I would think about it.

Collins moved quickly. He contacted old clients all over the world and confirmed there was enormous interest in Somaliland, which had been unhunted since the end of World War II. Collins returned to Somalia for another safari, and made up his mind to move there permanently. But back in Nairobi, Collins received a bombshell. President Shermarke, on a visit to his home province of Mijjertein, had been gunned down by his own bodyguard. Dougie's Somaliland safari dreams were shattered, and a shaken Collins mourned the death of another loyal old friend. In Africa one bullet changes everything.

Somalia fell with amazing rapidity into a state of anarchy following the death of Shermarke. *Shifta* raids into Kenya's Northern Frontier rapidly escalated. And amazingly, Dougie's book, *A Tear for Somalia*, was banned in Somaliland.

❖

UNDAUNTED, Dougie began writing again, drafting a new work, *Another Tear for Africa,* a sequel to his first classic. He was also writing poetry and short stories, which were quickly published.

In September 1970 Dougie was looking forward to his younger brother Edmund's first visit to Kenya. Together they would make a safari into the Furtherest Shag. Dougie had permits to hunt in Block 11 on the west bank of the Tana River for game birds like vulturine guinea fowl, francolins, and sand grouse. While in the desert he would have Edmund meet George Adamson, his old game warden friend, who now lived with his brother Terence and their world-famous family of lions at Kora camp, adjacent to Hunting Block 11. Dougie intended to surprise Edmund by returning to England with him for a brief holiday.

The two men set out from Nairobi in Dougie's Land Rover hauling a trailer loaded with safari equipment. Collins set up his camp a few miles downstream from thickly jungled Mballamballa island, a favorite haunt of elephants. From their scenic camp on the shady riverbank they could watch crocodiles emerging to sun themselves on sandbars that rose between the muddy streams. The chocolate waters are full of crocs that attack and kill riverine tribesmen and their animals with amazing regularity, yet the people accept the attacks with a strange, fatalistic resignation. When the streams between sandbars are low, it is not uncommon to see whole families wading across the river with the greatest nonchalance, oblivious to the crocodiles below the surface and the hippo in deeper pools.

At various places along the river flights of sand grouse came in to drink from the surrounding deserts, and in the evenings Egyptian geese and many ducks flew along the river. Shagbag's hunting clients were forbidden to shoot Egyptian geese, for "they mate for life," he would say. "If you shoot one the other gets very upset. Not cricket, old boy!"

On daily nature walks, Dougie explained to his brother the phenomenon of desert wildlife, and his particular fascination with huge roving herds of elephant that came to browse in the rich riverine woodlands. Behind the green snake of vegetation banking the river lay the formidable gray *borani* thorn desert—the Furtherest Shag—the home of Grevy's zebra, Hunter's hartebeest, gerenuk, wart hog, oryx, lesser kudu, dik-dik, and lion. In the evenings both men welcomed the cool breeze as it came up off the river to replace the languid heat of the day.

Elephants browsing in acacia woodland.

As the sun dipped low they would sit beside a campfire listening to the grunt of a lion or the shrill sounds of trumpeting elephants come to drink in the river, while cicadas throbbed in the undergrowth. Amid the new sounds of approaching night the brothers would sip a *wompo* whiskey and reminisce about their childhood days in faraway Nottingham, and the pranks they had got up to in their youth on their father's comfortable Aslockton, Nottinghamshire, farm. The family motto is *Obedienta melior quam sacrificia* (Obedience is better than sacrifice).

On September 10, 1970, the sun rose in a high white sky, as it usually does in the Northern Frontier. Instead of a grouse shoot that day, Dougie and Edmund started out on a short walk to a *mulka* (oxbow) where a sandbar jutted into the stream and a very large crocodile often basked. Dougie wanted his brother to shoot this particularly large croc as a trophy, and Edmund was keen to do so. During morning walks with Edmund along the riverbank on their way to shoot grouse, Collins habitually carried his big .470 Army and Navy double-barreled rifle as insurance, just as he would on any safari. His gunbearers, Buno and

Wario, carried shotguns, water bottles, and an ammo bag. Dougie had armed Edmund with a scoped Winchester .30/.06 for the croc hunt.

The hunters slowly followed a game trail that paralleled the river, winding in and out of dense thickets of *swaki* bush, doum palms, and Tana poplars. As the trail circled a thicket, Collins, who was leading the single-file column, heard and at the same time saw a buffalo break cover without warning. The buffalo appeared about ten feet from Collins in a full-out charge. Dougie had no warning, had seen no buffalo tracks, had heard nothing, not even the customary sound of rising tick birds that so often accompany buffalo and rhino. The buffalo already had great momentum, and as it came it kept its head lowered. There was no time to get his rifle to his shoulder. Collins swung from the hip and fired both barrels. The huge animal absorbed both shots without apparent effect. Collins had faced buffalo charges before. There was nothing new to him about this attack, except that in the past he had been deliberately hunting buffalo, or following a wounded animal. It was an unprovoked attack.

Even before Collins fired his shots, Edmund and gunbearer Buno had seen what was about to happen and jumped off the narrow game trail out of the way. The buffalo's horns hooked Collins, ripping his leg open from knee to thigh, and tossed him high in the air, as if he had been a mere puppet. Although the buffalo slammed into Collins with the force of an express train, Collins was conscious of coming down, of landing hard. Even in his dazed condition he knew this was it. This time the chips were down, and they were *his* chips. When Dougie landed the buffalo went after him again with insatiable fury. It ripped a horn into his thigh and shoved him along the ground, slamming Collins's head against a tree trunk.

As Collins came to, lying on his back bleeding, the buffalo was nowhere to be seen. Then he was aware of the rush of feet in the undergrowth and, fearful for his men's safety, he yelled, "Get behind me, get out of the way, I can cope!" It was vintage Collins. He could always cope, had always coped, whether with a wounded buffalo, or returning *shifta* fire. Collins was bleeding profusely. He could not get up. But nearby in the dust lay his .470 rifle. Collins reached for the heavy gun, and then he saw the buffalo watching him. Collins noticed blood from his shots oozing from the buffalo's chest.

Collins thought his number was up, for the buffalo made a sudden rush straight for him, but as it came a single shot rang out from the undergrowth. The shot did not drop the buffalo, but it distracted the animal momentarily, and it swerved away from Collins, who by then had made a desperate lunge for his rifle. Lying in the dirt he broke the gun, ejecting the spent shells, and quickly reloaded two 500-grain solids from his belt. Even as he lay on the ground slamming his rifle shut the buffalo was above him goring his thighs. Collins thrust his rifle up at the animal as it stood over him, and with the gun against the buffalo's chest, fired both barrels. The buffalo collapsed, falling across Collins's smashed and bleeding torso, trapping him with its massive bulk. Collins lost consciousness.

When Dougie came around he was aware of the awful silence, save for the flies attracted to congealing blood. He called out weakly, "Edmund, over here. I'm all right!" But there was no answer. Collins tried to move, but his smashed legs were pinned beneath the fallen buffalo. Collins called out again, "Buno, Buno. Wario, Wario, *cuja hapa!*" Still there was no reply, but soon the two gunbearers appeared near Collins, and with great difficulty the men rolled the buffalo off the fallen man. It was then that Collins saw his brother lying on the other side of the dead buffalo.

On his stomach Collins crawled over to Edmund, and even then as he placed his hand on his brother's brow and looked into his eyes he realized his beloved Edmund was dead. Overcome with grief, Collins tried to figure out what had happened. When the buffalo had made its second rush at him as he lay reaching for his rifle, a single .30/.06 shot had rung out. That was Edmund firing the light rifle, and although the shot had not killed the buffalo it had been sufficient to distract the animal and permit Dougie to get his gun, reload, and fire. On the ground with the buffalo pummeling him, Collins had fired both barrels into the animal's chest, but a solid bullet had exited the chest cavity and struck Edmund, who had rushed in to try to assist his brother. Dougie's .470 bullet exited the buffalo's rib cage and entered Edmund's heart, killing him instantly.

Collins again lost consciousness. Dougie's gunbearer, Buno, left Wario with Dougie while he ran back among the winding game trails along the riverbank. He ran for two hours in the crushing heat until he arrived opposite Mballamballa island. Buno waded across the Tana River, going warily from sandbar to sandbar until he reached Mballamballa village in Hunting Block 10.

On the bush telegraph Buno had heard that another *mzungu*

(European) hunter was camped upstream from Collins's camp, and the Game Department scout at Mballamballa confirmed white hunter Bwana "Ronnie" was camped two miles farther on. Buno had no difficulty finding the wheel marks of a Toyota Land Cruiser and followed them to Rene Babault's hunting camp. Babault immediately called the Flying Doctor Service in Nairobi on his radio and requested an aircraft to land at Garissa airstrip. Meanwhile Rene returned with Buno to fetch Collins. Dougie was in serious condition when he arrived at the hospital, and Edmund's body was taken for a postmortem.

Word of the tragedy swept like wildfire through Kenya, and Dougie's friends rallied around, but Dougie was inconsolable. Collins swore he would never hunt again. Later he wrote:

> Well, the sands of Africa have run out for me at last in the saddest possible way. . . . I am naturally severing all connections with Africa . . . but don't for one moment think, you sweet bastard, that I have lost my nerve. . . . If it hadn't been my brother I would have carried on a personal vendetta against all the bloody buffalo in the whole of Africa. I have always loathed them, the black, tricky, courageous, aggressive bastards.[2]

Douglas Tatham Ponsumby Shagbag Collins, a.k.a. Abdi Malek, a.k.a. Bwana Major, was bowing out of the heat, but it seemed he was taking the last cool breeze with him.

37.

KING OF THE CATCHERS

Carr Hartley was physically a most powerful man, just under six feet tall with the build of a heavyweight wrestler. It was not by accident the American press had dubbed him the "Toughest Man in the World." Carr began taking out professional hunting safaris before he turned twenty. He was famous not so much as a white hunter but as the best-known big game catcher in the business, supplying animals to zoos all over the world, from Japan to Israel. Carr also pioneered the translocation of wild animals in East Africa from threatened areas to wildlife reserves, long before anesthesia and darting methods had been developed.

Carr usually caught his game by lassoing from a speeding vehicle. Over the years he paid a high price for his daily handling of dangerous game. He was severely mauled several times by lion, twice tossed by rhino, trampled by a buffalo, and an oryx put a horn through his knee. In Carr's view elephant were the most dangerous of the Big Five, followed by buffalo, leopard, lion, and rhino, despite the fact that his most serious injuries were caused by lion and rhino.[1]

THOMAS AUGUSTUS CORKE HARTLEY was born at Nairobi on October 31, 1910, the son of an Irish coffee planter. He was the eldest of four children born to Lionel James and Eva Maude Hartley. Carr, as he was known, and his brother Lionel survived, but two of their siblings died in infancy. Just around the corner was more tragedy when their father died of plague, which was then sweeping through Nairobi. Hartley's widow married Percy Poolman, a Nanyuki rancher who fathered nine children, three of whom died in infancy.[2] But three of those children—Fred, Gordon, and Henry Poolman—were to make their lasting mark on the safari world. Eva was widowed again, but she hung on to Percy's Naro Moru ranch and raised her offspring with the help of her children's half brother, Carr Hartley. Carr became the patriarch of the entire Poolman-Carr-Hartley clan, and a father figure to the three Poolman boys. The clan looked to Carr for decisions and leadership, and his powerful personality greatly influenced their lives. The Poolman boys, especially the younger two, Gordon and Henry, owed their early career successes in the hunting world to Carr.

CARR HARTLEY was a good hunter and a clever businessman, although he only had two years of formal schooling. He got his first job at the age of fourteen, when he was hired by the Honorable Berkely Cole to help run Cole's sheep at Naro Moru, then a remote ranching region on the lower slopes of Mount Kenya. Two years later Cole died, and Carr, then sixteen, was managing 25,000 acres for a wealthy rancher named Major Sidney Armstrong at Naro Moru. In the same year Carr went after a cattle-killing lion, the first of many stock raiders that he shot.[3] Carr was careful with his money and supplemented his salary by hunting big-tusked elephant on his own licenses.

While in his late teens Carr shot a remarkable elephant at Kyonyo, Kenya. The tusks were almost the heaviest recorded in Kenya, weighing an amazing 162 and 167 pounds. It took Carr and his bearers two days to walk back to his vehicle carrying the enormous tusks.[4] Carr's hunting prowess came to the attention of Kenya's chief game warden, Archie Ritchie, who signed him up for buffalo- and elephant-control work.

In 1934 Carr bought 10,000 acres of land near the frontier town of Rumuruti, and in December of the following year he married his child-hood sweetheart, Claudia Daphne Randall. Daphne Carr-Hartley's family, the Randalls, and their kin, the Bastards (their real name), were very successful and dominated the Nanyuki farming country for the first half of this century. The Randalls took the cake for fertility with eight boys and six girls. Author Elspeth Huxley observed, "It was said that if you walked down a Nanyuki street and called out 'Bastard!' every second European would turn a head."[5]

Between 1936 and 1942, Daphne and Carr Hartley had four sons. The boys and their mother used "Carr-Hartley" as their surname to distinguish themselves from the other branch of the Hartley family. All the boys followed their father into careers with wildlife. As a child

Carr Hartley was twice gored by rhinos.

Mike featured in many movie productions, including Louis Cotlow's *Zanzabuku*, as well as some of the early Hollywood Tarzan films. As adults all the boys suffered an assortment of serious injuries from wild animals. One son, Brian Carr-Hartley, lost an eye. His brother Pat was also a successful big game catcher for many years. Both Mike and Roy Carr-Hartley are leading white hunters today.

Carr's Rumuruti Ranch carried many varieties of wild game, in addition to animals he had trapped or was holding for quarantine and international shipment to zoos. His most famous animals were two northern white rhino. They starred in many films and were so tame they could be ridden by strangers. The ranch became a base for moviemakers from Hollywood and Elstree, England, with Carr personally hosting stars of the caliber of Rhonda Fleming, Janet Leigh, MacDonald Carey, Victor Mature, and others. But the real stars at Rumuruti were Carr himself, his talented sons, and their menagerie of big game animals. Thirty-eight major movies were partly shot at Carr's ranch, which grew to cover 22,000 acres.

Actor Stewart Granger visited Carr's place during the filming of *King Solomon's Mines*, in which he and Deborah Kerr played leading roles. Granger badly wanted to see a wild black rhino. Carr soon located a rhino with a huge horn on his ranch. Granger thought it would be a great idea to include a rhino-hunting sequence in *Solomon's Mines*. For

Granger's benefit, Carr demonstrated how he was able to call wild rhinos by blowing into an empty cartridge case, which produced the same sound as a rhino's whistling snort. Granger was so impressed he proposed to Carr, and to J. A. Hunter, who happened to be Carr's guest at the time, that Carr should call this big rhino and get it to charge them. Granger hoped to be the "matador" on film who would shoot the charging rhino. Carr was willing to give the risky scheme a try, but when Granger approached the film's director with his plan, the man turned a doomsday shade of green. Much to Granger's chagrin the idea was dropped.

Carr's ranch became a sort of informal college for his half brothers, the Poolman boys, as well as for young hopefuls wanting to get into big game hunting or safari work. Among the better known youths who got a leg up with Carr's help was David Sheldrick, who switched from white hunter to become warden of Tsavo national park. The dashing young hunter Mark Howard-Williams, who was to die a sudden death, got started with Carr's help. Carr's most celebrated student was Brian Nicholson, who became first a white hunter then a warden known for his success in tracking down man-eating lions. Brian was later Tanganyika's principal game warden.

CARR'S BROTHER Lionel married an Irish girl named Diana who was serving in the British army in 1942. Lionel got a job as resident hunter based at Mac's Camp (later Mac's Inn), a roadside pub and hotel near the railway station of Mtito Andei (Place of Vultures), midway between Nairobi and Mombasa. The camp was owned by C. G. "Mac" McArthur, a former game warden and Safariland Ltd. stockholder. Lionel's job at Mac's Camp was cut short when he was killed in a light-aircraft crash at Voi in 1950. The pilot of the Tiger Moth was a British army sergeant named Bob Astles, who survived the crash although suffering a broken neck and other injuries in the accident. Years later the highly controversial and much disliked Astles gained infamy as bloodthirsty Ugandan dictator Idi Amin's "adviser." At the time of the crash it was widely rumored, but never proven, that it was "staged" by Astles because he was smitten with Lionel Hartley's wife, Diana. I asked Bob Astles if there was any truth to his alleged infatuation with Diana. He angrily scoffed at the "dammed lie, and ugly rumor," sarcastically saying, "I suppose I also deliberately broke my own neck in the accident—just to give it some credence."[6]

After Lionel's death, Diana took her two young children and stayed for a while with Carr Hartley's family at Rumuruti. There she met one of Carr's employees, an Austrian named Heini Demmer. Diana promptly went into an animal-trapping partnership with Demmer—to supply zoos—in direct competition with Carr Hartley, Diana's brother-in-law. Later still, Diana Hartley married Eddie Knodl, a chef at Nairobi's Norfolk Hotel.

Violence continued to stalk the family. Diana's own mother, Mary, was hacked to death with machetes by Mau Mau thugs who attacked the family's Nyeri farmhouse during the Mau Mau Emergency. Diana's seventy-year-old stepfather, G. A. Leakey, who was a blood brother of the Kikuyu tribe, was dragged off by the same gang and buried alive in October 1954. Gray and Mary Leakey are now in the same grave at Nyeri cemetery.

Diana (Hartley) Knodl also died tragically. She was killed by a "tame" lion while working on the Hollywood epic about professional animal catchers, *Hatari*. On November 1, 1960, Diana Knodl entered the lion's cage and it sprang on her. It bit her three times, on the chin, throat, and chest, then mauled her to death. White hunter Bill Ryan, who was on the film set nearby with stars John Wayne, Hardy Kruger, Red Buttons, and the actress Capucine, commented, "Diana should *never* have got into the cage with that lion. She didn't have a chance." Diana's only son, also named Lionel, began his professional hunting apprenticeship in 1970 with myself and Nick Swan. He was in the hunting business for seven years, until March 1977.

38

DEADLY LION HUNT

One of Carr Hartley's half brothers, Henry Poolman, was that rare being—a man utterly without fear. He was once described by a Nairobi newspaper as "a great bull of a man." Henry was six feet two of dynamite, and with the 220-pound physique of an athlete. In a tight corner he had no regard for his own safety. As a white hunter his cool head and toughness had won the respect of his peers, a decidedly picky lot of fellows, who considered him to be about as good as they get in the game.

Hunting had always been a daily activity for Henry, who like his white hunter brothers Gordon and Fred was a brawny Kenya cowboy and proud of it. He lived a frontier existence in the wide-open spaces of Naro Moru, with his rifle always close at hand. As a boy if he had flushed a bushbuck or some other antelope species while he was harvesting wheat, that animal was as good as dead—whether it was running, jumping, zigging, or zagging. Henry's old Mannlicher .256 rifle would fly to his shoulder, bark once, and that was the end of the business.

The self-reliant Poolman family was typical of pioneering families in the sparsely settled African highlands in the early fifties. They lived in a land where everything was used and nothing was ever wasted. At Naro Moru the plentiful game of the Laikipia Plains provided a fine selection of wild venison for the table. Surplus meat was sun-dried and spiced with pepper, salt, and vinegar to make beef jerky, or *biltong*. Bone marrow was seasoned with pepper and served as hors d'oeuvres, while the bones were boiled to make a base for soup. Hides were used in the manufacture of straps, reins, and furniture, horns provided glue, and animal fat was turned into soap and candles.

Rainbow trout could be caught in the icy snowmelt streams of Mount Kenya. Plum, pear, apple, and peach trees thrived in the temperate climate, yielding their fruit for preserves and jams; milk, cheese, and butter were provided by the farm's dairy herd.

Trips to Nairobi, one hundred miles away, were rare. More often the Poolmans would go to the small farming town of Nanyuki to purchase groceries or spare parts or, on infrequent occasions, to socialize or visit Carr's ranch at Rumuruti. On the lonely Poolman farm the main evening entertainment was an old-fashioned wooden-cased radiogram.

During Kenya's Mau Mau Emergency in the fifties, the Poolman boys had gained fame for their work with tracker teams. All three Poolmans became white hunters, but it was only Henry who went on to make a lasting name for himself in the safari world. Henry's early life was in stark contrast to that of most of his sophisticated and urbanized hunting clientele, but being more gregarious than his older brothers, he fitted easily into the milieu of international sportsmen who came on safari.

Henry took General James H. Doolittle, the famous U.S. Air Force hero and leader of the celebrated World War II raid on Japan, on a hunting safari in 1966, parts of which were televised in the United States. Doolittle, who returned with a full bag of exceptional trophies, including the Big Five, was exceptionally pleased with his white hunter.

Henry teamed up for a safari with his old friend Terry Mathews in March 1967. Ker and Downey outfitted the trip for clients Mr. and Mrs. Julian S. (Pete) Barrett, and Mr. and Mrs. Steve Spaulding, all from Buffalo, New York. Apart from big game trophies, the group hoped to collect a variety of Kenya birds for the Buffalo Museum of Natural Sciences. Terry Mathews, an expert ornithologist, would hunt with the Spauldings, while Henry Poolman would hunt with the Barretts. Operating from the same camp, the two white hunters made a formidable team.

As was the custom, a lion was among the Big Five trophies sought by Henry's clients. At thirty-six years of age, Henry Poolman had personally shot dozens of lions, and led clients into many more. A previous lion encounter several years earlier had left Henry a legacy of miniature railway-track scars over much of his body. On that hunt Henry followed a wounded lion into tall grass, getting off his shot just as the lion reached him. His bullet had been deadly, but not effective enough to kill the lion instantly. In the minutes it took for the lion to die from the bullet, the four-hundred-pound cat caught Henry and tore him apart, to the tune of 398 surgical stitches. His wrists, arms, and an ankle were broken. A weaker or smaller man would never have survived such an attack.

THE BARRETT-SPAULDING safari set out from Nairobi and headed first to the desert country of north-central Kenya. Camp was set up beneath umbrella acacias beside the dry watercourse of the Baragoi *lugga*, or sand river. The region offered specialized desert game, and the party hunted below the Lopet plateau for lesser and greater kudu, and the windswept El Barta Plains for *beisa* (oryx), eland, gerenuk, and Grevy's zebra.

While in the Northern Frontier, the party received word of a rampaging rhino on one of the big cattle ranches near Carr Hartley's place at Rumuruti. A rancher had requested help from the safari party to track down a very aggressive beast. Most important to the hunters, the troublesome rhino was said to have trophy horns. The safari broke camp right away and headed south. In those days rhino were common, but unusually big trophies were hard to come by.

Henry Poolman and Terry Mathews went together on the rhino hunt with clients Barrett and Spaulding. Eager African herdsmen showed them the spoor and the hunt was on. Tracking silently through wait-a-bit thorn scrub the hunters came upon the rhino, partly concealed by a thicket twenty yards away. At that moment the rhino got wind of the hunters and broke away across their front, rather than charging as Mathews and Poolman had anticipated. As the rhino thundered past, Spaulding and Barrett fired together and knocked the great animal down. It was a good trophy with a 21-inch front horn, and the clients and grateful ranchers were thrilled.

Mathews and Poolman moved to a camp over two hundred miles away in the Kuka Rombo controlled hunting area, known as Block 66. The eastern boundary of the block was Tsavo national park, and the southern boundary was the Tanganyika border at the foothills of Mount Kilimanjaro. The region is covered in light scrub and dry as a bone most of the year. Spiky-leafed sansevieria and thorn thickets are interspersed with rubbled black lava flows broken by tussocks of sun-bleached grass. Several spring-fed swamps at Kuka Rombo were popular with elephant and buffalo, and also with lion, who often lay in wait for prey, using the swamps as their private shopping mall.

Kuka Rombo is excellent hunting country—in those days good for the Big Five and for a bounty of plains game. The hunters had not been in camp long when a perspiring Game Department scout pedaled in on his bicycle and told them a rampaging elephant was demolishing millet crops and terrorizing villagers. It was decided Henry Poolman and Pete Barrett would go after the elephant.

Elephant raiders seldom carry big ivory, but the game scout hastily assured Henry this elephant had pretty good tusks. As a general rule heavy-tusked elephants have long ago learned that man is dangerous, and they have acquired heavy tusks because they are clever enough to stay away from man. In English the term "rogue elephant" is seldom used in East Africa, because "rogue" somehow smacks of overly dramatic connotations. Plain terms like *shamba* raider, or crop raider, are preferred by hunters. To the Africans a bad elephant is just that— *Ndovu mbaya!* (Bad elephant!). Raiding elephant are far more likely to be younger animals with little regard for danger. There is always the possibility that a bad-tempered elephant terrorizing people has been made that way—the product of an unpleasant encounter with man, and probably harboring an old wound. In which case such an animal may be extremely dangerous.

Setting out after the elephant, Henry's two experienced Kamba gun-bearers, Ethia and Gatia, led the way, followed by Henry, Pete Barrett, and the eager game scout. They soon picked up the *"mbaya"* elephant's spoor. Kuka Rombo is only two thousand feet above sea level, and March is the hottest and most humid month of the year preceding the monsoon season in April. Noonday temperatures can soar above the high nineties. It was a blistering day for a long tramp after elephant. The tracks led them across boulder-strewn plains, sometimes south, sometimes southwest. By early afternoon the elephant had entered a dense thicket of dried thorn scrub. Henry got a look at *ndovu mbaya* and was pleasantly surprised to see a fine pair of tusks. With the fingers of one hand cocked like a pistol, Henry pointed his index finger at his own temple, indicating to Pete that he wanted him to take a side brain shot. Barrett nodded in agreement.

In camp Henry had coached Barrett about vital shots for elephant. The brain shot on an elephant works well if the bullet is placed correctly, Henry had told Barrett. But if the shot is not well placed, the elephant will seldom fall to the shot, and if he does fall to a narrowly missed brain shot and is merely stunned, his recovery is likely to be swift, and possibly permanent. While Henry briefed Barrett about elephant hunting, he knew these shots are only performed well with some experience and under ideal conditions—when the wind is steady and the range short, ideally between twenty and thirty yards. An elephant's brain is about thirteen inches long from the side, and less than eight inches high. It is located at the ear, and forward just above the musth hole* and zygomatic arch—a relatively small target when encased in the enormous head.

Pete Barrett, an experienced American hunter, was about to face his first elephant at close quarters, and the prospect thrilled him. Maneuvering into a faint breeze, Henry got Barrett within twenty yards of the great beast. As the men slipped around a thorn thicket, the elephant's head came into view, and Henry gave the signal to fire. Barrett lined up his .458 Winchester's iron sights for a brain shot and squeezed off. The shot staggered the elephant but did not drop it. Barrett fired again, and as the elephant turned to take off, Henry also fired two quick shots from his .470 double rifle. Taking both Barrett's and Poolman's shots the elephant collapsed in mid-stride. It was a magnificent trophy with ninety-pound tusks. A crowd of excited villagers soon arrived to thank Pete and Henry for helping them out and making their village safe once more. The trip was going well for Barrett, who had now collected two of the Big Five.

AT KUKA ROMBO one morning Henry Poolman drove up a low rock kopje outcrop to scout the surrounding country. From the kopje, the keen-eyed Poolman spotted a trophy black-maned lion lying on a lava bed far off in the shadow of a patch of thorn. Poolman glassed the intervening terrain. He saw there was no way to make a direct approach toward the lion from their position—the country between them was far too open. He decided to walk in a wide half circle and, mindful of the wind, make his approach at right angles to the lion using a few thorn-bushes for cover.

It happened that one of Poolman's African gunbearers, Ethia, was ill and had remained in camp. To replace Ethia that day, Henry had brought along a young trainee gunbearer named David to assist veteran gunbearer, Gatia.

---

*Musth holes are located on either side of an elephant's head, from which fluid is secreted. The fluid comes from the temporal gland behind the eye. Musth holes are present in both the male and the female.

As usual Henry carried his double-barreled .470 rifle, and Barrett a .458 magazine rifle. Gatia shouldered a Czech-built 7mm Brno in case Henry had to make a long running shot. Most professionals do not like to use heavy doubles for long-range shooting. The 7mm would be handy if the lion was getting away, and a long shot was required to stop it. Some hunters also like to have a twelve-gauge shotgun on a lion hunt in case point-blank work is required, provided there is somebody to carry the gun. The advantage of two barrels and a charge of S.S.G., or buckshot, is favored by some, yet others prefer a heavy double or even a heavy magazine rifle in such situations.

Henry gave his shotgun to David, Ethia's replacement. The hunters began a careful approach sneaking from bush to bush. The nearer the hunters got to the lion, the thinner the cover became. The wind remained right, but the lack of cover was crucial. Henry figured that if they could reach a place where the line of brush ended and the lava flow began, they would be within one hundred yards of the lion.

Inching forward Henry took satisfaction on arriving at his chosen spot and hoped the group had not been seen by the lion. He paused to catch his breath, then raised his head to see whether the lion had discovered them or had changed position. Henry saw the lion, but at the same moment the huge cat saw him and, drawing itself up, stood broadside watching the hunters intently. At this point Henry knew there was no chance of getting any closer. Barrett had impressed Poolman with his good shooting at similar and longer ranges. Henry knew the ideal range for lion hunting is between forty and sixty yards, while one hundred yards is usually considered about as far as one should risk a shot. It is not that a well-placed bullet will not instantly kill a lion at this range, or even at much longer ranges, for almost any good bullet can do that, but it is more a question of accuracy. It is hard to shoot a heavy rifle well at longer ranges. If the first shot is not well placed on a lion, it will trigger a swift adrenaline response. There is little question subsequent body shots are, for the time being at least, going to do very little to slow him down. If that first shot is not immediately fatal, the lion may quickly become the most formidable terrestrial animal on earth. There is one more undisputed fact about an aroused lion: he is likely to be extremely brave. In the opinion of many experienced hunters a wounded lion is the most dangerous of the Big Five—the bravest of the brave.

Clearly, Henry Poolman had no qualms about getting Pete Barrett to shoot his lion from their position. Pete Barrett calmly aimed his .458

rifle just as the lion started to move off. The big, smoke-colored cat slid behind an acacia thicket, reappeared on the other side, and paused momentarily to check on the hunters. As the lion paused, Barrett was ready for him. He fired, but just as the fat soft-nosed 510-grain bullet left his rifle barrel, the big cat was already moving again. Barrett fired twice more as the lion bounded across the lava and over a low ridge. Pete Barrett thought he had missed the lion, but the two gunbearers—Gatia and the new man, David, both of whom had been standing behind the hunters on higher ground—insisted they had seen the lion collapse behind a lava ridge.

The hunters cautiously went over the ridge, and fifteen yards beyond it they found the lion lying motionless, facing away from them. The old-timer's credo, "It's the dead ones that kill you!" is African hunting dogma. It seems Henry Poolman was convinced the lion was dead. He saw no reason to put another hole in a magnificent lion skin. Henry reportedly said, "Congratulations!" At the sound of a human voice the lion raised its head, spun around, and with flattened ears and bared teeth came like a bullet straight for Pete Barrett.

Despite his size Henry Poolman moved with the agility of a cat. In what his colleagues know was a typical gesture, and later confirmed by Barrett and Gatia, Poolman sprang in front of Barrett to take the lion's charge himself. At the same moment he fired two shots simultaneously from his .470 double rifle. Henry's shots were so closely fired they sounded like one. The lion was in full charge by the time it reached Poolman, and while it is believed the lion took both of Henry's .470 bullets at point-blank range, they did not stop him. Instead the four-hundred-pound cat knocked Poolman over like a sack of cotton, and his rifle flew from his grasp. Even the impact with Poolman's muscular body hardly slowed the lion. It went over him intent on Barrett, and caught Pete, throwing him to the ground. While one arm was in the lion's jaws, Barrett fought back with his free arm. Behind the lion Henry was back on his feet, but he was unarmed. There was not a moment to lose, no time to search in the grass for his .470, reload, and shoot the lion again. Seeing the lion savaging his client, Henry seized the enraged animal by the tail, and with all his great strength he tried to haul the big cat off Barrett and deflect its ferocious attack upon himself.

While all this was happening in the blink of an eye, Henry's gun-bearer Gatia rushed in with the 7mm rifle, and quickly fired three shots into the lion's rib cage. The lion did not react immediately to the shots, for its adrenaline was up. With remarkable purpose it continued to savage Barrett on the ground, while Poolman tried to bodily tear the lion off his client.

In this frenzied melee of struggling men and a crazed lion, the series of events is not exactly known, but it seems that David, the replacement gunbearer, now wildly excited and probably very frightened as well, was facing the lion while Henry was behind the huge animal, desperately trying to drag it off Barrett. David leveled the shotgun at what he thought was the lion's head or body. Facing the lion from a few yards away, David hastily fired the twelve-bore shotgun. The deadly load of high-brass buckshot missed the lion and, at a range of only a few yards, the full charge plowed into Henry's chest, killing him instantly.[1]

MOMENTS LATER the lion succumbed to its many wounds and rolled off Barrett dead. At the start of the lion hunt, Jean Barrett, Pete's wife, had been left in Poolman's Toyota hunting car back at the rock kopje. From her elevated position she had watched the horror with binoculars and witnessed the dreadful scene of carnage. Now Jean Barrett rushed across the rocky plain to her husband. Henry Poolman lay dead, his chest ripped open by the shotgun blast, and near him lay the lion, which had quickly died of its wounds. Also lying on the rocky ground beside the lion was Pete Barrett, who was severely mauled.

Jean Barrett took charge. The ground was too rocky to get the car close enough to pick Barrett up, or to load Henry's body. With the help of the gunbearers Jean somehow got her husband across the lava flow to where she could maneuver the hunting car. But Henry's body was too heavy for them. The new gunbearer, David, stayed with Henry's body to keep the vultures away while Jean and Gatia raced off with Pete in search of help.[2]

Gatia, who held no driver's license, knew how to drive a car but only after a fashion. Jean Barrett remembers every event of that long day. She remembers the awful trails strewed with boulders, stumps, and pig holes. She remembers holding her bleeding husband in her arms, trying to brace him against the bumping car, as Gatia shot the car off rocks and trees. Somehow the journey to camp progressed, with Gatia driving like a frenzied little Martian hunched behind the wheel. During the terrible journey Pete Barrett drifted in and out of consciousness. He was bleeding profusely. Broken bones protruded from his arm, and he was in great pain.

When they reached camp they learned that Terry Mathews and the

Spauldings were out hunting. To her dismay Jean Barrett found that neither Gatia nor any of the safari crew in camp knew how to operate the radio telephone. Jean remembered that an American couple were doing research work at a camp nearby. The Americans had a radio and were able to contact Ker and Downey's office at Nairobi. The outfitter immediately dispatched a plane to Loitokitok, a Masai village on the northern foothills of Kilimanjaro, thirty miles from the safari camp.

With Gatia, Jean Barrett drove her husband to Loitokitok, where an African medical orderly at a small bush dispensary administered first aid while Pete awaited evacuation to Nairobi. When the aircraft arrived, Jack Block, Ker and Downey's chairman, and veteran white hunter John Sutton were on board.

In the meantime Gatia made the necessary report to officials at Loitokitok, then went to bring in Henry's body with the police, who would carry out an investigation. The lion was left where it fell. By the time Gatia and the investigators went back for it the next day, they found vultures and predators had devoured most of the lion carcass. For this reason it has never been certain how many shots hit the lion, or where the shots were placed, for the only trophy the Barretts retained from their terrible ordeal was the lion's skull, which had a broken jaw.[3]

In any event had the lion not sustained a broken jaw it would probably have killed Barrett. If Henry's longtime bearer, Ethia, had been along instead of trainee David, Henry would probably be alive today. As it was the luckless David was arrested by the Kenya police and investigated for murder. At the time there were wild, unfounded rumors that David had been hired to kill Poolman because of Henry's success against the Mau Mau during the dark days of Kenya's Emergency. None of these rumors proved to be true, for the police carried out a thorough investigation. David was eventually cleared of any wrongdoing, but after the ordeal he quit safari work, and Gatia too later gave up safaris.

Pete Barrett recovered from his wounds at Nairobi Hospital, and three weeks later returned with his wife to the United States. The real hero in this story is Jean Barrett. Before leaving Nairobi, the Barretts gave a check to Henry's widow to help educate their young daughter, Adelaide.*

---

*Texas-based Game Conservation International (GAMECOIN) established an educational fund for Henry's daughter in 1967. When the fund was ready Adelaide had left Kenya. GAMECOIN searched for Adelaide Sandra Poolman for fifteen years, and in 1982 traced her to England, where she received the fund from GAMECOIN's Harry and Gloria Tennison.

Shortly after the safari Pete Barrett wrote:

My left arm, wrist, and hand are continuing to improve, and I'll have almost complete use of them. A Texas friend who was camped near us [at Loitokitok] and who recovered Henry's body went back to the scene a second time, and salvaged the lion's skull. We determined that I had shot its right lower jaw, which possibly accounts for my wound not being worse than it was. Of course it was Henry who really saved my life as he hit the charging lion twice with a .470, and it was just about dead by the time it grabbed me. Its jaws didn't relax, though, until my gunbearer, Gatia, had put three more shots into its back and spine.[4]

39

KNIFE FIGHT WITH A LEOPARD

In the early sixties Mike Hissey made his entry among the ranks of Kenya's white hunters. Few men had more zest for life than Hissey, and hunting was his all-consuming passion. Mike's easygoing personality and finely tuned sense of humor made him the best of companions on safari. His privileged background was in contrast to the lives of the Poolman boys and most of the Kenya hunters of his day.

Mike Hissey was born in 1924 at Wokingham, Berkshire, in England, the son of a wealthy country gentleman who owned a large estate at Sidelsham, along the river Lodden. Mike recalled:

> When I was old enough to handle a gun, my father bought me a .410 double-barreled hammer shotgun. He gave me one box of cartridges and told me that was the last box of shotgun shells he was ever going to buy me. I could shoot rabbits, pigeons and wildfowl and sell them at Bracknell Market each week, and with the money keep myself in ammunition. Father was as good as his word. He never bought me another round of ammunition! When I was ten years of age my father allowed me to go with him on his shoots. He was a member of two syndicate shoots. One was at Cruxeastern in Hampshire, and the other at Didcot in Berkshire. A pheasant and a partridge shoot respectively. I used to help beating and sometimes stand with my father.
>
> One day the beaters were driving pheasants out of a chalk pit and the standing guns were around the lip of the pit. A gun that was with the beaters shot at a pheasant flying straight at us, from a range of about forty yards. The pellets hit my father in the top of his legs, and also hit me in the face and chest. Luckily we were

both well clothed as it was a cold winter day. My large coat buttons were shot to pieces, and my coat in tatters. Blood was running down my face and out of my mouth. A pellet had gone between my lips, broken a front tooth and cut my tongue. My father was wearing plus fours and Wellington boots and his boot was filling with blood from the pellet wounds in his leg and hip. My father grabbed me and took me on a sixteen-mile ride to Reading Hospital. The nurses stripped me and I well remember hearing the pellets falling on the linoleum floor, and rolling across the room as each garment was removed. We recovered quickly enough, and no permanent damage was done.[1]

Mike went to Bradfield College in Berkshire, which was situated in some of the best shooting and trout-fishing country. He and three friends regularly poached and averaged seventy-five pheasant per year. Mike's luck ran out the day he was caught red-handed poaching trout on a stretch of fishing-club water. The gentleman who nabbed Mike had a familiar face. He persuaded Mike to get in his car and took him to Lord Illiffe's mansion at Basildon:

I was ushered into the sitting room where his Lordship and her Ladyship were having afternoon tea. I was given a first-rate dressing down, and then I was asked to sit down to have a cream bun and join them for tea. I later realized that the gentleman who had caught me was the Prime Minister of England, Neville Chamberlain![2]

When World War II began seventeen-year-old Mike secretly went to Reading where he was "paid the King's shilling" and joined the Royal Navy without his parents' knowledge. He quickly made first lieutenant, then saw action in Normandy before sailing for India and the Arakan offensive. He made landings against the Japanese all the way from Chittagong to Rangoon.

In peacetime England Hissey thought he would live the life of a country squire. Instead he was astonished to discover the family estate had been sold. Mike learned of a farming scheme to benefit servicemen in Kenya, and he signed up in hopes of getting his own farm and to attend an agricultural course at Egerton College of Agriculture at Njoro. Lord Egerton of Tatton originally went to Kenya in 1938 to hunt with

Alan Black. Egerton liked Kenya so much he settled near Njoro, and gave eight hundred acres of his estate to provide training for those desiring an agricultural career.

One of three attractive English sisters at Egerton College caught Hissey's eye, and in March 1948 he married Daphne (née Northcote) in Nakuru. They settled on virgin land in Trans-Nzoia district, near Mount Elgon in western Kenya. In six weeks Mike had constructed a home made from bricks and thatch. He knew he had found his paradise:

> The Enderbess flats were crawling with game animals. There were vast herds of topi, and it was estimated there were over 4,000 on the flats alone. Also Jackson's hartebeest, waterbuck, roan, zebra, reedbuck, bushbuck, oribi, duiker, Rothschild's giraffe, and now and again lion crossed over from Karamoja, in Uganda.
>
> I bought a .470 double rifle by Webley and Scott from the Duke of Manchester, and I used this rifle until 1973. It was like my right arm when I was hunting.

Mike routinely assisted game wardens at Mount Elgon with control work, mostly buffalo and elephant. He was so successful the Game Department gave him complimentary elephant licenses to cover expenses. Control work began to take precedence over farming:

> I made safaris from Kimilili to the southern Uganda boundary on foot, taking several days each way and checking out reports on *shamba* raiding. I never shot a *shamba* raider unless damage was proved and the owner of the *shamba* had made efforts to protect his crops. I wanted to see an attempt to keep the elephant out either with stockades or fires. All the Kitosh and Mgishu [tribes] who lived along the forest edge were great elephant eaters. Eventually the *shamba* raiding got very bad in the Kimilili area. The Kimilili herd had increased to such a degree—to over 400 elephant—and for several years we took twenty-five cows per year out of this herd alone. One time 300 natives put up a temporary village to smoke the elephant meat.[3]

In 1957 Mike met Stan Lawrence-Brown at Kitale. Stan and his client, Marge Hopkins from Spokane, Washington, were on their way to the Cherangani Mountains to hunt eastern bongo. The two men hit it off so well that Mike joined Lawrence-Brown Safaris as a white hunter in 1961. He was teamed on his first professional safari with David Ommanney:

> I remember filming four leopard in one tree feeding on a zebra carcass. I was on my own in the leopard blind and Dave was to pick me up at sundown. He had gone with clients to hunt buffalo. I filmed the leopards for half an hour or so, when suddenly they all took off hurriedly. And there, standing beneath the bait tree, was a lioness. I had no rifle with me and only my camera and tripod. I backed out of the blind and moved out of the area without the lioness seeing me. I got to the track where Dave was to pick me up, but it was getting darker all the time. The bait was only fifty yards from the track, and when I looked down the track I saw more lions coming towards me. They saw me in the fast fading light and started to stalk me. I went to the nearest thorn tree and with my camera over my shoulder, I climbed up as far as I could.
>
> It rapidly became pitch dark and there was no moon. Then I heard a lion trying to climb the tree. I could hear claws scrabbling on the bark below me. It was the most uncomfortable three hours of my life waiting to see Dave's headlights come along that track. Then at last headlights appeared and the lions faded into the bush. Dave never saw them in his headlights. When I told him what had happened he could hardly believe it, until I showed him the claw marks on the trunk of the tree.[4]

MIKE HISSEY was next on safari with another of Stan's hunters, Nick Swan, and the Mull family from Wichita, Kansas. During a leisurely photographic run they saw a herd of Grant's gazelle whose attention was riveted to a patch of tall grass. Nick Swan was driving the doorless Dodge shooting-brake, and sensing something was amiss, he had his .577 double rifle loaded and across his knees. The client, J. A. Mull, was on the front seat beside Swan, and behind them Mull's daughter and a friend, along with Mike and two gunbearers. Nick slowly edged the car within twenty yards of the tall grass expecting to see a lion. Instead a big tom leopard broke cover and rushed with a growl straight for the car.

Nick just had time to stall the engine, grab his rifle, which was lying across his lap, push the barrels into the leopard's chest and fire. It seemed to fly straight at Nick. The heavy bullet blew the leopard back and it crumbled in a ball onto the grass. The leopard had a powder burn five inches in diameter on the front of its chest.

J. A. Mull had a leopard license and he told Nick it would please him to have this leopard on his license, as he would never forget this cat as long as he lived. If this leopard had got into the car nobody could guess how much damage might have been caused, not only to the girls but everyone else. On inspection we found the leopard had a wound caused by a sharp-horned animal that had pierced its stomach and exited through the hip. We thought it was probably caused by an oryx. In his trophy room, J. A. Mull has this leopard mounted in a springing position, with an oryx about to horn it![5]

In 1969 Mike Hissey went *mano a mano* with a leopard himself. The encounter came about during an action-packed foot safari with an American governor named Ammons. The safari's first camp was in the Northern Frontier at a place called Tum. Mike put the remains of a Grant's gazelle in a large cedar tree, with a perfect foot approach that allowed them to get into the blind unobserved:

It was a perfect setup presenting a broadside shot. The Governor fired and the leopard jumped out of the tree. I asked the Governor if he was happy with his shot, and he said yes. I went to the base of the tree and there was no cat lying there. So I called my gunbearers to bring the 12-bore and buckshot, and we tracked the leopard down a small dry riverbed with three-foot-high banks, and about six feet wide. We could tell the leopard had been shot too far back.

I was leading with my gunbearers; Maina behind me, and Makau behind him. Maina had the .30/.06 rifle, and Makau my .470 double. The leopard lay in ambush and let me go past, but as Maina followed me, the leopard came from behind to grab Maina. I swung around to take the shot as soon as I heard him growl, but he came in line with Maina, and I could not fire for fear of hitting Maina. Maina is a six-foot-tall man from the Nandi

Dawn at horse-and-camel camp on the Barsaloi sand river.

tribe. He is very powerful, and he took the leopard's charge holding the .30/.06 in front of his body like a stave. The leopard clamped his teeth into the wooden fore-end and the barrel, and with its claws around Maina's neck. Maina was thrown onto the riverbed, and was rolling about with the leopard on top of him. Then Maina grabbed the leopard's bottom jaw with one hand, and the top jaw with the other hand, while still trying to hold the leopard away from his body. But Maina was unable to keep the leopard's jaws apart, even with his great strength. The leopard was biting Maina through all his fingers and his hands. They were still rolling about in the riverbed, so I dropped the shotgun and took out my knife. Then I grabbed the leopard in a neck-lock with my arm from behind, and stuck my knife through its ribs into its heart. The leopard went on biting Maina through his hands, while I held on to it, but at last its eyes glazed over and it died. Maina was taken to the nuns at Baragoi Mission where he stayed for ten days. The sister in charge cleaned his wounds and stitched him up, and gave him tetanus and penicillin injections.

When we got Maina to Nairobi he had to have three operations on his hands to tie the ligaments severed by the leopard.
Governor Ammons gave Maina a goodly sum of money by way of
compensation for his wounds. Maina now lives on his farm near
Eldoret.[6]

Mike's troubles on Governor Ammons's safari were far from over. He
went to one of his favorite areas, known as horse and camel blocks,
which was administered by Mike's Egerton College roommate, game
warden Rodney Elliott. The only transport allowed in these hunting
blocks are horses and camels, which can be hired from the Game
Department:

We had been hunting elephant all day, and were returning to
camp. It was one of the rare occasions when I was riding a horse,
because as you know I prefer to walk. But I was really tired, and
did not expect to make it to camp before nightfall. I had two
trackers ahead of us keeping a sharp eye out for rhino, as we were
coming along a knife's edge on a mountainside. My gunbearer,
Makau, was walking beside my horse and we were discussing
where we should hunt on the morrow.

Suddenly one of the trackers ahead shouted that a rhino had
broken cover, and was coming fast towards us through long grass.
I drew my .470 from the saddle scabbard, and began to dismount. I
had one leg over the saddle when the horse heard the rhino coming. She shied and sent me flying. The next thing I remember was
Makau bending over me shouting that the rhino was coming for
us down the game trail. He got hold of my elbows and got me sitting up. My .470 was still in my hands. I shot the rhino at five
paces whilst still sitting in the path. The rhino turned into the
long grass, but did a short circle and came back again. Meanwhile,
Makau had me on my feet. The rhino broke cover and I fired,
braining him. It all happened so quickly. I looked around and
there was no sign of the Governor or his horse, and all the camels
had gone as well. After awhile the Governor turned up. Thank
God he was a good horseman. The camels were soon rounded up
and the party complete.

I tried to walk but found I could not manage it. There was
a numbness through my back. The numbness was soon replaced

by pain, and I thought I had slipped a disk. I was helped to a tree, but trying to take my weight on my arms, the pain was unbearable. The men got me on my horse and led it to camp. The safari ended next day when I found I was in big trouble with my back.[7]

Hissey had a crushed vertebra, and it was many months before he was fit enough to hunt again.

Terence Owen Mathews joined Safariland Ltd. in 1955. His first safari as a trainee hunter was for a movie appropriately called *Safari*, with Victor Mature and Janet Leigh. Soon afterward Terry changed his affiliation and worked for Ker and Downey. Major movie productions began to come his way: *Call Me Bwana* with Bob Hope and Anita Ekberg; *Sammy Going South*, starring Edward G. Robinson; then Hugh O'Brien in *Cowboy in Africa*. Mathews seemed to have an affinity for attracting big-name clients. There followed a spate of celebrity bookings, including two safaris with Stewart Granger, eleven with Joseph H. Cullman III (of Philip Morris), four with "Trader Vic" Bergeron (of restaurant fame), Robert Montgomery, and others.[1]

Terry formed his own firm, Mathews Safaris, in 1967 and hunted with crooner Bing Crosby and actors Phil Harris, David Janssen, and Texas governor John Connally. Crosby was so badly bitten by the safari bug he returned for seven more safaris with Mathews, sometimes with his wife and friends, sometimes alone.

Terry's future looked rosy, but the silver lining was shattered with a hunting accident in September 1968. Terry was bird hunting with a group of American clients at Salengai, southeast of Nairobi. The hunters advanced on foot across a short grass plain, driving francolin out of the grass as they progressed. A francolin rose with a flurry of wings between the line of shooters and beaters, and doubled back through the line. Walking behind the line in full view of the shooters was Terry Mathews with his gunbearers. A member of the party swung his shotgun behind the advancing line, drew a bead on the disappearing francolin, and squeezed off.

Terry was directly in the line of fire, and saw what was coming as the shotgun roared. He ducked and threw up his hands to cover his face. Terry took the full blast and was hit by thirty-nine pellets that struck his face and the backs of his hands and shoulders. His hands stopped five pellets, but a sixth went between his fingers and skated around on his eye.

In the hospital Terry remained optimistic, joking with friends. Terry's father, head of the East African Tourist Travel Association, masked his concern when reporters hassled him for a story: "Terry's hoping that clients will not now start trying to bag the *Big Six*— elephant, lion, leopard, rhino, buffalo . . . and hunter."[2]

Doctors thought there was a better chance to save Terry's eye with treatment in England, at London's Moorfields Eye Hospital. A few days later I visited Terry at Moorfields. "The great concern," Terry said, "is that this is my left, or master eye, that's been hurt. I can shoot pretty well off the right shoulder, but you know how it is."* Besides, if he were to lose the sight of one eye, his days as a white hunter would be over. Still joking about his terrible misfortune, Terry said, "I've already written to Winchester recommending the power of their shot!" His humor and courage were great, but Terry suspected this was the end of the road and a great safari career.

When Terry returned to Kenya in November 1968, he sported a black eye patch beneath his shock of unruly fair hair. He wore the eye patch of necessity, like a Moshe Dayan badge of honor, never complaining about the hand of fate. His name was already etched in the annals of safaridom, and clients wanted him any way they could get to go on safari with him.

As Terry was rehabilitated he continued to operate safaris from his office at Lavington Green, outside Nairobi. His booking chart was overflowing, and he hired freelance hunters to handle his safaris. As he progressed, Terry was able to go on safari but limited himself to photographic trips and film work.

All his life Mathews had been a painter and sculptor. As a sideline to the safari business Terry began sculpting wildlife figures, which he cast in bronze. Within a few years Mathews was even more famous as an artist than he had been as a hunter.

---

*Ten percent of East Africa's white hunters shoot off the left shoulder, because their left eye is the master eye, and not necessarily because they are left-handed.

◇

ANOTHER professional hunter whose promising career was tragically cut short by a client's bullet was William Henry (Bill) Winter. A handsome Alan Ladd look-alike, Winter had been in the Malayan police before he came to Kenya as a colonial police inspector during the Mau Mau Emergency. Winter stayed on in Kenya where he became a game warden at Nanyuki, and then later, a hunter. In 1975 Bill had been hunting professionally for five years when he met his Waterloo in the form of an enraged buffalo and a trigger-happy client.

Not far from Narok, in Kenya's Masai country, Winter's client wounded a buffalo. Bill, his gunbearer, and his client followed up, but the animal was waiting for them, and charged at short range. Winter fired, and although his shot killed the buffalo, its impetus carried the animal into him, knocking Bill down and breaking his leg. Winter lay pinned beneath the dead buffalo, and at that moment he saw his client rush in with a .375 rifle, aiming the weapon as if to give the buffalo an insurance shot. The memory of Henry Poolman was all too fresh. Bill shouted, "Don't shoot, he's dead. *Kufa!*"

"But," Winter told me, as he lay in Nairobi Hospital after the attack, "the client fired anyway. His bullet went into the buffalo's neck and exited into my leg, just above the ankle. The Flying Doctors got me out, and here I am, Bwana!"

Winter was in great pain, for the bones in his ankle had been shattered by the .375 bullet. He spent most of the next few years in and out of hospitals in Kenya and Switzerland. "They filleted my foot," Winter later said. "Now one leg is two inches shorter than the other." Bill Winter will never hunt again. Despite his "filleted foot" he keeps his hand in by outfitting photographic safaris.

A DATE WITH DESTINY

Unlike Terry Mathews, John Alexander did not at first appearance conform to the image of a white hunter. Although tall and distinguished in appearance, and always nattily dressed, the very British Alexander more closely resembled an urban engineer and surveyor—and indeed that is what he was. Well-educated and soft-spoken, John was more than a serious-minded academic, and his outwardly bookish appearance belied a deeper quest. The fact that he sought to ply his trade in bush country far from civilization was testament to an adventurous nature. Nevertheless, the courtly Alexander was an improbable candidate for professional hunter, but his transformation, when it came, was rapid and complete.

John Alexander's life in Africa started out with his arrival at the dusty railway station at Voi, one hundred miles from Mombasa. The hot scrubland and broken hills around Voi, barely known to the outside world, remained the isolated paradise of a handful of big game hunters.

Voi is bordered in the north and west by Tsavo national park, established in 1948, the year before Alexander arrived in Africa. Tsavo,* the largest national park in Kenya, straddles sixty miles of main road from Mombasa to Nairobi. It was selected as a park by the Game Policy Committee, which included white hunters, not because it had more game than other areas but because it was the only large piece of unoccupied land available.

Alexander's job was to survey the route for a water pipeline across the wilds of Tsavo and the formidable Taru Desert for the British colonial government. A pipeline was needed to carry water from the head-

---

*The first warden of Tsavo was Ron Stephens, who with a few African rangers guarded Tsavo's 8,000 square miles.

waters of Tsavo River, over one hundred and fifty miles inland, down to the residents of Mombasa on the Indian Ocean.

In 1950 Voi township consisted of a single dirt street bordered by a few ramshackle, Indian-owned *dukas* selling basic wares and provisions. The tiny settlement on the main Mombasa-Nairobi route came into being as the site for the junction of the Tanganyika Railway line, which branches off due south. Apart from the station and the railway's Dak bungalow (their guest house), Voi's most notable landmark was a small Bangalore-tile-roofed hotel that featured a bar frequented by itinerant hunters, railway officials, and sisal planters, as well as Tsavo's widely scattered park wardens. The modest Voi Hotel was the only stop on the road before Mac's Inn, sixty miles farther along on the corrugated dirt highway to Nairobi.

Alexander quickly fell under the spell of Africa and the Africans, and he enthusiastically adapted to his new life as frontiersman. As one of only a few European inhabitants in this vast bush country, John became friends with the park's wardens who occasionally assembled at Voi Hotel for riotous parties at the bar, led by David Sheldrick, Bill Woodley, Peter Jenkins, John Lawrence, Dave McCabe, and Scottish ivory hunter Bob Foster. Shortly after a new hotel manager named Henry Hayes arrived in the country from Yorkshire, he once dared call out "Time, Gentlemen!" during a well-attended impromptu party of wardens and white hunters. Henry, who was of ample proportions, was promptly carried kicking and screaming to the hotel freezer where he was locked up to cool off while the party resumed. After awhile his captors took pity, bought him a whiskey, then released him, and the party continued. Henry never again called "Time." When future parties developed, Henry took himself to bed, and the hunters and wardens would help themselves. Henry always found a pile of chits affixed to a metal stake on the bar next morning with everything accounted for.

BILL WOODLEY, the experienced bushman born on the Athi Plains, was amused by John Alexander's travails in the primitive environment. Woodley remembered Voi's spiny *commiphora* tree scrublands being so dense that if John had to sight a hill for a trigonometrical point he had to get a labor gang to cut a corridor through a mile of brush just to get a bearing. Living in big game country where his closest associates were hunters and wardens it was perhaps inevitable that the enterprising engineer from Birmingham would become more interested in game and hunting than in engineering. Alexander developed an all-consuming interest in wildlife and Tsavo park.

Bill Woodley's career as a warden must have seemed more challenging than Alexander's own. In 1955, at Bill's urging, John joined the Kenya national parks as a warden. In 1959 he was promoted at the behest of parks director Mervyn Cowie, who made him warden of Kenya's two mountain parks at Mount Kenya and the Aberdares, succeeding the first mountain warden, David Haywood. Once relocated to the highlands John delighted in frequent visits to view game at the nearby Treetops Hotel. Ironically, his own family had links with the Aberdare national park long before he came to Africa. His first wife, whom he married in England, was the great-great-granddaughter of Lord Aberdare.

As game warden, Alexander devised creative innovations, not all of them successful. One of the problems facing Alexander (and later Bill Woodley) was how to prevent elephants from raiding plantations that abutted the national parks' forests. Alexander had a trench dug by hand, six feet wide by six feet deep with a length of seven thousand yards, in hopes this would prevent elephant and other animals from leaving the park to raid crops. Alexander's elephant ditch did not present much of an impediment to elephant or buffalo, since they would break down the banks at certain spots and cross at these places. Alexander then installed electric fencing in combination with his ditch. That did not work either, because elephants had a way of getting around an electric fence. They would gang up on one of the herd members and shove the individual against the electric fence, shorting the current and flattening the fence. The herd thus left the park to raid corn and sweet potato *shambas*.

Bill Woodley arrived at Alexander's Aberdare park headquarters at Kiganjo, near Nyeri, on New Year's Day, 1959. He had come from Tsavo to assist John with preparations for a visit by England's Queen Mother. As it happened Alexander decided to quit the parks to become a white hunter, and Woodley took over from his friend. Woodley remained for a number of years as warden of Kenya's mountain parks, before returning to Tsavo.

ALEXANDER set up his safari operation at his home near Nanyuki. John was flexible enough to tailor safaris exactly to the needs and pockets of his clients. One of his clients was near stone broke Dian Fossey, who much later attained recognition as a gorilla expert. In 1963 Dian Fossey was staying at the Mount Kenya Safari Club at Nanyuki, and she introduced herself to one of the owners of the club, William Holden. Fossey told Holden she was looking for a white hunter to take her on a private safari through East Africa. Was there someone he might recommend?[1] Holden knew a man on the mountain he thought might be suitable named John Alexander. Fossey talked John into a you-bring-the-coffee, I'll-bring-the-sandwiches low-budget outing. When starry-eyed Fossey first met Alexander, then fortyish, she was the ultimate naive greenhorn in the wilds of Africa.

John, his complexion now ruddy from years in the sun, and his fair hair by now receding, had always had an eye for the ladies. Recently divorced, he was not inclined to turn down any safari work. Even with Fossey's limited budget Alexander nevertheless consented to take her on a tour, and guided her on what is generally regarded as the East African "milk run," an easy route taken by package tourists on their first trip to Africa. John took Dian to see Tsavo park, Ngorongoro Crater, the Serengeti Plains, and Olduvai Gorge, where he introduced her to anthropologists Mary and Louis Leakey.

Alexander later recalled Fossey with considerable distaste, not just because she was a heavy smoker and drinker, which he considered none of his business, but because he thought Fossey "moody" and a "bit neurotic." Alexander claimed that at the time of their meeting Fossey had never before even heard of mountain gorillas.[2]

Still, Alexander agreed to take Fossey on another safari, this time through Uganda and into the Congo to the Albert national park (now the Muhuavura national park). In neighboring Rwanda over this period, two tribes, the WaTutsi and the BaHutu, were killing each other in the thousands; the first years of genocide were barely reported to the international press. Zaire was also far from safe, with murderous soldiers roaming the countryside.

Despite the tribal unrest and general chaos then prevalent in Zaire, Alexander and Fossey continued with their safari into the eastern part of the country. At the village of Rumangabo they had hoped to pick up park rangers to act as guides. The only accommodation available was an old shed and it was here Fossey propositioned Alexander. "Here we've been three weeks on safari," she said. "We could have shacked up together and had a hell of a good time."[3]

Alexander apologetically turned her down explaining that he was already engaged. After being rebuffed Fossey despised Alexander, according to Harold T. P. Hayes, her biographer. Behind his back she began referring to John as "The Great White."[4]

At Albert national park, Alexander introduced Dian to a Belgian biologist named Jacques Verschuren, and he told Fossey about the gorillas[5] on the Virunga volcanoes straddling Rwanda, Uganda, and Zaire. While camped high on the Kabara Meadow, Alexander and Fossey encountered friends of John's, well-known wildlife photographers Alan and Joan Root, who were filming gorillas. The Roots took Dian out in search of her first gorillas. Although no contact was made, it was a thrilling experience and Fossey said she had "smelled them." It was certainly a turning point in her life. Fossey, by profession an occupational therapist, ultimately became famous as a dedicated gorilla preservationist.

When their safari returned to Kenya, Fossey and Alexander had a serious dispute over the money she allegedly owed him for extra mileage into Zaire, as well as for the rent of his movie camera and film he had bought for her, all amounting to $710. She told Alexander she would not pay another penny. Yes, she would, Alexander replied, or he would have her airline ticket impounded. When Alexander arrived to take Fossey to the airport the next morning, he found she had left town, having talked her way onto an earlier flight departing for Salisbury, Rhodesia[6] (now Harare, Zimbabwe). The animosity was not one-sided.

Years later there was worldwide publicity over the tragic murder of Alexander's former client. Dian Fossey, protector of mountain gorillas, was murdered by an unknown person or persons at her Kariasoke research camp in Rwanda in early 1985. Although they had not parted on good terms, John Alexander was greatly upset by the news. Dian had proved herself to be a dedicated gorilla researcher after all, and in that regard he felt that they had shared much in common as conservationists. "Hats off to her. Credit where credit is due," Alexander had generously said of Fossey's work.

Fossey was buried at Kariasoke camp beside the graves of gorillas killed by poachers on the Muhuavura volcanoes. To the Africans living in the region, the BaHutu, the WaTutsi, and the Batwa tribes, Fossey became known as Nyimachabelli (the woman who lives alone on the mountain). She liked the name so well that she wanted it on her gravestone. Her wish was granted.

The last photo of Ahmed, the elephant from Marsabit.

MOUNT MARSABIT, the lonely mountain paradise discovered by American explorer Arthur Donaldson Smith and made famous by wildlife photographers Martin and Osa Johnson, became a quest for Alexander. John made the acquaintance of a man named DeWitt Sage, who was revisiting Africa after an absence of many years. Sage had been on one of the early Martin and Osa Johnson safaris to Marsabit in a sort of jack-of-all-trades capacity, according to John. As such he had been among the first white men to explore Marsabit and its famous crater lake, which the Johnsons named Lake Paradise. Through DeWitt Sage and his tales of early days at Marsabit, Alexander's interest in the mountain was rekindled.

John Alexander made his own safari closely following in the Johnsons' footsteps, visiting all their camping spots at Marsabit, even going to the water hole they had named after their gunbearer, Boculy, to view elephant and buffalo. It was in 1959 on a visit to Boculy's water hole that John first saw the great elephant, Ahmed.

With his usual intensity, John became an expert on northern Kenya and its nomadic tribesmen. Alexander's favorite spot was Gof Redo, three miles from Marsabit on the North Horr road. The six-hundred-foot-deep crater, a perfect circle with a fine forest of euphorbia trees, is home to greater kudu. It was among these isolated deserts that Alexander came to feel most at home.

John had become so enthralled with the mystique and beauty of the mist-shrouded mountain that he built a permanent tented camp for tourists at Marsabit. Ahmed, the giant-tusked elephant, sometimes passed near Alexander's camp. On occasion Ahmed was on his own, but more often he was accompanied by two or more younger bulls. John remarked that these were seldom the same elephants and he wondered if there was some sort of roll call younger elephants responded to when the word was out for escorts for the great old patriarch. Nobody was able to give him any answer to this question, not even his friend Jerry Dalton,* who had been Marsabit's first warden, or Peter Jenkins, who is *the* expert on the region, having been warden there for many years.

There was much speculation about Ahmed when he was alive. How old was he? How heavy were his tusks? Where had he come from? Alexander observed that Ahmed's favorite food was the roots of a tussocky grass that grew to heights of over six feet after the rainy season. Ahmed would tear out the grass with his trunk, slap the roots against his leg to shake the earth free, and then stuff the roots into his mouth. John reported that during the rainy season Ahmed would sometimes go into the acacia country lower on Marsabit, returning to the higher elevations for most of the year.

Using Marsabit as a base Alexander conducted many camel safaris across the scorched Chalbi Desert. His caravans were superbly equipped and staffed with trained men. "Only greenhorns rough it!" he was fond of saying. When Ahmed, the famous big-tusked elephant, died of old age it was Alexander who wrote Ahmed's obituary, for by then he knew the animal personally.†

---

*In 1958 ex-Safariland hunter Dalton recovered massive ivory belonging to another big Marsabit elephant, Ahmed's predecessor, the legendary Mohammed, who died in October 1956. Mohammed's tusks weighed 141 and 117 pounds. Two and a half feet of the left tusk had been broken off. The right tusk measured 10 feet 8½ inches, the third world record for length.

†Ahmed died on the night of January 16–17, 1974. He was found by park ranger Corporal Wako, who had continuously guarded Ahmed for eighteen months. A life-size version of the elephant, complete with ersatz tusks, is displayed at Nairobi Museum (formerly the Coryndon Museum). Ahmed's actual tusks weighed 68 kilos (150 pounds) each.

◇

ONE NIGHT Alexander's Nanyuki home was raided by police, who entered without a search warrant. They claimed they raided John's home in search of illegal trophies. But it was a ruse, for no illegal trophies were found. Instead the police opened Alexander's gun safe and charged him with being in illegal possession of four guns without a firearms certificate, as well as possession of 324 rounds of ammunition in excess of those allowed on his license.

Alexander was also charged with being in possession of poison. The "poison" was actually 499 tablets of the common antibiotic tetracycline hydrochloride given to him by a departing client, a doctor, to use to treat Africans living far out in the bush who have no access to modern conventional medicines of any kind. Such a practice was common in Africa and continues to this day.

It turned out the four additional guns found in Alexander's armory were legitimate and belonged to one of the most respected men in the country, Sandy Field. Field was a former Uganda district commissioner and a keen hunter. For ten years Sandy had been the senior warden at the Serengeti national park. Field had left his guns in safekeeping with Alexander while he made a trip to England.

After the police raid John Alexander realized somebody was out to get him. It is a sad commentary that he needed the services of the most prominent criminal lawyer in the country, Byron Georgiadis, Kenya's Perry Mason. On December 1, 1972, the court magistrate, F. E. Abdullah, gave Alexander an absolute discharge on all counts brought against him by police at the Central Firearms Bureau. The magistrate said the prosecution of the case appeared to be more in the nature of vindictiveness and harassment, saying, "The court cannot condone the abuse of the process of law." The magistrate added that Alexander appeared to him to be a man of good character and had an unblemished record as a surveyor, a national parks warden, and a professional hunter and safari outfitter.[7] At the time John told me the trumped-up charges made his "blood boil."

Alexander seemed well able to roll with the punches, even those below the belt, but the low blows must have taken a toll, both personally and professionally. The final round came for John Alexander late on September 6, 1989. At the time John's Swiss wife, Elfi, was in Europe on business, and John was alone at his town home in the upscale suburb of

Langata, outside Nairobi. For some unknown reason John left the safety of his fortified home that night and ventured outside into the darkness. He was sixty-seven years old, but he was big, strong, and well able to look after himself. What drew him, unarmed, to the gated front entrance of his property is not known. What is known is that somebody struck John a massive blow on the forehead with a blunt instrument. John fell dead in his own driveway. Robbery was not the motive, as police believe little if anything was stolen. Like Dian Fossey's death, theories abound and lose nothing in the telling. Dian Fossey and John Alexander, so different in every way, were murdered by a person or persons unknown. And both foul murders have so far defied all efforts to solve them.

42.

THE PRINCE OF PRANKSTERS

Bryan Coleman is crafty and wily in all life situations, and in the bush he has that rare, special instinct only a few hunters possess. He considered himself part of the Kenyan landscape. "I was conceived in Kenya, born in England in February 1933, and returned to Kenya at the age of six months." His father, Inspector J. C. Coleman, was a pioneer policeman in the colony, a decorated veteran of twenty-one years' service. Inspector Coleman had miraculously survived many dangerous encounters. He once tracked a gang of murderers, and in the ensuing fight he was shot with a poisoned arrow, which is usually fatal within minutes.

Bryan was raised in an atmosphere of outdoor adventure. Like some hunters raised in Africa, he had the opportunity of doing extensive big game control work. Before he was twenty Coleman had developed a passion for mountain bongo hunts. Later, his searches for the western variety of bongo led him to Sudan and unexplored Zairean rain forests. He was so often successful peers regard him a "bongo specialist."

As a youth Coleman was apprenticed to old-timer Louis Woodruff, a gruff, rough-and-tumble hunter who had been in the business forty years. Woodruff did not believe in giving Coleman or anybody else shortcuts. He worked Bryan hard to gain his professional license. "Old Louis was tough," Coleman conceded, "but he taught me a lot. He loved a South African brandy called Mellow Wood. It sure mellowed *him* all right!" In 1959 Bryan Coleman joined David Lunan's company, White Hunters (Africa) Ltd.

COLEMAN was to become the most relentless prankster among the safari set. Full of good humor himself, Coleman nevertheless often stretched the good nature of his victims. Although his escapades were well known, he somehow always managed to find one more unsuspecting foil.

On safari Bryan was able to get away with his pranks because he was as skilled and fearless as the best of the hunters and he routinely delivered excellent results without much apparent effort. But events orchestrated by Coleman did not always go as planned. A Chinese businessman from California named Chow booked Bryan for a hunt in Kenya's Masailand. It soon turned into a bloody safari, with the first victim Chow himself. At the time Coleman was piloting his safari car. "We were driving cross-country and hit a pig-hole," Coleman recalled. "Chow was thrown forward and cracked his forehead against the windscreen, opening up a big gash." Without further ado Coleman stitched the wound up himself, and the hunt continued as if nothing had happened.

On another occasion Coleman and Mr. Chow were driving across country when the Land Rover's steering wheel suddenly came right off the column in Coleman's hands. The car was traveling about 25 miles per hour. Mr. Chow's jaw dropped when he realized Coleman was steering in an exaggerated fashion and the steering wheel was not connected to the rest of the car. "Here," said Coleman, lighting a cigarette, and without slackening speed, "you drive for a while"—as he handed the steering wheel to the astonished Chow. Somehow the car miraculously held its course.

If Mr. Chow was profoundly shocked, more was to come. Mr. Chow was taken into a large herd of buffalo on his hands and knees while the herd grazed among thorn thickets. Coleman crawled ahead of Chow closing the distance to a herd bull with a massive set of horns. At last they were close enough for Chow to make a killing heart shot. Forty yards from the buffalo, Coleman whispered to Chow, "Shoot!" Chow did as he was told. From a prone position Chow drew a careful bead on the bull and fired his .458. The buffalo took the shot and immediately raced off with the rest of the herd, headed for a valley covered in brush. "The buffalo was gut-shot," Coleman said dryly. Gut-shot is gut-wrenching for the professional hunter who has to go after wounded game. The hunters followed the buffalo to the edge of the thickets. There Coleman left Mr. Chow with two gunbearers, Kilunga and Sungura (Rabbit). Both gunbearers were experienced, especially Sungura, who had previously worked for Andrew Holmberg, a respected old-timer who holds the world's record bull buffalo.

Coleman picked up the wounded buffalo's spoor and tracked it on his own for a short distance. The buffalo's charge was so rapid and came from such a short range that Coleman for a moment did not realize what had hit him. But he knew soon enough, for when the buffalo tossed him, his rifle went one way and he went spiraling high into the air.

Coleman somehow landed smack on the animal's broad back, and there he hung on, sliding forward onto the neck so the massive horns could not gouge his thighs from the side. If Coleman was surprised, so was the buffalo. The baffled buffalo tore off, bucking to unseat its tormentor. Coleman hung on, realizing the moment he was unseated would be his last on earth. Suddenly the buffalo burst out of the thickets into the grassland with Coleman still on its back, hanging on for dear life. A startled Mr. Chow was standing about fifteen yards away, and he was even more surprised to hear Coleman's voice ringing out loud and true, "Adios!"

Badly shaken once more, Mr. Chow watched as the enraged buffalo again tried to unseat Coleman, tearing up the ground in great dust clouds, bucking this way and that. The gunbearers sprang into action. Sungura bravely raced alongside the buffalo and fired a couple of .458s into its shoulder without hitting Coleman's legs, bringing the buffalo and its rider down in a huge cloud of dust.

Coleman fell off the animal, but the buffalo was up in a jiffy and went after Coleman with a vengeance as he lay sprawled on the ground. The buffalo horned Bryan in the groin and thigh, while Sungura and Kilunga opened up on the animal in a ferocious barrage of shots fired at point-blank range. The buffalo fell over, this time for good, but to add insult to what was already a badly injured Coleman, it fell on top of him. At that point a dumbstruck Mr. Chow appeared and helped Sungura and Kilunga roll the 1,800-pound carcass off Bryan Coleman.

Coleman's long-suffering wife, Joan, recalled the radio telephone call she received from Bryan's camp. "He wanted me to send an aircraft to pick him up. He was perfectly calm, saying he had been 'scratched' a bit by a buffalo, but nothing to worry about." He was in fact severely injured with deep horn wounds in the groin and thighs, along with a mess of broken ribs.

COLEMAN continued to hunt Zaire (now Congo) despite formidable bureaucratic barriers. With a client named Lyn Herndon, Bryan hunted

Bryan Coleman with a western bongo from Zaire's forests.

on foot every day for a month in the steaming rain forests without turning up fresh bongo signs. He was convinced the area held trophy bongo, and he stuck with a gut feeling. His client wound up thirty-five days into the hunt with a trophy bongo with horns measuring 33½ inches. Soon afterward Princess Deidre of Sweden bagged a 34½-inch bongo trophy. During Deidre's safari Coleman and the royal party had a near mishap while hunting lion. Bryan and Deidre approached a lion bait on foot to check it and saw that the bait had been worked over by a lion. As they walked back to the car a big-maned lion exploded out of the bush. Coleman dropped the lion with a shot through the brain. At first Coleman reckoned the lion had been protecting its kill, but when he examined it he found the lion had a poacher's steel snare festering around its paw. It was enough to make any animal mad with pain.

BRYAN ONCE spent a season in Sudan for safari outfitters Laddy and Ada Wincza. When Coleman went to meet his clients at the crumbling airport at Juba, he was astonished to find the new arrivals were black Americans from Detroit.

"His name was Ethan Jacobson," Bryan said, "and he was one of the best clients I've ever had on safari. He was a good hunter, a good shot, and a ton of fun to be around." Ethan's companion was a polite and shapely black girl, a former bunny from the Playboy Club. Coleman simply could not let pass such a wonderful opportunity for a little fun. He learned that his friend and fellow white hunter, Austrian Prince Alfi von Auersperg, was also in southern Sudan, and better yet he was camped in the same area. That afternoon Bryan carefully primed his easygoing clients before driving to Alfi's camp. When they arrived, Alfi was still out hunting, but Coleman and his guests made themselves comfortable around the campfire with iced cocktails provided by Alfi's obliging camp staff. Just after dark they heard the prince's hunting car returning to camp.

Bryan rushed out to greet him. "Alfi, I'd like you to meet the new Minister for Tourism in Sudan. This is Pasha Ethan Jacobson bin Ali!"

Ethan Jacobson, the black American, looked suitably grave and ministerial. He stepped into the firelight, struggling to keep from laughing as he saw the startled expression on Alfi's face. Not knowing what significance a high-ranking Sudanese minister's visit might mean exactly, Prince Alfred von Auersperg collected himself and formally presented his German clients to the black dignitary. As soon as he could excuse himself from the exalted presence, Alfi hurriedly gave instructions to his camp headman to inform the cook there would be three additional V.I.P. guests for dinner. Bryan could hardly restrain himself as he watched Alfi scramble to get his camp staff organized in order to make the best possible impression on the "minister." Loving the commotion he had caused, Coleman winked at Ethan as they watched Alfi and his crew bring forth his finest wines and most exotic hors d'oeuvres.

Coleman was not about to let Alfi off the hook. Throughout a spirited five-course dinner served on fine china in the dining tent, Alfi engaged his special guest, "the minister," in conversation. "Do you think we will be able to get elephant permits on the east bank of the Nile?" Alfi inquired. Ethan looked stern, "It's a possibility, my friend . . . a possibility . . . We will have to wait and see."

Alfi was led into all sorts of compromising verbal traps, keenly egged on by the heartless Coleman. It was only after the feast had been consumed, and everybody gathered around the campfire for coffee and liqueurs, that Bryan let Alfi in on his little joke. History does not record exactly what happened after that, but surprisingly Coleman was allowed to live.

43

KEEPER OF THE FLAME

Old Bwana Charles Cottar, American patriarch of the Cottar clan, had left his mark on the safari world after following Teddy Roosevelt to Africa in 1910. Two of his three sons had gained considerable fame as hunters of renown. In 1939, Charles Cottar, his eldest son, Bud, gunbearers Mwaniki and Fundi, and two camp assistants rumbled across the Loita Plains of Masailand in their Ford safari car headed for their favorite campsite at the Barakitabu (difficult road) stream crossing.

Bwana Charles required a publicity film to advertise Cottar's Safari Service during a promotional trip he planned in the United States, and he was in search of dramatic wildlife footage for his sales pitch. With *campi* pitched Charles and Bud went out in search of suitable movie subjects. They soon put up an old rhino that suddenly charged. Bud was quick off the mark firing his .405 Winchester rifle. The shot broke the charge, making the rhino swerve away from the men at the last moment, but it did not knock the animal down. Before Bud could work the rifle bolt the rhino vanished into a *leleshwa* thicket. Bud left Bwana Charles behind with the heavy camera tripod while he followed the rhino. He had been gone a few minutes when Fundi tapped Charles on the arm to warn the old man as the bush crackled with breaking branches and the rhino bore down on them, coming straight for the old man. To Charles it was a wonderful opportunity to get exciting footage. He cranked the camera but had his gun ready. At the last moment Bwana swung his .405 Winchester and fired. By then the rhino was on him, sweeping its horns low and ripping upward, tearing Bwana's groin and thigh as the beast's two-ton impact threw Cottar to the ground. The rhino fell mortally wounded across Cottar's legs, pinning him. The gunshot and Fundi's urgent cry brought Bud running. The horn had ripped into Cottar's leg and passed through an artery. Despite Bud's efforts Charles Cottar bled to death in less than an hour.[1]

THE FOLLOWING year Mike Cottar, Bwana's middle son, thought by many to be the greatest bushman of his day, was hunting on the Serengeti corridor between the Grumetti and Mbalangeti rivers with a United States senator. Senator Costello wounded a buffalo and Mike Cottar followed it across a rocky hillside above the Grumetti River. Mike saw the buffalo in a thorn thicket and fired as the buffalo commenced a downhill charge. His first shot hit the buffalo and the beast stumbled but did not fall. Mike fired his second .470 barrel, hitting the buffalo in the brain and killing it instantly. But the momentum of the buffalo's rush carried its two thousand pounds down the hill, bowling Mike over as it fell.[2]

Rugged Mike seemed miraculously unhurt. He picked himself up, dusted his palms, and laughed the incident off. He had nothing more than a scratch or two to show for the encounter, or so he thought. But in fact the deadweight of the buffalo's body had ruptured Mike's enlarged spleen, a consequence of his numerous bouts with blackwater fever. Mike Cottar died suddenly on July 12, 1941. He was thirty-six years old.[3]

MIKE AND MONA Cottar's only son, Glen Calvin Cottar, was ten years old when his father was killed. By then the Cottar name was recognized in every remote hunting territory in East and Central Africa. The clan of pioneer white hunters, originally from Iowa and Oklahoma, now encompassed three generations, and had long ago established its reputation as the First Family of the safari business. The Cottars had taken their safaris into distant hunting grounds, into territory where no safaris had gone before. In the old days Glen's grandfather, larger than life Bwana Charles, had led expeditions that began in Nairobi and did not end until they reached Kathmandu. Glen's own father, like Bwana Charles before him, had ranged far and wide, taking safaris from Kenya to India, Nepal, and Indochina.

While Glen was still a boy, his family had left Nairobi to take up residence on the shores of Lake Victoria, at Musoma in Tanganyika, to make a new base for safaris and to operate a ferry service. At the small port of Musoma, Glen spent his waking hours hunting and fishing; sometimes he accompanied his father on expeditions after big game. On the family's doorstep was the vast Serengeti Plain, teeming with the world's greatest concentrations of wildlife. For a boy like Glen it was Paradise Found, but his carefree world abruptly ended with his father's death. Thereafter his mother, Mona, did everything in her power to prevent her son from following in his father's footsteps. She had seen it all. Old Bwana Charles had been terribly mauled by three different leopards, tossed by an elephant, hammered by a buffalo, and finally horned to death by a rhino. Mona had seen the ill effects and stresses on hunters' families for years. Divorces, deaths, disfigurements, blackwater and dengue fever, malaria, sleeping sickness, tick fever, bilharzia, car and plane crashes, broken bones, and maulings were routine in the white hunter's world. Mona knew the rootless, wandering life, the lengthy absences, and the financial instability of the safari business all too well. She did not want Glen to follow the same path.

Glen was sent to the Prince of Wales boarding school (in schoolboy slang the "Prince-O," but also known as the "Cabbage Patch" on account of a steady diet of that vegetable) back in Nairobi. His classmates included boys who would become white hunters—John Sutton, Dave Williams, John Dugmore, as well as future game wardens Brian Nicholson of the Tanganyika Game Department, Myles Turner of the Serengeti national park, and Peter Jenkins and Bill Woodley of Kenya national parks, along with Frank Poppleton of Uganda national parks.

His mother's fear to the contrary, Glen never doubted that his destiny was to carry on the family tradition. Not long after graduation Glen heard that a new safari outfitter, Eagle Safaris, was looking for somebody who would qualify as a trainee hunter. Eighteen-year-old Glen headed for town on his bicycle where he found the Eagle office on Delamere Avenue (now Kenyatta Avenue). Eagle's proprietors, white hunter Geoff Lawrence-Brown and journalist M. J. Turner-Dauncey, knew the Cottar name was legend in African hunting circles, and his pedigree was just what the doctor ordered for their fledgling firm. Glen was hired on the spot. Eagle had another trainee hunter, a former Prince-O schoolmate, Brian Nicholson, who would become one of the best known conservationists in Africa.

Soon afterward Glen joined the new firm of White Hunters (Africa) Ltd., headed by David Lunan. At the time White Hunters was managed

Glen Cottar, grandson
of Bwana Charles,
1974.

by Colonel Brett, formerly manager of Safariland Ltd. Brett left White
Hunters (Africa) Ltd. under a cloud and was replaced by Colonel Robert
Caulfield. In 1960, after Glen Cottar was fully licensed, he married
vivacious Pat Schofield, the daughter of English settlers from the Great
Rift Valley town of Nakuru. Cottar, always an optimist, also made the
big step of going it alone as an independent safari outfitter.

Now Cottar had the freedom to take his safaris wherever he pleased,
into distant and little-known country. He was the first hunter to penetrate the vast Moyowosi-Njingwe swamps in Tanzania on foot, long
before the era of amphibious vehicles. He and his client came out of the
swamps with a sitatunga antelope bearing record-class horns. The more
remote and unknown a region happened to be, the greater its attraction
for Glen Cottar. The time and expense of such explorations mattered
little to Glen. He surveyed Tanzania's almost unknown Lukwati and
Katavi areas, and cut many hundreds of miles of primitive tracks
through featureless *miombo* woodlands. His rewards were the
unspoiled landscape, unmarred by car tracks and, in many cases, even a
human footprint. His clients reaped the benefits of these "reccies" by
collecting outstanding trophies.

Glen had a devoted following of clients prepared to go with him
wherever he went. They put up with, or even enjoyed, all the Cottar
foibles, including the fact that Glen's safaris were always run on "Cottar Time"—as in "Irish Time." Glen's engaging personality was such
that he had loyal friends in every walk of life, from Kenya's first president and his family, the Kenyattas, to influential African businessmen

like Gideon Kago, tribal Masai chieftains, and simple cow- and goat-herds. It was said of Bror Blixen that he could laugh at a charging buffalo while deciding what his drink would be that evening, and the same could most certainly be said of Cottar.

Things went well for the well-liked Cottars. They had two children—a daughter, Tana, named for the famous Kenya river, was born in 1962, and a boy, Calvin, a year later. In time Calvin would take his own place in the family business. Glen bought a house on ten acres of woodland in Karen, west of Nairobi, where he and Pat built their safari headquarters. The Cottar household became a revolving door for hopeful young hunters, safari guides, and camp managers, whom the Cottars employed or just helped out.

IN MARCH 1965 Glen was in his favorite country, Loliondo, a highland savannah wedged between Tanzania's Serengeti national park in the southwest and Kenya's Masai Mara game reserve in the north. He was hunting with an old friend, a safari client from Argentina named Arturo, who was accompanied by his two young sons, Arturo junior and Guillermo. The rainy season had arrived early in Loliondo that year, and the grass was lush and green, attracting enormous herds of buffalo. Some of these buffalo herds were over five hundred strong. From small bachelor herds where the best bulls are usually found, in less than a week Glen and his clients shot no less than four exceptional buffalo, each with a record-book head of over 46 inches.

One afternoon the hunters went in search of a suitable lion bait and came upon an old, solitary buffalo that did not have much of a trophy head. Glen persuaded Arturo to shoot the buff as bait. The two men made a stalk on foot that brought them within sixty yards of the animal as it stood at the edge of a thicket. The buffalo received Arturo's bullet, but wheeled away as he fired again and again as it disappeared among the thickets. Glen sent for his car and left Arturo in the vehicle with his sons and a gunbearer. Arturo had long ago suffered an injury that made it difficult for him to walk long distances, and so he reluctantly agreed to remain behind while Glen and the trackers went after the buffalo.

That day Glen did not have his favorite .500 Rigby double-barreled rifle, for the rifle's mainspring had broken. He was going to follow up the buff with his standby .458 Winchester magazine rifle. Arturo generously offered Glen his own prized .500/.465 double rifle. Glen, a left-handed shooter and deep-down double-rifle devotee, gratefully accepted the loan. Accompanied by two young Kipsigis trackers, Arap Sambu and Getet, Glen set off after the buffalo.

The trio tracked the animal from a thicket across open short-grass plain to the next thicket, and so on through endless brush patches. There was a good blood spoor and Glen was confident the buffalo was badly hurt, and might even be down. As they were about to enter a thicket the hunters were warned of the buffalo's proximity by the sound of the animal's wheezing breath. At this place the brush was so dense they could not see the animal. Swarms of tiny sweat flies buzzed about the men's ears. Their footsteps were slow, deliberately placed, as nerves got strung out expecting the worst at any moment. With a sudden crash of breaking branches the buffalo tore off across a glade into another patch of brush. As it ran Glen got a fleeting glimpse of hide and fired, but he was uncertain what damage his bullet might have done.

Cottar let the buffalo go hoping his shot had weakened him. But this buffalo was different. There was no sign he was stiffening up or slowing down. On the contrary, he was leading the hunters into one nerve-wracking thicket after the other. There was still a discernible blood spoor, yet even that seemed to be diminishing. Worse still, the thicket-to-thicket tactic showed the buffalo was alert, was strong, was dragging out the suspense—awaiting its moment to launch its own deadly attack.

In the darkness of a brushy tunnel at a range of ten yards, Cottar saw what he believed was the motionless shape of the buffalo. As he stared into the gloom he could make out the curve of a horn and, following an imaginary line below the horn, Glen drew a bead where he thought the shoulder ought to be. The .500/.465 roared and the buffalo crashed away before Cottar could squeeze off his second barrel. Convinced the animal was now mortally wounded at last, Cottar and his men tracked it across a small plain as it neared another thicket. As they approached they could make out the vague shadow of a buffalo watching their approach. Glen fired, sure this time he would drop the animal in its tracks. Instead, the buffalo exploded from the bush and came straight for Cottar at a gallop. Glen waited until the buffalo's face was yards away, and as it lowered its horns to hook him, Cottar's second barrel boomed. The massive horns slammed into Glen, smashing him to the ground. The buffalo turned in mid-stride and raced back to work on the fallen man, horns down, hitting Cottar's legs as he desperately kicked. Glen tried to keep the horn tips from penetrating his chest by holding on to the horns as the beast worked him over. The buffalo kept its forehead close to the ground, its horn boss bulldozing Cottar as it tried to grind him into the dust and finish him off.

Glen later said that his regular tracker, a fearless man named Pissey, was not with him that day, and the two men he had were not as experienced. In Swahili Cottar yelled, "Grab the buffalo's tail," hoping this would distract the animal long enough to allow him to get away. "But," Cottar said ruefully, "nobody was *that* keen for a Victoria Cross!"

As suddenly as the buffalo had carried out its deadly attack, it just as quickly broke it off, heading for the brush at a trot.

In the center of the grassy glade Cottar lay bleeding from horn wounds in his thighs. His legs were ripped open, and the muscles torn away to expose bone on the calf of his leg. "There was an awful silence," Cottar recalled. "I felt nauseated, from loss of blood I suppose." He tried to get up, but could not. He well knew the ways of maddened buffalo and realized anything he did might trigger a fresh attack from his now unseen enemy. Glen looked for his rifle, which he could not find, nor were his trackers in sight. Afraid he might pass out, Cottar began to crawl, pulling himself along with his hands, clutching for small tufts of grass. He headed for a single spindly sapling standing alone on the little plain. He figured that if he could only reach the tree, he might somehow climb it. It was not a great solution to the crisis, but none other was in the offing. After what seemed an eternity Cottar made the base of the tree. He tried to pull himself up into the branches, but he was so weakened he could not manage it. As he looked up into the tree he was astounded to see one of his trackers perched on the topmost branch. Cottar whispered, "*Nyati iko wapi?*" (Where's the buffalo?).

This question brought immediate reaction from the terrified tracker. "Shh!" the man hissed nervously, and pointed. Glen followed the outstretched fingers with his eyes, and to his horror saw the buffalo a short distance away, standing in the open, its eyes upon him, its head hung low, blood dripping from its nostrils as it watched him intently. Cottar now knew that with this buffalo he had two chances left—slim and none. That is, providing he did not pass out and die from loss of blood first.

Glen whispered, "Quick! Pull me into the tree!"

His tracker nervously eased himself onto a lower branch of the sapling, and helped Glen up into the branches a few feet above the ground. The tracker kept hold of Glen, afraid he would fall, while Glen clung grimly to the tree trunk. He knew that to lose consciousness and fall would be the end of it all. Then Cottar heard the sound of a vehicle approaching. "It was the cavalry coming," Cottar said dryly. "I'd begun to think it was just the damn buffalo and us. And that buffalo had us pinned down!" The second tracker had raced to the car for help after Glen was attacked. Now the Toyota Land Cruiser crashed through brush in low-ratio gear and four-wheel drive, grinding down barriers of dense thorn beneath its tube-iron cowcatcher, recklessly flattening the underbrush as it came straight for Cottar. Just as the car reached Cottar's tree, the client and his two sons saw the buffalo, and Arturo quickly fired three .458 shots into it, dropping the massive beast in its tracks.

The safari rushed to Glen's camp, where his client immediately took charge, injecting Glen with an ampule of morphine and penicillin. The client cleaned Cottar's terrible wounds with disinfectant and swabs. Then he was bandaged and carried to the safari car. As space was needed for Glen to lie on the backseat of the Land Cruiser, Arturo's two sons remained behind in camp with Cottar's safari crew. Arturo, Kibet, and Pissey, Glen's headman, set out on the long drive to Nairobi, more than 250 miles away, most of it on narrow dirt roads. Glen's camp was more than twenty miles from the nearest road, which runs between the Serengeti and the Kenya border. A part of that main road had been cut by his own grandfather, Bwana Charles, and improved by his father, when Mike had led safaris across the Serengeti in the thirties.

After jolting across country Cottar's car passed the freshwater spring and wooded oasis known as Kline's Camp, and from the road his client saw the white glow of pressure lanterns in the awful blackness. Somebody was camped in this wilderness among the fig trees. It turned out to be American aviator Charles Lindbergh and his wife, on a photographic safari. Lindbergh told Cottar he had an aircraft parked at a nearby airstrip, and he generously offered to fly Glen to Nairobi at first light.

Cottar, now tranquilized with morphia, decided to push on to Nairobi immediately. Pissey hunched over the wheel of the Land Cruiser as its lights followed the graveled road back to Kenya and the Masai Mara game reserve. At Keekorok lodge Cottar's client hoped to find a visiting doctor, but they were out of luck. The safari car turned north again, jolting across washboard as it roared through the cold night. The exhausted party arrived at Nairobi Hospital thirteen hours after the attack.[4]

Glen's own father had died after a buffalo attack much less severe than his. While Glen was recuperating, and in an unusual moment of earnestness, he told me, "I know my client [Arturo "Art" Acevedo] saved my life with his quick thinking, and getting antibiotic and morphia into me. He's got *guts*. God bless him!"

44

PELIZZOLI'S PROMISED LAND

Alfredo Pelizzoli first arrived in Kenya by car. His overland route was an unusual mode of entry in the days when the sea and air provided the main access for international visitors to East Africa. In Alfredo's case, it was intended to be only the first installment on an around-the-world adventure. Tall, slim, brown-eyed, tanned, his dark hair fashionably over his collar, Pelizzoli might pass for an avant-garde movie director. A young man of the world, he smoked Gitanes, played very good tennis, drove a Jaguar, and knew good wine and European art. Despite all this sophistication, Pelizzoli was more than surprised by what he found in East Africa.

"In Kenya I knew I had already found what I was looking for," Alfredo said. "There was no point in continuing. The air and the game captivated me. I knew I would remain there for good. Kenya is the most magnificent country I ever imagined."

Alfredo Pelizzoli comes from the city of Verona, in northeast Italy. He had traveled and hunted extensively, making trips to the Far East and Africa before settling down to start his own publishing company back in Verona. In 1955 he sold his business and together with a friend patched up a vintage 1945 ex-army ragtop Jeep, then set off to drive around the world. Once in East Africa his southerly progress came to an abrupt halt, and he would go no farther.

At Nairobi Alfredo was not only enchanted by the country. He met a trim, intelligent beauty, the daughter of English settlers from Limuru, a tea-planting district northwest of Nairobi. Lisa spent her holidays at her parents' Limuru plantation, but she was being educated in England. Shortly after meeting Alfredo, Lisa Walker became Mrs. Pelizzoli. Theirs was to be one of the happiest and most enduring partnerships in the safari world.

◇

THE MAU MAU Emergency was still in progress, but for a sophisticated twenty-nine-year-old man like Pelizzoli, Nairobi was brimming with potential. Alfredo, being Italian, spoke little English and no Swahili, the languages of his newly adopted country. Used to overcoming minor obstacles he quickly learned both languages, and also the ropes of Nairobi's publishing industry. Amid forecasts of financial ruin, Pelizzoli created the first illustrated monthly color magazine in East Africa. He called his glossy production *African Life*. The venture was an immediate success. *African Life* featured stories about wildlife, tribal culture, travel, and adventure. Pelizzoli then started a crisply written weekly newsmagazine called *The Reporter*. It quickly became the premier news periodical in the country.

With his publishing ventures on solid ground, Alfredo set about enjoying Africa. He had made friends with hunters, who were often featured in his magazine, and he became so enamored with this band of characters he decided to become a white hunter himself. Alfredo bought his own game licenses and learned the country on hunting trips of his own. He made a series of long-range safaris to Somalia, Zaire, Congo (Brazzaville), Central African Republic, and Ethiopia. Then the Pelizzolis started their own safari business. Alfredo is unique in that his high-brow European social contacts were so extensive he was able to book safaris himself and then hire well-established white hunters (such as Bryan Coleman) to take out his safaris, with himself as "apprentice" hunter. Alfredo already knew he could never go back to his old way of life, and so he sold his publishing enterprises. In 1963 Pelizzoli achieved what had eluded so many before him, including many native-born Kenya cowboys. He became a full-time professional hunter.

When Alfredo had openings in his schedule he sought safaris as a freelancer for other outfitters. While hunting greater kudu in Uganda's Karamoja district, he promised himself he would return to Uganda to try for a difficult-to-hunt swamp-dwelling sitatunga antelope on the Sese islands, in Lake Victoria. Pelizzoli eventually found a client willing to enter the by-then ravaged country following Idi Amin's rise to power in a military coup.

Undeterred by Amin's camouflage-jacketed thugs in their dark glasses, steel helmets, and toting submachine guns, Alfredo and his client set out from Entebbe and sailed to the Sese islands, eight hours cess. Luckily my client was a veteran of many safaris, and he was patient. We cut some long poles and struggled across large areas of floating vegetation. The swamps were vast, and made up of papyrus and other plants. Sometimes we broke through the floating swamps, and fell into stinking deep water. Other times we had to crawl to distribute our weight better so that we would not fall through. We had to try and navigate around patches of open water where bad-tempered hippos had taken refuge.

Many days later, after much search, we opted to try a swampy inlet that looked very secluded on one of the smaller islands. But it was not easy to get to. We left the boat and made our way through the quagmire of mud and rotting vegetation towards a single distant tree on the shoreline. But the going was very noisy, and I feared that even if we did come across a sitatunga, these spooky animals would hear our approach and vanish.

With great effort we made it to the tree at the edge of the swamp. When we got to the tree we realized it was too frail to climb. But we had some rope with us, and we tied all the slender branches upwards together, until it looked like a spider's web. This strengthened the tree enough for it to support my weight. We had done all this in almost complete silence. I climbed the wobbly tree first, and as I got high enough to look over the swamp grass and tall papyrus, much to my surprise, far out in the swamp I saw three sitatunga all looking in my direction. One of the sitatunga was a very remarkable bull, with a fine head.

I unslung my rifle and took practice aim, balancing the fore-end on a piece of the rope we had used to tie up the tree. But with the wind the tree was rocking, and it was a very unsteady method. Still, if one timed it well, and waited until the wind dropped a bit and the movement of the tree stopped, I though a fairly good shot could be achieved!

I slowly descended the tree, and whispered instructions to my client, because the tree would not support the weight of both of us. It was an anxious time as I watched my client climb the tree, aim his rifle, and then the wind would come up in a little gust and the tree would rock and wobble. I was whispering to him to take all the time he needed. He could not get right to the top of the tree, and I was standing under him, holding one of his feet. I swear

Alfredo Pelizzoli.

distant, in an old government-owned diesel launch hired for the occasion. Pelizzoli camped at a small beach on the verdant Garden of Eden–like Bugala island, the largest in the Sese group, and set out to find the elusive sitatunga. The Sese island species of this aquatic antelope is by no means rare, but it is extremely hard to hunt, not only because of its difficult habitat, which is floating vegetation and papyrus swamps, but because the animal is extremely wary. Because of its spiraled-horn beauty and little-known habits, island sitatunga are a fascinating subject for study, and a great challenge for dedicated trophy hunters. The females are hornless, but old males occasionally have their horns tipped with bleached points, called ivory. Alfredo has vivid memories of his first Sese island sitatunga hunt:

> It was a foggy morning on Lake Victoria. The motorboat was called the *African Queen* and its layout was similar to the original version of the boat in Humphrey Bogart's movie. As we neared Bugala island and cut the motor we could hear majestic fish eagles screaming everywhere, and African darter birds were draped on dead trees along the shore. I was amazed how beautiful the islands are. Green rolling hills, patches of heavy forest, shining empty beaches. No people except the odd fishermen in their famous long-snouted wooden Sese canoes.
>
> We spent much time exploring swampy inlets without suc-

I thought he would never shoot. My arm went to sleep. Our small Sese tracker was standing around in the mud, hardly able to believe what these two crazy *mzungus* [Europeans] were trying to do. It seemed like an eternity, but at last my client's shot rang out, and I clearly heard the solid *thump* of the bullet, and knew the sitatunga was hit. His bullet had killed the sitatunga cleanly, and it fell where it stood.

We were very pleased, but getting to the sitatunga out in the swamp was a big headache. It was even more difficult to bring the animal back to shore, and it took us the rest of the day to do it. We were soaked to the bones. But it was worth it for the size and beauty of the trophy.[1]

That remarkable island sitatunga *(Sylvestris spekii)* had horns that measured over twenty-five inches, and won for Alfredo in 1975 the East African Professional Hunter's Association's highest award, the Shaw and Hunter trophy.

ON A SAFARI in northern Tanzania, one of Pelizzoli's clients wounded a lion, which made off into a densely brushed gully. His client was an elderly Italian gentleman who was mortified when he learned his shot had not immediately killed the lion. His client's anxiety was such that Alfredo tried to calm him, and walked him back to the hunting car.

Alfredo and his tracker got on the spoor of the wounded lion, but it was already late evening. They followed the lion until it was too dark to see. At first light Alfredo loaded up his .500/.465 Holland and Holland Royal and went after the lion.

Together with my head tracker, Guio, we picked up the spoor of the lion where we had left it the previous evening. There were small traces of blood on the leaves, and soon some of the blood signs were wet. Then we knew the lion was aware we were after him again, and he was moving silently ahead of us. The brush got thicker with each step.

We continued until there was suddenly a thunderous, gut-freezing roar as the lion leapt out of the dense foliage. It was just a flash and he swerved past us, disappearing into the brush.

Our knees knocking, we squatted on the ground to catch our breath until our will reasserted itself and once again we crept forward on his tracks very cautiously. We went a little distance and there was complete silence. But to our horror we noticed that the lion was circling around us, because we recrossed his tracks. We decided to pause, hoping the lion would think he had lost us.

I don't remember how long we waited before we continued. I tried to imagine how it would be when we met, how I would finish him off, or how he would finish us off. We moved on again, and several times we came across loops in his tracks like a figure eight as though he was checking whether we were behind him. Then for some reason he gave these tactics up and proceeded in a more or less straight line down the gully. We speeded up a bit, and suddenly we came upon him, but he saw us before we saw him. With a ferocious growl he was gone in the green thickets. We followed carefully, but the brush was so dense we could hardly see in the gloom. Then we realized it was not just the density of the brush that had cut down the light, but a big thunder cloud blotted out the sun. I looked at Guio, and he grimaced. And then we felt the first heavy drops of cold rain. The rain would obliterate the lion's tracks quickly enough, but I reasoned that it would also blot out some of the noise we made getting through the thick brush.

At a certain moment, the wind suddenly turned and came from behind us, and we had to make a wide sweep to outflank the lion. Then the rain began to fall very heavily, and my rifle felt slippery in my hands. I took the precaution of removing the safety catch, fearing I would fumble if I had to make a hasty shot. We were soaked and cold, and losing hope, but we went on anyway. Finally, among the dripping bushes we saw a yellow blob. I could see part of the lion's head and most of his soaked black mane. He had turned and was facing the direction he thought we were approaching from, and he was crouched, still as the sphinx. I shot him through the shoulder, and the roar of the gun for an instant drowned out the incessant drumming of the rain. The lion fell over dead, and we went to him and sat beneath the soaking bushes. I looked at my watch. We had been tracking the lion for six and a half hours. I lit two cigarettes, and gave one to Guio.

Such was our elation that we did not feel any fatigue at that moment.

But the lion is the only animal I know that, when dead, loses all his majesty, all his dignity. He looked like a miserable bag of skin scarred by a thousand battles. And I felt sorry for this magnificent lion at that moment.[2]

45

UGANDA, PEARL OF AFRICA

Before the 1960s white hunters were few in Uganda's past, and the country remained obscure as a safari destination. In 1962 a company called Uganda Wildlife Development Ltd., known as UWD, was formed at Kampala, the country's capital. The neighboring territories Kenya and Tanganyika had well-established safari industries, so UWD was eager to develop its own organization. On the eve of Uganda's independence the British Protectorate now regarded regulated hunting as an opportunity to earn foreign exchange, and big game was looked upon as a valuable renewable resource.

On October 9, 1962, Uganda became the second of Britain's three East African territories, after Tanganyika, to achieve independence. Milton Apollo Obote, the son of a cotton farmer from the Nilotic Langi tribe of northern Uganda, was elected the country's first prime minister. Shortly thereafter Obote also declared himself president, and emerged as the country's absolute ruler. Ultimately all Uganda's traditional tribal kingdoms, so carefully preserved by the British, were abolished. At the time more than a few expatriates elsewhere in Africa scornfully dismissed Uganda as a banana republic. But from the beginning Uganda was the only member of the East African triad states whose balance sheet was always black rather than red. Copper, cobalt, tin, gold, coffee, tea, cotton, rubber, vanilla, lumber, sugar, fishing, ranching, and other industries accounted for significant exports. But despite an outstanding national parks system, Uganda still lagged far behind its neighbors in tourism.

THE CAPITAL city of Kampala, whose name means "Hill of Impalas," is, like Rome, built upon seven hills. Kampala's broad avenues are

Karamoja is one of Uganda's finest game regions.

bordered with colorful blooms of bougainvillea, hibiscus, jacaranda, and the exotically scented frangipani. Large mango trees and stately Australian eucalyptus clothe its hillsides. Atop one of Kampala's hills is the residential area of Kololo where luxurious private villas are dotted amid wildly exotic vegetation, gardens, and lawns. On another hill stands the magnificent green-domed Bahai temple. Cresting two more hills, Rubaga and Namirembe, are the picturesque Catholic and Protestant cathedrals. The close proximity of Lake Victoria often brings heavy thunderstorms, and this part of Uganda is a shimmering green the year round. In the 1950s and 1960s Kampala was easily the most beautiful and well-kept city in East Africa.

Unlike Kenya and Tanzania, Uganda had a true multiracial society with a friendly cosmopolitan culture unrivaled on the continent. The white population was small, and settlement had never been encouraged there, as it had been in Kenya. The British administration had placed restrictions on foreigners owning large acreages of ranch and farm land, and as a result there was no competition for fertile areas, and relations between Africans, Asians, and Europeans were harmonious.

Uganda's inherited colonial infrastructure was rated the best among emerging African nations. The country's main airport at Entebbe was a major hub for international airlines traversing the continent from north to south and from east to west. Twenty-one miles away from Entebbe, Kampala boasted the respected Makerere University, as well as fine hospitals and advanced medical facilities. Kampala's shops were the best stocked in all East Africa. Imported goods of every description were readily and reasonably available.

UGANDA possessed certain species of game not found elsewhere in East Africa, such as the magnificent Uganda defassa waterbuck, Uganda kob (one small herd of kob existed on the Uasin Gishu plateau across the border in Kenya), Bright's gazelle, maneless zebra, Jackson's hartebeest, and Rothschild's giraffe, among others. Moreover Uganda, unlike Kenya or Tanzania, has two species of elephant, two species of buffalo, and two species of sitatunga.

Even as late as the 1950s Uganda's population of big cats was so plentiful as to be considered a dangerous nuisance and labeled "vermin." Nowhere else in East Africa can both chimpanzee *and* gorilla be found. With such a variety of climate and terrain Uganda has one of the most diverse and interesting bird populations on earth, and most certainly new species remain to be discovered there.

As there were no qualified hunters living in Uganda, UWD recruited hunters from Kenya and Tanganyika.* Hunters new to Uganda quickly concluded Winston Churchill had been right—it really was "The Pearl of Africa." Uganda's game fields turned out to be an unexplored big game El Dorado, and in a short space of time safari clients were producing world-record trophies of every species.

One of the first hunters in Uganda in 1962 was a youthful Nicky Blunt, son of a decorated World War I submarine commander who later became a Tanganyika game warden and the respected author of *Elephant*, a book detailing his extensive field observations. Nicky Blunt, easygoing, shy, and retiring, was an athlete and marathon run-

---

*UWD hunters included myself, Douglas Collins, Nicky Blunt, Dave Williams, Nick Swan, Owen Jeffries, Ken Jespersen, Robin Smith, Erik Andersen, Bruno Ferrari, Bill Pridham, Ernst Zwilling, Olaf Thunberg, Wahid Awan, Robin Hurt, J. Northcote. Kenya hunters often worked for UWD, including Fred Bartlett, Alfredo Pelizzoli, Glen Cottar, John Cook, Mohammed Iqbal, Tony Henley, Owen McCallum, Bill Jenvey, Walter Jones, Tom Lithgow, Bunny Ray, Kevin Torrens, Chris "Tiger" Lyon, Mike Hissey, and Garnet "Freddie" Seed.

ner, and perhaps the most gifted hunter in Uganda. Now based in England, Blunt is still in the safari business and hunts all over Africa.

AMONG UGANDA Wildlife's professional hunters was Erik Andersen. He was a tall, powerfully built, fair-haired, gray-eyed Dane. As a teenager during World War II, Andersen had fought in the Danish resistance movement. He arrived in Tanganyika from his hometown of Copenhagen after the war to operate drilling rigs. As a boy Andersen had hunted small game in Denmark, and in Tanganyika he was in his element. Bush living suited him and afforded him every opportunity to hunt on a daily basis. By the time he went to Uganda with the drilling firm he was already an experienced African hunter, having spent years in the back of beyond. Andersen was a friend of Uganda's chief game warden, John Blower. He suggested Andersen think about turning professional hunter, and he did so in 1962. His colleagues quickly realized Erik was an old hand at surviving perils in the African bush. When I first met him in 1962, the normally reserved Andersen had recently shot and killed an armed burglar during an exchange of fire at his isolated drilling rig in Karamoja.

A resourceful professional, Andersen could overcome any obstacle on safari. Once when he was hunting with an American woman their Land Rover was swept away in a flash flood while crossing what had moments before been a shallow stream. Erik employed his immense strength to escape from the car, dragging his terrified lady client as well as his gunbearer to safety on the bank, just as the car rolled over into the swirling waters.

The safari's only radio telephone had been inside his car and was destroyed, so Andersen couldn't radio Kampala (two hundred miles away) for another car. Neither could he risk crossing the still flooded river with his remaining vehicle, which was a five-ton Bedford baggage truck. Diving into the swirling river, Andersen attached a steel cable to the overturned car, then with the help of his twelve-man safari crew and a hand-operated Tirfor winch the powerful Andersen physically dragged the wrecked Land Rover from the river. In camp, working at night, Erik stripped the engine and gearbox himself, because both components were packed with fine sand and water. In order that his client would not lose any hunting time Erik used the Bedford truck as a "hunting car," and when that proved impractical because of the rough nature of the country, he simply hunted on foot. Over the next five days he obtained an elephant with tusks of ninety-four pounds each, a fine red-maned lion, a seven-foot leopard, and a record-class thirty-four-inch waterbuck for his much impressed lady client.

OWEN JEFFRIES was a fiftyish former district commissioner in Kenya. Owen more closely resembled an absentminded professor than a hunter. A bespectacled Englishman, slightly stooped, gray hair tousled, pink-faced, studious, and rumpled, Jeffries had hunted all his life as an amateur. During the Mau Mau Emergency, Jeffries, who spoke fluent Kikuyu, Somali, and Swahili, participated in operations against the Mau Mau in the Aberdare Mountains. No one would ever suspect that this mild-mannered, soft-spoken man had once been a "pseudo," dressed in rags with blackened face, in the wet highlands with a coterie of reformed Mau Mau gangsters, each carrying concealed Stirling submachine guns.

"During the entire Emergency he was incredibly brave," recalls former Ker and Downey hunter Peter Becker, who served with Jeffries and led his own tracker teams in the conflict. "He had absolutely no regard for his own life at all. He would stroll straight into a heavily armed Mau Mau gang and *boom!*"

Owen Jeffries had the driest and wittiest humor, but he was easily dismissed by casual acquaintances as a clever old chap who did not really amount to much. But Jeffries amounted to a whole lot, even though he humorously and steadfastly rejected the limelight and newspaper interviews. Jeffries was the most casual and fearless of professionals when working amid big herds of elephant (sometimes numbering around 2,000 animals, but more usually 200–300 individuals), which were then very common in Uganda.

Once, when Owen was watching a herd of several hundred elephant along the banks of the Weiga River in western Uganda, the wind suddenly turned and he faced a wall of confused, stampeding elephants. He reluctantly shot a bull in self-defense at the last possible moment, and as the animal crashed to the ground its momentum carried it a few remaining feet into Jeffries, sending him flying. Miraculously, he was not killed. Jeffries got up, dusted himself off, and calmly said with a chuckle, "Well, that's the first time *that* ever happened!"

It turned out that just a day previously this herd had been disturbed by game warden Robin Fairrie, who was capturing a young elephant for

Chipperfield's zoo in England. Fairrie was in the back of a fast-moving Land Rover, trying to capture the elephant. Then the Land Rover hit a large, brick-hard anthill concealed in tall grass. The open car bounced high in the air, and while it was airborne Fairrie was unceremoniously dumped into the path of the thundering elephant herd. Fairrie told me he had no idea why he had not been killed by the fall, nor why the elephants had not trampled him. The entire herd went tearing by as the unarmed Fairrie crouched in the dirt, certain his last moment on earth had arrived.

Jeffries finally settled into a comfortable hunting lodge Uganda Wildlife had constructed in the wonderful game country of the Semliki Valley, bordering Zaire. During his tenure at Semliki Jeffries produced many record trophies for clients, including several record-book kob, waterbuck, lion, northwestern red buffalo, and several good *cyclotis*, or forest elephant.

Jeffries led clients along the remote eastern shore of Lake Albert into virgin hunting and fishing places at Kaiso and Tonya. His greatest Nile perch weighed 169 pounds, caught off the Semliki flats.

THE AUSTRIAN hunter Professor Ernst Alexander Zwilling safaried in Uganda, usually with his own clients, whom he would escort to Entebbe from his home at Alland, near Vienna. A charming Old World gentleman, he was a most interesting companion. As a hunter he looked even less like a man of the bush than did Owen Jeffries. Zwilling more closely resembled a spindly, bald, pixie-eared elf. Although he looked puny Zwilling was an exceptional long-distance walker, and regularly hiked ten or eleven hours a day on safari.

Zwilling wrote twelve books over the course of a long hunting career. His best-known book, *Jungle Fever*, is a fine account of West African hunting. Ernst roamed over Africa long before the Second World War. He hunted French Equatorial Africa, and knew the desert regions from Fort Archambault to Lake Iro and the Aouk River. He had hunted the difficult Central African variety of greater kudu east of the Chari River, and into the mountains of central Chad territory. In 1931 Ernst was seriously hurt when a buffalo horned him in the stomach at the Mobun marsh in northern Gabon.

After the First World War Zwilling was a white hunter in the Cameroons, a forested West African country the size of Sweden. While in West Africa, Ernst had twice been the guest of the infamous and immensely powerful Sultan Rei-Bouba, who reputedly had eight hundred wives in his harem.[1]

Over his long and varied career Ernst hunted giant eland on the Mao Veimba River near the Chad frontier, and he said three thousand elephants could be found in the Chad Basin, broken up into six to eight herds. He had hunted his best elephant in the eastern part of Oubangi-Chari territory near the Belgian Congo border and the Sudanese frontier. His biggest tusker weighed 110 pounds and was taken here. But perhaps the most interesting thing about Ernst was his age. Nobody knew for certain how old he was, but in the early 1960s he was surely in his early seventies, and had recently married an Austrian girl named Helga, then in her early twenties. The couple had three children. Ernst was still supremely fit when he joined the ranks of Uganda's white hunters.*

AT THE TIME of Uganda's independence, John Blower was Uganda's chief game warden. He was a graduate of Edinburgh University, had served in Burma during the war, and in turn was appointed Conservator of Forests in Tanganyika, then warden of the Serengeti in 1952. During the Mau Mau period he commanded a Kenya police tracker team, before becoming Uganda's chief game warden.

Blower believed wildlife could only succeed outside national parks with the cooperation of the Africans. He figured that if local counties saw a financial advantage in protecting game, then they would support both anti-poaching and legal hunting by tourists. Blower was immensely important in shaping the country's wildlife policies. In 1963 he resigned as chief game warden to become manager of Uganda Wildlife Development. There was a small gathering at the Lake Victoria Hotel at Entebbe to officially inaugurate the new firm. Prince Bernhard of the Netherlands, a keen hunter, was the guest of honor as he was on his way to hunt in Tanzania.

Under Blower, UWD quickly became a leading outfitter, easily able to rival the largest firms in Kenya and Tanganyika in terms of clients, income, and quality trophies. Blower's original—and at the time controversial—ideas about wildlife conservation and hunting were breaking news.

---

*Ernst Zwilling was still hunting up to the time of his sudden death in Vienna in November 1990, and that, I think, would put him in his nineties.

As chief game warden he had proposed counties (or *saza*, chief's councils, as they were called) should benefit directly from income from tourist hunting licenses. He introduced a game quota system, the first of its kind in Africa. Annual quotas of game animals were allocated for each of Uganda's hunting areas. Once a quota was utilized no more of that species could be hunted in that area for the rest of the year.

Blower also did away with the hassles of red tape regarding game licenses for tourists. He introduced a "minister's permit," which cost $14 and allowed the tourist hunter to take a single trophy animal of each male game species, provided it was available on quota. At the time in 1962, Kenya, Tanganyika, and elsewhere required tourist hunters to purchase an expensive nonrefundable basic game license in advance, costing $150. Sought-after species required the purchase of nonrefundable "supplementary" licenses for game such as elephant, lion, leopard, roan, and so on. Blower thought the flaws in the system warranted a change in the law. Uganda's safari clients paid for trophies *after* the safari. This was beneficial to the tourist hunter who only paid for what he actually shot. On the other hand, the professional was relieved of pressure to allow an inferior trophy to be hunted simply because the client had already paid for his permit in advance and wanted his money's worth. Blower's policies were so fair and so successful, they were embraced by Tanzania, and to a lesser extent by Kenya as well.

It was a sad day when John Blower left to become chief game warden of Ethiopia.* Safariland's Ken Jespersen was Blower's replacement. Jespersen had already worked at UWD as a hunter for several years. He remained manager at UWD until 1969. In that year a record 100,000 foreign tourists visited Uganda.

WHILE PRESIDENT Obote was out of Uganda on January 25, 1971, he was overthrown in a military coup d'état staged by Idi Amin and the Uganda army, and in less than one week Amin established rule by decree. At first almost all Ugandans welcomed Amin because they were

---

*John Blower wrote Ethiopia's first game ordinance, demarcated national parks, and implemented game laws. He discovered the hitherto unknown existence of Mrs. Gray's lechwe, thought only to occur in Sudan. Blower went to Nepal as wildlife project manager, then in 1974 to Indonesia to plan national parks. He returned to Africa as a wildlife consultant to Sudan, then Burma for four years, followed by wildlife consultancy jobs in Bhutan, Somalia, and Bangladesh. The Netherlands recognized Blower's outstanding conservation work and in 1981 awarded him the Order of the Golden Ark.

glad to see the end of the left-leaning, autocratic Obote, who had never-theless guided Uganda to comparative peace and prosperity. But Amin's sudden rise to power would soon be regretted. For years even expatriate residents of Kampala, as well as the rest of Africa and the world, would have no inkling of what was really going on in Uganda.

The new president, self-styled Field Marshal Idi Amin Dada, had humble beginnings. In 1946 Idi joined the King's African Rifles as an assistant cook, but he did well in the colonial British army. He was keen, husky (six foot four), immensely strong, cheerful, and willing to take orders, and after rising to the rank of corporal was considered "offi-cer material." In 1953 Amin had served with British security forces in Kenya during the Mau Mau Emergency. He also became heavyweight boxing champion of Uganda. With these heady credentials Amin, after becoming president of Uganda, proclaimed himself "Conqueror of the British Empire." There were still plenty of people who regarded him as no more than an amusing buffoon, or even as a likeable chap, and indeed, he could be both charming and amusing. But Amin's murderous misrule and the doings of his brutal army were nothing to joke about. Over 300,000 Ugandans were butchered during Amin's short reign. Yet even then few in or outside Uganda knew the extent of atrocities and genocide perpetrated by Amin's army against its own citizens. Not only would Uganda's people suffer, so would wildlife—in a very big way. Churchill's once glorious Pearl of Africa would not be a safe place for man or beast for nearly a generation. In the end Uganda's hunters and tourists enjoyed less than ten great years. Uganda was never able to ful-fill its promise as safari country.

46.

COMPANY OF ADVENTURERS

Safari hunting in East Africa was forever changed by the masterly blueprint of Brian Nicholson, a former white hunter turned game warden. The disciple and successor of C. J. P. Ionides, the "Father of the Selous game reserve," Nicholson conceived a plan for administering Tanzania's expansive wildlife regions. In 1965 he changed most of the vast former controlled hunting areas, or CHAs, into hunting concessions that could be leased by outfitters from the government for two or more years at a time. Nicholson also demarcated the Selous game reserve's 20,000 square miles of uninhabited country into 47 separate concessions. Concessions were given a limited quota of each game species, and outfitters were expected to utilize quotas as fully as possible, but not exceed them.

Nicholson's plan gave outfitters exclusive rights over hunting lands, providing powerful incentives for concession holders to police their areas, develop tracks, airfields, and camps, and, most importantly, preserve the wild game. When the system was put into effect, it was the larger outfitting organizations—safari outfitters who could muster the resources to bid and who had a clientele sufficient to fulfill the trophy quotas Nicholson had set (done in order to provide government revenue by way of fees for anti-poaching operations, development, and research)—that moved quickly to buy up the leases on the most desirable blocks of land. Smaller safari companies who could not compete on their own banded together and formed alliances so that they, too, could obtain hunting territories.

To meet the challenge, Kenya hunters Glen Cottar, Alfredo Pelizzoli, and Reggie Destro founded an alliance known as Afriventures in 1970. The group, all of whom headed their own established safari firms, eventually managed the largest number of concessions in Tanzania's unsurpassed big game country. Reggie Destro's calm and decisive personality combined well with Glen Cottar's exuberant enthusiasm and Alfredo Pelizzoli's shrewd business acumen. The Afriventures trio grew to include a diverse set of characters. Prince Alfi von Auersperg of Austria was invited to join the group, as was the Danish hunter Jens Hessel and the Frenchman Rene Babault. Completing the partnership were Englishman Derrick Dunn, Kenya-born brothers, David and Anton Allen, and Brian Herne.

DESTRO, the patriarch of the group, had his own brand of slightly roguish Old World charm. He was the most likeable of men, and had long been a mainstay in the hunting world. The son of an Italian father and a Scottish mother, Reggie was raised in Kenya. His father, John Destro, arrived in British East Africa with pioneer William Northrup McMillan as manager of the American's celebrated Juja Estate at Ol Donyo Sabuk, the "Mountain of Buffaloes." Destro senior had previously been an aide during McMillan's ill-fated Blue Nile explorations of Sudan and Abyssinia in 1903–1905.[1]

Reggie's family had a cattle ranch not far from where Nairobi's Jomo Kenyatta Airport is now located. In those days the Destro place was alive with Thomson's and Grant's gazelle, Coke's hartebeest, eland, wildebeest, zebra, wart hogs, cheetah, and cattle-raiding lion and leopard. Reggie became a hunter after World War II with Ker and Downey before creating his own firm, managed by his wife, Cecilie.

Destro took his young neighbor, teenaged Bill Woodley, on one of his early elephant hunting safaris. During their safari Reggie and Bill stalked within twenty yards of a big bull elephant in the thorn jungles surrounding the Makindu railway station. Reggie signaled for Bill to take a heart shot. Bill fired, and much to his surprise the elephant took off at full speed, then wheeled around and charged. Bill threw up his rifle and fired again, this time trying for the only shot offered him, a tricky frontal brain shot. His bullet was a touch high, missing the brain by an inch, but that did not stop the bull. On it came at full speed in a huge cloud of dust, bent only on Woodley's destruction. As Bill frantically worked the bolt of his .375 magazine rifle, he was rocked by the thunderous boom of Reggie's big Schuler .500 double rifle as it exploded beside him. The elephant collapsed in mid-stride, skidding to a halt less than a yard from Bill. When the dust settled Destro calmly offered Woodley a Clipper cigarette. "Reggie held his lighter to my cigarette, and I couldn't help but notice his hands were steady as a rock. Not so with my hands or knees," Bill recalled. Thereafter Woodley credited Reggie with saving his life. Destro had always used his Schuler .500 double rifle with deadly effect, but he later switched and became the first professional hunter to convert to the American-built .475 O.K.H. (O'Neil, Keith, Hopkins) magazine rifle.

Destro once told of a large and cunning leopard that lived on a big rock kopje surrounded by open grassland. Many hunters had tried to get this huge old leopard, but he had outfoxed them all. There was no way to make a concealed approach to a bait set in a tree beside the rockpile. Hunters had tried moving the bait to trees several hundred yards away from the rocks, but the crafty leopard would never cross the open space in daylight. He fed on the baits in the dead of night then retired to his stronghold among the rocks. One hunter had built a good blind at the edge of the rocks near a bait tree, but the leopard never fed on this bait in daylight, either.

Every time a hunter tried something new the leopard seemed to pick up on it. Hidden among the high rocks the big cat had a bird's-eye view of events below. When hunters used a car to drop them off at a blind, the leopard never showed. The Maharajah of Mayhem, Eric Rundgren, got the idea that "salting" the bait would tempt the leopard into feeding while there was still enough light to shoot. In fact, the leopard did feed on the bait lightly coated with salt, but only after dark. Rundgren continued to feed the big cat and he said that it once came on the bait late in the evening, but he could not get close enough for his client to shoot without being seen. Rundgren then built a portable blind by bending the boughs of green saplings laced with fresh leaves into a dome large enough to hide himself and a client. With a gunbearer driving the car Eric had slowly gone past the bait, and while the vehicle was momentarily parked between the bait and himself, he and his client removed the blind from the car's roof and hid in the blind. The car drove on with Rundgren and his client concealed in the blind, but the leopard never showed up. Rundgren had been frustrated enough to arrive at the rocks with his entire camp crew to organize a "beat," but this also failed, for the kopje was broken with huge piles of rocks where numbers of leopard could easily elude the largest party of beaters.

Reggie Destro had observed the leopard with his binoculars over the course of several safaris. He discovered the leopard had a habit of some-times appearing late in the evening on a massive boulder where it could look out over the plains. Destro and his client made their way to a shallow gully formed by storm runoff. They were able to get within a few hundred yards of the rocks by crawling unseen in the ditch, which became more shallow as they advanced, until there was no cover at all.

In full view of the leopard and the rocks Destro and his client wriggled on their bellies across the open plain in single file, so close together that from a distance they resembled a large serpent. The hunters wriggled a few yards at a time then paused motionless for several minutes before advancing straight for the kopje. Seventy yards from the rocks a perspiring Destro dared look up and saw the fascinated leopard lying on a rock watching them, just as a house cat might watch a lizard.

Destro, keeping his eyes downcast, for he was a firm believer that eye contact with your quarry kicked in a predator's suspicious sixth sense, resumed the wriggling approach until he was forty yards from the base of the rocks. The sun was fast dipping over the horizon, but his strategy was working so far. Destro paused again, and slowly looking above he saw the intrigued leopard sitting up, watching intently. Destro whispered to his client to crawl alongside for his shot. It was almost anticlimactic when the client fired from his prone position and bagged the leopard. Destro's knowledge of cats and their curiosity had combined with his unusual hunting skills to win the contest.

Destro had enormous influence with Afriventures hunters. His experience combined with Cottar's daring and Pelizzoli's far-sighted tactics resulted in the group managing eleven major Tanzania hunting areas, the largest operation of its kind.

ONE OF the more colorful characters to join the Afriventures group was dashing Austrian Prince Alfred von Auersperg. Alfi's boyhood home at the scenic alpine town of Kitzbuhel was not far from the fashionable resort of Schloss Mittersell, a castle originally built in the fifteenth century as a summer palace for the bishops of Salzburg. The schloss had an interesting history, having served in the 1930s as a popular resort patronized by an elite list of guests that included Cole Porter and Princess (later Queen) Juliana of the Netherlands and her husband Prince Bernhard, who spent their honeymoon there.[2] In 1956 young Alfi was at Schloss Mittersell where he met an American beauty named

Martha "Sunny" Crawford. Sunny was the daughter of a self-made Pittsburgh oil and gas multimillionaire, George Crawford.[3] After a glamorous high society courtship, and a Greenwich, Connecticut, wedding in 1957, Alfi and his bride settled at Haus Auersperg, their luxurious alpine chalet at Kitzbuhel. Alfi went on numerous trips to Africa to indulge his love of big game hunting over the next nine years. The flaxen-haired prince sporting the trademark year-round tan of the follow-the-sun jet set was an Olympic-class skier who had twice won the famous Hahnen-Kamm race at Kitzbuhel, no mean feat in a land famed for its steep mountains and competitive skiers. A versatile athlete, he excelled at track and field, and twice represented Austria in international golf competitions. While Alfi was in Africa, his wife Sunny grew restless, and the storybook couple drifted apart. Sunny obtained a divorce in 1966, and in the same year made a fateful second marriage to Claus von Bulow.[4]

At first most professional hunters regarded Alfi as a happy-go-lucky playboy prince, one among the many wealthy and titled sportsmen who would hire a white hunter for a month or two, then return to their more natural environment amid the salons of Vienna, Munich, and Paris. But it turned out Alfi was not just another client. He was determined to be a white hunter. He had risen from the ranks of amateur hunters, training under Reggie Destro to earn full membership in the East African Professional Hunter's Association. His perseverance won over any colleagues who doubted the seriousness of his intentions.

Aristocratic hunters were not uncommon in the history of African safaris, but it was unusual for East African hunters to accept an outsider, no matter how blue his blood, as one of their own. In contemporary times other Kenya hunters with a handle to their names included Polish Count "Stas" Saphiea, Belgian Count Rudi Van der Stegen, Italian Marchese Francesco Bisletti, and Alfi's cousin, Tanzania hunter Count Franz "Ferry" Meran, all of whom operated safaris in the 1960s and 1970s.

Alfi possessed the cool poise of a natural hunter. A good example of this was the day one of Alfi's German clients wounded a buffalo. With his tracker and a colleague Alfi spoored the beast for several miles through Masailand thickets until the faint blood spoor dried up. At that point Alfi paused to give his tracker time to regain the spoor. Without warning the wounded buffalo charged out of a thicket twenty yards from Alfi. The prince coolly stopped the buffalo with a shot between the eyes. His colleague measured the distance separating Alfi and the buffalo. The fallen buffalo's nose was four feet from where Alfi had stood. With typical sangfroid, he made light of the affair, saying he had received plenty of warning from the snapping branches as the buffalo broke cover. Despite Alfi's nonchalance, it was a magnificent piece of shooting.

On another occasion near Voi, Alfi, his client, and two trackers stayed on the spoor of a giant elephant for two days. When they caught up with the bull Alfi was astonished to see how big the tusks were and knew he was looking at a magical hundred pounder. Alfi maneuvered his client to within twenty-five yards of the elephant for a side brain shot. The client fired but missed the brain. Alfi saw the dust fly off the side of the elephant's head, too high to do any good. The elephant whirled and took off. Without a word Alfi left his astonished trackers and client and sprinted after the elephant. The elephant was running through light woodland as if the devil were after him. Alfi said that to add to the confusion the bull ran right into a small mating herd of perhaps thirty elephant that scattered in alarm as the old bull charged through them. Alfi ignored the confused herd and, keeping his eye on the back of the disappearing bull, was surprised to see the elephant suddenly halt and turn, raising its trunk to test the wind. Then it ran off at right angles to Alfi, who seized his chance and sprinted after the elephant. Alfi pulled up and fired a single .458 bullet, dropping the fast-moving animal in its tracks from a range of sixty yards. Few hunters would have been able to maintain the sustained speed and duration of such a marathon and still be steady enough for a precision shot with a heavy rifle at the end of it.

RENE BABAULT had come aboard soon after Afriventures's inception. He was born in France in 1926, then raised in East Africa and the Belgian Congo where his father had been a prominent entomologist. As a youngster Rene had explored the Ituri rain forests where he hunted in company with bands of Efe pygmies. When Babault's relatives in Zaire moved to the village of Gabiro, known as the gateway to Rwanda's once-magnificent Kagera national park in northern Rwanda, Rene was able to further indulge in his passion for hunting. Like the great Brazilian hunter, George DeLima, Rene came to hunt all over Africa from Zaire to Chad, from Cameroon to the Central African Republic. In

Kenya Babault had been a leading white hunter for David Lunan's renamed Hunters (Africa) Ltd.

David and Anton Allen are the sons of incorrigible English Gypsy hunter, Bunny Allen. As stepbrothers they shared little in common physically, but both inherited Bunny's love of hunting dangerous game and his irrepressibly rakish and mischievous nature. While the dark-haired David started his career in wildlife as a Kenya game warden at Nanyuki, his tall, blond brother cut his teeth in Tanganyika working for old-timers Russell Bowker-Douglas and George Dove. The Maharajah of Mayhem, Eric Rundgren, pronounced Anton "a bit of a fire eater but a brilliant hunter."[5] In 1959 Anton was mauled by a leopard that had been wounded by a client near the Malagarasi River in southwest Tanganyika. Some time later he was seriously injured by a buffalo in Kenya and wound up with a broken pelvis. It was Anton's second near deadly encounter with an enraged buffalo, but he accepted the event with the savoir faire typical of the Allen clan.

A DANE named Jens Hessel settled with his wife at Mweiga, on the foothills of the Aberdare Mountains, not far from the Allens' safari headquarters at Nanyuki. He had been a freelance white hunter for several years as well as a bush pilot before he joined Afriventures. Specializing in flying safaris Hessel has appeared in movie productions, including *Out of Africa*, in which he was the pilot flying as Finch Hatton in the yellow biplane.

The only Tanzania-based hunter invited to join the group was Derrick Dunn from Arusha. Red-haired and powerfully built, Derrick was affectionately known to the Africans as Bwana *Singizi* (Mr. Sleepy) because of the shape of his drooping eyelids. Dunn had taken up elephant hunting as a youth in Nyasaland (now Malawi), then moved to Tanganyika in 1956, and turned professional with Lawrence-Brown Safaris, before going into the safari business for himself. Derrick was awarded the Shaw and Hunter Trophy twice, in 1971 and 1972, the only man apart from Syd Downey to be so honored. On the first occasion Derrick's client, R. M. Zimmerman, obtained a 47½-inch East African sable antelope at Rungwa, Tanganyika. On the second Paul Deutz obtained the outright world record Cape buffalo (a bull), which measured 59⁵⁄₁₆ inches, taken at Maswa, south of the Serengeti. The record still stands.

In 1973 Brian Nicholson resigned as principal game warden of Tanzania to manage the Afriventures group based in Nairobi. By then Afriventures was ranging far beyond East Africa and the demand grew for first-class pilots willing to fly into regions where only the most basic airfields had been carved out of the bush, and navigational beacons were unknown. The hunters found soul mates in a Nairobi firm called Kenya Air Charters, whose pilots were household names in the safari world: John Falconer-Taylor, Heather and Jim Stewart, Giles Remnant, and Pat Dale. All were outstanding in emergency situations and willing to fly anywhere at short notice. Pilots had become an integral part of safaris, and in the dangerous business of bush flying, each hunter had his favored pilot. A first choice for many was the glamorous blonde, hazel-eyed Heather Stewart. Heather carried on the proud East African tradition of daring female pilots begun back in the 1930s by Maia Carberry and the romanticized Beryl Markham. The daughter of British expatriates, she was born in Nigeria and arrived in Kenya at the age of eighteen to be married. Later, on the occasion of Heather's second marriage, she had been given flying lessons. From that time on, piloting became her life.

Heather knew East Africa's hunting areas as few pilots did, and her flying skills rivaled the best of her male colleagues. In a sea of endless bush, forest, or sand dunes, Heather could locate and memorize exact locations where hunters had chopped out rough airstrips. After making an initial low pass to scare off animals grazing on the strip, she would zoom in, followed by a huge cloud of dust as she "painted" her aircraft onto the most basic postage-stamp field. From her pressed khaki pilot's uniform to her manicured fingernails, the fashion-cover blonde with a fine sense of humor was all business where flying was concerned. Beating off mosquitoes, amorous clients, and hunters alike, Heather has put her heavily loaded aircraft down in places many old pilots would refuse to consider, yet her safety record is impeccable.

The bonds of friendship and shared interests endured for the Afriventures hunters, and their combined strengths enticed them into riskier and even more remote territory.

47

HAVE GUN WILL TRAVEL

By the 1970s most East African hunters were as comfortable in the cockpit of a small airplane as they were behind the wheel of a Land Rover or Toyota. Those who did not fly often traveled beside the pilot as spotters for vague landmarks. In countries where flying was done by dead reckoning, most hunters were as skilled as any navigator at locating bush landing strips, which they had carved out of the uncharted terrain. More than ever before, safaris ranging outside East Africa required the use of light aircraft. In some of these unknown places it was accepted that great opportunity often went hand in hand with great risk.

PERHAPS NO professional hunter of recent years has more personified the "Have Gun Will Travel" aspect of the modern-day sportsman than Robin Hurt. Robin emerged in the 1970s to become one of the most successful of his generation. Born in London in April 1945 he began his career as a stooge (learner-hunter) with Ker and Downey, then in the mid-1960s joined Uganda Wildlife during the heyday of safaris in that country. A son of Kenya game warden Roger Hurt, who raised his children on a farm at Lake Naivasha, Robin had never wanted to be anything but a hunter. Tall, well-built, and quick-witted, Hurt has an engaging personality and considerable charisma. He is also that rare being in the safari world, a white hunter who understands business. His success has been remarkable.

In a quest for new frontiers Hurt has covered much of the African continent. If a client desired a giant eland in Central African Republic, or a red lechwe in Zambia, or a bongo in Sudan, Hurt willingly obliged.

Along the way he attracted a fine group of young hunters to his firm, all of whom came with old-style qualifications, traditions, and pedigrees.*
In 1973 Robin was awarded the Shaw and Hunter Trophy for a 54-inch buffalo taken by his German client, Dr. F. K. Flick. The same buffalo also won the MacDonald Trophy for Hurt. Despite his constant hunting Robin only once suffered a physical setback. The incident occurred near Tanzania's Monduli Mountain. Hurt's client had hit a leopard low with a .375, breaking its shoulder. Reasoning that the brush was so thick he would only have a chance to shoot at close range, Hurt grabbed a 12-gauge shotgun, and gave his usual weapon of choice, a .500 Evans double rifle, to his tracker. Robin knew the leopard would be hard to see in the low light of dense brush, and he figured the spread of Double-O buckshot pellets would give him a better chance of stopping the cat. Moments later the leopard went for him and Robin fired the shotgun as the cat reached him. The range was so close his buckshot entered the leopard's neck in a tight pattern with no time to spread.

The leopard knocked Hurt down, and he lost his grip on the gun. Robin struggled with the leopard as it mauled his arms and legs, then it abruptly drew away from Hurt, as if exhausted by the attack. Robin realized the shots had taken a toll as his gunbearer quickly finished the leopard with a shot from the .500.

Robin Hurt has dominated the African hunting scene through the 1980s and 1990s, and he operates Robin Hurt Safaris based in Arusha.

LIKE ROBIN, Tony Seth-Smith was another adventurous hunter who came of age during the 1970s. He also hails from an old Kenya family whose roots are buried deep in African soil. His father, Donald, and uncle Martin were both prominent pioneer white hunters who came to Kenya in 1906. As a boy Tony learned to hunt with D'robo honey hunters on the Mau escarpment near his family's farm at Njoro. He graduated from Oxford and returned to Kenya as a game warden in 1961. Three years later he turned professional and joined Hunters (Africa) Ltd. As a hunter Tony was extremely successful, twice winning the MacDonald Trophy for getting the best buffalo for clients. Shortly afterward his luck with buffalo ran out and he was badly gored.

---

*Kenya hunters employed by Robin Hurt at this writing are: Roy Carr-Hartley, Simon Evans, Rick Hopcraft, Barry Gaymer, Alick Roberts, and Danny McCallum.

In 1970 Tony won the Shaw and Hunter Trophy,* for a record lion with a skull length measuring 14⅛ inches and a width of 9 inches, giving it a total score of 23⅛ inches. Seth-Smith recalled:

> Lions roared continuously all around camp within 100 yards until just before dawn, so much so that at half past five in the morning—bearing in mind the main object of the safari was a good lion—I got Tim [Havens] out of bed, cleaned the oil out of one of his rifles, and he and I sneaked out of camp in the direction of the last roaring.
>
> As it began to get light enough to see, a bit of what looked like a large black bush got up from 50 yards ahead of us, and walked into the gully to our right. We sat down behind a bit of cover and waited for it to get lighter. Some five minutes later we were rewarded by this magnificent lion stepping out of the gully. Havens killed the lion with a well-placed shot. Tim's comment was, "What do I do now for the rest of the 21 days?" It so happened we went on to get an excellent leopard and elephant just under the 100-pound mark.[1]

ONE OF the more daunting safari destinations was the vast nation of Zaire, the former Belgian Congo,† which covers 905,365 square miles in Central Africa. Its tropical rain forests, home to the pygmies, are also inhabited by elephant, bongo, and a good variety of forest game. Nothing is easy in Zaire. Merely getting about the countryside is both difficult and dangerous. Armed soldiers of undefined loyalties roam everywhere. Yet the irresistible lure of hunting Zaire drew the likes of Glen Cottar, Bryan Coleman, and a few other Kenya hunters including Robin Hurt, all of them ready to brave the tangle of logistic and bureaucratic hurdles to establish camps among the great rain forests and savannah woodlands.

Cottar was the first of the East African hunters to return to Zaire after the series of brutal wars and internal unrest that had isolated the

---

*The East African Professional Hunter's Association awarded the Shaw and Hunter Trophy to only nineteen individuals.

†Zaire was known as the Congo prior to 1971. In 1997 Zaire was again renamed Congo.

country for years. Glen's heavily laden safari convoy inched across Kenya and Uganda to the forests near Isiro (formerly Paulis) in north-eastern Zaire. With enormous difficulty Glen made his way through unknown jungles and was rewarded for his efforts by tracking down and getting two hundred-pounder elephants for clients, as well as some outstanding western bongo trophies. The western bongo (B. eurycerus eurycerus) differs from its much rarer eastern cousin (found only in Kenya) with a generally lighter chestnut coloration and a different habitat. The eastern bongo is found only in highland montane forests, while the western variety lives in warm lowland forests in some west and central African countries.

Cottar, for whom no horizon was too far, set up a base camp for himself and the Afriventures hunters near a small village amid savannah woodland known as Dika, named after a Mangbetu chief. As the hunters grew familiar with the country it became evident poaching was commonly sanctioned by what passed for officialdom.

Nevertheless Cottar and his colleagues hunted from Dika through two seasons. At the end of March 1973 Glen returned to Kenya, leaving Bryan Coleman at Dika. Coleman and his clients had just taken another record-class bongo and planned to hunt through April. With no warning Zaire's government declared radio telephones illegal and banned their use. Radios are an integral part of safaris and a lifeline in the event of injury. As Coleman and his clients mulled options Zaire made a second pronouncement banning safaris. Both Cottar and Coleman believed Zaire's government wanted no foreign eye-witnesses or scrutiny of its poaching rackets. Coleman knew the country's undisciplined soldiers needed no encouragement to rough up guests who had become unwelcome by their government, and his clients wanted to clear out right away. Despite the ban on radios Coleman called Nairobi. To allay the air charter company's concerns about flying to Zaire, the wily Coleman suggested a flight plan that followed a roundabout course approaching Isiro, an official airport, from the north, via Juba in Sudan, rather than directly from the east. He assured Nairobi he would obtain flight clearance. The Afriventures safari crews broke camp and quickly drove north to Sudan, then east on a ten-day drive to Nairobi. At Isiro Coleman and his clients scrambled aboard the aircraft as Bryan waved his clearance, a sheet of blank paper. The pilot wasted no time in getting airborne and raced for the Sudan frontier.

◇

GLEN COTTAR and some of his colleagues were eager to hunt in Sudan following the 1973 cease-fire that temporarily ended the seventeen-year civil war between the Muslim north and the Christian and animist south.* The crumbling town of Juba, on the west bank of the upper Nile, became a safari supply center of sorts and was the port of entry for planes arriving from Nairobi. Sudan was known for its heavy-tusked elephants, exotic tribal life, mysterious maladies including "green monkey disease," and inclement, scorching climate. Juba itself, deprived and dilapidated after years of turmoil, was still home to a few Greek and Lebanese merchants who controlled its meager trade.

Sudan was considered a last frontier by some who had been on safari everywhere else. Among its devotees were Alfi von Auersperg and the gregarious Irishman Liam Lynn. In Juba the fair-haired Lynn turned a luminous shade of pink, his skin permanently flushed from the heat. The burly hunter became so enamored of Juba's charms that he set up camp on the bank of the Nile, where fellow hunters and sundry travelers could shelter in thin shade beside the great river. Liam ingeniously acquired a beer distributorship, the equivalent of a gold mine in thirsty Sudan. For a short time he was a cult classic in safari lore.

Hunters faced a special set of hazards in Sudan. The most basic supplies were unobtainable, and the logistics of getting food and spare parts from Kenya were both expensive and difficult. In addition, well-armed poachers from Zaire and Central African Republic were active in most west-bank hunting areas.

Glen Cottar casually brushed aside near insurmountable difficulties that turned others back. He was the first to hunt west of the Nile to Yambio, Tembura, and Wau, and the first to obtain a western bongo in Sudan after the war. Glen's clients hunted giant eland, sitatunga, and Mrs. Gray's lechwe for a series of back-to-back safaris. Seeing that others followed him to Dinkaland territory, Glen, true to the Cottar credo, which proclaims a loathing for any sort of "beaten track," recrossed the Nile at Juba. He headed up the east bank far beyond the old Nile town of Gondokoro, once a British outpost and bastion of law and order that had

---

*Heather Stewart piloted the first outfitters to Sudan after the war, accompanied by Glen Cottar, Reggie Destro, and myself.

Elephant among borassus palms near the Sudan-Uganda frontier.

long since succumbed to the torpor of its stifling climate, neglect, and indifference.

Over a period of months Cottar led his fast-moving, multivehicle Suzuki caravan across the roadless Nile valley eastward as far as Boma and the Ethiopian frontier. Turning south again Cottar hunted the vast unknown region of game fields north of Torit and Kapoeta. It was virgin territory, trackless and untouched since Karamoja Bell's ivory safaris had marched beyond Morua Akipi seventy years earlier. It was rugged, hard country, beyond the reach or desires of most humans, yet to Cottar it was immensely rewarding and worthy of the title Cottar Country.

Glen is one of the few hunters who, like George DeLima and Robin Hurt, really did hunt all over Africa.

48

THE EMPEROR AND THE PRINCE

By the end of 1973 Kenya was the sole remaining tourist destination in East Africa. While the neighboring country of Uganda was still in the throes of military anarchy, Tanzania surprised the world on September 7 by issuing an overnight ban on all hunting and photographic safaris within its territory. Government authorities moved quickly to seize and impound foreign-registered Land Cruisers, supply trucks, minibuses, aircraft, and equipment.

The stunned collection of safari clients as well as sundry mountain climbers, bird-watchers, and beachcombers who had been visiting the country at the time of the inexplicable edict were summarily escorted to Kilimanjaro airport outside of Arusha to await deportation. The residue of tourists stranded without flights were trucked to the northern town of Namanga where they were left on the dusty roadside to cross into Kenya on foot. All tourist businesses, including the government-owned Tanzania Wildlife Safaris, were closed down. No government refunds were ever made to tourists or to foreign or local safari outfitters.

Back in Kenya, members of the East African Professional Hunter's Association realized time was running out. It was increasingly apparent that their own existence, as well as that of the nation's wildlife, was dependent upon the uncertain will and whim of the government. Unabated public attention focused on escalating poaching activity that had become a festering thorn in the side of some local politicians. In December 1976 political opponents of Kenya Minister for Tourism and Wildlife Mathews Ogutu went so far as to state that Ogutu's own Ministry for Tourism and Wildlife harbored poachers. The pressure had reached the boiling point and some action had to be taken.

Alfi von Auersperg, 1974.

During the 1970s not even the most pessimistic professional hunters thought a total hunting ban would ever actually come to pass in Kenya. There had never been any mention of it in government circles. After all, Kenya was historically the safari capital of the world. When the measure was enacted it was a bitter blow to those who had chosen to believe that they could fight the tide, that they could work hand in hand with government, and that the situation could be saved. A leading Kenya conservationist, Dr. Iain Douglas-Hamilton, an authority on the African elephant, wrote, ". . . and so a seventy-year-old tradition was killed off with the stroke of a pen. For all those years it [hunting] had been properly regulated until the corruption of the game department destroyed it."[1]

Prince Alfi von Auersperg was one of the few members of the hunter fraternity who was not unduly fazed by the abrupt end of safari hunting in Kenya in 1977. The irrepressible Austrian took the loss of his Kenya business in stride and remained as cheerful as ever, just as when he and fellow hunters had suffered major financial losses before, first in Tanzania, next in Uganda, then Kenya, Zaire, and, finally, Sudan. Alfi cast his gaze across Africa in search of new hunting grounds. This time the former French colony of Ubangi Shari, later known as French Equatorial Africa then renamed Central African Republic (CAR), appeared in his optimistic line of sight. Along with several Afriventures colleagues, the prince took more than a passing glance at the huge landlocked plateau located above the Zombieland that was then Zaire.

The penniless territory operated from year to year on huge deficits. Then as now it was a poverty-stricken nation encompassing 240,534 square miles, an area slightly smaller than the state of Texas. The economy was only able to survive on massive injections of foreign aid, received mainly from France, its principal backer. Another significant contributor was the apartheid regime of South Africa.

The country's prolific game region is mostly grass and scrubland with an average altitude of 2,000 feet, with rivers draining south to the Congo and north to Lake Chad. Open, well-watered savannah covers most of the area with an arid corner in the northeast and tropical rain forest in the southwest.

By the time Alfi became interested in the Central African Republic, hunting safaris had already been regionally developed, mostly by French hunters. Some of these men were recognized as fine bushmen, and of the old-timers the best known was the great Claude Vasselet. Yet new, younger French hunters had emerged since Vasselet's golden days in the fifties and sixties. There had always been a strong current of Francophone resistance to foreign or non-Francophone white hunters, especially those arriving from the formerly British Kenya.

While the Central African Republic's hunters did not particularly mind the occasional foreign safari, they were not prepared to welcome permanent foreign competition in their midst. Ker and Downey hunter Myles Turner had noted this attitude way back in the early fifties when the country was still French Equatorial Africa. In more recent times the American hunter Bert Klineburger—who has hunted in more countries worldwide than any hunter in history—had penetrated the Francophone curtain and for a number of years made a series of successful safaris to what is now Central African Republic, just as he had in *haut* Zaire.

THE CENTRAL African Republic was ruled by the iron fists of a former soldier, the maniacal Jean Bedel Bokassa. Some African leaders in newly independent countries modeled themselves after disparate characters from history. Ghana's president Kwame Nkrumah professed admiration for American president Abraham Lincoln, a figure celebrated in Africa for his emancipation of black people from white domination. Uganda's Idi Amin claimed Adolf Hitler as his hero. Bokassa meticulously crafted his own image to match that of his inspiration, a simple man born in Corsica of Italian lineage, the French emperor Napoleon Bonaparte.

The pint-sized, pigeon-chested Jean Bedel Bokassa had long worshipped Napoleon's grandeur, dazzled by tales of France's glorious Napoleonic era. On December 4, 1977, the former African soldier crowned himself Emperor Bokassa. He renamed his poverty-stricken domain the Central African Empire.

Bokassa had invited the Pope and every African head of state to attend his coronation. All African leaders, with the exception of Sir S. Raugoolam of Mauritius, politely declined to appear at an occasion that most considered an embarrassment to Africa's emerging nations. Bokassa had erected his own counterpart to Notre Dame Cathedral, calling his version Notre Dame de Bangui Cathedral, in the middle of the bush. Although Pope Paul sent his regrets, an emissary was sent from Rome to say mass.

Bokassa had ridden to his coronation site in Bangui stadium in a green coach drawn by six white horses and emblazoned with gold emblems built to replicate that of Napoleon. On its roof were mounted five golden eagles. A French-tutored military band preceded Bokassa. In another coach rode Bokassa's two-year-old son, Crown Prince Jean Bedel, dressed in a formal military uniform. Behind in yet another coach rode Empress Catherine Bokassa, the number-one wife, a former airline hostess. Elsewhere were various other wives, including a buxom bleached blonde and ex-barmaid from Bucharest called La Roumaine, along with at least fifty-four known Bokassa children.

The coronation throne was in the shape of a giant golden eagle with twelve-foot wingspan and weighing two tons. The emperor's crimson train was thirty-feet long, trimmed with ermine and carried by an honor guard. Bokassa had lifted his own bejeweled crown, studded with two thousand diamonds, and placed it upon his own head, just as Napoleon Bonaparte had done. Then he had crowned his Empress Catherine with a diamond tiara. In the ensuing celebration the thirsty coronation party consumed 40,000 bottles of wine and 20,000 bottles of champagne imported from France. The whole shebang cost a cool $30 million. In Washington, the United States was not overly amused by the gross extravagance of the self-proclaimed emperor's coronation expenditure, and economic aid to the empire was promptly suspended.

The splendor of Bokassa's coronation was in stark contrast to daily life in the crumbling capital city of Bangui, whose near-starved populace loiter amid the rubble of trash, yellow pye dogs, foraging goats, pigs, scavenging ravens, open sewers, all crowded on smashed streets of broken tar and red dust. The shops in town were mostly Lebanese-owned. Among the denizens of the capital there was no pretense of upward mobility. That dream had dwindled since independence in 1960, even though the French government in Paris still helped with infusions of aid to keep the leaky ship of state somehow afloat, receiving in return a measure of the country's diamonds, peanuts, and iron ore.

The wide and sluggish Ubangi River coils its way through the city amid mud-and-thatch huts and cracked-block shacks with rusting corrugated iron roofs. In Bangui's dusty bazaars women enshrouded in black *bou-bous* crouched over stinking dried fish, cassava, and pyramids of withered tomatoes. Fly-blown smoked monkey, crocodile steak, and slabs of blackened snake were among proffered delicacies. Across the river lay Zaire, hidden by the beginnings of its vast, mysterious rain forests.

WHAT ATTRACTED Prince Alfi von Auersperg and his colleagues to the Central African Empire was its well-deserved reputation as wonderful game country. The nation is home to some of the best wildlife populations north of the equator. Safaris were divided into savannah hunting and forest hunting. The two regions, when both could be hunted during the course of a safari, offered a fine selection of game.

Alfi well knew Kenya, Uganda, and Tanzania were hard acts to follow in the safari world, but after the overnight closure of legal hunting in Kenya, he liked to say there was nowhere to go but up. Yet gaining entrée to operate in the Central African Empire required the personal blessings of the head of state himself, Emperor Bokassa. It had been that way in Idi Amin's Uganda. When this aspect became apparent, Alfi good-naturedly shrugged off the gibes of his colleagues. Somehow he would wangle an interview with the emperor.

In 1978 Alfi presented his proposition to Bokassa in Bangui. The emperor and the prince reached an agreement allowing Afriventures to operate safaris. No bribes were asked, and none were paid. And that may have been a strike against Alfi.

The two men were strange bedfellows—the popular, blond, aristocratic European prince and the self-proclaimed emperor, a Mbaka tribesman reputed to still indulge in his ancestors' practice of cannibalism, a despot who fed enemies and sundry prisoners convicted in his kangaroo courts to the swarms of ravenous crocodiles he maintained at his infamous Kolongo "palace."

Never one to be troubled by bizarre African personalities, Alfi was jubilant as he returned to Kenya with Bokassa's agreement. Alfi's colleagues pooled safari crews, vehicles, and aircraft for the enterprise. Not all Alfi's intimates were enamored of the plan, among them his mentor, Reggie Destro, who thought Alfi and the others mad to attempt the scheme. But Alfi's enthusiasm was infectious.

As with Zaire and Sudan, outfitting luxury safaris from Kenya was a mammoth logistical nightmare. Alfi's well-assembled vanguard rolled out of Kenya in a rumble of dust headed for the inland empire. Day after day the convoy of trucks and hunting cars plowed through, billowing dust and sand, crawling over boulders, crashing into potholes, stopping only at dusk to camp by the roadside. For twelve long days and nights the procession lumbered across northwestern Kenya, through Sudan, and on to Bangui.

Just as the heavily loaded safari carrying African staff and precious truckloads of equipment neared the capital, Emperor Bokassa's men seized the vehicles, taking as prisoner the Kenyan safari crews, along with the convoy's escort, a trainee hunter from Tanzania named Trappe.

When the news was relayed to Alfi in Nairobi, the prince, along with his young third wife, Bea (Beatrice), and Danish hunter Jens Hessel, immediately flew their single-engine aircraft to Bangui. There Alfi and Jens were taken by Bokassa's men to a hotel and placed under house arrest. For some reason Bea von Auersperg was allowed to move about Bangui freely. Alfi gave her a credit card and instructed her to slip away and get on the first UTA flight to Paris. Alfi knew President Giscard d'Estaing personally, and Bea was sent to seek his assistance and intervention. Giscard d'Estaing was a fellow hunter who had made his own safaris to the former French colony. He was well acquainted with Bokassa.

In Bangui, the safari crews were jailed. Through a friend Alfi learned that he and Jens were also about to be incarcerated at the infamous Ngaragba prison. Up until then no charges had been preferred against Alfi or the Kenya safari crews. Alfi had not been allowed to communicate with Bokassa.

Alfi was savvy enough to realize that real charges were unnecessary in order to wind up in the clink, or even as fodder in Bokassa's crocodile abattoir. Both Alfi and Jens knew that even if they could get airborne and get away, their aircraft did not have the range to make it even as far as Tambura, just across the Sudanese frontier, or to Yambio (neither of which normally had supplies of avgas), much less to Juba, 913 miles away as the crow flies, where avgas was then still available. If they were to make a run for it, they would not be able to land at the tinpot towns of Bangassou or Mobaye in the Central African Empire, either, because they would surely be expected, and where, in any case, fuel was only occasionally available.

While Bea was away in Europe, Alfi made serious attempts to get his men freed from Bangui jail, but his efforts went nowhere. Then one day at the Bangui hotel, and still under house arrest, Alfi met an old friend, a hunter who had previously worked in Mozambique. At great personal risk to himself this hunter volunteered the use of his savannah camp where he had a stock of avgas. The camp was conveniently between Bangui and the Sudan border.

Somehow Alfi and Jens escaped from the hotel without being shot, and made it to the airport. Hessel, who is one of the best bush pilots in Africa, quickly got their plane airborne. Almost immediately the hunters realized they were being pursued by the only military aircraft the Empire possessed, a vintage DC3 cargo plane. Hessel figured the pursuit plane would follow knowing they did not have the range to escape the country, and would run out of fuel before reaching Sudan.

Hessel flew along the Ubangi River until a cumulus cloud appeared. Jens climbed into the clouds and lost his pursuer. Alfi and Jens found their hunter friend's camp, where they landed and were royally entertained with dinner. In the predawn light next day they were on their way to Sudan. At Juba the hunters refueled once again, then headed for Nairobi.

In Kenya Alfi haggled with Bokassa's government for the release of the safari crews, and some weeks later he won their freedom. The Kenya Safari Workers Union wasted no time in castigating Alfi in the Nairobi press about the arrest of the safari crews. Afriventures was never able to reclaim any impounded vehicles or equipment, and the loss was total. But Alfi was not one to dwell on misfortune. He continued to base himself in Kenya and led safaris to Zambia, beginning with one for R. S. "Dickie" du Pont,* an old friend and experienced safari aficionado from Delaware.

---

*Richard S. du Pont was one of many safari clients who made generous contributions to various African governments and private organizations for anti-poaching operations. He presented an aircraft to Kenya, as did Mrs. F. M. Kellog. Other American benefactors included J. A. Mull, John M. Schaefer, and Chuck W. Ennis Jr.

49

ONWARD PASSAGES

The political and social changes that ensued in East Africa following the closure of legal big game hunting brought to a close a singular way of life for Nairobi's white hunters. With the end of the East African Professional Hunter's Association, the continent's largest professional hunting community was broken up, never again to be a powerful and cohesive force in the management of wildlife. The hunter colony, once so important to the region as proponents of a carefully regulated wildlife industry, was no longer wanted.

A number of former hunters could not, or would not, wrench their roots from the soil of Africa. Yet some packed up and moved farther south or elsewhere, where they continued to lead a hunting-based existence in countries where that was still possible. None ever claimed to find a place that matched the stunning game country of Kenya, Tanzania, or Uganda—but they found acceptable alternatives and bought a bit more time.

DAVE LUNAN, the handsome Kenya-born hunter who had been Gregory Peck's look-alike stand-in during the filming of *The Snows of Kilimanjaro*, joined the contingent of old-guard hunters who began new lives in Australia. The quiet-spoken Lunan had conducted safaris for some of the world's best-known celebrities since founding White Hunters (Africa) Ltd. Even before the hunting ban, Dave made his last safari in Kenya in 1974 with Dr. Herman Tarnower, the celebrated Scarsdale diet doctor who was subsequently murdered in the United States by a gunshot fired by his lover, Jean Harris.

What may have ultimately convinced Dave Lunan to depart the land of his birth was not the end of big game hunting, but an event that occurred in Nairobi on May 3, 1968.[1] After a hunting safari Dave and a lady friend were at his home on Lower Kabete Road when they were attacked by a gang. As Dave recounted:

> I heard the sound of footsteps in the passage leading from the kitchen, and thought it was my servant. I put my head around the door and was immediately struck by a stone. I saw a stranger and charged at him. While I was grappling with him the rest of the gang ran in from the kitchen and began cutting me down with *simis.** They pulled me into my bedroom and asked me for money and firearms.[2]

Lunan, who had been badly slashed by a sword across the face, arms, and back, also had a finger chopped off in the attack. Other fingers were slashed but not entirely severed. One robber held his arm while another slashed off his wristwatch. The house was looted and the telephone line cut. Dave was losing blood fast as the gang rolled up valuables in bedsheets and dragged them to Lunan's Mercedes Benz, in which they drove away. Lunan's servants had been unable to help him because the gangsters had first entered their quarters, stripped them of their clothes, beat and tied them up before robbing them and raping the cook's wife.

As he prepared to sail away from Kenya there remained one more unhappy episode. At Mombasa's Kilindini docks all of Dave's earthly possessions, including a lifetime of African memorabilia and a treasured collection of photographs, were stolen.

From Australia Dave Lunan wrote: "I left Kenya in 1975 when I was optimistic enough to believe that it couldn't get much worse! I think that period was the start of the worst poaching and decimation of forests."[3]

ROBERT RUARK'S hunter, Harry Selby, had moved from Kenya to Botswana and settled at Maun back in the early 1960s. Selby helped develop Botswana's safari industry and pioneered tourist attractions such as Khwai River Lodge, the Xugana Island Camp in the Okavango

---

*Pointed, double-edged stabbing swords, 20–25 inches long.

Delta, and Savuti Safari Camp in the Chobe game reserve. Selby's colleagues know that it was not simply Selby's hunting ability that set him apart. He is a man of character who has dominated the field for fifty years, and Botswana is now his home.

BUNNY ALLEN, Kenya's earringed English Gypsy who led safaris for stars such as Ava Gardner and other Hollywood beauties, is still a shameless ladies' man. He lives with his tolerant American wife, Jeri, in an Arab-style coral-block bungalow he built himself near Shella beach, on remote Lamu island. After retiring to Lamu in 1977, Bunny's gunbearer and confidant for more than a thousand hunts, Tabe Arap Tilmet, and his family followed him to Lamu. Tabe died there in 1983 and is buried near casuarina trees on a low hill nearby. Like Tabe, vigorous, ninety-three-year-old Bunny plans to bury his bones in Kenya, but not, of course, for a very long time.

THE OLD Polish lion, Laddy Wincza, and his wife, Ada, had already been forced to shut down safari businesses in Tanzania and Kenya, so their antennae were quick to catch a whiff of ill winds, this time from their Sudanese safari operation. Before anybody else, Wincza foresaw the collapse of hunting and Sudan's free fall back into bloodshed, anarchy, and a protracted civil war. Laddy and Ada decided to make a break with East Africa, no matter how painful. For the Winczas there would be no pitiful farewells. It was simply not their style. Together with their daughter, Eve, they sailed away to what was to be their final refuge, the Republic of South Africa.

The resilient old military officer, still of ramrod-straight bearing, his profile as firm and sharp as ever, stoically made a new start in yet another African country. In Johannesburg Laddy purchased the venerable Rowland Ward firm, famous for its wildlife art, books, and artifacts. His plan was that Ada and Eve would operate the store, and Laddy would get in some hunting, but he remained desperately homesick for Kenya. Then, in 1984, Ada cabled: "Laddy died 17th November." Later she wrote:

> It is uncanny but he predicted the day (exactly) of his death. After he passed away I discovered in the garden a cement piece with his name and the date 17-11. The garden boy was absolutely shaken

when I showed it to him. Laddy scribbled it six years ago! But it
was covered with ivy and I never had seen it. Now, due to the terrible drought the ivy dried out and I saw the inscription.[4]

PRINCE ALFI VON AUERSPERG continued to jet between Europe and
Africa, indulging his love of big game hunting wherever possible. His
former wife, now Sunny von Bulow, lapsed into a coma in 1981. The
reasons for Sunny's coma have been the subject of speculation ever
since. The mystery led to two trials of her husband, Claus von Bulow,
for attempted murder. At his second trial, in Rhode Island, von Bulow
was found not guilty. Sunny remains in an irreversible coma in New
York City.

Even after the hunting bans in Kenya and Tanzania, Alfi kept a
home at Karen, outside Nairobi, which he used as a base for safaris
elsewhere in Africa. In 1983 he left Nairobi and returned to Haus
Auersperg in Kitzbuhel, as he usually did during the spring monsoon
rains in East Africa. There a cruel twist of fate awaited him. Alfi's sister,
Hetti, wrote:

> On April 14th Alfi was on his way from Linz to Salzburg where he
> had been meeting with safari customers. He was with Alexander
> [his son] and there was heavy rain and the car aquaplaned [went
> into a skid]. Alexander remembers that the car turned over twice,
> Alfi never letting the steering wheel go. Alexander was propelled
> out of the side window into the meadow whilst Alfi crashed
> through the windshield on the asphalt autobahn. They took them
> to the nearby hospital—and had to cut a window in Alfi's head.
> Alexander only had a few stitches on the head. Next day they
> were transported to the Salzburger *klinikum* to Professor
> Diemath, where he remained.[5]

Alfi von Auersperg remained in a coma in Salzburg for nine years. On
June 19, 1992, he made his last safari into the Furtherest Shag. He was
fifty-six years old.

"They closed the town [Kitzbuhel]," Alfi's daughter, Ala, wrote,
"and we were able to bring him through with a beautiful horse-drawn
cortege, surrounded by family and friends. We have buried him between
the Horn and Hahnen-Kamm mountains and I cannot think of a more
beautiful place for him to rest."[6]

ALFI'S NEMESIS in the Central African Republic, self-proclaimed Emperor Jean Bedel Bokassa, was forced to flee his country following a French-backed army coup d'état in 1979 and spent years in exile. In 1986 Bokassa was allowed to return to his homeland. He was tried by the Bangui regime and found guilty of murder, cannibalism, infanticide, and the misappropriation of $170 million of public funds, but his death sentence was commuted to life in prison. In September 1993, during a general amnesty, he was released at the age of seventy-three. The former emperor, who had once declared himself a Muslim convert in an effort to woo aid from Libya's Muammar Qaddafi, just as Idi Amin had, became a Christian again and claimed to be the Thirteenth Apostle of Christ. Bokassa died of a heart attack in Bangui on November 3, 1996.

◇

FOR MANY of the old-guard hunters leaving Africa was easier said than done. The former Somali Gendarmerie officer, Douglas Tatham Collins, known variously as Shagbag or Abdi Malek, had been one of those who left Africa "for good" long before the hunting ban. Dougie had been emotionally and physically battered following the tragic accident in which his brother was killed by a stray gunshot as Dougie was gored by a buffalo. Collins had left for England, but once there he yearned for the Furtherest Shag in which he had spent most of his life. He returned to Kenya to resume his hunting as a professional through the 1970s.

By the mid-1980s Douglas Collins's old comrade, former white hunter turned conservationist George Adamson, the subject of the film *Born Free* and a subsequent series of books and movies, was living at a remote place called Kora, in the northern deserts of Kenya. Considered the savior of lions by much of the world, Adamson was sometimes a figure of controversy in Kenya, where his semi-tame lions had attacked and mauled a number of Africans as well as Mark Jenkins, the son of George's friend, game warden Peter Jenkins.

To keep his lions it was necessary for George to relocate to an area devoid of significant human settlement. Adamson had obtained permission from the Kenya government to establish a camp in the thornbush country near the Tana River, in what had been Hunting Block 11A. By coincidence, George's settlement was sited beneath a cluster of rock kopjes not far from the place on the Tana where Dougie's tragedy

Prince Bernhard of the Netherlands and George Adamson test elephant-jaw plumbing at Kampi ya Simba.

had occurred. Soon afterward one of George's lions, Boy, who had previously mauled Mark Jenkins, attacked George's assistant, an African named Stanley, who knew Boy well and was able to handle lions. George heard Stanley's strangled cries from the camp and rushed into the brush to find Stanley firmly held in Boy's jaws. As soon as he saw George, Boy dropped Stanley and calmly walked off for about twenty yards. George shot Boy through the heart. Stanley died of his wounds within ten minutes. Some time later George was hospitalized when another of his lions mauled him. After that, George Adamson, who was living with his brother, Terence, asked his old friend Dougie Collins to come and give him a hand with his lion rehabilitation project, and Dougie gladly accepted.

Fame, if not fortune, had followed the lion guru George Adamson to Kora, and it was not long before a steady stream of celebrities and devoted fans were making the dusty pilgrimage to Kampi ya Simba. Most visitors brought offerings for their genial hosts, the most welcome gifts being fruit, vegetables, and *wompo* (whiskey) for evening libations.

Collins and Adamson, the two old white hunters with flowing, shoulder-length silver hair, always cut a memorable swath as they held court in their desert domain. Both were tanned, grizzled, and shirtless. And both reveled in their life in the bush. Dougie was usually clad in his coastal kikoi or lungi (colorful woven cotton cloth worn around the waist by men on the East African coast) and Somali sandals; George in his frayed khaki shorts, puffing contentedly on a pipe.

Across the Tana River north of Kampi ya Simba the harsh desert thorn lands are inhabited by nomads who are predominantly Somalis, as well as the ever-present hair-triggered *shifta* (bandits). Both Collins and Adamson were well accustomed to the perils of the hostile territory of the Northern Frontier and accepted it as the price they paid for living among lions in the Furtherest Shag.

In 1989 Douglas Collins left Kampi ya Simba to go to a hospital in England for more treatment of his old buffalo wounds, which still troubled him greatly. On his way back from England to Kampi ya Simba, tragedy once again derailed Dougie's life. As soon as he disembarked from his flight at Nairobi, Collins heard the news that was already being relayed around the globe: George Adamson had been murdered at Kora. A letter from Collins told it all:

> By now you will have heard of the brutal killing of old George Adamson just outside this camp by *shifta* thugs armed with automatic rifles as he rushed in his clapped-out old Land Rover— armed with a .38 pistol only—to the aid of one of his staff who had gone to the airstrip to collect guests for lunch. Two of the staff were killed with him. As you know his whole life was devoted to lions and he died like one, heroically and with much courage.
>
> We buried him here last Saturday next to his brother, Terence, with about fifty Europeans and about the same number of Africans attending the funeral. A volley was fired over his grave and a bugler from the Kenya Rifles beautifully blew the Last Post and Reveille at which I shed yet another tear. Most poignant. When I was here last I built up a cairn of attractive quartz stones over Terence's grave and presently I am doing the same for George with a desert rose planted at the head.

At first, before reality set in, George Adamson's friends and followers were determined to carry on his lion rehabilitation camp at Kora, despite being surrounded by Somali *shifta*. Douglas Collins, the old desert warrior, did not hesitate to take up the mantle:

> Although on my return to Kenya I still had not quite recovered from my operation at the King Edward VII Hospital for Officers I was asked if I would take over. I am sure there would be no other volunteers!
>
> Have a guard of 6 Police and a Sergeant in camp. They are shagged with fear. The staff are shagged with fear and so am I— until I receive the personal arms I have asked the Director for. Presently I am digging weapon pits inside the camp perimeter being watched by curious and wondering eyes by our three half-grown lion cubs who share the camp with us. I said I would stay for six months but unless Leakey does his stuff on arming me— all I have at the moment is a Somali sword and a catapult with ball bearings as my ammo! I shall beat a retreat to Muthaiga Club.
>
> In memory and deference to George I have made but one change here. As you know he was another St. Francis of Assisi. All were fed at this camp. Lions both wild and tame. Jackals. Dik-Dik. Guinea fowl. Doves. Go-Away birds and the like, including a troop of Vervet monkeys who would hang from the *makuti* roof peeing in the soup and doing the odd boo-boo on the corn beef sandwiches. Yesterday I got one up the bum with a ball bearing and they now look at me from the outside with mournful and beseeching eyes of brutality. I remain unmoved.
>
> I am no St. Francis. I am a Shagbag. There is, of course, a real danger here, for a few days ago a gang shot up a bus travelling from Mwingi to Garissa with a Land Rover and armed police escort. They were all killed and their automatics stolen. Some 12 people on the bus were also killed and many wounded. Disturbing news indeed.
>
> I am hoping the authorities will have made contact with the gang and wiped them out. I wonder? For if they are Somalis, and I think they are, they can cover fifty miles a day on foot and leave all behind them floundering in their wake. I remember so well from Ogaden days.[7]

Despite Dougie's brave optimism, it was soon clear the situation at Kora was untenable. The camp was closed, and the surviving members

Abakunya Gumunde.

of George's family of lions were split up. Nevertheless, Collins remains indefatigable, convinced his home will always be Kenya. He now lives on a remote Indian Ocean beach north of Mombasa, but occasionally makes safaris "up-country" to Muthaiga Club to share a *wompo* or two with old chums. Already acclaimed as the author of *A Tear for Somalia* and *Another Tear for Africa*, Dougie's *Tales from Africa* has recently been published.

ABAKUNYA Gumunde, the athletic Giriama tribesman who served as Tony Archer's gunbearer and tracker, was, like many of his colleagues, a reformed poacher. Abakunya's poaching days ended when he was arrested at Tsavo national park by former hunter turned conservationist Bill Woodley. Woodley sent Abakunya to jail for ivory poaching, and while there, the tracker had a change of heart.

On his release from prison Tony Archer hired him, and Abakunya became an ex-officio member of the Archer family and Tony's closest friend. After the ban on legal hunting in 1977, Abakunya retired to his village at Kasikini. And it was at Kasikini on June 7, 1989, that a gang of Somali *shifta* raided Abakunya's village. Unarmed Abakunya was shot down in cold blood.

BILL WOODLEY knew the Aberdare Mountains as no other man did. He had patrolled the rugged mountains on foot, and he had piloted his aircraft over the bamboo jungles, steep gorges, and windswept moors countless times. After the bitter days of fighting during the Mau Mau uprising, Woodley had returned to his beloved mountains and recruited former enemies from the Mau Mau as wardens and game scouts, all of whom became valued friends.

On a lonely ridge overlooking a valley where elephants caked with red mud can still be seen drinking from icy trout rivers in the Aberdare salient, there is a simple stone marker about three feet tall. Set in the marker is a modest copper plate that has been defaced by vandals. It is just possible to read, in part:

IN MEMORY OF
BILL WOODLEY **1929–1995**
Who served the National Parks of Kenya with dedication for 44 years.
1948–1959 1978–1992 Tsavo National Park
1959–1978 Mountain Parks
This is one place Bill left for us all
"ALPHA CHARLIE ECHO, OVER AND OUT"

TERRY MATHEWS had made the transition to photographic safaris after losing an eye in a shooting accident. He also became a renowned wildlife sculptor. In an effort to raise money for rhino rescue operations, Mathews donated a life-sized concrete sculpture of a rhino with its calf; it is displayed at the entrance to Nairobi national park.

On Saint Valentine's Day 1987 Terry and the American photographer Peter Beard, accompanied by an armed African game ranger and a couple of American Broadcasting Corporation cameramen, entered the park to make a film publicizing the plight of rhinos facing extinction. As Terry was filmed with a wild rhino cow and her calf in the background, a couple of tourist minibuses turned up. Visitors to Nairobi park are forbidden to leave their cars, but upon seeing Mathews and his party (who were exempted from the rule on this occasion) on foot, the tourists piled out of their vehicles to get photos. This rowdy intrusion upset the rhino.

The armed park ranger assigned to stand guard during the filming was distracted by the tourists and went to order them back to their vehicles. At that moment the rhino charged the Mathews party. Terry was unarmed, but he grabbed a stone and threw it at the rhino, hoping to turn it, but the rhino came on with its horns lowered. Mathews stood his ground, bellowing at the rhino, giving others in the party a chance to escape. Terry hoped the rhino would swerve or abort the charge. But on it came at full speed. The rhino's horn swept low, scooping upward, goring Terry, puncturing his thigh, ripping into him. Terry weighed a muscular 220 pounds, but he was tossed skyward over ten feet. He came down on the stony ground with a bang that broke his leg. The rhino wheeled and made off with her calf.

Although the park is adjacent to the modern capital city of Nairobi, the place where Terry's accident occurred is in a less accessible southwestern section of the park's forty-four square miles. It was ninety minutes before an ambulance reached Mathews. He had suffered massive wounds. In March 1987 there was hope for Terry's recovery, and his wife Jeanne wrote:

> The rhino's horn somehow missed his arteries, spleen, kidney, heart and lungs. But it tore part of the lining of his colon and penetrated his thigh. He was wearing a heavy belt which he reckoned saved him being completely torn open. The horn still entered 16" through his abdominal and pelvic cavity, breaking two ribs with the tip of its horn.[8]

At Nairobi hospital Terry's long agony was just beginning. By 1996 Terry had made fifty trips to England from Kenya for medical attention. Terry and Jeanne live near Nairobi where he produces his wildlife sculptures.

ONE FORMER hunter who thrives in modern Africa is Alfredo Pelizzoli. In the old hunting days Alfredo explored the most isolated beaches in Kenya. One day as he rested on a white coral beach called Kiwayu,

Alfredo was astonished to see a bull elephant emerge from the forest and calmly walk along the Indian Ocean shore before browsing at the forest's edge. Convinced he had found his new utopia, Pelizzoli decided to build an exclusive dream camp at this place. To do this he had to overcome enormous logistical obstacles, including ferrying building materials by dhow from Mombasa. At Kiwayu camp the menu consists of simple luxuries such as lobster, crab, and shrimp caught fresh each day, along with gourmet Italian pasta dishes. Visitors include celebrities who wish to escape the public eye and share Alfredo and Lisa Pelizzoli's paradise on earth.

KENYA, Tanzania, and Uganda are each finding their path into the next century. Kenya is still the safari capital of East Africa, at least so far as photographic safaris are concerned, but Nairobi is no longer a Wild West town. Today in the capital multistoried glass-and-concrete office buildings and hotels tower over the city center. The once game-filled plains surrounding the metropolis are no longer occupied by countless herds of game. Instead they are home to several million people. The country remains a major tourist destination, and the international hub for all commerce in the region. But there are danger signs. The human population has exploded. Almost all northern Kenya areas, where herds of elephant once roamed, are sometimes unsafe because of Somali bandits. On the brighter side, corrupt game officials have been replaced, elephant and rhino populations are again on the increase, and there is hope for their continued recovery.

NOW, IT is late in the 1990s. On a broad plain as the sun cools and evening brings slanted light to the short-grass plain, it turns from yellow to Serengeti gold. At the edge of the plain broken granite kopjes edge the skyline. There are dark groves of trees near the kopjes, and among the trees a herd of sable antelope feeds quietly. The sables' scimitar horns glint with the fire of diamonds when the light catches them. Sliding the binoculars around the edges of a low ridge it is possible to pick out a nice herd of greater kudu browsing amid scrub thickets. The kudu cows and young are led by a massive horned male with at least two and a half full twists, and tipped with "ivory"—a prime candidate for the top line in Rowland Ward's *Records of Big Game*.

On the open plain a herd of Thomson's gazelle grazes, and with them a troop of Burchell's zebra. If you look east there is a column of Grevy's zebra approaching. The stone verandah on which we sit is the home of Bryan and Joan Coleman. Bryan, the Prince of Pranksters, still likes a practical joke or two. But this evening he is more introspective than usual. The iced beer we sip is not Tusker. It is Budweiser. The prolific herds of wild, free-roaming game we view are African, but we are not in Africa. We are in the beautiful hill country of Texas, and the Prince of Pranksters is lord of all we survey. He manages this 12,000-acre property and all its denizens, both human and animal. Coleman is the bwana here. He has easily made the transition to Texas from the good old safari days. "Look at the size of that Grevy," he exclaims. "She's about to foal down!"

There is no hunting at present on Coleman's exotic "game ranch," as it is called in the United States. But there are numerous exotic ranches with wild Asian and African game where it is possible to hunt. Many ranchers on these big properties long ago gave up cattle in favor of African and Asian game. Good hunting and good conservation go hand in hand in Texas. Raising wild game that runs free is more profitable than raising cattle, I am told. It is somehow reassuring to know there is such a thriving population of African and other big game in the Western Hemisphere.

And what of the golden days in Kenya, Tanzania, and Uganda? To the old-guard white hunters, an empty plain or vacant desert scrub without herds of game is anathema. Times have simply changed too much, and there is no going back to what used to be. Most premium game areas outside national parks and game reserves have vanished forever under cultivation or settlement, or massive habitat destruction. Those unfortunate animals with the potential for a high cash return with little risk continue to be the target for well-armed poachers.

Paradise lost? Perhaps. But the passing of the golden age of safaris in Kenya, Tanzania, and Uganda in no way dims the memory or the magic of those days. For those who witnessed life in East Africa during those times, for those who saw it all—nothing will ever compare. For the white hunters, and for those who journeyed with them on safari, East Africa was Paradise Found.

No one will deny that the countdown for East Africa's free-ranging wildlife had begun back in the 1970s. Poaching, political turbulence, habitat destruction, and climate all played a part. The decade began with a catastrophic drought in Kenya, during 1970–1971, in which warden David Sheldrick estimated that Tsavo national park alone lost as many as 10,000 elephant. At the same time Uganda's thriving elephant herd of around 40,000 was reduced by half following Idi Amin's bloody 1971 coup d'état as camo-jacketed thugs went on a rampage, machine-gunning entire herds of elephant.*

The year 1973 brought rapid inflation to prices paid for elephant ivory and rhino horn, which marked a drastic turning point for the fate of those two species. Prior to that time tusks had sold for "a pound a pound"—one pound of ivory fetched a Kenya pound, then worth about $2.80. Within a few short months the price jumped to more than $50 per pound and presidents, politicians, and peasants all scrambled to grab their share of black market lucre as jetloads of illicit tusks departed East Africa for Far Eastern carving factories. Over the same period rhino horn soared from $24 per pound to $400 and more. The main markets were North Asia, where rhino horn was highly prized as both an aphrodisiac and a panacea for an assortment of ailments, and North Yemen, where it was used in the manufacture of dagger handles.

Traditionally the safari hunter never accounted for more than a fraction of the rhino and elephant taken in East Africa. Those clients who hunted rhino and elephant valued their trophies, and these were not for sale. Safari clients traditionally spent a good deal of time and money in

---

*Ian Parker estimated Uganda lost half its elephant population in less than two years.

search of a particular trophy, and more than a few left empty-handed only to return year after year in a sometimes mythical quest for just one outstanding specimen. For many of these individuals safari life and the physical aspects of a hunt were infinitely more rewarding than actually securing a trophy. For most professionals worth their salt, a rhino's front horn had to be at least sixteen inches to be considered a trophy candidate, and many never permitted a horn of less than eighteen or twenty inches to be taken. Even in the heyday of safari hunting in the early 1970s, when Kenya's rhino population was estimated at 20,000, rhino licenses were far more often purchased than used. In 1972, for example, although thirty-four clients purchased rhino licenses, only nineteen animals were actually shot, and most of these animals had been reported to the Game Department as aggressive to humans or destructive to farmer's crops. Yet official records show that in 1972 Hong Kong alone imported a thousand rhino horns from Kenya. Within a few months poaching quickly accelerated and got out of hand as the price of horn skyrocketed, and rhino were decimated by poachers in every habitat, including national parks.

Over the same period damage inflicted upon the elephant population by ivory poachers was just as alarming. The Kenya Game Department was accused of numerous abuses in regard to elephant permits. Chief beneficiaries of the department's largesse were sundry officials and the *WaBenzi* (crooked big men), so named because they could afford Mercedes Benz cars and were up to their ears in the ivory-poaching racket. Some Game Department officials and *WaBenzi* poachers had been observed, identified, and reported operating boldly and with impunity at Masai Mara game reserve, Tsavo national park, South Horr Valley (an elephant sanctuary), Meru game reserve, Mount Kulal, and Ukambani, among other places.

A Kenya Game Department researcher named Peter Jarman organized a Nairobi seminar in 1973 of scientists, conservationists, hunters, ranchers, researchers, and elephant experts. The gathering was historically important because it was the first time anybody had risked speaking out publicly on such a touchy subject. At the time of Jarman's meeting the elephant population of Kenya was still relatively healthy, but all knew the poaching situation was escalating by the hour and was cause for considerable alarm.

At the time, Tsavo national park and its environs had a *known* elephant population of at least 35,000. Prior to the seminar John K.

Mutinda, Kenya's chief game warden, had estimated that there were 50,000 elephant in the country, although at the seminar this figure was disputed by accredited experts, who estimated Kenya's elephant population at roughly 167,000, of which 49,000 elephants had some form of protected status in national parks or game reserves.[1]

Ian Parker, who heads Wildlife Services, a private wildlife consultancy, shocked the seminar by saying ivory worth $160 million would leave Africa in 1973—the equivalent of up to 200,000 massacred elephants.[2] In pit bull fashion Parker bravely went for the jugular, exposing ivory rackets with irrefutable data. Ian connected the high number of elephant permits issued with the newly increased value of ivory. Afterward reprisal was swift for the man who had dared organize the seminar. The fearless expatriate Peter Jarman was sacked by the government two weeks later.

As predicted, during the first five months of 1973 the toll on elephant was significant. No less than 149 tons of ivory were officially exported from Kenya, with the unaccounted for portion being a staggering 88 tons.* The Wildlife Clubs of Kenya claimed this tonnage represented from 10,000 to 25,000 elephants killed illegally.[3] A single cargo composed of eight hundred elephant tusks was intercepted at Nairobi's Embakasi Airport, followed shortly thereafter by the priceless cargo's mysterious disappearance.

IN THE FACE of increasing international outrage at such statistics, it was perhaps inevitable that the most convenient scapegoats were the white hunters. Though few in number, they were well known and highly visible. In the last week of October 1973 the Kenya government implemented a ban on elephant hunting, ivory trading, and dealings in elephant products. Privately, chief game warden John Mutinda assured the East African Professional Hunter's Association that the ban on legitimate ivory hunting would only be temporary, and that it was the intention of his department to lift the ban as quickly as possible. It was not lost on either side that the only group of human beings with the means and incentive to protect and sustain the region's wildlife, apart

---

*Thirty-one tons came from government control hunting, and a small portion was "found" ivory, removed from elephants that had died of natural causes, or through drought, as well as ivory passing through Kenya from other countries.

from a few overworked and underfinanced game wardens as well as the likes of Douglas-Hamilton, had been effectively removed from the action.

The results of the ban were immediate. Organized poaching gangs, now no longer hindered by the surveillance of professional safaris, were striking with confidence and audacity. As the deadly toll escalated, it was obvious to hunters and wildlife personnel in the field that the effects of the ban were far worse than had been predicted. In the famous elephant country of Kenya's Northern Frontier deserts and in other isolated regions, the elephant's fate was swift and certain. AK-47 assault rifles and other modern weaponry soon supplanted the more traditional snares, poisoned arrows, traps, and spears. Poachers traveling in four-wheel-drive vehicles were equipped with chain saws to cut through the heads of elephant to more efficiently remove ivory.

In 1977 the sudden closing of all hunting in Kenya brought more of the same. In the first six months following Kenya's ban on all legal hunting, poachers slaughtered 1,040 elephant, 235 rhino, and 20 leopard, according to one news report. People living in the Kenya bush knew that the actual numbers of animals slain in remote areas and never discovered were vastly greater.

TWENTY YEARS ago, in 1979, there were an estimated 1.3 million elephants living in Africa, and now there are only an estimated 500,000 or fewer left. Tanzania had a thriving elephant population as recently as 1976. Ian Parker and Dr. Iain Douglas-Hamilton counted 110,000 elephant in the Selous game reserve, 44,000 at Ruaha, 3,000 in the Serengeti, 3,000 at Tarangire, and 500 at Manyara. Parker estimated Tanzania held a total of 350,000 elephants.[4] By 1989 poaching had reduced those numbers by more than 80 percent, and the decline continued in free fall.

According to Clive Spinage's authoritative book, *Elephants*, between 1979 and 1989, 691,000 elephants died in Africa, from which 8,000 tonnes (8,818 tons) of ivory were recovered to fuel the insatiable demand in the Far East.[5] Roughly half of Africa's elephants were poached in the ten-year period between 1979 and 1989.

In 1989 the United Nations Convention on International Trade in Endangered Species, known by the acronym CITES, acted to end a decade of massacres of Africa's disappearing elephant herds. The convention's 136 member states enacted an international ivory-trading ban by which it sought to protect the future of the African elephant. Once in force in 1990 the CITES ivory-trading ban went a very long way toward arresting the elephant's drastic decline.

In June 1998 CITES voted to partially reverse the ivory-trading ban, and Zimbabwe, Botswana, and Namibia will now be allowed to sell 60 tons of stockpiled ivory to Japan. The stockpile was accumulated from poachers, from elephants shot as so-called rogues, and from others that died of natural causes.* All three countries have large elephant populations. Zimbabwe has about 52,000 elephants, reckoned by pro-elephant traders to be double the optimum number that can be carried on available land. Botswana's burgeoning elephant population is upward of 68,000, and even dry Namibia has 7,000 elephants.

Proponents who favor lifting the ivory-trading ban say they will use proceeds from the sale of ivory to fund conservation and development projects. They have long argued that since the African elephant is not endangered, ivory should not be regarded as the product of an endangered species. In poor African countries it is impossible to gain sympathy from hard-pressed small farmers for protection of elephants, or for that matter any other animal. Adult elephants that daily consume 300 to 600 pounds of food can rapidly wipe out pitiful fields of hard-won corn, cotton, cassava, or other crops, destroying a family's, or entire village's, sole sustenance and income overnight. To ask these victims to grant protection to elephants while their own survival is in dire jeopardy simply is futile. Even in Kenya, where the elephant population has been devastated by poaching, there are still enough of them around to account for an estimated 80 percent of the reported crop damage suffered by subsistence farmers.

Critics, however, point out that a CITES panel of experts sent to Zimbabwe, Botswana, and Namibia to assess those nations' ability to control the ivory trade found that none had adequate enforcement capabilities and none would be able to determine the origins of ivory in their stockpiles.[6]

Those who oppose the CITES decision to relax the ivory-trading ban are alarmed for the future of the elephant. Some Kenya conservationists, notably Richard Leakey, director of the government's Kenya

---

*This controversial resolution would permit Zimbabwe, Botswana, and Namibia to resume ivory trading with Japan in March 1999, provided certain CITES conditions are met.

Wildlife Service, who played a part in having the CITES ban on ivory trading implemented in 1989, insist that elephant herds have not recovered from poaching over the last quarter century.[7] If ivory trading is legalized there is little doubt it will provide incentive for poaching all over Africa. It has been shown that once the 1989 CITES ban was implemented the bottom fell out of the ivory market. There is no doubt the ban has been effective, causing ivory prices to plunge, along with the demand for tusks.

Those conservationists and old-guard hunters who strongly oppose legalizing ivory trading say that creating a market for ivory would spur anew another African elephant holocaust like the one that raged through the 1970s and 1980s. They believe illicit ivory can easily be funneled into those countries allowed to trade in ivory, and it will be impossible to keep tally of what is and is not legitimate. They point out that elephants migrate across vast borders between different countries, and those borders are in any case porous for ivory smugglers. They ask why anybody would want to dismantle such an effective anti-poaching policy as the ivory-trading ban.

GAME MANAGEMENT is a topic much discussed and debated by old-guard hunters and conservationists alike. Tony Archer, an active and respected Kenya hunter for over forty years, mirrors the opinions of most of his colleagues who decry the resumption of ivory trading, but not necessarily of limited culling, if it is absolutely necessary and as a last resort. Archer proposes that in those countries that have reached maximum elephant carrying capacity, industrialized nations should step in, join together, and form a rescue squad to subsidize and buy culled ivory, then stockpile it at an equivalent of Fort Knox. Archer and most of his colleagues believe that safari hunting in those few countries overstocked with elephant is a legitimate, although limited solution to the problem, and should continue.

On the other hand, while most hunters decry the resumption of ivory trading, almost to a man they believe legal hunting of range animals, and in some cases elephants and predators as well, should be allowed on private land. Unless individual landholders preserving game are permitted to harvest it, range animals are doomed, since there will be no incentive to protect them. In Kenya some ranchers have carefully preserved and protected resident herds, for which they have received no compensation since 1977. In many cases their herds of range animals are at or way above carrying capacity. It is only reasonable that they want to reduce their stock and see a return on their preservation efforts.

LESS THAN fifty years ago Kenya's human population was 5.2 million. Today it is close to 30 million. Only about one-fifth of the country receives sufficient rainfall to raise cash crops, and in many areas the burgeoning human population has moved to marginal lands formerly inhabited by wildlife. Encroachment has disrupted and, in some cases, severed traditional wildlife migration routes. It has also created competition for grazing and watering points.

Since 1977 at least 400,000 wild animals in Kenya have vanished and continue to disappear at a rate of 2 to 3 percent per annum, according to government surveys. Most game live outside national parks, where policing is difficult at best and villagers often take matters into their own hands. To survive on marginal lands local people have taken up hunting for meat. Hard-pressed villagers seek out common plains animals like Grant's gazelle, hartebeest, waterbuck, oryx, gerenuk, and small forest animals such as bushbuck and duiker. It is believed that for these species the decline has been more than 50 percent.

In Africa land must be productive for people. It is argued that wildlife which has a price on its head by way of a license or utilization fee will receive protection from the rural population, who benefit economically from those animals when they are hunted legitimately. More particularly, high-priced wildlife such as elephant will be protected. It is further argued that if wildlife is properly utilized with well-administered hunting and culling programs, Africans will benefit and be encouraged to regard wildlife as an important resource that will improve their livelihoods. The notion that preserving wildlife in Africa can only be achieved provided that game pays for itself is not new. John Blower, Uganda's chief game warden, proposed and successfully implemented these and other conservation ideas back in 1961.

The government's Kenya Wildlife Service, a separate entity from the private consultancy, Wildlife Services, is exploring ways to make wildlife profitable for locals and give them incentives to protect game. Small farmers are frequent victims of crop-raiding animals, and few receive compensation for their losses. People living in isolated regions must also be given incentives to protect wildlife. It should be remembered that in many areas where the land is so poor that it will not sustain domestic stock, wild game thrives.

Yet the simple incontrovertible fact is that in countries with a per capita income of a few hundred dollars a year, there is little hope for a species such as rhinoceros when the current price fetched by its horn is more than $30,000 per pound. The few living descendants of those magnificent beasts that roamed East Africa for thousands of years now commonly graze in fenced enclosures, watched over by the wary eyes of armed sentries.

On a more positive note, in August 1998 Tony Archer reported that Kenya's rhino population has increased slightly and is now between 450 and 500 animals, although five were recently poached on two Laikipia ranches. With the ivory-trading ban still in force, Archer believes Kenya's elephant population has rebounded also, and may currently number around 25,000.

These relatively small successes in what has been a momentous slide toward oblivion for wildlife demonstrate that cautious recovery is not only possible, but it can definitely be achieved. With international assistance, restraint on incursions into wildlife habitats, incentives for landholders, and an effective anti-poaching policy, there is still an opportunity to arrest drastic wildlife declines and preserve Africa's unique heritage.

SOURCE NOTES

1. The First White Hunters

1. Marcus Daly, *Big Game Hunting and Adventure 1897–1936* (London: Macmillan, 1937), p. 161.

2. Peregrine Herne, *Perils and Pleasures of a Hunter's Life* (Philadelphia: Keystone Publishing, 1854), p. 77.

3. Interview with Donald Ker, *African Life* (Nairobi), August 1957.

4. Emily Host, *East African Annual 1951–1952* (Nairobi), p. 73.

5. Carl Akeley, *In Brightest Africa* (New York: Garden City Publishing, 1927), p. 154.

6. Theodore Roosevelt, *African Game Trails* (New York: Charles Scribner's Sons, 1910), p. 179.

7. Ross W. McGregor, *Kenya from Within* (London: George Allen & Unwin, 1927), p. 97.

8. Elspeth Huxley, *Out in the Midday Sun: My Kenya* (London: Chatto & Windus, 1985), pp. 22–26.

9. Noel Simon, *Between the Sunlight and the Thunder* (Boston: Houghton Mifflin, 1963), p. 64.

10. A. Blayney Percival, *A Game Ranger's Note Book* (London, 1924), p. 56.

11. Ibid., p. 63.

12. W. S. Rainsford, *The Land of the Lion* (New York: Doubleday, 1909), pp. 176–77.

13. Ibid., pp. 183–84.

14. Ibid., p. 216.

2. Nairobi, Wild West Town

1. R. O. Preston, *The Kenya Graphic* (Nairobi: Colonial Printing Co., n.d.).

2. Elspeth Huxley, *White Man's Country* (London: Macmillan, 1935), vol. 1, p. 63.

3. Sir Charles Eliot, *The East African Protectorate* (London: Frank Cass, 1905), p. 73.

4. Huxley, *White Man's Country*, vol. 1, p. 87.

5. W. Robert Foran, *A Cuckoo in Kenya* (London: Hutchison, 1936), p. 154.

6. Huxley, *White Man's Country*, vol. 1, pp. 251–52.

7. Jan Hemsing, *Then and Now, Nairobi's Norfolk Hotel* (Nairobi: Sealpoint Publicity, 1975), p. 45.

8. Tom Murray Smith, "Old Timers," *African Life*, June 1959.

9. S. E. White, *The Rediscovered Country* (New York: Doubleday, Page, 1915), p. 41.

10. J. A. Hunter and Dan Mannix, *African Bush Adventures* (London: Hamish Hamilton, 1954), p. 179.

11. Huxley, *White Man's Country*, vol. 1, pp. 225–56.

12. Hemsing, *Then and Now, Nairobi's Norfolk Hotel*, p. 28.

13. Foran, *A Cuckoo in Kenya*, p. 58.

14. David Edward Herne, pers. comm., Diani Beach, Kenya, August 1979.

15. Murray Smith, "Old Timers."

16. Ibid.

17. Ibid.

3. Hunter on the Lunatic Express

1. Mary Gillett, *Tribute to Pioneers* (Nairobi, n.p., n.d.).

2. J. A. Hunter, *Hunter* (London: Hamish Hamilton, 1952), p. 25.

3. W. Robert Foran, *Kill or Be Killed* (London: Hutchison, 1933), p. 64.

4. Flash Jack and the King

1. Winston Churchill, *My African Journey* (London: Hodder Stoughton, 1908), p. 189.

2. *British East Africa Directory*, 1908–1909.

3. Hunter and Mannix, *African Bush Adventures*, p. 111.

4. John Boyes, *Company of Adventurers* (London, 1929), pp. 275–77.

5. Huxley, *Out in the Midday Sun*, p. 43.

6. Sir Geoffrey Archer, *Personal and Historical Memoirs of an East African Administrator* (Edinburgh and London: Oliver & Boyd, 1963), p. 38.

5. Yankees on Safari

1. B. H. Jessen, *W. N. McMillan's African Expeditions and Big Game Hunting in Sudan, Abyssinia, and British East Africa* (London: Edwin Arnold, 1906), p. 44.

2. Edgar Beecher Bronson, *In Closed Territory* (London: A. C. McClurg, 1910), p. 2.

3. Ibid., p. 6.

4. Ibid., p. 8.

5. Ibid., p. 63.

6. Kenyon Painter, unpublished diaries and *The London Evening Standard*, February 25, 1913.

7. Painter, unpublished diaries.

8. Maud Painter, unpublished diaries, 1911–1913.

6. THE HUNTER'S HUNTER

1. J. G. Millais, *Far Away Up the Nile* (London: Longman's Green, 1924), pp. 215–16.

2. Rainsford, *The Land of the Lion*, p. 76.

3. Ibid., p. 78.

4. Ibid., p. 79.

5. Bill Judd, unpublished diaries, 1911.

6. Rainsford, *The Land of the Lion*, p. 80.

7. William D. Boyce, *Illustrated Africa, North, Tropical, South* (Chicago and New York: Rand McNally, 1925), p. 447.

8. Ibid.

9. Ibid., p. 455.

10. David Edward Herne, pers. comm., Ngorongoro, Tanganyika, December 1957.

11. Jack Judd, pers. comm., Nairobi, Kenya, July 18, 1956.

7. FUNGA SAFARI!

1. Akeley, *In Brightest Africa*, p. 152.

2. Ibid., p. 52.

3. Ibid., p. 150.

4. Herbert "Pop" Binks, pers. comm., Nairobi, Kenya, June 10, 1959.

5. Roosevelt, *African Game Trails*, p. 272.

6. Ibid., pp. 140–41.

7. W. Robert Foran, *The Elephant Hunters of the Lado* (Clinton, N.J.: Amwell Press, 1981), p. 223.

8. Roosevelt, *African Game Trails*, p. 457.

9. Ibid., p. 485.

10. Ibid., p. 586.

11. bid., p. 571.

12. Akeley, *In Brightest Africa*, p. 77.

8. THE ELEMENT OF STYLE

1. Roosevelt, *African Game Trails*, vol. 1, p. 47.
2. Emily Host, interview with Philip Percival, *Comment*, April 22, 1950.
3. Roosevelt, *African Game Trails*, pp. 26–27.
4. Ibid.
5. Murray Smith, "Old Timers."
6. Ibid.
7. George Eastman, *Chronicles of an African Trip* (Privately printed, 1927), p. 32.
8. Ibid.
9. *East African Standard*, May 4, 1926.
10. Kathleen Seth-Smith, unpublished diaries, 1926.
11. Anthony Cullen, *Syd Downey's Africa* (London: Cassell, 1959), p. 7.
12. Murray Smith, "Old Timers."
13. Host, interview with Philip Percival.

9. A WHITE HUNTER CALLED BLACK

1. Dennis Lyell, *African Adventures* (London: John Murray, 1935), p. 251.
2. Er Shelley, *Hunting Big Game with Dogs in Africa* (Columbus, Miss., n.p., 1924), p. 33.
3. Sir Frederick Jackson, *Early Days in East Africa* (London: Edwin Arnold, 1930), pp. 382–83.
4. Sir Alfred Pease, *The Book of the Lion* (London: John Murray, 1913), p. 283.
5. Percival, *A Game Ranger's Note Book* (London, 1924), p. 81.
6. Ibid., p. 82.
7. Akeley, *In Brightest Africa*, pp. 74–75.
8. Ibid., p. 156.
9. Pascal James and Eleanor Imperato, *They Married Adventure* (New Brunswick, N.J.: Rutgers University Press, 1992), p. 97.
10. Bill Jenvey, pers. comm., Queensland, Australia, October 14, 1993.

10. THE SHORT MYSTERIOUS LIFE OF FRITZ SCHINDELAR

1. Herbert "Pop" Binks, pers. comm., Nairobi, Kenya, June 10, 1959.
2. Hunter and Mannix, *African Bush Adventures*, p. 178.
3. Ibid., p. 179.
4. Ibid., p. 180.
5. Herbert "Pop" Binks, *African Rainbow* (London: Sidgewick & Jackson, 1959), p. 129.
6. Ibid., p. 130.
7. Percival, *A Game Ranger's Note Book*, pp. 81–84.

11. War Clouds on the Equator

1. C. J. Wilson, *The Story of the East African Mounted Rifles* (Nairobi, 1927), p. 4.
2. Brian Gardner, *German East* (London: Cassell, 1963), p. 49.
3. Charles Miller, *The Lunatic Express* (London: Macdonald, 1971), p. 521.
4. Wilson, *The Story of the East African Mounted Rifles*, p. 36.
5. *Handbook of Tanganyika Territory* (London: Macmillan, 1930), p. 81.
6. Lyell, *African Adventures*, pp. 45–46.
7. Baron Bror von Blixen-Finecke, *African Hunter* (New York: Knopf, 1937), p. 85.
8. Ibid., pp. 274–75.
9. Wilson, *The Story of the East African Mounted Rifles*, p. 5.
10. Ibid., p. 50.
11. Brian Herne collection, order grounding 2nd Lieut. Bell by Major Wallan, Mbuyuni 26-4-1916.

12. Frontiersman in Africa

1. Charles Cottar as told to Edison Marshall in an article by Marshall, *Field & Stream*, December 1938.
2. Evelyn (Cottar) Reidy, "Charles Cottar," unpublished ms.
3. Mona Cottar, interview, Nairobi, Kenya, April 22, 1974.
4. Mary Gillett, *Tribute to Pioneers* (Nairobi, n.d.).
5. Evelyn (Cottar) Reidy, "Charles Cottar's Family," unpublished ms.

13. The Honorable Bedar

1. Errol Trzebinski, *Silence Will Speak* (Chicago: University of Chicago Press, 1977), p. 84.
2. Isak Dinesen, *Letters from Africa, 1914–1931*, ed. Frans Lasson, trans. Ann Born (Chicago: University of Chicago Press, 1981), p. 412.
3. Frederick B. Patterson, *African Adventure* (New York: G. P. Putnam's, 1928), p. 56.
4. Ibid., p. 82.
5. Ibid., p. 57.
6. J. A. Hunter and Alan Wyckes, *Hunter's Tracks* (London: Hamish Hamilton, 1957), pp. 68, 69.
7. Ibid., p. 70.

14. BARON OF THE BUNDU

1. G. F. V. Kleen, *Bror Blixen: The Africa Letters* (New York: St. Martin's Press, 1988), p. xvii.
2. Thomas Dinesen, *Merry Hell: A Dane with the Canadians* (London: Jarrolds, 1929), p. 254.
3. Lasson, trans. Born, *Isak Dinesen: Letters from Africa, 1914–1931*, p. 19.
4. Blixen-Finecke, *African Hunter*, p. 26.
5. Huxley, *Out in the Midday Sun*, p. 62.
6. Kleen, *Bror Blixen: The Africa Letters*, p. xv.
7. Blixen-Finecke, *African Hunter*, p. 177.
8. Ibid., pp. 102–103.
9. Carlos Baker, Ernest Hemingway's letter of August 19, 1949, to Charles Scribner, in Carlos Baker, *Ernest Hemingway, A Life Story: Selected Letters* (New York: Charles Scribner's Sons, 1969), p. 665.
10. Kleen, *Bror Blixen: The Africa Letters*, p. xix.
11. Blixen-Finecke, *African Hunter*, pp. 120–21.
12. Kleen, *Bror Blixen: The Africa Letters*, p. xv.
13. Blixen-Finecke, *African Hunter*, p. 119.
14. Kleen, *Bror Blixen: The Africa Letters*, p. xvii.
15. Ibid.
16. Kleen, *Bror Blixen: The Africa Letters*, p. viii.
17. Errol Trzebinski, *The Lives of Beryl Markham* (New York: W. W. Norton, 1993), p. 193.
18. Ibid., p. 194.
19. Tony Archer to Jan Hemsing, *Ker and Downey Safaris: The Inside Story* (Nairobi: Sealpoint Publicity, 1989), p. 185.
20. Blixen-Finecke, *African Hunter*, p. 175.
21. Ibid.
22. Dennis Holman, *Inside Safari Hunting* (London: W. H. Allen, 1969), p. 51.
23. Gustaf "Romulus" Kleen, pers. comm., Drottingholm, Sweden, September 29, 1995.
24. Huxley, *Out in the Midday Sun*, pp. 65–66.
25. Olga Anastasia Pelensky, *The Life and Imagination of a Seducer* (Athens, Ohio: Ohio University Press, 1991), p. 174.
26. Ibid., p. 148.

15. THE ROYAL SAFARIS

1. Pat Ayre, *African Life*, February 1959.
2. Tom Murray Smith, *The Nature of the Beast* (London: Jarrolds, 1963), p. 82.
3. Patrick Chalmers, ed., *Sport and Travel in East Africa, an Account of Two Visits, 1928 and 1930: Compiled from the Private Diaries of HRH the Prince of Wales* (London: Philip Allan, 1934), p. 83.
4. Huxley, *Out in the Midday Sun*, p. 64.

5. Blixen-Finecke, *African Hunter*, p. 192.
6. Ibid., pp. 191–95.
7. Chalmers, *Sport and Travel in East Africa*, pp. 80–83.

16. TRAILBLAZERS OF THE TWENTIES

1. Mona Cottar, pers. comm., Karen, Kenya, June 22, 1977.
2. Paul Hoefler, *Africa Speaks* (New York: Blue Ribbon Books, 1931), p. 144.
3. Donald Ker, *African Adventure* (Harrisburg, Pa.: Stackpole, 1957), p. 12.
4. Ibid., p. 13.
5. Donald Ker interview (by Canuk [M. J. Turner-Dauncey]), *African Life*, August 1957.
6. Donald Ker, *African Adventure*, p. 16.
7. Hemsing, *Ker and Downey Safaris*, p. 8.
8. Edie Ker, *Around the Campfire* (Privately printed, 1988), p. 12.
9. Ibid., pp. 12–13.
10. Bunny Allen, *Second Wheel* (Clinton, N.J.: Amwell Press, 1985), p. 277.

17. SYD DOWNEY AND THE MASAI MARA

1. Hemsing, *Ker and Downey Safaris*, pp. 22–23.
2. Ibid., p. 23.
3. Anthony Cullen, *Syd Downey's Africa* (London: Cassell, 1959), p. 9.
4. Hemsing, *Ker and Downey Safaris*, p. 22.
5. Cullen, *Syd Downey's Africa*, p. 9.
6. Sheila Herne, pers. comm., December 25, 1955.
7. East African Professional Hunter's Association ruling on complaint by Mr. Donald Ker against Mr. Sydney Downey, arbitrated by Mr. Andrew Fowle of the EAPHA's Committee, Nairobi, April 12, 1936.
8. Edie Ker, *Around the Campfire*, p. 14.
9. Negley Farson, *Behind God's Back* (New York: Harcourt, Brace, 1950), p. 288.
10. Hemsing, *Ker and Downey Safaris*, p. 141.
11. Count Gregers Ahlefeldt-Bille, *Tandalla* (London: Routledge & Kegan Paul, 1948), p. 47.

18. WARDENS, LIONS, AND SNAKES

1. C. J. P. Ionides and Dennis Holman, *Mambas and Man-Eaters* (New York: Henry Holt, 1966), p. 34.
2. Ibid., p. 40.
3. Ibid., p. 57.
4. Ibid., p. 78.

5. George Adamson, *Bwana Game* (London: Collins and Harvill Press, 1968), p. 101.

6. Ibid., p. 103.

7. Ibid.

8. Ibid., p. 104.

9. Ibid., p. 105.

19. A Wartime Alliance

1. Kenneth Gandar Dower, *Abyssinian Patchwork* (London: Frederick Muller, 1949), p. 18.

2. Ahlefeldt-Bille, *Tandalla*, p. 8.

3. Dower, *Abyssinian Patchwork*, pp. 207–10.

4. Cullen, *Syd Downey's Africa*, p. 20.

5. Edie Ker, *Around the Campfire*, p. 56.

6. Ibid., pp. 56–57.

20. Safariland

1. Canuk, "The Old School," *African Life*, January 1959.

2. Ibid.

3. Bill Jenvey, pers. comm., Queensland, Australia, February 15, 1992.

4. Ibid.

21. On Safari Again

1. Cullen, *Syd Downey's Africa*, p. 62.

2. Edie Ker, *Around the Campfire*, p. 71.

3. Ibid., p. 71.

4. Ibid., pp. 71–72.

5. Farson, *Behind God's Back*, pp. 288–89.

6. Ibid., p. 298.

22. Heroes of the Silver Screen

1. David Lunan, pers. comm., Martin Gosnells, West Australia, December 14, 1992.

2. Ibid., January 20, 1993.

3. Stan Lawrence-Brown, pers. comm., Kijungu, Tanganyika, August 9, 1960.

4. Ibid.

5. Bunny Allen, pers. comm., Lamu, Kenya, November 20, 1992.

6. Ava Gardner, *Ava, My Story* (New York: Bantam Books, 1990), p. 179.

SOURCE NOTES \\ 425

7. Alan Wykes, *Nimrod Smith* (London: Hamish Hamilton, 1961), pp. 121–22.
8. Murray Smith, *The Nature of the Beast*, p. 130.

23. LUNAN'S WHITE HUNTERS

1. Tony Henley, *Round the Campfire* (Clinton, N.J.: Amwell Press, 1989), p. 134.
2. Ibid.
3. White Hunters (Africa) Ltd., 1957 brochure.

24. THE TANGANYIKA HUNTERS

1. Canuk, "Safari Profile, Russell Bowker Douglas," *African Life*, February 1958.
2. Hemsing, *Ker and Downey Safaris*, p. 119.
3. David Ommanney, pers. comm., Asheville, North Carolina, August 15, 1984.

25. THE MOTH AND THE FLAME

1. Lea McCallum's recollections of her brother, pers. comm., Arusha, December 1958.
2. Peter Hirsch, *The Last Man in Paradise* (New York: Doubleday, 1961), pp. 53–54.

26. CLARY'S WORLD RECORD

1. Clary Palmer-Wilson, pers. comm., Hurricane, Utah, February 4, 1992.
2. Laddy and Ada Wincza, *Bush and Plains* (Clinton, N.J.: Amwell Press, 1983), p. 45.
3. Clary Palmer-Wilson, pers. comm., Hurricane, Utah, August 4, 1992.
4. Ibid.
5. Ibid.

27. THE ENEMY WITHIN

1. Wincza, *Bush and Plains*, pp. 72–73.
2. Ibid., pp. 89–90.
3. Erik Andersen, pers. comm., Kampala, Uganda, July 18, 1968.

426 // SOURCE NOTES

28. THE HASSANS OF MOMBASA

1. Ikram Hassan, unpublished diaries, 1946–1950.
2. Ibid., 1947.
3. Ibid., 1953.

29. AFRICAN ODYSSEY

1. George DeLima, pers. comm., São Paulo, Brazil, October 6, 1992.
2. Ibid., May 25, 1992.
3. Ibid., October 6, 1992.

30. THE MESSAGE OF MAU MAU

1. Mike Hissey, pers. comm., Diani Beach, Kenya, November 10, 1979.

31. HEARTS OF DARKNESS

1. Chuck W. Ennis Jr., *Diary of a Hunt* (San Antonio: privately printed, 1964), p. 70.
2. "White Hunter's Skill Tracks Down Gangs. Anti Mau Mau Teams Formed," *East African Standard*, January 7, 1954.

32. THE BAMBOO BADLANDS

1. Hemsing, *Ker and Downey Safaris*, p. 192.
2. Fred Bartlett, pers. comm., Otjiwarongo, Namibia, June 6, 1993.
3. Ibid., November 9, 1993.
4. F. D. Corfield, *Historical Survey of Mau Mau* (London: HMSO, 1960), pp. 31–51.
5. Mike Prettejohn, pers. comm., Mweiga, Kenya, October 6, 1993.
6. Dennis Holman, *Elephants at Sundown* (London: W. H. Allen, 1978), p. 72.
7. Ibid.
8. Guy Campbell, *The Charging Buffalo* (London: Leo Cooper in association with Secker & Warburg, 1986), p. 59.
9. Mike Prettejohn, pers. comm., Mweiga, Kenya, August 6, 1993.
10. Campbell, *The Charging Buffalo*, p. 60.
11. Myles Turner, *My Serengeti Years* (London: Elm Tree Books, 1987), pp. 6–9.

33. Out of the Forest, Into the Bush

1. Peter Becker, pers. comm., Francistown, Botswana, February 7, 1994.
2. Peter Becker, pers. comm., Madeira, Portugal, April 22, 1994.
3. Mike Prettejohn, pers. comm., Mweiga, Kenya, August 6, 1993.
4. Kenya Game Department, Annual Reports 1960–64.
5. Mike Prettejohn, pers. comm., Mweiga, Kenya, August 6, 1993.

34. The Maharajah of Mayhem

1. Hemsing, *Ker and Downey Safaris*, p. 191.
2. Ibid., p. 191.
3. Holman, *Inside Safari Hunting*, p. 214.
4. Fergus McBain, pers. comm., Northampton, West Australia, January 29, 1993.
5. Pablo Bush Romero, *"Shikar" in India, "Safari" in Tanganyika* (Mexico: privately printed, n.d.), p. xvii.
6. Holman, *Inside Safari Hunting*, p. 231.
7. John Alexander, pers. comm., Nairobi, March 7, 1977.
8. Holman, *Inside Safari Hunting*, p. 186.
9. Erik Andersen, pers. comm., Greek river camp, Karamoja, Uganda, January 8, 1967.
10. John Sutton, pers. comm., Palm Beach, Florida, November 10, 1991.
11. Chuck W. Ennis Jr., pers. comm., San Antonio, Texas, September 10, 1997.
12. Mike Prettejohn, pers. comm., Mweiga, Kenya, August 8, 1993.

35. A Tale of Two Hunters

1. Hemsing, *Ker and Downey Safaris*, p. 117.
2. Ibid.
3. Robert Stack, *Straight Shooting* (New York: Macmillan, 1980), p. 232.
4. Ibid., p. 233.
5. Ibid., p. 239.
6. Hemsing, *Ker and Downey Safaris*, p. 117.
7. John Fletcher, pers. comm., Pacific Beach, California, November 6, 1991.
8. Ibid.

36. The Wanderings of an Officer and a Gentleman

1. Douglas Collins, *Another Tear for Africa* (Clinton, N.J.: Amwell Press, 1984), pp. 88–89.
2. Douglas Collins, letter to author, Mombasa Club, November 7, 1970.

37. KING OF THE CATCHERS

1. Carr Hartley, pers. comm., Nairobi, November 11, 1974.
2. Sheila Carr-Hartley, pers. comm., Amanzimtoti, South Africa, May 25, 1993.
3. Ibid., June 25, 1993.
4. Sheila Carr-Hartley, pers. comm., Natal, South Africa, March 9, 1993.
5. Huxley, *Out in the Midday Sun*, p. 126.
6. Bob Astles, pers. comm., Kololo hill, Kampala, Uganda, November 20, 1975.

38. DEADLY LION HUNT

1. Gatia, pers. comm., Nairobi, Kenya, March 22, 1967.
2. Mrs. Jean Barrett, pers. comm., Buffalo, New York, October 11, 1991.
3. Jack Block, pers. comm., Nairobi, Kenya, March 1967.
4. Pete Barrett, letter to Chuck Ennis, Buffalo, New York, January 20, 1968.

39. KNIFE FIGHT WITH A LEOPARD

1. Mike Hissey, pers. comm., Diani Beach, Kenya, June 17, 1978.
2. Ibid.
3. Ibid.
4. Mike Hissey, pers. comm., Brackley, Northants, England, June 2, 1980.
5. Ibid., May 1, 1980.
6. Mike Hissey, "Lucky Escapes," unpublished ms., May 1980.
7. Mike Hissey, pers. comm., Brackley, Northants, England, June 2, 1980.

40. THE BIG SIX

1. Hemsing, *Ker and Downey Safaris*, p. 113.
2. "Wounded Hunter Flying to Britain in Effort to Save Eye," *East African Standard*, September 7, 1968.

41. A DATE WITH DESTINY

1. Harold T. P. Hayes, *The Dark Romance of Dian Fossey* (New York: Simon & Schuster, 1990), pp. 76–77.
2. Ibid., p. 79.
3. Ibid., p. 93.
4. Ibid., p. 96.
5. Ibid., p. 84.
6. Ibid., p. 101.
7. *East African Standard*, December 2, 1972.

43. KEEPER OF THE FLAME

1. Evelyn "Dutchie" (Cottar) Reidy, pers. comm., Augusta, Georgia, June 2, 1981.
2. Mrs. Pat (Cottar) Imison, interview, Karen, Kenya, June 20, 1979.
3. Brian Herne, "The Cottar Clan," *Tanzania Safaris* (Clinton, N.J.: Amwell Press, 1981), pp. 38–39.
4. Glen Cottar, pers. comm., Karen, Kenya, July 21, 1979.

44. PELIZZOLI'S PROMISED LAND

1. Alfredo Pelizzoli, pers. comm., Langata, Nairobi, August 4, 1991.
2. Ibid.

45. UGANDA, PEARL OF AFRICA

1. Ernst Zwilling, *Jungle Fever* (London: The Travel Book Club, 1956), p. 156.

46. COMPANY OF ADVENTURERS

1. Jessen, *W. N. McMillan's Expeditions*, p. 44.
2. William Wright, *The Von Bulow Affair* (New York: Delacorte Press, 1983), p. 15.
3. Ibid., p. 8.
4. Ibid., p. 26.
5. Holman, *Inside Safari Hunting*, p. 270.

47. HAVE GUN WILL TRAVEL

1. A. M. D. Seth-Smith, pers. comm., Nairobi, Kenya, October 4, 1992.

48. THE EMPEROR AND THE PRINCE

1. Iain and Oria Douglas-Hamilton, *Battle for the Elephants* (New York: Viking Penguin, 1992), p. 113.

49. ONWARD PASSAGES

1. *East African Standard*, July 19, 1968.
2. David Lunan, pers. comm., Martin Gosnells, West Australia, December 14, 1992.

3. Ibid.

4. Ada Wincza, pers. comm., Johannesburg, South Africa, January 5, 1985.

5. Princess Henrietta (von Auersperg) von Bohlen und Halbach, pers. comm., Kitzbuhel, Austria, April 14, 1983.

6. Ala (von Auersperg) Isham, pers. comm., New York, October 28, 1992.

7. Douglas Collins, pers. comm., Kora National Reserve, Kenya, September 12, 1989.

8. Jeanne Mathews, pers. comm., Nairobi Hospital, March 3, 1987.

EPILOGUE: A RACE AGAINST TIME

1. Douglas-Hamilton, *Battle for the Elephants*, p. 41.

2. Ibid., p. 42.

3. "The Hunting Ban," Wildlife Clubs of Kenya, July 1977, p. 3.

4. Douglas-Hamilton, *Battle for the Elephants*, p. 103.

5. C. A. Spinage, *Elephants* (London: T. & A. D. Poyser, 1994), p. 262.

6. CITES, "The Elephant: Back to the Bad Old Days?" August 11, 1998.

7. Richard Leakey, pers. comm., Karen, Kenya, November 1997.

BIBLIOGRAPHY

Acevedo, Arturo F. *Humor in Adventure: The End of an Era, U.S.A.* N.p., 1996.

Adamson, George. *Bwana Game.* London, 1968.

Ahlefeldt-Bille, Count Lauvig Gregers. *Tandalla.* London, 1948.

Akeley, Carl. *In Brightest Africa.* Garden City, N.Y., 1927.

Allen, Bunny. *First Wheel.* Clinton, N.J., 1984.

———. *Second Wheel.* Clinton, N.J., 1985.

Amin, Idi. *Uganda Second Year, Second Republic.* Kampala, 1973.

Anderson, Major G. H. *African Safaris.* Nakuru, 1946.

Arbuthnot, Thomas S. *African Hunt.* New York, 1957.

Archer, Sir Geoffrey. *Personal and Historical Memoirs of an East African Administrator.* London, 1963.

Aschan, Ulf. *The Man Whom Women Loved.* New York, 1987.

Baker, Carlos. *Ernest Hemingway: A Life Story.* New York, 1969.

Baker, Sir Samuel. *The Nile Tributaries of Abyssinia.* London, 1867.

Baldwin, William C. *African Hunting and Adventure.* London, 1894.

Baldwin, William W. *Mau Mau Manhunt.* New York, 1957.

Barclay, Edgar N. *Big Game Shooting Records.* London, 1932.

Barnes, Alexander T. *Across the Great Craterland to the Congo.* London, 1924.

Bauer, Erwin. *My Adventures with African Animals.* New York, 1968.

———. *Treasury of Big Game Animals.* New York, 1972.

Bauer, Erwin, et al. *A Treasury of African Hunting,* ed. Peter Barrett. New York, n.d.

Beard, Peter. *The End of the Game.* London, 1965.

Bell, W. D. M. *Karamoja Safari.* London, 1949.

Binks, H. K. *African Rainbow.* London, 1959.

Boyce, William D. *Illustrated Africa, North, Tropical, South.* Chicago, 1925.

Boyes, John. *King of the WaKikuyu.* London, 1911.

———. *Company of Adventurers.* London, 1929.

Blixen-Finecke, Baron Bror von. *African Hunter.* New York, 1936.

Bronson, Edgar Beecher. *In Closed Territory.* London, 1910.

Bulpett, C. W. L. *A Picnic Party in Wildest Africa.* London, 1907.

Burrard, Major Sir Gerald. *In the Gun Room.* London, 1951.

Burton, Richard F. *First Footsteps in East Africa.* London, 1894.

Campbell, Guy. *The Charging Buffalo*. London, 1986.

Chalmers, Patrick R. *Sport and Travel in East Africa*. London, 1934.

Chanler, William Astor. *Through Jungle and Desert*. London, 1896.

Chapman, Abel. *Savage Sudan*. London, 1921.

Churchill, Winston S. *My African Journey*. London, 1908.

Clayton, Anthony. *Counter Insurgency in Kenya 1952–60*. Nairobi, 1976.

Cloete, Rhena. *The Nylon Safari*. London, 1956.

Collins, Douglas. *A Tear for Somalia*. London, 1960.

———. *Another Tear for Africa*. Clinton, N.J., 1984.

Corbett, Jim. *Treetops*. New York, 1956.

Corfield, F. D. *Historical Survey of the Growth and Origins of Mau Mau*. London, 1960.

Cotlow, Lewis. *Zanzubuku*. London, 1956.

Cott, Hugh. *Looking at Animals: A Zoologist in Africa*. New York, 1973.

Courtney, Roger. *African Escapade*. London, 1939.

Cranworth, Lord Bertram. *A Colony in the Making, or Sport & Profit in East Africa*. London, 1912.

———. *Kenya Chronicles*. London, 1939.

Cullen, Anthony. *Syd Downey's Africa*. London, 1959.

Cullen, Anthony, and Sydney Downey. *Saving the Game*. London, 1960.

Cumming, Roualyen Gordon. *The Lion Hunter*. London, 1911.

Daly, Marcus. *Big Game Hunting and Adventure 1897–1936*. London, 1937.

Dickinson, F. A. *Big Game Shooting on the Equator*. London, 1907.

Dinesen, Isak. *Out of Africa*. London, 1937.

———. *Letters from Africa 1914–1931*, ed. Frans Lasson, trans. Ann Born. Chicago, 1981.

Dinesen, Thomas, V.C. *No Man's Land*. London, 1929.

Donaldson-Smith, A. *Through Unknown African Countries*. New York, 1897.

Douglas-Hamilton, Iain, and Oria Douglas-Hamilton. *Battle for the Elephants*. New York, 1992.

Dower, Kenneth Gandar. *The Spotted Lion*. Boston, 1937.

———. *Abyssinian Patchwork*. London, 1949.

Dracopoli, I. N. *Through Jubaland to the Lorian Swamp*. London, 1914.

Dugmore, Major A. Radclyffe. *The Wonderland of Big Game*. London, 1925.

Dunbar, James T. *Big Game Hunting in Central Africa*. London, 1912.

Dundas, Sir Charles. *African Crossroads*. New York, 1955.

Dutton, E. A. T. *Kenya Mountain*. London, 1929.

Dyer, A. *The East African Hunters*. Clinton, N.J., 1979.

Eastman, George. *Chronicles of an African Trip*. Rochester, N.Y., 1927.

Eliot, Sir Charles. *The East African Protectorate*. London, 1905.

Ennis, Chuck W., Jr. *Diary of a Hunt*. San Antonio, Tex.,1964.

Farson, Negley. *Last Chance in Africa*. New York, 1949.

———. *Behind God's Back*. New York, 1950.

Fleischmann, Max C., *After Big Game in Arctic and Tropic*, Cincinnati, Ohio, 1909.

Foran, W. Robert. *Kill or Be Killed*. London, 1933.

———. *A Cuckoo in Kenya*. London, 1936.

———. *A Breath of the Wilds*. London, 1958.

———. *A Hunter's Saga*. London, 1961.

———. *The Kenya Police*. London, 1962.

———. *The Elephant Hunters of the Lado*. Clinton, N.J., 1981.

Fossey, Dian. *Gorillas in the Mist*. New York, 1983.

Fox, James. *White Mischief*. London, 1982.

Gardner, Ava. *Ava, My Story*. New York, 1990.

Gardner, Brian. *German East*. London, 1963.

Gilbert, Martin. *The First World War: A Complete History*. New York, 1994.

Gillett, Mary. *Tribute to Pioneers*. Nairobi, n.d.

Granger, Stewart. *Sparks Fly Upward*. New York, 1981.

Gregory, J. W. *The Foundation of British East Africa*. London, 1901.

———. *The Great Rift Valley*. London, 1896.

———. *Under the Sun*. Nairobi, 1951.

Grogan, Ewart S. *From the Cape to Cairo*. London, 1902.

Guggisberg, C. A. W. *Simba*. Philadelphia, 1961.

———. *Early Wildlife Photographers*. New York, 1977.

Gunter, John. *Inside Africa*. London, 1955.

Harris, Captain Cornwallis. *The Wild Sports of Southern Africa*. London, 1839.

Hayes, Harold T. P. *The Dark Romance of Dian Fossey*. New York, 1990.

Haywood, Captain C. Wrightwick. *To the Mysterious Lorian Swamp*. London, 1927.

Hemingway, Ernest. *The Green Hills of Africa*. New York, 1935.

Hemingway, Mary. *How It Was*. New York, 1951.

Hemsing, Jan. *Then and Now, Nairobi's Norfolk Hotel*. Nairobi, 1975.

———. *The New Stanley*. Nairobi, 1976.

———. *The Beauty of Amboseli*. 1993.

———. *Naivasha and the Lake Hotel*. Nairobi, 1987.

———. *Ker and Downey Safaris: The Inside Story*. Nairobi, 1989.

———. *Keekorok Game Lodge, Masai Mara Game Reserve, and Samburu Game Lodge, Samburu Game Reserve, Kenya*. Nairobi, n.d.

Henderson, Ian, and Philip Goodheart. *The Hunt for Kimathi*. London, 1958.

Henley, A. M. H. *Round the Camp Fire*. Clinton, N.J., 1989.

Henrickson, Aage. *Isak Dinesen—Karen Blixen*, trans. William Mishler. 1988.

Herbert, Agnes. *Two Dianas in Somaliland*. London, 1908.

Herne, Brian. *Uganda Safaris*. Clinton, N.J., 1979.

———. *Tanzania Safaris*. Clinton, N.J., 1981.

———. *Desert Safaris*. Clinton, N.J., 1984.

———, et al. *The Complete Book of Hunting*, ed. R. Elman. New York, 1980.

Herne, Peregrine. *Perils and Pleasures of a Hunter's Life, or, The Romance of Hunting*. Philadelphia, 1854.

Hill, M. F. *Permanent Way*. Nairobi, 1949.

Hirsch, Peter. *The Last Man in Paradise*. New York, 1961.

Hoefler, Paul L. *Africa Speaks*. New York, 1931.

Hollis, A. C. *The Masai, Their Language and Folklore.* Oxford, 1904.
———. *The Nandi, Their Language and Folklore.* London, 1909.
Holman, Dennis. *Inside Safari Hunting.* London, 1969.
———. *Elephants at Sundown.* London, 1978.
Hoyt, Edwin P. *Colonel von Lettow-Vorbeck, Guerilla.* London, n.d.
Hunter, J. A. *White Hunter.* London, 1928.
———. *Hunter.* London, 1952.
Hunter, J. A., and Dan Mannix. *African Bush Adventures.* London, 1954.
Hunter, J. A., and Alan Wykes. *Hunter's Tracks.* London, 1957.
Huxley, Elspeth. *White Man's Country.* 2 vols. London, 1935.
———. *Out in the Midday Sun.* London, 1985.
Huxley, Julian. *Africa View.* New York, 1943.

Iliffe, John. *Tanganyika Under German Rule 1905–1912.* Dar es Salaam, 1969.
Imperato, Pascal James and Eleanor M. *They Married Adventure.* New Brunswick, N.J., 1992.
Ionides, C. J. P. *A Hunter's Life.* London, 1965.
Ionides, C. J. P., and Dennis Holman. *Mambas and Man-Eaters.* New York, 1966.
Itote, W. *"Mau Mau" General.* Nairobi, 1967.

Jackson, Sir Frederick. *Early Days in East Africa.* London, 1930.
Jessen, B. H. *W. N. McMillan's Expeditions and Big Game Hunting in Sudan, Abyssinia, and British East Africa.* London, 1906.
Johnson, Osa. *I Married Adventure.* New York, 1940.
———. *Four Years in Paradise.* New York, 1944.
Johnston, Sir Harry. *The Kilima-Njaro Expedition.* Farnborough, 1886.
———. *The Uganda Protectorate.* 1902.

Kaggia, B. M. *Roots of Freedom.* Nairobi, 1975.
Kariuki, Josiah Mwangi. *Mau Mau Detainee.* London, 1963.
Keith, Elmer. *Guns and Ammo for Hunting Big Game.* Los Angeles, 1965.
Kenyatta, Jomo. *Facing Mount Kenya.* London, 1937.
Ker, Donald. *African Adventure.* Harrisburg, Pa., 1957.
Ker, Edie. *Around the Campfire.* Alexandria, Va., 1988.
Kimambo, I. N., and A. J. Temu. *A History of Tanzania.* Nairobi, 1969.
Kinloch, Major Bruce. *The Shamba Raiders.* London, 1972.
Kitson, F. *Gangs and Counter Gangs.* London, 1960.
Kittenberger, Kalman. *Big Game Hunting and Collecting in East Africa 1903–1926.* London, 1929.
Kleen, G. F. V. *Bror Blixen: The Africa Letters.* New York, 1988.

Lane, Margaret. *Life with Ionides.* London, 1963.
Lasson, Frans. *The Life and Destiny of Isak Dinesen,* trans. Clara Svendsen. London, 1970.
Laws, R. M., I. C. S. Parker, R. C. B. Johnstone. *Elephants and Their Habitats.* Oxford, 1975.
Leakey, L. S. B. *Mau Mau and the Kikuyu.* London, 1953.
———. *Defeating Mau Mau.* London, 1954.

Leed, Eric J. *No Man's Land. Combat and Identity World War I*. London, 1979.

Lettow-Vorbeck, General Paul von. *My Reminiscences of East Africa*. London, 1920.

Lewis, I. M. *Modern History of Somaliland*. New York, 1965.

Lovell, Mary. *Straight On Till Morning*. London, 1987.

Lyell, Dennis. *Memories of an African Hunter*. London, 1923.

———. *African Adventures*. London, 1935.

Majdalany, Fred. *State of Emergency*. Boston, 1963.

Markham, Beryl. *West with the Night*. London, 1943.

Marshall, Edison. *Shikar and Safari*. New York, 1947.

———. *The Heart of the Hunter*. New York, 1956.

Martin, David. *General Amin*. London, 1974.

Matthiessen, Peter. *Sand Rivers*. New York, 1981.

Maxwell, Marius. *Stalking Big Game with a Camera*. London, 1924.

Meikle, R. S., and M. E. Meikle. *After Big Game*. London, n.d.

Meinertzhagen, Colonel Richard. *Kenya Diary, 1902–1906*. Edinburgh, 1957.

———. *Army Diary, 1899–1926*. Edinburgh, 1960.

———. *Middle East Diary, 1917–1956*. New York, 1960.

Melland, Frank H. *Through the Heart of Africa*. Boston, 1912.

Mellon, James. *African Hunter*. London, 1975.

Millais, John G. *Wanderings and Memories*. London, 1919.

———. *Far Away Up the Nile*. London, 1924.

Miller, Charles. *The Lunatic Express*. London, 1971.

———. *Battle for the Bundu*. New York, 1974.

Moise-Bartlett, H. *The King's African Rifles*. Aldershot, Eng., 1956.

Molloy, Peter. *The Cry of the Fish Eagle*. London, 1957.

Moore, Audrey. *Serengeti*. London, n.d.

Moorhead, Alan. *The White Nile*. New York, 1960.

———. *The Blue Nile*. New York, 1962.

Morden, William and Irene. *Our African Adventure*. London, 1954.

Morkel, Bill. *Hunting in Africa*. Cape Town, 1980.

Mosley, Leonard. *Duel for Kilimanjaro*. London, 1963.

Moss, Captain A. H. E. *My Somali Book*. London, 1913.

Mowat, Farley, *Woman in the Mist*. New York, 1987.

Mungeam, G. H. *British Rule in Kenya 1895–1912*. Oxford, 1966.

Murray Smith, Tom. *The Nature of the Beast*. London, 1963.

Muruiki, Godfrey. *A History of the Kikuyu 1500–1900*. Oxford, 1974.

Mwapwele, D. W. K., ed. *Tanganyika Notes and Records 1961–1971*. Dar es Salaam, 1971.

Neumann, Arthur. *Elephant Hunting in East Equatorial Africa*. London, 1898.

Newland, V. M., and L. Tarlton. Foreword by Ewart Grogan. *Farming and Planting in B.E.A.* Nairobi, 1917.

Ochieng, William Robert. *An Outline History of the Rift Valley of Kenya*. Nairobi, 1975.

Oswald, W. Cotton. *Big Game Shooting*. London, 1894.

Pakenham, Thomas. *The Scramble for Africa.* New York, 1981.

Pakenham, Valery. *Out in the Noonday Sun.* New York, 1985.

Patience, Kevin. *Steam in East Africa.* Nairobi, 1976.

Patterson, Frederick B. *African Adventures.* New York, 1928.

Patterson, Lt. Col. J. H. *In the Grip of the Nyika.* London, 1909.

———. *The Man-Eaters of Tsavo.* London, 1907.

Pavitt, Nigel. *Kenya: The First Explorers.* London, 1989.

Pease, Sir Alfred. *The Book of the Lion.* London, 1913.

———. *Edmund Loder: A Memoir.* London, 1923.

Pelensky, Olga Anastasia. *The Life and Imagination of a Seducer.* Athens, Ohio, 1991.

Percival, A. Blayney. *A Game Ranger's Note Book.* London, 1924.

———. *A Game Ranger on Safari.* 1928.

Potocki, Count Joseph. *Sport in Somaliland.* London, 1900.

Powell-Cotton, Major P. H. G. *A Sporting Trip Through Abyssinia.* London, 1902.

———. *In Unknown Africa.* London, 1904.

Preston, R. O. *The Genesis of Kenya Colony.* Nairobi, n.d.

Prickett, R. J. *Treetops: The Story of a World Famous Hotel.* North Pomfret, Vt., 1987.

Rainsford, W. S. *The Land of the Lion.* New York, 1909.

Rice, Edward. *Captain Sir Richard Francis Burton.* New York, 1990.

Riefenstahl, Leni. *Leni Riefenstahl: A Memoir.* New York, 1987.

Robertson, H. J., and A. Davis. *Chronicles of Kenya.* London, 1929.

Romero, Pablo Bush. *Mexico and Africa from the Sight of My Rifle,* Mexico, n.d.

———. *"Shikar" in India, "Safari" in Tanganyika.* Mexico, n.d.

Roosevelt, Kermit. *A Sentimental Safari.* New York, 1963.

Roosevelt, Theodore. *African Game Trails.* New York, 1910.

Ruark, Robert. *Something of Value.* New York, 1955.

———. *Horn of the Hunter.* London, 1954.

———. *Uhuru.* London, 1962.

———. *Use Enough Gun.* London, 1957.

Sand, Rudolph. *Afrika Stadig Vildt.* Copenhagen, 1962.

Schaller, George. *The Serengeti Lion.* Chicago, 1972.

Schillings, C. G. *With Flashlight and Rifle.* 2 vols. London, 1906.

Shelley, Er. *Hunting Big Game with Dogs in Africa.* Columbus, Miss., 1924.

Sherbrooke-Walker, Eric. *Treetops Hotel.* London, 1961.

Sibley, Major J. R. *Tanganyikan Guerilla.* London, 1971.

Simon, Noel. *Between the Sunlight and the Thunder.* Boston, 1963.

Sommer, François. *Man and Beast in Africa.* New York, 1954.

Speke, John Hanning. *What Led to the Discovery of the Source of the Nile.* London, 1864.

Spinage, C. A. *Elephants.* London, 1994.

Stack, Robert, with Mark Evans. *Straight Shooting.* New York, 1980.

Stanley, Henry M. *In Darkest Africa.* 2 vols. London, 1890.

Stoneham, C. T. *Mau Mau.* London, 1953.

Strage, Mark. *Cape to Cairo.* New York, 1973.

Sutton, Richard L. *An African Holiday.* St. Louis, 1924.

Swayne, Major G. H. C. *Seventeen Trips Through Somaliland.* London, 1885.

Taber, F. Wallace. *Assignment Safari.* Denver, 1951.

———. *Safari Sagas.* Denver, 1955.

Thomas, Elizabeth Marshall. *Warrior Herdsmen.* London, 1965.

Thomson, Joseph. *To the Central African Lakes and Back.* London, 1881.

———. *Through Masailand.* London, 1885.

Thurman, Judith. *Isak Dinesen: The Life of a Storyteller.* New York, 1982.

Tolan, John. *No Man's Land.* New York, 1980.

Treatt, Stella Court. *From the Cape to Cairo.* London, 1928.

———. *Sudan Sand.* 1930.

Trzebinski, Errol. *Silence Will Speak.* Chicago, 1977.

———. *The Lives of Beryl Markham.* New York, 1993.

Turner, Myles. *My Serengeti Years,* ed. Brian Jackman. London, 1987.

Varian, H. F. Foreword by Ewart S. Grogan. *Some African Milestones.* Oxford, 1953.

Verdcourt, Bernard, and E. C. Trump. *Common Poisonous Plants of East Africa.* London, 1969.

Vesey-Fitzgerald, Desmond. *East Africa Grasslands.* Nairobi, 1973.

Visram, M. G. *On a Plantation in Kenya.* Mombasa, 1987.

Ward, Rowland. *Records of Big Game: Editions 1907–9, 1935, 1962, 1964, 1988.* London.

Wardenburg, Fred. *Operation Safari.* N.p., 1948.

West, Richard. *The White Tribes of Africa.* New York, 1967.

White, Stewart Edward. *The Land of Footprints.* New York, 1912.

———. *African Camp Fires.* New York, 1913.

———. *The Rediscovered Country.* New York, 1915.

Wilson, C. J. *The Story of the East African Mounted Rifles.* Nairobi, 1927.

Wincza, Ada. *Masai the Magnificent.* Nairobi, 1973.

Wincza, Laddy and Ada. *Bush and Plains.* Clinton, N.J., 1983.

Wolverton, Lord. *Five Months Sport in Somaliland.* London, 1894.

Wright, William. *The Von Bulow Affair.* New York, 1983.

Wykes, Alan. *Nimrod Smith.* London, 1961.

Young, Francis Brett. *Marching on Tanga.* London, 1917.

Zwilling, Ernst A. *Jungle Fever.* London, 1956.

DIARIES AND LETTERS

Alan Black, letters, papers, notes, and documents, 1906–1930.
Peggy (T.M.) Brown, diaries and letters, 1931–1990.
Major Douglas Tatham Collins, letters, notes, and articles, 1956–1998.
Chuck W. Ennis Jr., diaries and letters, January 1958–1998.
Ikram Hassan, diaries, letters, and notes, May 1951–1973.
Mahmoud Hassan, diaries and letters, 1951–1952.
David Edward Herne, diaries and letters, 1896–1935.
J. W. Judd, diaries, 1907–1927.
Kenyon Painter, diaries, August 1909–June 1936.
Maud Painter, diaries and letters, 1911–1929.
Donald Seth-Smith, diaries, 1916–1917.
Kathleen (Bailey) Seth-Smith, diaries, 1926.
Martin Seth-Smith, diaries, May 1908–1909.
Published history: *The Family of Black of Over Abington 1694–1924.*

UNDATED PRIVATELY PRINTED ACCOUNTS

Bakr, Abu. *Early Recollections of East Africa.*
Barberton, Renshaw Mitford. *Elgon Caves.*
———. *The Sitatunga of Kipsain.*
Breton, Peter Le. *Life on the Mountain.*
———. *The Cherangani Highway.*
Pharazyn, Marjorie. *Early Settlement in the Trans Nzoia.*
W., S. *Kitale Township—Early Days.*
Williams, D. K. *The Kakamega Gold Rush.*
Woods, Angela. *Northern Cherangani, Kaibuibich.*

MAGAZINES, PAPERS, REPORTS

Re: John Alexander, prosecution of. "Police Had No Search Warrant." *East African Standard,* Nov. 28, 1972.
Re: John Alexander, prosecution of. *East African Standard,* Nov. 30, 1972.
Re: John Alexander, prosecution of. "Professional Hunter Discharged on Firearms Charge," *East African Standard,* Dec. 2, 1972.
Alexander, John. "A Tribute to Ahmed." *East African Standard,* Dec. 7, 1973.
———. "Ahmed and a Legend Dies at Marsabit." *East African Standard,* Feb. 18, 1974.
Re: John Alexander, murder of. *East African Standard.* Sept. 7, 1989.
Re: John Alexander, murder of. "John Alexander Killed by Two Head Blows." *The Karen'Gata Chronicle,* Sept. 9, 1989.
Re: John Alexander. "Church Window Memorial for Murdered Man." *The Karen'Gata Chronicle,* Dec. 22, 1990.

Blower, John H. "What Uganda Offers the Hunter," *Safari* magazine, July 1969.

———. "The Kidepo," *Uganda Wildlife and Sport*, 3, no. 1, Feb. 1962.

———. "Safari in Uganda." *Crane Magazine*, Dec. 1973.

Bulletin, Mountain Club of Kenya, March 1949, September 1949, April 1950, June 1950.

Collins, Douglas. "White Eyes Versus the Shifta." *African Life*, August 1958.

East African Railways and Harbours Magazine, Oct. 1957, Feb. 1958, Aug. 1958.

"80 Trophies from New Style Hunt." *The Reporter*, Sept. 6, 1962.

Elgon, John. "Veteran Hunter Looks for New Fields to Conquer." Re: Bill Ryan. Friday Diary, *East African Standard*, Feb. 27, 1970.

Foree, Kenneth, "Black Hunters Leave Memories." *Dallas Morning News*, May 15 1966.

"Game Hunters Close Shop," *East African Standard*, Aug. 27, 1977.

Hassan, Ikram. Re: A. G. Candler. *East African Standard*, Aug. 30, 1949.

Hemsing, Jan. "Nairobi and Its New Stanley." *Africana* magazine, 4, no. 3, 1970.

———. "A Long Life and a Very Full One for Leni." Re: Leni Riefenstahl. *Weekend Standard*, Dec. 10, 1976.

———. "When Kenya Led the Way, Aero Club of East Africa," *Golden Jubilee Year Commemorative Review*, 1927–1977.

Herne, Brian. "Game Hunting in Tanzania." *The East African Standard*, September 19, 1978.

———. "Winning Bid." *Gamecoin* magazine, Spring 1989.

———. "Appreciation. Prince Alfred von Auersperg." *Gamecoin* magazine, Fall 1992.

Host, Emily. "The Professional Hunters of East Africa." *East African Annual* 1951–1952.

"Hunting Feud." *The Reporter*, Sept 1, 1962.

"King of the Wa-Kikuyu." *East African Annual 1951–52*.

Marshall, Edison. Re: Chas. Cottar. "On the Ivory Trail." *Field & Stream*, Dec. 1938, Jan. 1939, Feb. 1939, Mar. 1939, April 1939.

Murray Smith, Tom. "The Old Timers." *African Life*, June 1959.

Rodwell, Edward. "Noon Gun." Coast Causerie, *Mombasa Times and Daily Nation*, Oct. 1946.

———. "When Whiskey Was 23 Cents a Pint." *Safari* magazine, March 1970.

———. "Balloonatics in Nairobi." *Aero Club of East Africa*, 1977.

Russell, Nick. "Recognition for the Hunters." *East Africa Standard*, July 13, 1966.

Seth-Smith, A. M. D. Courtesy of re: Mrs. Bailey. "White Woman Charged by Two Rhinos." *East African Standard*, May 4, 1926.

Tester, Laurence. "The First Royal Safari." *Uganda Wildlife and Sport*, Sept. 5, 1959.

Track (International Professional Hunter's Association magazine), 1971, 1972, 1973.

Turner-Dauncey, M. J. "Interviews." *African Life*, Oct. 1957–July 1961.

"Uganda Angus." *The Reporter*, Sept. 6, 1962.

Scientific, Wildlife, and Natural History Publications

Darroch, R. B., Mikael Samson, and others. "Some Notes on the Early History of the Tribes Living on the Lower Tana." *Journal of the East Africa and Uganda Natural History Society.* Nov. 1943.

Denning, Lord. *Lord Denning's Report.* Sept. 1963.

Du Bois and Walsh. "Republic of Kenya. Minerals of Kenya." *Ministry of Natural Resources. Bulletin* 11, 1970.

East African Wildlife Journal, Aug. 1969, Dec. 1973, Dec. 1976.

East Africa Protectorate. *Queen's Regulations. Preservation of Game,* 1897. An ordinance enacted by His Britannic Majesty's Commissoner for East Africa.

Game, no. 11, 1904.

Kenya, Colony and Protectorate of. His Majesty King George V. An Ordinance to Amend the Ordinance, 1928 and 1955.

Kenya Colony Game Ordinances of 1921, 1926, 1928.

Kenya Ministry of Tourism and Wildlife, Tourism Market Report, 1977–1978.

Kenya Past and Present. Issue 6, 1975.

Kenya Past and Present. Issue 8, 1977.

Mackinder, Halford. "A Journey to the Summit of Mount Kenya." *British East Africa. Geographical Journal* (London), no. 5, 1900.

Moreau, R. E. "Mount Kenya: A Contribution to the Biology and Bibliography." *Journal of the East African Natural History Society,* April 1945.

Quiggin, A. H. *Trade Routes, Trade and Currency in East Africa.* Rhodes-Livingstone Museum, Livingstone, Northern Rhodesia, No. 5, 1949.

Regulations for the Protection of Wild Animals in the German East African Protectorate, June 1, 1903.

Republic of Kenya. Game Department Annual Reports 1963, 1964, 1965.

Republic of Kenya. Game (Preservation and Control) Ordinance, 1970.

Richard J. J. "Volcanological Observations in East Africa." *Journal of the East African Natural History Society,* 1945, 1947, 1948.

Royal National Parks of Kenya Reports, 1960–1961.

Schutte, Dr. H. K., P. J. Howison, and B. A. Blacquiere. *The Mount Kenya Expedition 1951–1952.* Cape Town, South Africa.

Stockley, Lt. Col. C. H. "Mammal Notes. Nature in East Africa." *The Bulletin of the East Africa Natural History Society,* Aug. 1950.

Tanganyika Fauna Conservation Ordinance, 1951.

Uganda Government. Game (Preservation and Control) Ordinance, 1964.

Uganda National Parks Handbooks, 1962–1971.

Uganda National Parks, *Report and Accounts of the Trustees,* Dec. 1953, June 30, 1970.

Weerts, Maurice D. "The Late Mr. Antonin Besse and the Ethiopian Resistance During the Years 1935 to 1940." *Journal of Ethiopian Studies,* July 1970.

ACKNOWLEDGMENTS

A very special thanks to Diana, whose enduring patience over the long years of research for this project was sorely tested. She somehow managed to get all the potatoes into the sack without mashing them. This book would never have been completed without her considerable assistance.

Many of the people who helped so generously have died since I began this project, but they are not forgotten. Chuck W. Ennis Jr. encouraged and assisted me with every facet of the story, as well as with photographs, diaries, and audio and video tapes, and allowed quotes from his book, *Diary of a Hunt*, 1964. Chuck's rhino photograph is on the cover of this book. My grateful thanks also to Marge Ennis.

Thanks to Mike Richmond for allowing quotes and photos from *The Aero Club of East Africa's Golden Jubilee Year Commemorative Review, 1927–1977*; Richard S. du Pont for his elephant sketch and for photos, and to Zavell's Inc., and Smith Photographers, and the late Zavell N. Smith, Mrs. Marian Smith, and Allan F. Smith, for use of Zavell's photographic collection; Bernard Kunicki for his Tiva River photo; Douglas Tatham Collins, for continuous correspondence from 1956 to date. Dougie's sisters, Marisia Le Ber and Barbara Ellis, for family history; Armando Conde for photos and data from his 1958 safari with Douglas Collins and my late brother, David Herne; Lisa and Alfredo Pelizzoli for quotes and photographs from their magazines, *African Life* and *The Reporter*, and for Alfredo's hunting stories; Frank Bowman for photos and reminiscences about safaris with Robert Ruark; Bill Jenvey for data from the post–World War II safari era; the late Bill Ryan for data and photos over a period of thirty years, and to Bimbetta Lincoln MacVeagh; Cynthia and Margaret Downey for data and photographs; Edie Ker for allowing quotes from her book, *Around the Campfire*, 1988. Donald Ker, Syd Downey, and Robert Ruark were generous with anecdotes and opinions. The late Bob (R.P.) Brown offered numerous anecdotes, and was the best company on safari. Bob was one of the few people Alan Black sought out socially, and in whom he confided.

Thanks to Margaret Kummerfeldt and her family for much assistance, photographs, and data about her father, Kenya game warden Blayney Percival, and quotes from *A Game Ranger's Note Book*, and Joy Berseford-Pierce, Philip Hope Percival's daughter, for photos and scrapbook data. Virginia Reidy went beyond the extra mile with extensive data about the Cottar family. Virginia's mother, the late Evelyn "Dutchie" (Cottar) Reidy, generously gave unpublished manuscripts. Thanks to the late Mona Cottar who gave numerous taped interviews and use of photos; Glen and Pat Cottar assisted with photographs, stories, documents, and interviews. Thanks also to Calvin and Tana Cottar; Pat (Cottar) Imison for interviews; Joan (Cottar) Kennedy for data and background about her father, Bud (Charles Jr.) Cottar; Sheriff Allen B. Cottar; Bill Ellis for photos and recollections of Bwana Charles Cottar from boyhood visits to Bwana's sister, Mrs. Emma Derrington, in Kansas, also for his generous gift of vintage Cottar's Safari Service brochures; Mrs. Julian S. (Jean) Barrett for her eyewitness account of events leading to her husband's mauling by a lion and the death of Henry Poolman; Esther Spaulding for much help and photos of the ill-fated Barrett-Spaulding safari; Tanganyika's first director of National Parks, Peter Molloy, and his wife, Yvonne; Myles Turner, Gordon Poolman, and the late Sandy Field, all wardens at Serengeti national park; the late John Owen, director, Tanzania national parks; Uganda national park's senior warden, Frank Poppleton, and his wife, Inge; Iain Ross, warden, Kidepo Valley national park, Karamoja, Uganda, for photos, data, and reports; Uganda chief game warden John Blower for photos and a great deal of assistance; Major Bruce, also a former chief game warden of Uganda (and Malawi), and Elizabeth Kinloch; the late Ian Grimwood, chief game warden of Kenya; the late George Adamson. Bill and Ruth Woodley were generous with help and great hospitality on many occasions over the years while he was warden at Tsavo and the Aberdares. Thanks to former principal game warden of Tanzania, Brian Nicholson; Sheila and Bryan Carr-Hartley for correspondence and family background; Roy and Sue, and Mike and Judy Carr-Hartley for use of Carr's scrapbooks; Robert Stack (with Mark Evans) for allowing quotes and photos from his book *Straight Shooting*, 1980; Bryan and Joan Coleman for photos, news-cuttings, and quotes from Joan's book

Zebra Stew and Safari Baloo; Tony Henley for correspondence, photos, anecdotes, and quotes from his book, *Around the Campfire*, 1989; Mrs. R. Hamilton of Lonhro Ltd., Nairobi, for use of a historic Norfolk Hotel photo.

My late uncle, Jack Judd, gave me Bill Judd's diaries, photographs, and news clippings, and Jack's firsthand account of his father's death. An aunt, Sheila Kirkham, related the story of Eddie Grafton's death. Grateful thanks to Alyson and Bill Kneib for accounts of life in pre-independence Tanganyika and the development of Missouri Coffee Plantations at Arusha, along with photos, diaries, and papers of Kenyon and Maud Painter; German film icon, Leni Riefenstahl, and Leni's assistant, Hanni Lanske, for photos; Kay Turner for allowing quotes from *My Serengeti Years* by Myles Turner, edited by Brian Jackman, 1987; the late Ikram Hassan, his wife, Dr. Bilquis Hassan, and his sister, Razia Hassan, for use of Mahmoud and Ikram's photos, diaries, and papers. The von Auersperg family went to great lengths to assist me. Thanks to Princess Hetti (von Auersperg) von Bohlen und Halbach for family history and photo albums; Prince Alexander von Auersperg; Princess Annie Laurie "Ala" (von Auersperg) Isham. Thanks to Ada and the late Laddy Wincza for photos and quotes from *Bush and Plains*, 1983, and Ada's *Masai the Magnificent*, 1970, also for data regarding Ian MacDonald's character, leopard mauling, and death; John and Nancy Schaefer for so much help in so many ways; the late Clary Palmer-Wilson for numerous interviews, correspondence, and photos. M. G. Visram allowed me quotes from *On a Plantation in Kenya*, 1987; F. Wallace Taber for photos and quotes from *Safari Sagas*, 1955, and *Assignment Safari*, 1951; the late Kenneth Foree of the *Dallas Morning News*; Edward Rodwell of the *Mombasa Times and Daily Nation*, and for data from his Coast Causerie columns. Thanks to *East African Standard* and *Uganda Argus*; *Daily Nation*; and the *Karen'Gata Chronicle* for references. Thanks to Christopher Powell-Cotton for photos and much data from the Powell-Cotton Museum, Kent, England. Thanks to the late Major W. R. Foran for stories, photos, and quotes from a wide assortment of published data. Erwin and Peggy Bauer gave much help, advice, and photographs. Thanks to George Laycock for photographs. Thanks to Andrew and Judy Holmberg for correspondence, stories, photos, and news accounts.

Grateful thanks to Marianne Wirenfeldt Asmussen, Director of the Karen Blixen Museum, Rungstedlund, Denmark, for generous help with photographs and frequent assistance, and to Rungstedlundfonden, Copenhagen, Denmark; Frans Lasson for use of photos, and much help; Hans Berggreen of Det Kongelige Bibliotek, Copenhagen, Denmark; G. F. V. "Romulus" Kleen for correspondence, photos, and anecdotes about his uncle, Baron Bror von Blixen-Finecke; Jorge Alves DeLima Filho, for photos and much correspondence. My mentor, the late Edgar DeBono, gave correspondence, photos, and opinions, of which he had a great many. Thanks to John Fletcher for anecdotes, photos, and accounts of control hunting with Eric Rundgren; Kenya game warden Ken Smith for permission to use his photograph of George Adamson and Prince Bernhard of the Netherlands; Allan Lodge of Rhodes House Library, Oxford, and the Bodleian Library, Oxford; Wallace Dailey, Houghton Library, Theodore Roosevelt Collection, Harvard University; David Lunan for correspondence, photos, and much help. Grateful thanks to Peter Becker for photos, news items, and accounts of tracker teams and pseudo–Mau Mau operations.

Thanks to the late J. A. and Hilda Hunter for his views on man-eating lions, and many pleasant visits to their home at Makindu and, later, Hunter's Lodge at Kiboko. Thanks to the late Alan Black for reminiscences and several books. Thanks to David and Dilys Ommanney for correspondence and the account of Dave's leopard mauling; to Terry and Jeanne Mathews for photos and correspondence; to A. M. D. "Tony" and Sara Seth-Smith for family diaries, letters, and photos; to John Sutton for accounts of hunting with Eric Rundgren; to Mike Prettejohn for correspondence, photos, and hunting stories; to Tony and Rose Dyer for photos, correspondence; to the old EAPHA for photos and archival material; and to Arthur McGreevey for photos and safari stories. Thanks to the following: Raoul Millais; Arturo Acevedo; Mrs. Peg Pearson; Wolfgang and Traudi Rizy; Russell R. Waterhouse; Paula McGehee; the late Mohammed "Bali" Iqbal; Bill Morkel; Mohammed Akbar; Jilla Lynn; Colm Lynn; Mrs. Elfi Alexander for photos, correspondence, and news accounts; John Wroe for photos and data about Alan Black's cars; Janet Hurt; Robin Hurt for photos, hunting stories, and his account of a leopard mauling; the late Bob Foster, Mrs. May Foster, and Peter Head for photographs and family history; Sylvia and Don Ward for photos, news accounts, letters, and papers; Barbara "Midgie" S. Connors; Dr. Jim Holmes for photos; Lewis Mull for photos; Daphne Hissey and the late Mike Hissey for photos, correspondence, and use of Mike's unpublished manuscripts; Marianne Rolleri; Mardie Fraser;

Alexander Maitland; Fergus McBain for photos and much correspondence; Dave and Verity Williams; the late Dr. C. J. Cross and Marcia Cross; the late Barbie Adcock; Tony and Betty Archer for data and photos; Erik Andersen; Shah Awan; Wahid Awan; Bill and Barbie Winter; the late Herbert K. "Pop" Binks; the late John Boyes Jr.; the late Russell Bowker Douglas; Mrs. Constance Bowker Douglas; the late Jack Block; the late Rene and Joanna Babault; Ronnie and Barbara Boy; Shirley Brown; Francesco Bisletti; Nganga Kariuki; Bella Hinkhouse; John DeVilliers; Wilson and Elizabeth Brown; Tony and Alison Davies; Peter Johnson; Peter Davey; Paul and Joanie Deutz; Derrick and Heidi Dunn; the late George Dove; Mike Dove; Adrian T. Sada; Julio Escamez; Francis and Robert Foster; Neil Forgan; Peter Saw; Alec Forbes-Watson; the late Robin Fairrie; Ruth Fletcher; Patsy Hellerman; the late Nick Swan and Moira Swan; Patrick Hemingway; Peter and Renata Hutchence; Dr. Pascal James Imperato; Angela Wilson; Hilary Jackson; Ron Kidson; Dr. Walker and Stephanie Kemper; Bert and Brigit Klineburger; the late Stan Lawrence-Brown; Mrs. Ronnie Lawrence-Brown; George Lanham; James Mellon; Gisella Meyer; Ruth McNiven; the late Slim and Molly Medcalfe; the late Jim Midcap; Crane Midcap; Norma Midcap; Wendy Pierce; the late Bunny Ray; Mrs. Kay Ray; the late Charles Whitead. Thanks to Pablo Bush Romero for allowing quotes from two of his books, "Shikar" in India, "Safari" in Tanganyika, and Mexico and Africa from the Sight of My Rifle, and to Mrs. Elsey Bush Romero; Adelaide Roughton; the late Don Hopkins; Mrs. Marty Six; the late Dr. George Six; Dr. Eric and Anne Six; Steve Smith; Monty Brown; Rudolph Sand; Heather Stewart; Betty Silverson; the late Mrs. Gloria Stewart and James Stewart; Errol Trzebinski; Colonel Dale Wykoff; the late Professor Ernst A. Zwilling; Yarka Ondricek; Nadine Johnson; Galen Black; the staff at the Museum of the Cherokee Strip, Enid, Oklahoma; and the Society for Physical Research, London; Alan Wesenraft at the University of London Library; Mona Brittain and Paloma Humphries at Pacific Beach Library, California; Jean Cogan and Connie Mullins at La Jolla Library, California; Caroline D. Marais, San Diego Central Library; Carlsbad, California, computer guru Howard Monell, who did what nobody else was able to do—translate my CPM data to DOS.

Thanks to the following for use of copyright material: Carol Christiansen for assistance, Bantam, Doubleday, Dell Publishing Group, Inc., New York, 1990, reprinted from Ava Gardner's Ava, My Story; Anthony Pekarik for assistance; reprinted with the permission of

Simon and Schuster from *The Dark Romance of Dian Fossey* by Harold T. P. Hayes, copyright © 1991; Lydia Zelaya for assistance; excerpted with permission of Scribner, a Division of Simon and Schuster, *Ernest Hemingway: Selected Letters, 1917–1961*, edited by Carlos Baker. Copyright © 1981. The Hemingway Foundation, Inc. Thanks to Fiona Beatty, Peters, Fraser and Dunlop Group, for permission to quote from *African Bush Adventures* by J. A. Hunter and Dan Mannix, Hamish Hamilton Ltd., 1954, and *Hunter's Tracks*, by Alan Wyckes, Hamish Hamilton Ltd., 1957. Thanks to Elaine Iles, Rutgers University Press, for permission to quote from *They Married Adventure* by Pascal James Imperato and Elanor M. Imperato, 1992. Thanks to Judy Wilson for assistance, Ohio University Press, for permission to quote from *Isak Dinesen: The Life and Imagination of a Seducer* by Olga Anastasia Pelensky, University Press, Swallow Press, 1991. Thanks to Tony Dyer for photographs and quotes from *The East African Hunters*, Amwell Press, New Jersey, 1979, Monica Sullivan, Amwell Press, and the old EAPHA, Tony Dyer and Tony Archer for quotes from *Elephant Hunters of the Lado*, 1981. Thanks to Bunny Allen for photos, correspondence, interviews, and quotes from his books, *First Wheel* and *Second Wheel*, 1984 and 1986. Thanks to Angela T. Colangelo for assistance, Dell Publishing, Delacorte Press, for permission to quote from *The Von Bulow Affair* by William Wright, 1983. Thanks to Paul Rodger of Random House (U.K.) Ltd. for permission to quote from Elspeth Huxley's *Out in the Midday Sun*, published by Chatto & Windus (U.K.) 1985. Thanks to Joel Cameron Head, of McGraw Hill, New York, for permission to quote from *The Heart of the Hunter* by Edison Marshall, 1956; to Henry Holt for permission to quote from *Mambas and Man-Eaters* by C. J. P. Ionides and Dennis Holman; to Perry Cartwright, University of Chicago Press, for assistance with *Silence Will Speak*, 1977, by Errol Trzebinski. Thanks to Duncan Barnes, Editor-in-Chief, *Field & Stream* for permission to quote from *On the Ivory Trail* by "Bwana" Charles Cottar as told to Edison Marshall, published in the December, 1938, issue of the magazine; by kind permission of the Estate of Elspeth Huxley for permission to quote from *White Man's Country*, Macmillan and Company, Ltd., London 1935. Thanks to Douglas Collins for permission to quote from his books, *A Tear for Somalia*, 1960, and *Another Tear for Africa*, 1984. Thanks to Jan Hemsing for generous correspondence and allowing quotes from *The Beauty of Amboseli*, 1993; *Naivasha and the Lake Hotel*, 1987; *Keekorok*

Game Lodge and Samburu Game Lodge; Then and Now, Nairobi's Norfolk Hotel, 1975; *Ker and Downey Safaris, The Inside Story*, 1989. Thanks to Lisa Herman for much assistance and for help with tracking sources; copyright © 1988 by G. F. V. Kleen, from *Bror Blixen: The Africa Letters* by G. F. V. Kleen, reprinted by permission of St. Martin's Press, Incorporated. Thanks to Fredrick Courtright; from *Lives of Beryl Markham* by Errol Trzebinski. Copyright © 1993. Reprinted by permission of W. W. Norton & Company. Inc.; to Ron Hussey and Rose Marie Cimarino for assistance; extracted from *Syd Downey's Africa*, by Anthony Cullen, Copyright © 1959 by permission of Simon and Schuster. Thanks to Carol Christiansen, Doubleday & Company, Inc., for allowing quotes from *The Last Man in Paradise*, by Peter I. Hirsch, New York, 1961. Thanks to Sam Moore and Florence Eichen for assistance; from *Battle for the Elephants* by Iain and Oria Douglas-Hamilton, Copyright © 1992. Used by permission of Viking Penguin, a Division of Penguin Putnam Inc. Thanks to Duncan Carsons at HarperCollins for granting permission to reference passages from George Adamson's *Bwana Game*, London, Collins and Harvill Press, 1968. Grateful thanks to Kyle Weaver of Stackpole Books, Inc., for permission to quote from Donald Ker's *African Adventure*. Acknowledgment is made to Frederick Patterson and G. P. Putnam's Sons for quotes from *African Adventures*, New York, 1928. I should like to apologize to any heirs and holders of copyright whom, despite diligent search, I was unable to locate to request permission to quote.

Thanks to those brave and cheerful gunbearers and trackers, the finest hunters of all: Longolla Lakiti, Ethia, Gatia, Dominico Orego, George Opio, George Opondo, Freddy Aboy, Buno Ndolo, Tipapa, Wario, Gholo, Kipsang, Kimatai, Mohammed, Issa Bendere, Saidi Juma, Hassani, Saidi bin Ali, Enduyai, Bokari, Bithoka Mutuo, Wambua Kitonga, Mapigano, Mutua Muta, Mutisa, Kamau Njeri, Muli Mulei, John Muyasa, Wilson Chepko, Mwalimu Tarre, Mwalimu Manza, Gholo, Abdullah Abdulahi, Musau Musyoki, Mohammed Ardo, Peter Mutio, Mwangi Chege, Mwakanyanga, John Okola, Lucas Ocheng, Caleb Okech, Kulet ole Lespet, Leposo ole Tameno, Baden arap Kipchelat, Franzio Orket, Palo Lokimat, Bokari, Tameo, Mwalimu Koreh, Aden Koreh, and thanks to Henry Katabazi, who is not a hunter but the best diplomat and camp manager in Africa.

PHOTOGRAPHIC CREDITS

5, from *With Flashlight and Rifle* by C. G. Schillings. 8, 68, from *African Game Trails* by Theodore Roosevelt. 11, 63, from *In Unknown Africa* by P. H. G. Powell-Cotton. 17, 21, 65, Northrup McMillan. 28, courtesy T. E. Matsila, Kenya Railways. 30, 74, 89, 157, 183, EAPHA Archives. 35, John Boyes Jr. scrapbooks. 45, 47, 48, Bill and Alyson Kneib collection. 51, 56, 195, 208, Brian Herne collection. 81, Don and Sylvia Ward. 85, Angela Wilson. 97, 111, Karen Blixen Museum, Rungstedlund. 101, from *The East African Mounted Rifles* by C. J. Wilson. 106, Glen and Pat Cottar. 119, Bernard Kunicki. 121, 128, G. F. V. Kleen. 142, from *Big Game Shooting on the Equator* by F. A. Dickinson. 144, Mona Cottar. 151, 212, 306, 312, Chuck W. Ennis Jr. 163, 179, Erwin A. Bauer. 168, Mrs. Hammond and Lonhro Ltd. collection. 177, Lewis M. Mull. 181, Frank Bowman. 189, David Lunan. 192, Bunny Allen collection. 234, Razia Hassan. 243, Jorge Alves DeLima Filho. 260, Bimbetta Lincoln McVeigh. 276, Mike Prettejohn collection. 283, 404, Tony Archer collection. 295, Robert Stack. 301, Armando Conde. 330, George Laycock. 341, 348, Bryan Coleman collection. 353, and elephant sketch, Richard S. du Pont. 361, Francesca Pelizzoli. 367, 388, Iain Ross collection. 390, Alfi von Auersperg. 401, Ken Smith.

INDEX

The youngest professional hunter ever licensed in East Africa, Brian Herne has had a career spanning thirty years. He is one of only seventeen individuals awarded the Shaw and Hunter Trophy—known as the "Oscar" of the African hunting world. Mr. Herne has also received awards for his photography, including Japan's prestigious Asahi Pentax Award. The founder of the international professional hunter's magazine *Track*, he has written for numerous outdoor and hunting magazines. A second-generation Kenyan, Mr. Herne now lives in southern California.